THE LIFE AND LETTERS OF
ANNE ISABELLA, LADY NOEL BYRON

PUBLISHED BY

Constable & Company Limited
London W.C. 2

.

BOMBAY
CALCUTTA   MADRAS
LEIPZIG

Oxford University
Press

.

TORONTO

The Macmillan Company

ANNABELLA MILBANKE AT ABOUT TEN YEARS OLD

From the full-length portrait by Hoppner

THE LIFE AND LETTERS

of

ANNE ISABELLA, LADY NOEL BYRON

from unpublished papers
in the possession of the late Ralph, Earl of Lovelace

By

ETHEL COLBURN MAYNE

With an Introduction and Epilogue by

MARY, COUNTESS OF LOVELACE

and twelve illustrations

" Her life was spring and winter"

LONDON

CONSTABLE & CO LTD

1929

PRINTED IN GREAT BRITAIN BY ROBERT MACLEHOSE AND CO. LTD.
THE UNIVERSITY PRESS, GLASGOW.

PREFACE

THIS book is by no means intended to revive what is called the " Byron Scandal." Its purpose is to give a portrait of Byron's wife and widow at each stage of her development ; and that portrait has been drawn chiefly from a great mass of documents preserved by the present representatives of the Byron posterity. Of these documents the history may be read in two previous publications, *Astarte* (by the late Earl of Lovelace ; new edition, 1921) and *Ralph, Earl of Lovelace : a Memoir* (1920), by Mary, Countess of Lovelace, the widow of Byron's grandson.

I need not recapitulate that history ; all I need say here —but this I wish to say with every possible emphasis—is that when words are put into the mouth of any person whatever who figures in these pages, those words have invariably been quoted verbatim from the documents. In no single instance has my invention played the smallest part. There is no useful method of reference to otherwise unpublished papers ; the documents I especially allude to must therefore be described. They consist of Lady Byron's " only two important narratives of her married life " (*Astarte*, p. 21, new edition), and were written during and soon after the separation proceedings for the information of her legal advisers, to whom it was necessary that she should give grounds—in the first instance for her resolve to live apart from her husband ; in the second, for the proceedings which made her daughter Ada a ward in Chancery.

Thus a great part of the documents here relied on derive their value from Lady Byron's universally recognised truthfulness—by no one more explicitly and fully recognised than by Byron himself ; and her testimony was accepted as entirely authoritative by the two distinguished lawyers, Stephen Lushington, LL.D., and Sir Samuel Romilly, with the result that she gained her point as regards the terms of separation and the care of her child.

Later, she frequently set down in writing reminiscences of her life with Byron. In these compositions she was more concerned to excuse than to accuse him; yet it is remarkable that between the two there is no sort of inconsistency to be found. Seeking to trace the source of their tragic relations, she preserved the same truthfulness; the sole difference is that in the later writings she was freed from the necessity of defending her resolve to escape from his hostility, and to protect her child from the possible guardianship of Mrs. Leigh.

I shall say no more on this point; my readers will judge for themselves.

My thanks are due above all to Mary, Countess of Lovelace, for constant interest and aid in my arduous task. Also to Mr. Harold Child, who was prevented by circumstances from writing the Life which I have now written, and who gave me the use of his full and valuable notes for that purpose. I owe acknowledgments for permission to quote from copyright letters to Colonel John Murray, Mr. J. A. Ingpen, and Mr. Ernest Benn. The last-named granted me the use of two letters, and some words of text, from the very interesting *Memoir of Mrs. Anna Jameson* by Mrs. Steuart Erskine, published by Mr. Fisher Unwin in 1915, before his firm was incorporated with that of Mr. Benn. From Mrs. Belloc Lowndes I received some valuable conjectures regarding her grandmother's, Mme. Swanton Belloc's, imputed "biography" of Lady Byron. (See Appendix II.)

To M. André Maurois I am indebted for an act of courteous consideration in the postponed publication of his forthcoming Life of Byron. It was felt by him that my book should be the earlier to appear, since it had been in preparation for a longer time than his on Byron, and since in both the Lovelace Papers were for the first time available as part of the material for the marriage and separation periods. I need not say how warmly I appreciate this gracious and sympathetic action.

ETHEL COLBURN MAYNE.

CONTENTS

APPENDICES

LIST OF ILLUSTRATIONS

ix

INTRODUCTION

BY MARY, COUNTESS OF LOVELACE

THE village of Kirkby Mallory, which stands ten miles west of
Leicester and four from the site of the Battle of Bosworth
Field, was once the home of the ancient family of Mallory.[1]
They passed away from it in 1389. Somewhere about 1570
it came into the possession of John Noel of Whellesburgh
through his wife Amy Fowler, and for some 350 years since
then, the neighbouring manors of Wellesborough—as it is
now spelt—and Kirkby Mallory, have been held together by
their descendants. John Noel was the younger brother of
Sir Andrew Noel, knight of Dalby, co. Leicester, who was the
ancestor of the earls of Gainsborough.

It was John Noel's great grandson, Sir William Noel, second
baronet of Kirkby Mallory, who about the year 1650 married
Margaret Lovelace, daughter of John, second Lord Lovelace
of Hurley by his wife Anne Wentworth, Baroness Wentworth
in her own right. Three generations later, Sir Edward Noel
sixth baronet, succeeded in right of his great grandmother
the aforesaid Margaret Lovelace, as ninth Lord Wentworth
of Nettlestead (Suffolk).

The full story of the ancient barony of Wentworth would
form a chapter in English history. The first holder Thomas
Wentworth, an offshoot of the Yorkshire Wentworths, served
Henry VIII in various capacities and was raised to the
peerage by him. The second holder was the last English
Governor of Calais. The fourth fought and ruined himself in
the cause of Charles I, who had created him Earl of Cleveland.
His only son having pre-deceased him, the earldom died with
him, but the barony continued in the person of his young
grand-daughter, Henrietta Wentworth. She, poor pretty
child—for she was scarcely more than that when she and
Monmouth first met and danced into each other's hearts at
the Court of Charles II—was born to a tragic fate. Mon-

---

[1] Their connexion with Sir Thomas Malory, author of the *Morte d'Arthur*,
appears to be uncertain.

mouth could not make her his wife, for he had been given in marriage as a boy to the heiress of Buccleuch (the great lady to whom Sir Walter Scott's *Last Minstrel* is supposed to have chanted his lay), but for many troubled years their lives were closely united. When Monmouth, after the discovery of the Rye House Plot, fled for his life, Henrietta and her mother concealed him for months in the " vastness and intricacy " [1] of their old house at Toddington in Bedfordshire. Later, Henrietta followed him to Flanders. On July 1, 1685, was fought the battle of Sedgemoor, followed by Monmouth's flight and capture, the dreadful hours in the Tower of London, and his death on the scaffold, July 15, with Henrietta's name upon his lips. Within a few months she too had died, as was said, of a broken heart.

The barony now reverted to a sister of Henrietta's father (Anne Lady Lovelace) and as before mentioned came down through her daughter Margaret after various vicissitudes to her descendants the Noels.

Edward Noel, Lord Wentworth (later created a Viscount) and his wife Judith Lambe of Farndish, Bedford, seem to have been distinguished and cultivated persons. The present Kirkby Hall, a dignified eighteenth century pile, was built by him. He was ambassador at Venice, and his wife is remembered for her friendship with Angelica Kauffmann, whom she introduced into English society. Lord and Lady Wentworth had four children, Thomas, tenth baron and second viscount, Judith, Elizabeth and Sophia Noel, and of these four persons, their friends and manner of life, we possess a very full record in a mass of correspondence, ranging from the year 1767 to 1802, which was found preserved at Kirkby Hall. Judith Lambe Lady Wentworth having died early, her children were entrusted by their father to the care of his unmarried sister Mrs. Mary Noel, who seems to have acted towards them as the tenderest of mothers. The best letters in the collection are those of this excellent old lady, full of homely wit and keen observation, and next after them come those of her favourite niece Judith, who was married in January 1777 to Ralph, eldest son of Sir Ralph

[1] From a contemporary letter to the Earl of Rochester.

Milbanke of Halnaby in Yorkshire and Seaham in Durham. Within a few months the two younger sisters were also married, Elizabeth to Mr. (afterwards Sir James) Bland Burges, later a prominent figure in literary and political circles, and Sophia to Nathaniel Curzon, son of Lord Scarsdale. Both sisters died early. Old Mary Noel remained at Kirkby to keep house for her bachelor nephew who had now succeeded his father, but she spent much of her time in her own little London house, whence sheaves of gossip from her pen travelled down for years at frequent intervals to Judith Milbanke in the North. Here is the first letter that she sent to her " best-beloved " after her marriage :

KIRKBY, January 10, 1777.

MY DEAR MRS. MILBANKE

As Mr. Hulse leaves us to-day I can't forbear letting you know by him that we are all well, tho' I spent but a melancholy day yesterday, for my eyes made themselves full amends for the fortitude I shew'd in your presence, and even now, (fool that I am) my tears blot my paper, and all for what ? why truly because the first wish of my heart is fully accomplish'd, for what have I ever so ardently wish'd, or pray for, as to see you united to an Amiable & worthy man, and no one who knows Mr. Milbanke so well as we do here, but must know he has one of the best of hearts ; May God Almighty grant you to be long long the happy possessor of it, as I am sure you will always sincerely and indeed endeavor to perform the Solemn vow you made yesterday in his presence. . . .

Give my particular love to Mr. M.

I feel all the rashness of such a comparison, but surely this may remind some of us (at least a little) of Madame de Sévigné writing to Mme. de Grignan.

The letter to " Mrs. Milbanke " was soon followed by others to the newly married " Mrs. Burges " and " Mrs. Curzon." Hardly anyone in the whole circle of intimates was ever endowed with a Christian name. The brother is always " his Lordship " or " your Brother," never " Tom " after he had ceased to be a boy. But all this formality of address never impairs for a moment the complete intimacy and affection which united the old foster-mother to her nurslings. We get many a picture of the old easy-going hospitable life of the provincial gentry of those days. It was frankly social and little else. The men had their Quarter Sessions and their Yeomanry duties, the women cared for the welfare of the villagers, but nobody founded societies or sat on committees, or worried themselves about schemes for public welfare. The only allusions to politics consist of occasional abuse of some member of the opposite party. The great interest in life was to observe and detail the doings of neighbours and relations, and to that end there were continual visits and sojournings in each others' houses. All this, as people of the old generation will realise, was not unlike what still went on in country neighbourhoods only fifty or sixty years ago ; but in these letters are touches from a more remote past.

We hear for instance of a lady of high degree who could not show herself to visitors because " she had ink'd her face for the ringworm." We gather that it was quite common—if you could afford it—to drive about to call upon your neighbours in a coach-and-six ; but that even that magnificent horse-power did not entirely obviate all inconvenience from the very bad roads. In the South of England coals were apt to be both scarce and dear. It behoved you to be cautious in deciding what relatives to stay with in October. In an impecunious or stingy house you might find only " empty grates and painted boards " until after the first of November. There was much drinking, but only in extreme cases do the women take it very seriously. In one letter Mrs. Milbanke bemoans herself that if certain guests come they will make " Mil " tipsy every night (Thank goodness he had now ceased to be " Mr. M.", at least to *her* !) In another letter she rejoices that he has been good and sober for many weeks. " Old Aunty " suffering much in health during a hot summer, her devoted niece implores her not to give way to " light drinks," and is reassured by promises that she will not drink anything whatever but *Porter and Madeira*.

The Milbankes were a very happy couple. Her earlier letters are full of encomiums of the " best of Husbands " and of " the best Creature living (you know who I mean);" and of descriptions of " the greatest kindness and attention ever shewn a Woman." If this tenderness becomes less vociferous as time goes on, it is plainly still there, and they were scarcely ever apart.

They lived quietly at the modest house overhanging the sea at Seaham in Durham, then only a fishing village,[1] paying occasional visits to old Sir Ralph Milbanke at Halnaby, to Lord and Lady Darlington at Raby Castle, to Sir Thomas and Lady Liddell at Ravensworth, and to other hospitable houses, and diverting themselves now and then in lodgings at Durham or Newcastle for the local race meetings. In 1790 Ralph Milbanke became M.P. for Durham county, and a part of the year was henceforth spent in London.

There was but one cloud on their horizon—they were childless. For the wife, at all events, consolation came when after the death of her sister Mrs. Curzon in 1782, one of her two orphan children, " little Sophy " (afterwards Lady Tamworth), was put under her care, and became in all respects as a daughter to her. Thenceforth Old Aunty's maternal heart is continually fed with details about this charming child, and with as much as can be gleaned about her brother Nathaniel Curzon who, in the absence of the father abroad, remained with the grandparents Lord and Lady Scarsdale.

But the blank was not really filled. There are signs that now and then wild hopes sprang up, only to die quickly. Many years passed ; and at last—at last—on January 1, 1792, Mary Noel is able to write to Mrs. Milbanke : " No need my dearest Milly for Liquor when I received your delightful letter on Saturday. I was tipsy with joy, for to tell you the truth as my love is great so was my fears, and your friends may laugh at me as much as they do at you, for I added every possible distemper to those you gave yourself, but thank God my fears are now all over, and I look forward now as patiently as I can," etc. etc. The good old lady, a mother only in heart, exhausts herself in collecting information and advice from experienced friends about the great business of

---

[1] Seaham Harbour is now a town surrounded by collieries, and a large shipping centre for the coal trade. It was sold by Sir Ralph Milbanke somewhere about the year 1820 to Frances Anne Vane-Tempest, Marchioness of Londonderry, for its agricultural value, the mineral wealth that lay under it being then undiscovered. It was the Londonderry family who later made the Harbour.

bringing a child into the world ; and when Mrs. Milbanke finally decides not to take the risk of the long journey to London, rejoicingly sets forth to rejoin her at Seaham for the event. Here in May 1792, fifteen years after marriage, was born the little daughter destined henceforth to be the centre of all joys and sorrows to her adoring parents. Of course they had looked forward to " a fine boy," but there are few signs of disappointment. The child was christened Anne Isabella, Anne being the name of the Duchess of Cumberland, who had been for years offering her services as Godmother.

Pages could now be filled with the constant allusions to the " little Angel," her beauty and intelligence, etc., etc. " When she *frowns* she is the image of Milbanke—when she smiles she is like *me*," writes her mother. The first event in her little life was the death of her grandfather Sir Ralph Milbanke, when she was six years old. " Annabella cannot comprehend our change of appellation. She is quite disconcerted about it and says she will not have her Papa called Sir Ralph." The family now migrated to Halnaby for part of the year, but Annabella was still happiest at Seaham. " Annabella has taken a prodigious fancy to Nat (Curzon) and made strong love to him for the few days they were together."

In September 1800, Sophia Curzon was married to Lord Tamworth.[1] " I feel like *a lost thing* for want of Sophy," writes Lady Milbanke ; and little Nancy Milbanke, as in these early days we are still permitted to call her (how much better than the ponderous " Annabella ! "), lost the companionship of a very dear elder sister.

Less than two years later the correspondence comes to an abrupt end. Mary Noel, the dear and revered Old Aunty, passed away after a few days' illness, comforted by the presence of her best-beloved adopted daughter, her " First Darling."

It is time to turn the page and listen to the story of a new generation.

MARY CAROLINE LOVELACE.

[1] Eldest son of the seventh Earl Ferrers.

CHAPTER I

THURSDAY'S CHILD

May 17, 1792 ; Ascension-Thursday.

The date, or an approximate one, and the event which was to mark it had been looked forward to for nine months and fifteen years by Mr. and the Hon. Mrs. Ralph Milbanke of Seaham Harbour in the county of Durham, but then living at Elemore Hall in the same county. When it became certain that the radiance of Ascension-Day would touch the newborn head, there was besides the old birthday-rhyme to be consulted. *Thursday's child has far to go.* Like other oracles, it was ambiguous ; the Milbankes smiled and sighed and wondered.

And when the hour came, did some faint grudge against slow destiny come with it ? A daughter—the child so long awaited, so probably to prove an only one. . . . There had been letters in the suspensive months : " I look forward to the dear little fellow's appearance " ; " I cannot pay a compliment to the sex at the expense of my veracity." In this vein Mrs. Milbanke's aunt and brother had written. She herself, indeed, had taken an attitude : " I shall be quite as well pleased with a daughter." But the child would in all probability succeed to a title and great possessions ; so she had borne unresentfully the clamour for a boy. That was the penalty attached to such expectant motherhood as hers.

Though disappointment must have been, it quickly ceased to be—for mother and father, at any rate. They had their " little angel " at long last, and they settled down to a fond rivalry of worship. So did Mrs. Milbanke's aunt, Mrs. Mary Noel, who had come to Elemore Hall for the event ; and she was already an adept at worshipping nieces, great or otherwise. She had chosen this baby's mother, Judith Noel that was, from

Judith's two sisters to be her best-beloved ; she had later taught herself to be (in a measure) content with—a great-niece indeed, but not her best-beloved's daughter. Only an adopted one, this little Sophy Curzon whom Judith Milbanke had taken to herself on the death of her sister Sophia ten years ago. But Sophy's nose was evidently not put out of joint on the Ascension-Day of 1792 ; for on the following 8th of June, she sat down and—queer little girl she must have been !—composed a long letter to the baby. It was the solemnest of letters, full of effusion (" your lovely and expressive countenance "—to an infant who, less than a month old, can scarce have been either lovely or expressive of much beyond material needs) ; full too of advice which might almost be called admonition ; but breathing such fervent sentiment as does away with her having had to puzzle out the vile phrase that has wounded many a childish heart. Sophy's letter was passed round in the family, and Lord Wentworth, Judith Milbanke's brother, wrote : " Indeed I agree with you that it is a marvellous performance."

And what was the " barley-sugar " daughter's name, or names ? Two had been chosen. Anne, for the Royal godmother —this was the Duchess of Cumberland, long solicitous to sponsor Judith Milbanke's first child ; and Isabella, for we know not whom. Anne Isabella : a troublesome combination, soon telescoped into Annabella, with frequent relapses to the Nancy of babyhood. At six we already read the statelier name. " Annabella . . . will not have her Papa called Sir Ralph."

But her Papa had to be called Sir Ralph, for he had succeeded to the baronetcy ; and this brought about another change as well, likewise unwelcome to the small personage, who had already experienced a removal. Soon after her birth the family had gone from Elemore to the " modest house overhanging the sea " at Seaham, with trees of the same age as herself springing up round each wing. There, when she was only eighteen months old, had occurred a domestic upheaval—the Itch had invaded the household. One of the servants, thus afflicted, had been afraid to tell, and the revelation came in the form of Baby's taking it. The rumpus was immense ; in the middle of it the mistress herself was attacked by the humiliating scourge. Her sufferings were aggravated by one of " Clermont's " most harassing displays of character. This was Annabella's nurse, later to be her governess—and the Mrs. Clermont who was later still to be cast for a star-part in the Byron Separation-Drama. From the itch-episode it does seem to emerge that Mrs. Milbanke was more or less under her thumb—afraid of her, just because she was so devoted. A malady most incident to mistresses ; and taken advantage of to some extent by Clermont, who would not go out for her daily airing, would not exchange a word with a nursemaid to whom she attributed the mischief. " She is *resolved to go*," moaned poor Judith in many a distracted letter to Aunt Mary. But at last the storm died down ; Clermont did not go, and the itch did. Annabella had been very good during the visitation, and she was gooder still when at five came the scarlet-fever. She took her physic " like a heroine."

So she had learnt some lessons from life before she had to learn, too, that Papa must be called Sir Ralph, and that part of the year must henceforth be spent away from Seaham—at Halnaby Hall in Yorkshire, a few miles from Darlington. But Annabella never took to Halnaby. Seaham was—and always remained—far dearer to her than the handsome red-brick seventeenth century mansion in Yorkshire, with its Frenchified interior and its furniture to match.

We who know her story might well regard the dislike for Halnaby as something in the nature of presentiment ; for it was there that she spent the honeymoon which Byron called the treaclemoon, and it was in the big red-curtained bedstead there that, on the nuptial night, she heard her bridegroom cry so loudly that it wakened her : " Good God, I am surely in Hell ! " He had had a nightmare ; there was firelight shining through the ruddy bed-hangings—how effective to shout of hell where another man might have murmured tamely of another spirit-world ! Sensational, Byronic ; and so, Byron shouted.

Presentiment or not, Annabella was indifferent to the splendours of Halnaby. When she looked at herself in one of " the pair of extravagant gilt mirrors in the Chinese-Chippendale style," what sort of a little person did she see ? We have no portrait of her at six, when she first looked in them ; but we do possess a character-sketch by her mother. " She is excessively talkative and entertaining *if she likes* people, and very coaxing to her favourites ; and she will judge *for herself* and cannot be *made* to like anybody. She dances very beautifully ; I never saw feet and ankles so well placed as hers, and Watts (her dancing master) says she has the strongest knees and ankles of any child he ever taught. Her *Pas grave* and *Balancez* in the minuet is *perfect*."

When at ten she was painted by Hoppner, the portraitist whom Northern gentry then most patronised, the picture shows a child with " the fairest skin imaginable," thick straight brown hair, a rounded head and face, a light but not slender form, and the most serious of countenances—a sense of responsibility already marked in the concentrated gaze at whatever she may have been told to fix her eyes upon, and in the resolute small mouth with its slightly contracted underlip. One slim sandalled foot comes forward as though for dancing ; the other, well behind, assists her in preserving the poise of which her mother was so proud. It is indeed a strikingly graceful little figure, and somehow a touching one. That dutiful gravity, that earnest submission to the hour's demand—though common to children's portraits—seem in this one to proceed from deeper sources, to foreshadow the Annabella of twenty-three, and of many another year with hours more rigorous than that in which Hoppner posed her for his picture.

When she was thirty-nine, Annabella Byron posed herself for what she called an Auto-Description. Thursday's Child, from the Far-to-go, looked back at the little girl on the seashore and wrote :

Few of my pleasures were connected with realities—riding was the only one I can remember. When I climbed the rocks, or bounded over the sands with apparent delight, I was *not myself*. Perhaps I had been shipwrecked or was trying to rescue other sufferers—some of my hours were spent in the Pass of Thermo-pylæ, others with the Bishop of Marseilles in the midst of the Pestilence, or with Howard in the cheerless dungeon.

What was the consequence in regard of my pursuits and studies ? That none were agreeable to me which had not some reference to sentiment, to the exhibition of human nature in moving situations. . . . It could not be supposed that I should

ANNABELLA MILBANKE

After the portrait by Hoppner at Ockham Park

confine my idealism to the realms of Fiction. [It] was soon applied to living materials, and I smile on looking back to some of which my heroes and heroines were compounded. Those were my idols—but they dwelt in a secret shrine. . . . I never spoke of these—passions, I must call them. They were sacred.

About the age of 13 I . . . began to throw my imagination into a home-sphere of action—to constrain myself, from religious principle, to attend to what was irksome, and to submit to what was irritating. I had great difficulties to surmount from the impetuosity and sensitiveness of my character. When misunderstood, I felt bitterness and despair —when ridiculed, an excess of false shame—when unjustly accused, the madness of pride to such a degree that I have struck my head with my hand till I have staggered back. It was this stage of my character which prepared me to sympathize unboundedly with the morbidly susceptible—with those who felt themselves unknown.

From want of means of comparison, I was not sufficiently sensible of the real blessings of my lot, and was always craving for the excitements which it denied—excitements which it requires long years to teach us are incompatible with the ends of human existence.

She was only eight when Sophy Curzon married Lord Tamworth, and left the Seaham household. The match was frowned upon by Earl Ferrers, Lord Tamworth's father ; he made himself so obnoxious that Lady Milbanke was driven to write him a scathing letter, the draft of which has been preserved. Whether it was sent or not we do not know ; at any rate it was the sort of letter which to write is a pleasure of the keenest, and Judith Milbanke —eloquent, downright, mistress of vehement rebuke—very evidently enjoyed writing it. But love prevailed in the end, though the Tamworth pair were long ostracised by the " Erl-King," as Lord Ferrers was nicknamed by Sophy and her champions.

In much later years Annabella wrote of this parting from her elder sister :

I had prayed for that event—it was, I thought, to ensure her happiness ; but when the time came, when I passed her vacant apartment next to mine, the misery of my loss became insupportable to me. I remember feeling, for the first time, as if the actual scene was visionary. . . . I made one attempt to confide my despair ; I encountered a contemptuous sort of reproof, and I shrank into an existence of solitary reverie.

She had been passionately devoted to Sophy, but timidity had held her from expression of " that indwelling fervid feeling." " I was too fearful of intruding." At night she had, like all of her type, been wont to picture situations in which she might serve Sophy as she loved her, and " romantic love assumed in my estimation the rank of an exalted virtue."

Il n'y a pas d'enfantillage. When Paul Bourget wrote those words, he might have had in mind just such a child as this. So much of what she was, both in her bloom and her maturity, is implicit in the two narratives from which I have quoted that though they were composed many years later, we feel that so the child did even then confront experience. Her defects are no less manifest than her qualities—the emotional force, and the morbid sensibility ; the reserve, and the proud withdrawal into a self-centred world of reverie ; the ardent dreaming, and the absorption in an ideal of " perfection," with its extravagant demands upon herself and others.

However, she was only eight when Sophy married, and Sophy's image was soon replaced by that of another young lady-in-love. This was the Harriet Bland of whom (in both narratives) she writes as " beautiful, lonely, and romantically devoted." And again, she never showed this passionate admiration.

> It burst forth only after I had said a farewell which, as I then expected, was the last. For some days I wept in every interval of solitude, and I am certain that during the year and a half which elapsed before I heard of her death, her image was constantly present in my mind.

But tears and intervals of solitude were not all. One traditional delight of little girls was not, indeed, among her delights. Aunt Mary Noel tells us that " Annabella was never fond of a doll." We need not interpret this exclusively as lack of the maternal instinct—too simplified explanation of what in her was a complex trait. Like all children, she loved make-believe, and her make-believe always implied self-devotion ; but it implied as well a struggle against adverse destiny from which *she* was to be the rescuer. " Like a boy "—and just as much like a girl, if the girl is one with an impulse to protect the conscious, not the merely helpless, struggler. That impulse was strong in Annabella Milbanke ; in Annabella Byron it became supreme, excessive— the expression of an almost fanatical ideal. The helplessness of infancy and childhood did not awaken it ; she had too much of intellectual pride for that. The mind must take part before she could feel devotion ; mere tendance, as on babyhood, made little appeal to her imagination. Thus we find her writing to her mother about her own baby : " I talk of it for your satisfaction, not my own, and shall be very glad when you have it under your eye." And we observe the neuter pronoun, to most young mothers inconceivable.

Magnanimity—that was the spur. But not blind magnani- mity! Part of her formidable incorruptibility, this was. Devotion was not to be a reason for denying the weaknesses of its objects. So early as her seventh year she sounded that note. Some one asked her if her father were not always right. She answered : " Probably not. Sometimes right, sometimes wrong, as we all are." The questioner's face, as these words fell from the lips of seven, should have been worth seeing.

At nine she was given an allowance of £20 a year, paid quarterly by Sir Ralph's estate-agent. She was to give her own receipt— an impressive arrangement which does not either explain or commend itself. But everything seems to have been designed to develop the serious fold in her nature. At ten, the poor infant was reading Smollett's History. There were no Little Arthurs and Mrs. Markhams in those days, but surely there must have been somebody more indulgent than Smollett for childish minds ? She summed up her impression with scornful lucidity : " There seem to have been more weak kings than wise ones."

Reading the letters of her maternal uncle, Lord Wentworth, we divine that Annabella harked back to the collateral side. Certainly there did not come from father or mother the tinge of pedantry which made her, through life, alternately the anxiety and the amusement of her friends. Neither Ralph nor Judith Milbanke had an ounce of pedantry about them ; and so there was much to redress the balance. Her companionship with

" Dad and Mam " was close and refreshingly unceremonious. As a daughter she was quite without solemnities, lavishing pet-names and nicknames on both, calling her mother Judy, her father " chicken," " old goose," and (for a change) " Bright Daystar." She never lost this vein with them, even when life had played its evil trick upon her.

A devoted couple, these parents—as childless and long-childless couples so often are. Ralph might now and then get " as drunk as poison " (his wife's phrase), like nearly every other man in those days ; Judith might always display that extreme of solicitude about the affairs of those she loved which caused her to be " managed " by such people as understood the art, and vituperated by the son-in-law who never managed anybody, least of all himself. But we have only to read her daughter's reminiscences of the daily life at Seaham, to realise that Lady Milbanke's fussiness was the outcome of warmhearted energy.

> Amongst the many interests that engaged the zealous good offices of my Parents, I never saw any preferred to the comfort of the labouring poor. It then seemed to me as a mere matter of course that the best horse should be sent many miles for the best Doctor, to attend on Rustics who are usually consigned to the Parish Medical Officer—that the finest Claret should be taken out of the Cellar to be applied to the exhausted Patients in a Tenant's house. I did not think that property could be possessed by any other tenure than that of being at the service of those in need. It was all so simple ! Yet my Mother put a spirit into it—she did not leave it to servants. She saw that the execution was as good as the Intention.

But the Lady Bountiful was by no means all of her. Like so many men and women of her time, she was a champion letter-writer. Long screeds, and very vivid and amusing ones, went almost daily to Aunt Mary, who responded in kind ; and when Annabella was five (for everything was dated by Annabella) there arose a craze for patchwork, to which Judith succumbed. She was already a practised spinstress ; she and Aunt Mary had been wont eagerly to compare notes about their wheels ; but when patchwork dawned on the horizon of country-house visits, the wheel was eclipsed. " Spend a guinea on small pieces of linen. Borders—all sorts of colours. . . . *Staring* flowers and leaves. They are cut into *Hexagons*, and mixed with white in a particular manner." And one day in the June of 1798—Annabella six—Aunt Mary in London received from her best-beloved a letter which must have had many parallels in recent years. " Do ladies *à mon âge* cut their hair behind ? I long to do it, because it would be so comfortable for riding." And Aunt Mary replied :

> They are all cut shortish—that is long enough to curl, hang all blowsy, and stick out a mile from the head behind ; but . . . it is not at all particular to have it cut, and as to *votre âge* there is no such thing ; everybody dresses as girls.

So they were doing it all in those far-off days—and saying it all too ; and on the 30th of July, Judith, aged 46, at last summoned courage to cut her hair, and everyone said she looked younger for it.

She was the grey mare ; and Ralph seems only passively to have kicked in the traces. " Ralph, as usual," did not do this or that as he had been expected or commissioned to do—phrase which how many wives have written and will write ! Judith was his complement—practical, impulsive, swift in action, kindly as he but a good deal more clear-sighted, except perhaps where Clermont was concerned. " A dasher in her day . . . pettish and tiresome, but clever." So she was to be described by the best man at that wedding which turned out so sadly different from her own.

The best man found a more indulgent word for Ralph. " An honest red-faced spirit, a little prosy, but by no means devoid of humour " ; and the bridegroom never included his father-in-law in the fulminations which he incessantly poured upon the Milbanke household in days to come. Turning again to Annabella's reminiscences, we find a character-sketch of the father to whom she was so warmly, if so judicially, attached :

> His kindliness and cordiality won every heart ; his good-nature was as constant as spontaneous—not called out by particular occasions, or by gratified feelings, but ready at all times for man, woman, and child. Sterne has hit upon such a character in Uncle Toby, but my Father's mind was far from being as limited. Of Shakespeare, Otway, Dryden, he was a devoted admirer, pointing out or reciting to me their finest

passages. . . . Perhaps this superabundance of poetical feeling unfitted him for practical life. He could not deal with men, tho' he could gain their love. He had no weight as an M.P.—tho' so often elected because he was personally popular. The Prince Regent showed him favour as a jovial companion, but that was all, except invitations to his Wife and Daughter. . . . He was indifferent as to sects and denominations—friendly to Quakers and Wesleyans. . . . He was energetic in his attendance on Parliament—would go to London from Seaham in snow, 270 miles, 3 days and nights ; and even when gouty, to give his silent vote for the Emancipation or against Pitt's measures.[1]

In the Evenings, I remember when we were alone, Musical performances by my Father on the Violin, by my Mother on the pianoforte—Handel, Corelli, and other old composers ; or Cards—when I was included occasionally, as partner at Casino or in Cribbage or Commerce. I would rather have amused myself, and was but a poor player. At Chess I succeeded better and learned to beat my Mother, who never shewed talent for that game, tho' extremely fond of it—

Here the reminiscences break off.

The couple were "scarcely ever apart" ; but unfashionable though this was, they were by no means a dull provincial pair of Northern county-people. Their connections were too many, and too variegated, for that. The most exciting of these—but the least often visited—was Ralph's sister Elizabeth, Viscountess Melbourne, brightest star in the constellation which then rained influence on London society, cleverest great lady of her time, and possibly most unscrupulous too ; at any rate, a connection of whom there was always something to hear and (if one happened to take it so) disapprove. Judith did take it so. Lady Melbourne was, indeed, the crumple in the roseleaf, the "in-law" whose name would oftenest crop up when things went wrong between the happy pair ; for it was felt by the wife that the sister had too much influence over simple-minded Ralph, and that she used it to her own advantage solely.

However, there were plenty of other connections and plenty of other friends ; plenty of race-meetings, too, in Durham and Newcastle, to which the Milbankes would go off " by themselves "

---

[1] In 1812 Sir Ralph retired from Parliament, " after twenty years of neglected Whiggery, and the loss of all his property over elections." (*Astarte*, pp : 359-60.)

SIR RALPH MILBANKE

After the portrait by Reynolds at Ockham Park

to stay in lodgings. And moreover, Sir Ralph had been M.P.
for Durham County for two years before their daughter was born,
so that part of the year was always spent in London.

Not a dull household, we see, and by no means an uncultured
one. We may suspect that the library was dearer to Papa and
Annabella than to Mamma, who was taken up with her patchwork, her garden, her riding. She liked visiting the neighbours
and tenants, with a friendly finger ready to stick in everybody's
pie, and consequent plums to bring back for the Jack Horners at
home, writing their verses and reading their Milton and Cowper
and Campbell. Ralph could write verses as well as appreciate
them. By a dazzling great lady in London he was described as
" old twaddle Ralph " ; and as this was Elizabeth, Duchess of
Devonshire,[1] it does seem to point to his being something of a
bore. For Lady Elizabeth, in the Duke, had learnt what " the
personified quintessence of English apathy " could be ; she
suffered *him* because he was a Duke besides, but she must have
known all about masculine dulness.

However, Ralph was not a twaddle for his daughter. She
was on the gayest of easy terms with Papa, who was obviously
the favourite parent. Mamma was good company too, and
(much more critically) loved ; but Papa could write verses,
could teach her to write them herself, and moreover could make
jokes of a kind which—oddly enough—delighted his daughter as
child, young lady of the London seasons, wife, mother, and
heroine of tragedy. These were harmless little ribaldries about
women's legs, ankles, and skirts ; about fleas and even lice—
creatures surely taken on trust by the young lady of Hoppner's
portrait, who nevertheless compared herself to both in her second
London season. " As gay as a Flea, and as smart as a Louse."
The latter clause is reassuring ; she cannot have known much
about the Louse.

But the poetry was Papa's chief charm. They vied with one
another in composition—would enclose copies of verses in their

[1] The " Inseparable " of Georgiana, Duchess of the same Duke of Devonshire, throughout that exquisite creature's life. Georgiana was Reynolds's
Beautiful Duchess, and heroine of the famous " Kiss for the vote " episode,
during Charles James Fox's candidature in 1784. She died in 1806 ; and
Lady Elizabeth Foster, born Hervey, who had been for years the Duke's
mistress, became his Duchess in 1809.

letters ; and if most of these were of the frivolous order, Annabella at least could be serious—not to say solemn—in metre too.
In Seaham village lived a poet, " an unfortunate child of Genius "
—one Joseph Blacket, a cobbler's son, whom her parents actively
befriended.   Whether they took him seriously as poet, or (like
Byron) very much the reverse, Annabella was impressed by
his attempts.   One of the early records is a copy of verses to her,
" on her presenting the author with a beautiful edition of
Cowper's Poems "—just a year before Blacket's death in 1810,
at twenty-three.

Annabella was then seventeen, a girl absorbed in things of
the mind, writing about anything and everything, setting up a
private magazine, which still survives in a large quarto manu-
script-book, and bears the marks of most private magazines—
scrupulous professionalism in the matter of titles and arrangement, handwriting of inhuman perfection ; the whole designed
as for an eternity of zeal . . . and gradually, gradually, the
tailing-off for *that* year, and the phoenix rising from the fair
reproachful pages with the new one—to soar another while,
again sink to earth, again spread resolute pinions, and so on until
at last it dies indeed.

The magazine might be abandoned ; poetry was not.   Blacket
had died ; but there was another victim of genius—much longer
dead—to be mused upon.   This was the Irish Thomas Dermody,
who had drunk himself to madness and death in 1802, when
Miss Milbanke was only ten years old.   In 1809 she wrote the
Lines supposed to be spoken at the Grave of Dermody.   It is one of
the earliest of her compositions extant.   Let us read some of these
lines ; for they belong in a dual sense to her story.

> Degraded genius ! o'er the untimely grave
> In which the tumults of thy breast were still'd,
> The rank weeds wave, and every flower that springs
> Withers, or ere it bloom.   Thy dwelling here
> Is desolate, and speaks thee as thou wert,
> An outcast from mankind, one whose hard fate
> Indignant virtue should forbid to weep. . . .
> The innate consciousness of greater powers
> Than one in thousand know to estimate
> Will with the frown of restless discontent
> Oft mark his brow who owns them. . . .

These, with some other verses, were sent to Byron for his opinion in 1812, by Annabella's cousin-by-marriage, Lady Caroline Lamb. He liked the Dermody lines " so much that I could wish they were in rhyme." They might, indeed, have been written expressly to please him whose brow was so well acquainted with the frown of restless discontent ; but he praised other pieces too, and then went on to say :

I have no desire to be better acquainted with Miss Milbanke ; [1] she is too good for a fallen spirit to know, and I should like her better if she were less perfect.

We shall see how little he knew himself—or how well he knew Caroline Lamb—when he wrote that invidious praise ; but for our moment Miss Milbanke is still at Seaham, still earnestly writing poetry, and as a contrast making shoes. This activity was a by-product of the French Revolution. Girls were, for some reason unexplained (to the intelligence of the present writer, at any rate), taught to make their own shoes, and Annabella learnt like the rest—apparently under Clermont's supervision, for the magazine displays an advertisement of " Messrs. Milbanke and Clermont's superior style of cutting shoes for ladies of fashion." Shoes, it is true, were fragile affairs, made of the thinnest kid or satin ; ladies of condition never wore any kind of leather. So these " pedal vestments " may have been as practical as most others were.

Poetry and shoemaking were part of the daily round ; a grander ambition was taking shape. *Translations from Horace.* The quarto volume should see the finished achievement ; meanwhile a note-book was good enough. It duly received the first attempt under that sanguine heading. Three lines and a half of English verse . . . and then this phoenix sank for evermore amid its scanty ashes. What had Papa thought of the scheme, we wonder ? Infatuate though he was, we cannot doubt that Papa had chuckled to himself.

[1] They had met at Melbourne House.

CHAPTER II

1811

THE FIRST LONDON SEASON

" ARRIVED at the age of 17, I was anxious to postpone my entrance into the world, of which I had formed no pleasing conception." They did not hurry her, for not only seventeen but eighteen was allowed to pass ; at nineteen, though, a young lady really had to come out. Surprisingly enough, her parents did not see her through the first London season ; for when in the spring of 1811 she took the plunge, it was from Lady Gosford's,[1] daughter-in-law of an old friend of Lady Milbanke's, and the " M.G." of Annabella's correspondence. " M.G." was one of her two great friends at this time ; the other, " M.M.", was Miss Mary Millicent Montgomery. Here we see the protective impulse at work, for of these two intimates Lady Gosford was an unhappy wife, and Miss Montgomery a confirmed invalid. Annabella's letters are full of references to both, throughout the early years and for many years afterwards.

The initiation was comparatively dull ; or it may be that we, in our frivolity, would have liked to read of new acquaintances more dazzling than the most erudite of professors and editors, and a Mr. Walpole who was writing " a serious work on literature." But Miss Milbanke, aged nineteen, seems to have enjoyed her evenings with these gentlemen much more than that on which her Aunt Melbourne took her to the Opera. All she had to say about the Opera was that it was " a considerable fatigue to me, who do not take pleasure in flirting or listening to squalling."

She wrote this to Mamma, whose prejudice against Lady Melbourne may have coloured the report. In the article of

[1] Born Mary Sparrow. Her brother married Lady Olivia Acheson, daughter of Viscount Acheson, afterwards Earl of Gosford.

flirting, at any rate, the next season was to give it the lie. For whatever she may have thought about flirtation—that name for a delightful minor art at the birth of which Johnson's Lord Chesterfield assisted, hearing it "fall from the most charming lips in the world"—she must have demurely practised it in 1812, when suitors flocked around the girl who in 1811 had only two. One was a nebulous Mr. Mackenzie; the other was Lord Auckland's heir, George Eden. He was strongly supported by Lady Melbourne; but Annabella applied her own standard, and George Eden was refused. He wrote her, in the July of this year, a touching letter: "Be a friend to my mother and sisters [1]— I have taught them to love you, and *they* need not unlearn it." The Aucklands were old friends of the Milbanke family; so "agitation" and "a distressing state of confusion" had to be gone through later, in the season of 1812. But all was well; the parents had not borne malice, and George Eden as a suitor seemed to be happily disposed-of. He was not, as we shall see.

This conquest could not, however, be reckoned among London triumphs, for Eden was a friend of Annabella's childhood. During the first immersion it is plain that she never, in the worldly sense, found her feet at all. In the Auto-Description we read of 1811:

> I met with one or two who, like myself, did not appear absorbed in the present scene—and who interested me in a degree. I had a wish to find amongst men the character I had often imagined—but I found only parts of it. One gave proofs of worth, but had no sympathy for high aspirations—another seemed full of affection towards his family, and yet he valued the world. I was clear-sighted in these cases—but I was to become blind!

Lady Gosford may have had her own ideas about her friend's comparative failure. Already she had bantered Annabella upon her extreme seriousness, for in an early letter to M.G. we read: "I have so frequently written what might afford a just opportunity for wickedness"—wickedness here standing for no more

---

[1] One of these sisters was the Emily Eden who wrote, among other novels, *The Semi-Attached Couple*—an Austenish story which has been reprinted with notable success in very recent years.

than teasing. Such opportunities she was to afford so long as she lived; for she had a sense of fun but not of humour, could laugh at other people but only very seldom at herself, and even in the letters to her parents, full of little impertinences as they are, the only child is manifest—the petted darling, able to smile at them for adoring her, but not at herself for being adored. " I am a sweet chicken, a barley-sugar daughter. . . . I am tired of paying compliments to myself, but you may send me as many as you like."

There was bluff, perhaps, in her boast that she believed " a civil war will ensue because I cannot divide myself or be in two places at once " ; but she *had* begun to pick and choose between invitations—avoided a ball (" a ball is a public nuisance ") by going into the country ; would not visit another house because the hostess's venison was high ; was in short the slightly spoilt child and the " blue " young lady with a sharp tongue and pen. In her sedulously-kept diary there are blighting comments on most of the people she met ; such as on the Mr. Walpole of the serious work on literature : " His face is rather pretty, and his manners of the same cast." A Mr. White is ambiguously presented : " He possesses powers of rapid elocution " ; a Mr. Robinson is " clever, but afraid people will not notice it " ; and the renowned Miss Lydia White (a prominent Blue) is judged not to be confident of her own powers of attraction, and therefore willing to admit " persons of *common* sense " to her parties. But it is conscientiously added : " This may be from good-nature too."

No unusual experience—this sense of disillusionment on first encountering London. But about one of her new acquaintances she had this to say : " She has more humility than I have "— so there were searchings of heart as well, of a kind which persisted throughout life. And with reason ; for there was a vein of spiritual pride in Annabella Milbanke, always to be reckoned with despite the efforts at subdual. In this first season, when she merely passed amid the crowd, there was little to dazzle her ; and she abounded in complacent severities, believing that of London she had now taken the measure, was intellectual mistress of the glittering deception—which, for that matter, she never honestly confessed to enjoying, even in the subsequent days of triumph.

That in 1812 she did enjoy it like any less sublime young lady, there is no question ; but the note of scorn was kept up and even emphasised. It was an attitude like another, and one which affords many of those " just opportunities for wickedness " ; though in days very soon to come, it could impress—yet also stir to an indulgent defence of " the world "—a more extravagant but more humorous, more ironic attitudiniser than herself.

At one point she certainly does differ from most girls, and evidently from her mother, in that throughout her entire correspondence we never find an allusion to dress, either of her own or others. Yet for an emancipated spirit the fashions of the time offered a fine occasion for satire. Looking nowadays at a number of *La Belle Assemblée* for 1812, we shiver as we look. It was a very cold winter, but morning-dresses " continue to be made in white muslin, which is more fashionable than anything else." Indeed, it was considered indelicate to wear anything else ; " a woman habited in cloth is less feminine than if she were clothed in transparent gauze." A drawing shows us a lady sitting out-of-doors in October. She wears nothing in the shape of a wrap but a shawl, which we should call a scarf, of rose-coloured Chinese silk " thrown negligently over the shoulders." Very negligently, for it covers only one ; and the cambric gown is cut low, with long sleeves it is true—but what were these in an English October ! The shoes are of straw-coloured kid, thin as may be, and very shallow. Leather had been called by *La Belle Assemblée* " quite gothic and canaillish." Furs were held to be " gross "—not, as now, for humanitarian reasons ; white muffs could be tolerated, but " the bear-muff and tippet was visible in Hyde Park, on Sunday last, only with a few grisettes and dowagers of the bourgeois." So scathing a remark would put an end to any budding craze. Even cashmere shawls (first worn in Europe by Napoleon's Josephine, who liked them as well or even better than our Victoria was to like them) were shuddered at by *La Belle Assemblée*. " Totally destitute of every idea of ease, elegance, or dignity."[1]

Miss Milbanke was to be described as " rather dowdy-looking " on the eve of her wedding ; but there is nothing in her girlish

[1] Quoted from *La Belle Assemblée* in *Our Grandmother's Gowns*, with preface by Mrs. Alfred Hunt. 1884.

letters or diaries to show that she despised the fashion. Nothing, it is true, to show that she revered it either; yet we might have expected that she to whom the Opera was fatiguing and a ball a public nuisance would have exercised her satiric vein upon the deadlier follies of *La Belle Assemblée*. Here too she evidently submitted to the hour's demand, as at ten she had submitted to the white muslin gown and long trailing scarf in the Seaham seashore portrait. But in the portrait that seashore was fictive, symbolic merely of her childhood's home.

She was back there, settled down into the old life, in the September after this trial-trip—writing Reflections on Gratitude and how to keep it alive. Reflections on gratitude usually mean that we are not feeling it, and indeed she said as much.

> Will not a temporary mortification, a worldly disappointment, extinguish that gratitude which should have influence lasting as my life? I know the temptation that has before caused me to yield, will come again. Be not this added to the instances of my guilt!

Nineteen—and truly youth alone could have been capable of that Reflection.

But there was always poetry. Campbell, just then at the top of his short-lived vogue; Ossian, the unreadable of to-day; Milton—and with the New Year of 1812 a Captain Boothby (met during the London season), as a visitor with whom to read the last, but not the other two. For he did not admire either Campbell or Ossian; and indeed he seems to have been a person of delicate discriminations, though not advanced in thought. They were reading *Paradise Lost*; he said that "he believed almost all the events in it." Only almost; and he went on to point out a passage in Book X which proves that, when diction was his theme, he knew what he was talking about. It occurs in Eve's speech to Adam:

> "While yet we live, but one short hour perhaps,
> Between us two let there be peace."

The simplicity of these words was their beauty, said Captain Boothby—a hint which, whether he designed it or not, Annabella would have done well in taking to herself. She did not so take it, then or ever; but it is clear that he occupied her thoughts, as they said in those days, for he figures largely in her diary wherein (how like her it was !) she made a list of his good qualities. There were no bad ones—in the list, at any rate. But the following entry says, or sighs : " Captain Boothby left us on the 6th "— and there an end of him, except for a visit he paid in March at Seaham. Annabella was away from home, and Sir Ralph reported to her that Boothby seemed much upset.

A Reverend Mr. Darnell followed in this January of 1812. He too read Milton. This time it was *Comus*, and the whole party joined in, Annabella and her guests taking the various parts. They did the Trial-Scene from the *Merchant of Venice* too, and she " never heard anyone read with more discriminating judgment than Mr. Darnell." So Captain Boothby was forgotten, whatever he may have hoped.

1811, and the New Year of 1812. There was nothing of Byron's to be read at that time, beyond his early verses and *English Bards and Scotch Reviewers*. July had seen him back in England after the Greek tour—a young man of twenty-three, not yet " in society." He had returned to encounter that succession of tragic deaths which inspired the fantastic will wherein he asked to be buried beside his dog ; Newstead was only just cleared of bailiffs ; the eternal question of Rochdale was dragging its weary length. He had a poem in his pocket, but one of which he had a very poor opinion. It was the eclipse before the dawn, for the poem in his pocket was *Childe Harold*.

The only link of which he was at this time conscious between him and Miss Milbanke was his acquaintance with Joseph Blacket's poetry and fate. He thought slightingly of the poetry, as she was to learn ; and not less slightingly of the patronage which, in his view, had done the poor young cobbler more harm than good.

But for us who now reflect upon these two there was another link, more intimate and far more poignant. They were both the only children of their houses—a circumstance which, in his own person, was one of Byron's pet vanities. " The fiercest animals have the fewest numbers in their litters." In the list of

his connections with such litters which he long afterwards made,
Byron did not forget his wife ; but how different, in its superficial likeness, was the only childhood of each ! He, the son of
separated parents—one a dissipated spendthrift ; the other a
woman of violent, ungovernable temper, the most injudicious,
most unlivable-with of recorded mothers, with whom he lived
and from whom he suffered throughout infancy, boyhood, and
early adolescence—inured to penury and ostracism, badgered,
infuriated, disgraced, embittered. And she, the darling centre
of her parents' every thought and hope ; scarce knowing what
dissension was, not knowing at all what penury, ostracism,
disgrace in any form can bring of bitterness and anger—a girl of
inexperience so profound that her gifts of the mind worked rather
to narrow than to broaden her perceptions. With her brown
head bent upon her poets and her poems, she lived in an imaginary
world, intensifying all that was to wreck her in the actual one.

Byron's disastrous boyhood taught him a lesson which she, in
her Atlantis of home-worship, never learned—the necessity for
making allowances. They were to be wrecked, both of them ;
to be in fault, both of them—he far more than she in fault ; yet
there are moments when irresistibly we feel that rigour in her
shows forth against some quality in him—call it mere mutability,
if we will—which might have . . . not indeed saved that foredoomed marriage ; but at least, had she possessed it, brought
about an hour less agonising than that in which " she walked
about the room, her whole frame shaken with her sobs, imploring
his servant to ' remember ' the farewell message that he had been
unable to hear."

The daughter of the house at Seaham and Halnaby never went
to school. That too was out of her knowledge—that communal
life which teaches things so different from those taught by home-
life, and especially to a girl without brothers or male cousins.
It is true that girls of her rank did not in those days leave home
for school. It was then not even thought of ; she could not have
regretted the loss of an experience which was entirely out of her
reckoning—yet, leaving that social circumstance aside, we can
hardly doubt that it would have been well for her to be plunged
into an atmosphere more bracing than that of Seaham adoration.
A typically home-bred girl, unversed in the lessons petty

enough in themselves—which school-life thrusts upon the consciousness, married Byron in the persuasion that she could suffice
to him, that her qualities of heart and mind could prevail against
" the world," and what Byron had been in the world. Had she
known but that little more of struggle, emulation, need of self-
assertion, need no less of self-effacement, there might have been
the ghost of a chance for her. Marriage with Byron was fatal
for any type of woman ; but Annabella's disaster might have
proved less tragically bitter for herself, in that it might have
awakened less malignity and resentment in him, had she ever
been forced to recognise a standard different from her own. That
was the only one she knew, and it was not enough. She was
always the Annabella who at eight had " shrunk into an existence
of solitary reverie," because someone told her she must not fret
over Sophy Curzon's departure. That single standard of hers
she applied to everything : not because she was arrogant, but
because she was ignorant. So, when life gripped her by the
throat, she had no kind of measure for the adversary's power.
She fought heroically—under that personal standard ; prevailed,
and knew herself the vanquished ; did right, and longed to have
been able to do wrong :

> I can remember wishing it was right to give up all for one
> —even to be a slave or victim. . . .   There was a burning world
> within. . . .   I had given up all that was congenial with youth
> —the imagination of what *might have been* was all that remained.
> —The touch of every hand seemed cold.   I could look on tears
> without sympathy.

CHAPTER III

1812

THE TRIUMPHANT LONDON SEASON

In 1812 Sophy Tamworth wrote to Lady Milbanke of Annabella :
" It is not every day that she is likely to meet with a Mind which
ought to claim kindred with one so superior as hers."

Sophy, as we know, had done this sort of thing in the schoolroom ; and for posterity it is no worse than laughable. But the
atmosphere it suggests is bad for superior minds, sedulously
making themselves more and more superior. Annabella was now
reading Cowper's *Iliad* and annotating every second line ; she
was studying Alfieri with the family-solicitor's daughter ; for
relaxation condescending to *Evelina*. In *Evelina* she was disappointed, like a good many more of its readers—more perhaps
than make the confession. There was study of Southey,
Wordsworth, and Coleridge as well, for everyone was reading
them ; and moreover at this time she met in Durham a Mrs.
Southey who knew Coleridge and did not at all like him.
" Intolerably self-sufficient," said Mrs. Southey, and she de-
plored her famous relative's devotion to him. The " Lakers,"
as Byron called them, were making themselves strongly felt, and
(at this moment) Southey most strongly of all. So Annabella
waded through *Madoc*. She found some passages wearisome,
but was convinced that Southey would one day be ranked high
" among the ancient poets." Her prophecy may have come true,
for it is impossible to tell what she meant by it. She was often
guilty of this woolly kind of writing.

So the days ambled by—studious, complacent on the surface,
but with an undertow of the restlessness and irritability to which
the Auto-Description confesses. There is a letter from Annabella to her mother of February 9, 1812, when they were both

at Seaham. She was aching for M.M. and London, though she
thought it was only for M.M., now iller than ever. The parents
wished her to stay at home ; the spoilt child had made them a
scene during the day. They had yielded, of course ; and in her
room at night she wrote this letter, feeling ashamed of herself
but not directly acknowledging it. She would wait a fortnight,
she said, because Papa was not well ; but in a fortnight, go she
must. The expressions are dutiful and loving ; but it is clear
that her parents had been deeply wounded, and unable to conceal
their pain.

It was quickly forgotten, and in less than her fortnight she
started for London and Lady Gosford's. On the way she wrote
home from every stopping-place. Her letters are pervaded by
a theme which so often reappears—even in the after-stages of
the Separation-Drama—that it is worth dwelling on for a moment.
That theme is mutton-chops. From Wetherby, in this February,
she told Sir Ralph that she had dined on " *fleecy* mutton-chops."
Enough, one would think, to make her order anything else when
she got to Grantham next day. But no. She ordered mutton-
chops, ate " twice two, and frightened the waiters." And afterwards mutton-chops are so constantly reported on for praise or
blame that we cannot but recall Byron's fantastic dislike to seeing
a woman eat, and remember too that (as he wrote to Lady
Melbourne during his first stay at Seaham as Annabella's
betrothed) she was " never well for two days together." It does
emerge from her letters that she was inclined to be greedy. We
read of her eating too many peaches (with her own commentary
of " Beast ! "), of a goose-pie being clamoured for by both her and
" B."—to which demand Mrs. Clermont (then in London) adds a
postscript pleading for a small sample of the same north-country
dish for herself. All through Annabella's correspondence with
her parents, especially after the separation, food plays a large
part, with a frequent corollary of " biliousness " and its varying
remedies.

Arrived in London, at the Gosfords' house in Cumberland
Place, she wrote from bed next morning that she was wearied
with happiness. " Such a welcome—and M.M. looking better
for a moment, but soon pale and weak again." But this was the

one cloud. The season of 1812 was to prove a triumph. She was for the first time complimented on her bloom, and adds complacently : " My complexion has become so clear, my eyes so lively, and my muscles so round that I have not looked so well this year past." And again :

> I am quite the fashion this year. Mankind bow before me, and womankind think me somebody. But without jest I am certain that I am better liked in company, probably because I am stronger, and more able to exert myself in scenes of dissipation.

Naturally, after this, the old folks at home wanted a miniature. She went to see Hayter, then just establishing his reputation, and reported : " You must pay *Twenty* for me—I cannot get done decently for less." It was not thought too much for the barley-sugar daughter, and Hayter was engaged. He decided to paint her with her hair loose, " as he says that formal arrangement of dress is not consistent with my character." In this she obeyed him ; yet the long loose hair in the picture does not succeed in conveying any effect of informality—which, to modern eyes and minds, is by no means a characteristic of Miss Milbanke. She declared that Hayter had never seen *her* countenance, " because it is under the depressing influence of shyness in his presence." Miss Montgomery went with her to one sitting, " to make your chicken smile upon the picture-maker. She is in high beauty—at least as far as her snub face can be—and grinning from ear to ear."

In Hayter's miniature—the only picture of the grown-up Annabella Milbanke that we possess—she certainly is not grinning from ear to ear ; but M.M.'s was no doubt a generalised impression of her looks during the triumphant season. It was a self-conscious countenance that Hayter saw, or at any rate rendered— the countenance of a young lady unmistakably sitting for her portrait. Not a pretty young lady, yet one whom we can imagine to have been (as Byron said of her to Medwin) piquante. The snub face of M.M.'s fond disparagement is clearly capable of just the sort of fun that we find in Annabella's letters ; but the thin lips, though sweet in expression and with a prophetic sadness hovering about them, are as clearly lips that will not laugh at

ANNABELLA MILBANKE IN HER TWENTIETH YEAR

After the miniature by Hayter

life's more elaborate bad jokes. Even if we knew nothing about her, this picture would speak to us of a girl who was going to take things hard. It is the face of one whose character was, as her mother wrote to her in 1816, " like *Proof Spirits*, not fit for common use." One of the consummate phrases which this group of people frequently struck off, it was tenderly felt, yet reveals a clear perception of where the danger lay. Resolution is in the wide strong cheek and firm reticent lips—resolution so tyrannous as to destroy its possessor rather than let her accept the weakness of compromise.

Posterity may read all this into Hayter's miniature, but there was respite before it came true. She had her day, in the shape of a London season's triumph. That she should go everywhere was a matter-of-course for Lady Melbourne's niece and Lord Wentworth's presumptive heiress. Miss Milbanke was a " match " ; yet this is not enough to account for her success in the season of 1812. She must have been genuinely attractive to men, for suitors and partners came in battalions. Among her admirers was Augustus Foster, son of Elizabeth Duchess of Devonshire by her first husband ; and he, though notoriously susceptible, was faithful to Annabella for quite a long time. The Duchess would have liked the match ; she would even have urged her son to refuse the offered appointment of British Minister in Washington, if Miss Milbanke had not fancied America. But Miss Milbanke did not fancy Augustus. His mother wrote to him :

> She persists in saying that she never suspected your attach-
> ment to her, but she is so odd a girl that though she has for some
> time rather liked another, she has decidedly refused him,
> because she thinks she ought to marry a person with a good
> fortune, and this is partly, I believe, from generosity to her
> parents, and partly owning that fortune is an object to herself
> for happiness. In short, she is good, amiable, and sensible, but
> cold, prudent, and reflecting.

This does not convince us, whatever it may have done for Augustus, who as a member of the powerful Devonshire House group had every prospect of a brilliant future.

George Eden, though definitely rejected the year before, still hovered about her ; and there was another *parti* in the person of Lord Jocelyn, Treasurer of the Household to the Prince Regent. Much favoured by Lady Gosford, he was " ugly, bandy-legged, very tall, ungraceful," and (not surprisingly) he failed to please, though she wrote with complacent indulgence in her diary : " His love appears at times in Society to oppress his feelings, which however he commands in a manly manner."

General Pakenham—described by M.M. as a " wild Irishman " —was early on the scene in 1812. Dates seem to show that he, whose Christian name is never mentioned, was Lord Longford's eldest son ; so here was yet another *parti* to disprove Lady Betty. Annabella at first thought his manners " too silken " ; then he began to please her by the enthusiasm he showed for Lord Wellington, who was his brother-in-law, and under whom he had been fighting in the Peninsular Campaign. But this impersonal way of winning a girl's heart could not prevail against two serious drawbacks—the " strong tendency to insanity in all the Paken-hams," and the lurid view taken by Annabella of Lady Wellington. " She is under the sway of a ruling passion—*bloodthirsty ambition.*" A week after she met him, Miss Milbanke's standard was in appli-cation : " His opinions are not founded on the same principles as mine." Ten days later he had been refused ; but :

> Gen. Pakenham has called here, as he requested that Lady Gosford would allow him to surmount the awkwardness of a first interview with me when there were no spectators but himself. He told her that he has now submitted to reason, and that he will never think again of his presumptuous hopes.
> I met him with cordiality. He said : " I am grateful for your friendship—be assured you shall never repent it." I replied, " I have perfect confidence in you ; " and we then talked as if nothing of this nature had ever passed between us.

The bloodthirsty Lady Wellington wrote a very handsome letter ; Lord Gosford was relieved by her refusal of the General—everyone, in short, approved of her behaviour, herself included.

> My purpose was to prevent his encreasing (*sic*) his malady by a conduct that could only proceed from his unconsciously cherishing a remain of hope. I am quite satisfied with the part I have acted in regard to him—I meant it for his good, and I am sure that it has proved so.

The General, thus edified, went back to the Peninsula to do great things at Salamanca on July 12. So Miss Milbanke could continue to feel satisfied.

The Army, always obedient to suggestion, took up the tale ; for the following admirer was a Major Dickens. She definitely favoured him ; " but pray do not let Judy fancy that I am in love with him—whatever I *may be*." This oracular saying ended in smoke ; Major Dickens left for the East Indies without proposing, whether disappointingly or as a tacitly-rejected suitor there is nothing to show. But he seems to have had a better chance than the others.

With the next lover, coming events began to cast their shadows before. William Bankes, with £8000 a year, had been an intimate of Byron's at Cambridge, had brought Byron and Hobhouse together (in *his* day unsuccessfully), had been " father of all mischiefs," and finally had written, when the early poems came out, a letter which produced in reply one of Byron's most characteristic displays of human nature.[1] Annabella wrote of him at the beginning of the season : " One of my smiles would encourage him, but I am niggardly of my glances." Nevertheless he called so often, always to find her absent, that she had " some idea of returning his cards to him, for his own pocket's sake." He rushed upon his fate, and like the rest was dismissed. The friendship with Byron had been kept up ; in after-days they were to condole with one another on their common failure to please Miss Milbanke.

A Mr. Francis Cunningham, on his introduction, was frankly appraised in a suitorial light—from force of habit possibly, for he does not seem to have qualified ; and on one night at the Opera there were so many admirers in the box that she never was able to look at the stage. She should, on that night, have remembered her strictures in 1811 when Lady Melbourne took her to the Opera, " and it was a considerable fatigue to me who do not take pleasure in flirting." But flirting has a dual aspect, according as we are active or inactive in it.

[1] This was in 1807. Byron's letter may be read in *Letters and Journals*, vol. i. (March 6, 1807), and in *Byron* (second and revised edition, 1924, p. 74), by the present writer. Bankes became famous as a traveller, explorer, and discoverer. " He has done miracles of research and enterprise," wrote Byron to Murray in 1820.

She would have been quite too superior a mind if all this had not elated her, and her parents' anxiety was a source of great amusement. " I must not look about for a spouse, if you feel the hours so long without me." Then she propounded a brilliant idea of opening " my " house in Portland Place and giving a dinner of fourteen persons. A list of guests was enclosed, " and I shall ask some men who cannot think I am in love with them." She gave this dinner in April ; but by that time there was only one man who interested her, and—though not yet aware of it— she *was* in love with him.

But let us regard her for a little longer as the fancy-free young girl who could enjoy a London season in all its length and breadth. True, she attended lectures, and of the heaviest kind : somebody on Mnemonics, somebody else on Geology—these latter she not only attended but analysed ; and, for light relief, Campbell's discourses on poetry at the Royal Institution. Campbell was still the fashion ; she analysed him too, and liked the lectures except when he " strove to be witty." She quotes one effort : " I cannot forgive him this expression : ' A Sinking Fund of Imagination.' " It strikes modern ears as inoffensive—even happy.

She read enormously, finding time and energy we wonder how. A list of her books makes the unregenerate blood run cold, though she did include some novels—Miss Edgeworth's and Beckford's sensation-making *Vathek*, in which she detected the source of some passages in the Book of the Season, " Lord Byron's *Childe Harold*." *Childe Harold*'s only rival in her poetic reading was *The Faërie Queene*. That was a reckless undertaking for the height of the London season ; she may not, like so many of us, have quite finished *The Faërie Queene*. One morning she went with a party to the British Museum, and saw the Library " throughout "—a smaller library in those days possibly, to be so seen in the course of a morning.

But for the most part it is of parties and dances, theatres and country-house visits that her letters and diary tell. Though she was conscientiously on the look-out for " excellence," excellence is less amusing to write about than the follies and weaknesses which she seems to have found so much more frequently. Her perception of these was often just, if some of the remarks are so violently phrased as to instil a reaction in favour of her victims. Old Lady Cork, notoriously unlovable, can scarcely have been so horrific as this : " She gave additional proofs of her cowardly insolence—she is to be shunned by all who do not honour iniquity " ; and Lady Holland—familiar to our imaginations as a formidable hostess—must have been seriously put out when Annabella first saw her with a " countenance which said she was capable of determined malice." Nor did Royalty escape. Of the Duke of Clarence, who particularly noticed her one night, all she had to say was : " How disgusting he is ! "

So too with many of the parties. At one, " comfort was absent " ; another house was " a wretched prison which reminded me of Lord Byron's description of Solitude—' with none to bless us, none whom we can bless ' " ; a bachelor-dinner was summed-up in a single word : " Dullness," and the ball to which she went on was no better. To these last two she was taken by her mother, when in May the parents came to London. They had come suddenly, altering plans which had apparently been immutable. Their reasons we shall see ; but apart from these and the restiveness they awakened in her, it is not inconceivable that the elated heart-breaker, the adored of M.G. and M.M., found it dull to be maternally looked-after.

Annabella's affection for her mother seems to have been of the kind which flourishes best in absence—no unusual state as between mother and daughter. There is an entry in the diary where this is almost explicit. " Mrs. Hervey evidently dislikes me. . . . I guess that she thinks me in some respect deficient in duty to Lady Mil." She certainly preferred her equally infatuated and far less fidgety Papa ; was never satisfied with the post unless there were some of " Dad's pothooks," and the home-baked loaves sent her daily from Seaham were always lightest when he had been the baker. She said he was the best nonsense-maker she ever knew : " his letters ought to be transmitted to posterity." [1] Flatteries like these were not lavished on Judy ; the best she received in that sort was a con-

---

[1] Yet scarcely any letters of Sir Ralph's to her are to be found among the Lovelace Papers, though there are quantities of Lady Milbanke's—in later years, Lady Noel.

fession that her "buttery" speeches made her daughter very happy.

Sir Ralph got all the pet jokes about fleas, of which this season inspired many ; he also got a letter about the Lord Mayor's Ball on Easter Monday—a somewhat snobbish one, in which the girl who belonged to the most fashionable set in London has a little too much to say about Cockney nature and vulgar vanity. But if this letter is snobbish, it is certainly not priggish. "What most amused me was the Superfine Ladies taking up their gowns all round before they seated themselves. Till I was acquainted with the custom, I thought the action had rather a *suspicious* appearance." Sir Ralph—"honest, red-faced spirit"—should have enjoyed this touch.

In her diary the Lord Mayor's Ball was much more solemnly treated :

> I could not have imagined the difference which really exists between the City gentlefolk and the Western fashionables. I had supposed that when there was less *refinement*, there would be less *art*, but this theory is completely destroyed by a view of the guests at a Lord Mayor's fête. Vanity there prevails in as strong a degree, and is more gross in its operation, because it is not corrected by *taste*, a purifier that often to a certain degree supplies the place of morality in Fashionable society. In the shape of the dresses Nature was horribly caricatured.

The concluding sentence is her sole reference to dress during the two London seasons of her girlhood !

She was herself slender and very small, "exquisitely finished," " her figure perfect for her height," as Byron said in describing her to Medwin after the separation ; and the roundness of her face made him give her the nickname of "Pippin"—which she delighted in while delight was allowed to survive in her.

This little person, making her caustic observations at the Lord Mayor's Ball, was likewise busy in the dazzling circle to which she belonged. The Lambs loomed large there, and on the eve of a week-end at Brocket Hall—the Melbournes' smaller country-place in Herts—she wrote to Sir Ralph that she wished there were to be

> a mixture of other animals with the *little sheep*. I do not like incessant *bleating*. Lady Caroline baa-a-a-a's till she makes me sick. Indeed that verb is so much the fashion among all the set,

that it is practically conjugated through all moods and tenses.
. . . The Greville set have a different favorite. Theirs is the
languid, listless, languishing, lifeless *sha*—the constant exclamation of any member of that illustrious society.

Besides these two sets there is the potent company of the
Blues, who maintain a very independent situation in the
Politics of Fashion, seldom forming alliances with *ba* or *sha*, and
preserving their characteristic *bray* in its native purity.

I, poor mortal! though admitted occasionally to view these
admirable people, cannot catch the *innocence*, nor the *elegance*,
nor the wisdom.

The Devonshire House drawl of that period is notorious ; we
know less about the " sha," which certainly seems to touch
bottom in imbecility ; in the " bray " attributed to the Blues
(with whom she ought surely to have felt some affinity) we
suspect that she was practising cheap wit. Since she belonged
in some sort to each of the three circles, this passage is a good
example of the satiric detachment which was her chosen attitude
to the world. Welcome her though it might, she was resolute
to scorn it, to confess none of its weaknesses as her own.

She too, for all that, had her jargon. A phrase which is
frequent in her letters, as in those of her mother and Sophy
Tamworth, may have been of purely Milbanke coinage, but it
has a flavour of the slang which fashionable close corporations
invent with every season. This one has unusual prettiness.
" High honeysuckle "—that was it ; they used it in telling of an
encounter which had seemed formidable in advance, but had
after all passed pleasantly enough. " I was in high honeysuckle " ; " it was all high honeysuckle " ; and the impression
given is that there was thunder in the air of Arcadia.

The leader of the Lambs was Lady Melbourne, and she was
dazzling enough ; but there was a still more dazzling little sheep
to be studied. Lady Caroline Ponsonby, daughter of the third
Earl of Bessborough and Lady Henrietta Spencer,[1] had been
married to William Lamb, Lord Melbourne's second son, in 1805 ;
and Annabella's admirer-to-be, Augustus Foster, had written of
the event to his mother (at that time still Lady Elizabeth Foster) :
" I cannot fancy Lady Caroline married. I cannot be glad of it.

---

[1] Daughter of the first Earl Spencer, and sister to Reynolds's Beautiful
Duchess (of Devonshire).

How changed she must be—the delicate Ariel, the little Fairy Queen. It is the first death of a woman." But his mother had been able to tell him that Caroline had not yet died. She had made of her wedding an unforgettable occasion—had flown into a rage with the officiating Bishop, torn her lovely gown to pieces, fainted, and been borne out senseless to the carriage. This does not suggest an Ariel; but Caroline had many other nicknames, and among them was Young Savage. She was bewilderingly charming, though not a beauty, with her tiny slender form, fawn-flaxen hair, immense dark eyes, and sweet drawling voice. "Not pretty, but worse"; astonishingly versatile, unconventional to the verge—and beyond it—of eccentricity, dressed like no one else and always exquisitely, of sensibility so excessive that in her childhood the family doctor had feared insanity . . . here was a challenging study for an analytic and superior mind. At first she was no more than half-disapproved of, though the praise given with one hand was mostly taken back with the other.

> I was more pleased with Ly. C. Lamb than before, because I thought that when she was silly, she was really *unmeaning*, not *artificial*. She seems clever in everything that is not within the province of common sense.

> Lady C. Lamb does not do justice to her own understanding. She conceals its power under the Childish manner which she either indulges or affects.

In these passages there is little sign of surrender to "Caro's" charm. They were to be involved in each other's tragedy; but at this time they were no more than rival cousins, each with an acknowledged superiority to the mere crowd of women, each aware of it—and one already caught up in the relation which was to destroy them both.

It was on the 10th of March, 1812, that Byron "awoke one morning and found himself famous"; and to Caroline Lamb, Queen of the Drawing-Rooms, a very early copy of *Childe Harold* was lent by Samuel Rogers, powerful as she in the same circles. Instantly Rogers was summoned to Melbourne House, where the William Lambs were then living.

> "I must see him—I am dying to see him!"
> "He has a club-foot," said Rogers, "and he bites his nails."
> "If he is as ugly as Aesop, I must see him!"

She soon saw him—of course to behave differently (at first) from " all the other women." Her hostess led her up—she submitted to that—for introduction. She looked at him fixedly for a moment ; then turned and walked away.

" Mad, bad, and dangerous to know." So she wrote in her diary that night. But though she wrote those words, she was listening while she wrote them to other words, sounded from deeper depths. " That beautiful pale face is my fate " . . . Such rubbish as any schoolgirl might have thrilled to ; but for Caroline Lamb it came true.

And in the same month, Annabella Milbanke was to write in *her* diary of her first meeting with Byron—to write **how** differently, how far less arrestingly ; yet to the same issue.

CHAPTER IV

1812

INTRODUCTION TO BYRON

THUS far we have travelled with Thursday's Child—a girl unlike other girls, and very conscious of it. Even her idea of being different was unlike the commonly accepted one ; unlike Caroline Lamb's, for instance. Waywardness, caprice, eccentricity in dress or behaviour—these Annabella Milbanke scorned. It was on a difference in spirit that she prided herself, while enjoying what might be enjoyed by one so aloof. Absurdity lies in wait for such an attitude ; there have been those " opportunities for wickedness " which she, with the humility and candour no less characteristic of her than spiritual pride, acknowledged to be just. A girl like this, when she is aware of her effect on others, becomes a pathetic figure as well as an absurd one. She struggles against the only things which uphold her—her sense of judgment, her incorruptibility, her Narcissus-like gaze at the disparaged yet cherished image of herself. " She has more humility than I have." Early in her contact with London, Annabella had written that in her diary ; and all her life she wrote it in her heart. But those around her could not read her heart—or only a very few of them.

Now, inured to the social scene, well-practised in rejecting men's hands at any rate—whatever scepticism about their hearts may trouble heiresses—she stood before her little great world as an acknowledged success. Fancy-free, more " grateful " because happier, as critical as ever but with more indulgence in her view of others' weaknesses, and perhaps inwardly wishing that the exultant boast to her mother : " Cupid has not even left his card for me " were not quite so well justified . . . let us look a moment longer at this Annabella, before (in Byron's phrase) the Fates change horses.

34

On March 15, a Tuesday, she dined at Lady Melbourne's. The "Williams" were there, and she thought William Lamb self-sufficient. We know that like the rest of us (and like Annabella), William Lamb had his affectation. This was to seem indolent, phlegmatic, used-up. At a family-gathering there was good opportunity for practice; moreover, he may have been genuinely tired of the principal topic as recorded in Annabella's journal—*Childe Harold*, poem and poet, about both of which his wife had lost her head in authentic Caro-fashion.

Annabella could not join in that discussion, for she had not read *Childe Harold*. And she let another week go by before she did read it, possibly in the service of her difference from other women in general and Caroline Lamb in particular. But on the following Sunday she surrendered to the spirit of the season, and began. Two days later she had finished the two cantos of which it then consisted; in her diary for March 24, she set down her opinion.

> It contains many stanzas in the best style of poetry. He is rather too much of a *mannerist*, that is, he wants variety in the turns of his expression. He excels most in the delineation of deep feeling, and in reflections relative to human nature.

So the best things passed her by. But that was not her fault; the Byron Legend was already rampant, and *Childe Harold* was read in its light. Deep feeling and human nature—it was on these that fashionable London fastened. A life so darkly mysterious, passions so fulgurant, bitterness and scorn so scathing . . . the East was merely the setting for all that, in the season of 1812. And then they met him, and he was Harold to the life!

Annabella met him the day after that entry in her diary. It was at Caroline Lamb's morning-party for waltzing at Melbourne House. Waltzing was, ironically enough, the secondary craze of the Byron Season. It had only just been introduced; there was much prejudice against it—shared by him who resented any form of the dancing he could not join in. Elizabeth Duchess of Devonshire would not permit it at Devonshire House; but the young Duke was resolute to practise somewhere, and the other Queen Elizabeth—Lady Melbourne—had no prejudices about waltzing or anything else. So Caroline could give her party, to

which Miss Milbanke was invited. Lord Byron was invited too,
and came. These were the early days of his affair with Caroline ;
he was as yet indulgent.

That night Miss Milbanke wrote in her diary :

Saw Lord Byron for the first time. His mouth continually
betrays the acrimony of his spirit. I should judge him sincere
and independent—sincere at least in society as far as he can be,
whilst dissimulating the violence of his scorn. He very often
hides his mouth with his hand when speaking. He professed
himself very partial to music, and said he could not understand
how any one could be indifferent to it. It appeared to me that
he tried to control his natural sarcasm and vehemence as much
as he could, in order not to offend ; but at times his lips
thickened with disdain, and his eyes rolled impatiently. Indeed
the scene was calculated to shew human absurdities. There
was the listless gaiety which so surely bespeaks the absence of
enjoyment. Waltzing was in vain attempted to give animation ;
Music was listened to *as a duty* ; *Thought* was engrossed by *self*.
What a picture of the first-rate society of London ! Of the
company there I remember Lady Jersey—gentle and elegant
as usual ; Lord and Lady Kinnaird—she good-natured, he
superfine ; Miss Mercer Elphinstone—incomprehensible. I
suspect that she thinks it becoming to her situation to be
assuming,[1] and that the encouragement she unfortunately meets
with has encreased this disagreeable habit, which may conceal
a rightly disposed heart. She was very roughly obliging to me.
Mrs. Lamb—sensible amidst this contagious folly.

Dined in Seymour Street with MM, and went afterwards with
her to Mrs. G. Knight and Lady Charlemont's. Mrs. Knight
told me authentic anecdotes of Lord Byron which gave me much
concern, as they indicated feelings dreadfully perverted.

Next day she wrote to her mother :

My curiosity was much gratified by seeing Lord Byron, the
object at present of universal attention. Lady C. has of course
seized on him, notwithstanding the reluctance he manifests to
be shackled by her. What a shining situation she will have in
his next satire ! He appears to be a very independent observer
of mankind—his views of life participate that bitterness of

---

[1] She was a very great heiress, *suo jure* Baroness Keith. In 1817 she
married the Comte de Flahault, subsequently Ambassador to Vienna,
Berlin, and (1860) London. It has been said that Byron proposed to her in
1814 ; but on the testimony of his letter to Annabella in 1813 this does not
seem to be true (see p. 59).

Spirit which (as I hear) makes himself wretched. He quarrelled with all his family, and this was the cause of his foreign travels. Young Knight is acquainted with him, and was very much shocked at hearing him say, " Thank Heaven ! I have quarrelled with my mother for ever." He is so very proud that the shadow of advice even from the kindest motives, has excited his indignation to the highest degree and *for years*—which happened with regard to his sister. She had suggested that it would be better if he left his name with some common acquaintance. In consequence he would not speak to her for very long. It is said that he is an infidel, and I think it probable from the general character of his mind. His poem sufficiently proves that he *can* feel nobly, but he has discouraged his own goodness. His features are well formed—his upper lip is drawn towards the nose with an expression of impatient disgust. His eye is restlessly thoughtful. He talks much, and I heard some of his conversation, which is very able, and sounds like the *true* sentiments of the Speaker.

I did not seek an introduction to him, for all the women were absurdly courting him, and trying to *deserve* the lash of his Satire. I thought that *inoffensiveness* was the most secure conduct, as I am not desirous of a place in his lays. Besides, I cannot worship talents that are unconnected with the love of man, nor be captivated by that Genius which is barren in blessings—so I made no offering at the shrine of Childe Harold, though I shall not refuse the acquaintance if it comes my way.

" I really thought," she adds, " that Lady Caroline had bit half the company and communicated the *Nonsense-mania*."

But if Caroline could talk nonsense, she could also say in six words what Annabella failed to say in ten times six. " Mad, bad, and dangerous to know "—comparing that with " his views of life participate that bitterness of spirit " and the rest, we get a flashlight on the two women. Both meant that Byron was fascinating and frightening ; both, on their introduction to him, might with equal truth have felt what only one felt : " That beautiful pale face is my fate." Caroline Lamb rushed on her fate with all her selfish, reckless devotion, knowing herself the doomed one, quite sincerely believing herself prepared to suffer. . . . Annabella foresaw nothing. She came home ; like Caroline, she wrote her diary ; unlike her, she abounded in comments on his mannerisms, his tricks of countenance. Yes—she had seen

Lord Byron, and she recognised that for an event which demanded lengthy treatment in diary and letter home. But to the writer of diary and letter nothing had happened ; no beautiful pale face was Miss Milbanke's fate—though to hear baleful anecdotes about him on the evening of that waltzing-party might give her " much concern." Complacently she could say that she had not sought his acquaintance, but were that acquaintance to come her way. . . . It did not come her way until the 14th of April, though the night before there had been a party at the Gosfords', of which she wrote to her father :

> I have been so rakish that I have not had time to bestow on the dullities of Seaham. On Monday . . . there was a party here, at which Lord Byron . . . shone with his customary glory. He certainly is very shy, and in consequence our acquaintance did not proceed that night, as I had not leisure to concert an attack on him. Indeed I was tormented by that impudent Bankes, who seems really to consider me as his property and will not understand any rebuffs. I have at present transferred my inclination for the Black Coats to the Red—Gen. Cole, Col. Bathurst, Col. Armstrong, etc.

Delightful to hold off—to be different ! But the hour had struck. Next night she went with Mrs. George Lamb to a supper-party at Lady Cowper's, " where for the first time I conversed with Lord Byron."

It was of Joseph Blacket—their ready-made link—that they talked, and she was " much pleased by the humanity of his feelings on the subject." In this entry she carefully details other conversations, " with Lord Erskine, Mr. Lewis, etc."—a trick that women practise, even in their diaries, when one voice sounds too persistently through the memory of an evening. For already she had written to her mother :

> I have met with much evidence of his goodness. You know how easily the noblest heart may be perverted by unkindness— perhaps the most easily a *noble* heart, because it is the more susceptible to ungenerous indignities. . . . At Lady Cowper's Lord B. and I had some very pleasing conversation—at least I thought it so. Lord B. is certainly very interesting, but he wants that calm benevolence which could only touch my heart. He is very handsome, and his manners are in a superior degree such as one should attribute to Nature's gentleman.

She was capable of that ; but soon Nature rebelled, and it was
a girl like other girls who wrote after another party at Caroline
Lamb's : " Lord Byron is without exception of young or old
more agreeable in conversation than any person I ever knew. . . .
I think of him that he is a very bad, very good man." The longer
words in the dictionary could not, however, be entirely neglected,
and she added : " *Impulses* of sublime goodness burst through
his malevolent *habits*."

It must have been a wonderful morning-party at which that
could happen ; the parents at home can hardly have failed to
divine something more than the fashionable interest in the lion of
the season. If they had seen the diary for that day, their anxious
hearts would have trembled.

> I continued my acquaintance with Lord Byron, and was
> additionally convinced that he is sincerely repentant for the
> evil he has done, though he has not resolution (without aid) to
> adopt a new course of conduct and feelings.

Thursday's Child had set her foot upon the Far-to-go when
she wrote the words : " without aid."

> " Do you think there is one person here who dares to look
> into himself ? " was one of his abrupt questions at a party
> where—in the crowd—I felt that he was the most attractive
> person ; but I was not *bound* to him by any strong feeling of
> sympathy till he uttered these words, not to me, but in my
> hearing—" I have not a friend in the world ! " It is said that
> there is an instinct in the human heart which attaches us to the
> friendless. I did not pause—there was my error—to enquire
> why he was friendless ; but I vowed in secret to be a devoted
> friend to this lone being.

But that was kept for the Auto-Description.

Humorous indeed, if it were not so piteous, that just this girl
should have fallen in love at first speech with Byron ; more
humorous still, if it were not a commonplace with his type of
libertine, that Byron's fancy should have been caught by just this
girl. But a commonplace it is ; and hence the incredulity so
often expressed about his ever having loved her is surely short-
sighted. She was the most piquant of " changes " for him in

that spring and summer of the Byron Fever.   True, she like the rest was immediately fascinated, and he must have been conscious of it ; but her way of being fascinated had all the appearance of difference from the other women's way.   With her seriousness, her earnestness, the touch of absurdity in her dignity (which yet survived it), and above all her devout, pathetically obvious faith in the whole machinery of the Byron Legend—past evil, present penitence, and future resolution (not without aid) to adopt a different course . . . with all this she had her fascination for him who, though so recently a conqueror in " the world,'' had already added a feather to the panache by his paraded scorn for it.

She struggled against the subjugation.   They met, again at Caroline Lamb's (with whom Byron was by this time deeply involved), and the talk turned on novels, *Evelina* among them. We know that Annabella had been disappointed in *Evelina*. Now she heard Byron defend it against William Lamb ; and it was probably with a vague sense of relief in being able to disagree that she wrote : " Justly attacked by William Lamb.''   So too with her comment on his remark at another party, where he spoke of the caprice natural to her sex—" with the greatest gravity, as if it was an acknowledged truth which I had too much sense to deny.''   One can almost see the reminiscent smile, the lingering on the words.   And then again she would feel safe— and unsafe.   " His attention was so modest and respectful that it could not create mistrust, and deserved confidence.''   Easy to read between those lines ; she must almost have done it herself.

There is a kind of cruelty in thus looking over her shoulder, in forcing open this Maiden's Blush, the rose of whose budding she had so vague a consciousness.   She could always be complacent about men's attentions ; even there we catch the note, though beneath it breathes as audibly an encroaching fear.   But the vogue aided her delusion—the compulsion laid upon them all to unravel, if they could, the enigma of Byron's persecution, misery, repentance.   To them he was the Harold of the Paphian girls, the Newstead harems (in cold reality represented by the women-servants), the Marble Heart—marble because so noble, yet so perverted by the evil influences it had known.

So on April 26 there was another letter home ; and it was

enough to bring the anxious parents up to town in a fortnight. We can imagine Judy—always on the fidget about any one she loved, and how much on the fidget about Annabella it is more comfortable not to guess—reading this effusion, bringing it to Sir Ralph ; and even he, the dallier, the truster to chance, recognising that the sooner they could see for themselves the better.

> He is indeed persecuted to the greatest degree by those who know nothing of him except what they have learned from prejudice. On the other side he is as violently and unjustly exalted—but this affords him no gratification, for he has too much penetration not to perceive that his *talent* alone is considered, and that there is no *friendship* in all this *mouth honour*. He has no comfort but in *confidence*, to soothe his deeply wounded mind. I consider it as an act of humanity and a Christian duty not to deny him any temporary satisfaction he can derive from my acquaintance—though I shall not seek to encrease it. He is not a dangerous person to me. . . .
> *I* cannot think him destitute of natural religion—it is in his heart.

But before the parents arrived, something had happened.

Caroline Lamb had suddenly fallen ill, and there had come an urgent message from her to Miss Milbanke. Miss Milbanke must come at once to see her ; it was vital that she should come. Annabella understood the situation. Her comment on the summons was : " I shall exert my influence to prove to Lady Melbourne that there is no danger in my meeting Lord Byron." So the " temporary satisfaction " had evidently been visible.

Her poems had just then been submitted to Byron ; he had not yet written to say what he thought of them. Entrusted to Caroline that they might be so sent, had they struck her as a good card to play ? Would they show him that the writer was a little prig ? She was by no means a spiteful woman ; still, there are promptings of the jealous heart. . . . And there was something else. Before he met the other he had spoken of her to Caroline, saying how much he admired her, how superior she seemed to all the rest ; and Caroline had been " all acquiescence and approbation," until the temporary satisfaction became evident. Then, getting frightened, she had remembered George Eden. What had become of his suit to Miss Milbanke ? No one had ever been told. Annabella was much with him—perhaps she was only waiting to be asked ?

This kind of Perhaps can easily be turned into Certainly, and that was what Caroline had done with it. She had told Byron that the attachment was mutual, salving her conscience by the knowledge that her sister-in-law, Mrs. George Lamb, had told him the same thing. George Eden was Annabella's frequent partner at the dances ; and moreover, were not the Aucklands more friendly than ever before with her ? Surely, this could be doing her no wrong. . . . But Caroline Lamb was Caroline Lamb —a creature of generous impulses, if a creature torn by jealous fear. She fell ill between her jealousy and her remorse ; and (always histrionic) could not rest until both had been acknow-ledged. The most dramatic confession—to whom could that be made ? To whom but Annabella ? Annabella was accordingly summoned, and on the 2nd of May she came.

Her diary says merely : " Went in morning to Lady Caroline Lamb, and undeceived her by a painful acknowledgment. . . . Received Lord Byron's opinion of my verses."

The painful acknowledgment we must suppose to have been that she had refused George Eden. There was nothing painful to acknowledge about Byron, since all she knew of herself in regard to him was known as well to Caroline. And Caroline knew more—his opinion of the verses, and not only his opinion of *them* :

> She certainly is an extraordinary girl ; who would imagine so much strength and variety of thought under that placid countenance ? . . . I have no desire to be better acquainted with Miss Milbank (*sic*) ; she is too good for a fallen spirit to know, and I should like her more if she were less perfect.

The first clause was read to her, as we know from a future letter of hers to Byron. There she sat, before her a countenance which at no time was placid ; the wide dark eyes observing her, the ashen-gold hair, cut short like a boy's (or more pertinently, like a page's, for Caroline had a mania for pages) enhaloing the pathetically invalidish head ; and in her ears the low caressing voice which was one of Caro's greatest charms. Her own " placid countenance." . . . So placid, was it ? Had one not, when unjustly accused, felt " the madness of pride to such a degree that I have struck my head till I staggered back ? " Had one not had " great difficulties to surmount from the impetuosity and sensitiveness of my character ? " How little Lord Byron knew about one ! But Caroline was watching. She must not suspect that anything was felt beyond a mild gratification in his praise of the verses—must think that the personal comment passed unheeded. It would not be forgotten—it was not forgotten ; meanwhile she could only get away as soon as might be.

The interview altered her intercourse with Byron—altered too the entries in her diary. " Lord Byron was there, with an improved countenance and manners " ; " Lord Byron there—he spoke satirically of one of my *best* friends whom he did not know except by sight and report. This was evidently an effect of that irritability which renders him so wretched." On the last day of May : " Lord Byron was there, but we never spoke." Next evening : " Lord Byron was there in gentle mood. From a strange hurry of spirits, he is apt to repeat the same question, though his memory is good."

Meanwhile her parents had hurried to London. It was now that she found so many parties worse than dull ; now that she wrote a paper on the Delight of a Solitary Hour : " Who can reproach a solitary hour with dullness ? It has often the blessing of Heaven. . . . I pity the being who is not conscious when alone that *he is a friend*—a friend to his friends." A little later on her reflections were occupied with Moonlight. " Such is the illuminating effect of one being who is dear to us." She wrote that in a blank interval between the 12th and the 31st of May ; it was on the 31st that she met Byron again at last, and " we never spoke."

All this was the result of Caroline Lamb's manipulation. Both had been made self-conscious ; Byron, moreover, had been told that she was engaged, or as good as engaged, to George Eden. . . . The triumphant season was spoilt for Miss Milbanke. She might meet him at one party and observe his " propensity to coquetry " ; after another record that he had been " very good-natured " to her ; but though she stayed later at the dances where he was not, the diary received such plaints as " wearied with want of tranquillity, and found no pleasure." So little pleasure that soon the entry became : " Danced not " ; and not long afterwards her diary was given up for good.

She made instead a list of the men she had come to know better during the season. Twenty names are included, all of them nonentities ; one—not a nonentity's—is left out.

Tedious to multiply the indications of which there are so many ; but two are interesting. There was a moment of confessed unhappiness, which took the form of another reflection—this time on Discontent.

> Certain descriptions of feeling awaken our *sympathy with ourselves*, and from such the mind which fears itself shrinks, though it be not guilty, with scarcely less of dread than if it were. " Look on't again I dare not."

Easy to divine the author of those descriptions of feeling ! Was it at this time or earlier that she wrote some feebly satirical lines entitled *The Byromania* ? It was in that season, at any rate, after she had met him.

THE BYROMANIA

> Woman ! how truly called " a harmless thing ! "
> So meekly smarting with the venom'd sting.
> Forgiving saints !—ye bow before the rod,
> And kiss the ground on which your censor trod. . . .
> Reforming Byron with his magic sway
> Compels all hearts to love him and obey—
> Commands our wounded vanity to sleep,
> Bids us forget the *Truths* that cut so deep,
> Inspires a generous candour to the mind
> That makes us to our friend's oppression kind.
> Amusing Patroness of passing whim
> Which calls the *weaker* sex to worship *him*,
> See Caro,[1] smiling, sighing, o'er his face
> In hopes to imitate each strange grimace
> And mar the silliness which looks so fair
> By bringing signs of wilder Passion there.
> Is Human nature to be cast anew,
> And modelled to your Idol's Image true ?
> Then grant me, Jove, to wear some other shape,
> And be an anything—except an Ape ! !
>
> A.I.M. 1812.

[1] Note in A.I.M.'s handwriting : *Lady Caroline Lamb.*

And then the season of 1812 was over, with its triumphant beginning and its troubled end. She left London with her parents, and amused herself by writing Characters in the French manner of various people whom she had met—Lord Jocelyn, Lord Palmerston (" devoid of party spirit, of public spirit, or of spirit of any kind "), Mr. Ward, Lady Caroline, Mrs. George Lamb. . . . Not until October 8 was a Character of Lord Byron attempted. By that time something had happened which made it a peculiarly absorbing effort.

CHAPTER V

1812-13

BYRON'S PROPOSAL

THE season of the Byron Fever : no need to re-tell the hackneyed tale of what it had meant for him. Two circumstances ruled it —his sudden fame, and the Caroline Lamb affair. But there were two others, more relevant for Annabella's biographer— his close friendship with Lady Melbourne, and the " temporary satisfaction " he found in her niece's society.

His withdrawal from Caroline began its long series of critical moments in June. In August she was taken by her mother to Ireland, there to remain at least a month (by her own account, three months), incessantly writing to him, and " in a state very little short of insanity, and my aunt describes it as at times having been decidedly so."[1] Early in September Byron wrote to Lady Melbourne that he wished the affair to end, and certainly it would not be renewed by him. But whatever he might wish the end was not in sight, as Lady Melbourne at least never doubted, knowing her daughter-in-law.

Friends—were Byron and the great Elizabeth mere friends ? She was sixty-two ; he, twenty-four. Sufficient answer, we might think ; but this is not the only instance of Byron's feeling the spell of a woman much older than himself. Lady Oxford, the only one of his mistresses to whom he always referred with gratitude, was nearly double his age at the time of their liaison. He said that the autumn of a beauty like hers was preferable to the spring in others ; and whatever may have been the truth about his intercourse with Lady Melbourne—by himself

---

[1] *Letters of Harriet, Countess Granville*, i. 40, 41. This was Lady Harriet Cavendish, daughter of the fifth Duke of Devonshire. Lady Bessborough (Caroline Lamb's mother) was sister to Georgiana Duchess of Devonshire, mother of Lady Harriet.

ELIZABETH, VISCOUNTESS MELBOURNE

After the engraving from Reynolds at
Ockham Park

described in his diary as friendship, but to his wife as something
very different indeed—there is no question that the magic she
still possessed was potent for him as it had been for many other
men. He wrote to her in a strain of enchanted admiration,
well-laced with his characteristic ribaldry, but unmistakably
sounding the lover's note. Of course she enjoyed it ; a woman
who could write her delightful mockingly tender letters, does
not refuse herself that diversion even at sixty-two. But in one
of them she said : " I told you I would teach you friendship, and
so I will." His diary of 1813 seems proof that she did, despite
the obscene boastings he was afterwards (by some accounts)
to make. They belonged to the period of pseudo-insanity in
1815.

In 1812, at any rate, the intrigue with Caroline in all its phases
was being confided to her mother-in-law. She was not surprised,
but wrote to him reproachfully of the sorrow he was causing her
—for William Lamb was by very far her favourite son. Byron's
answer of September 13 not only declared that he wished the
affair to end, but made a confession which did come as a surprise.
" I was, am, and shall be, I fear, attached to another." He gave
the name : Miss Milbanke. He had never, he said, seen a woman
whom he esteemed so much.

It was a surprise, and a relief. Now there was hope of ending
the Caroline scandal once for all. But Lady Melbourne replied
by asking him if he was sure of himself. There she displayed her
insight, for his answer is an amusing vacillation between the wish
to settle down (if so it might be) with Miss Milbanke, and heroics
about " reparation " to Caroline. Of the heroics her mother-in-
law made short work. They would be much beyond his power,
she said ; moreover Caroline was no novice and could not be
looked upon as a victim. " Poor Annabella ! " she went on,
" her innocent eyes . . . will improve *if* she should be in love
with you. Eyes require that sort of inspiration. . . . Do you
think you can manage both her and C. ? Impossible ! "

But she did not more definitely discourage him ; and before
September was over he wrote that he should like of all things to
become a candidate, " were it only for the pleasure of calling
you *aunt*." Then comes an ominous word : " My only objection
would be to my *mamma*, from whom I have already by instinct

imbibed a mortal aversion." However, he was ready to try;
" and if this fails, anything else."

Reading that, and many other flippancies to Lady Melbourne,
there are two things to remember—the woman to whom he was
writing, and the persecution from Caroline Lamb to which he
was then being subjected. " Anything else " which might put a
stop to that would be welcome ; while to Lady Melbourne
effusion about another woman was out of place, unless well-
spiced with flippancy. At all events he did try. Early in
October, through her aunt, he made Miss Milbanke a formal
proposal. On October 12 she wrote to Lady Melbourne,
declining it.

She was at Richmond with her parents. It was on a Thursday
(October 8) that Thursday's Child sat down to compose her
Character of Lord Byron. The proposal-by-proxy had reached
her then, for she took some days before she answered it. Strangest
of reactions—to vivisect the man who now had confessed (however unsatisfyingly) to her instinctive sense of attraction between
them ! That she had felt this we have seen ; then came the
blazing publicity of the Caroline affair, her interview with
Caroline, Byron's subsequent aloofness—and she had put it all
away from her : " ' Look on't again I dare not.' "

Now she was forced to look on it again. He *had* found that
satisfaction, and wanted it to be more than temporary. Her
heart had leaped as she read, but there was a monitor to be
obeyed before she listened to a mere heart. Aware (as she afterwards told him) that he could " excite affection," she was still
uncertain whether he could " inspire esteem." That spectre had
always haunted her ; now it appeared in all its dismal majesty,
and she gazed loyally into its leaden eyes. Affection, disgusted
by the dowdy rival, withdrew ; but Annabella could not quite
forget that it was there. To which mute presence should she—
ought she to—give her allegiance ? Suppose one wrote a
Character of Lord Byron ? That might clarify one's feelings.

The passions have been his guide from childhood, and have
exercised a tyrannical power over his very superior intellect.
Yet amongst his dispositions are many which deserve to be
associated with Christian principles—his love of goodness in

its chastest form, and his abhorrence of all that degrades human nature, prove the uncorrupted purity of his moral sense. In one of his juvenile poems he says :

"I love the virtues that I cannot claim."

There is a chivalrous generosity in his ideas of love and friend-ship, and selfishness is totally absent from his character. In secret he is the zealous friend of all the human feelings ; but from the strangest perversion that pride ever created, he endeavours to disguise the best points of his character. He has felt himself wronged, and he scorns to show regard to illiberality of opinion by condescending to a justification. . . . When indignation takes possession of his mind—and it is easily excited—his disposition becomes malevolent. He hates with the bitterest contempt ; but as soon as he has indulged those feelings, he regains the humanity which he had lost—from the immediate impulse of provocation—and repents deeply. So that his mind is continually making the most sudden transitions —from good to evil—from evil to good. . . . He laments his want of tranquillity and speaks of the power of application to composing studies, as a blessing placed beyond his attainment, which he regrets.

He is inclined to open his heart unreservedly to those whom he believes *good*, even without the preparation of much acquaint-ance. He is extremely humble towards persons whose character he respects, and to them he would probably confess his errors—

There she broke off.

But she had clarified her feelings. The enigma of Byron unravelled or not, the enigma of *them* was. And she wrote to her aunt :

I endeavour not to yield to any decided preference till my judgment has been strengthened by longer observation, but I will not assign this as my only motive for declining. . . . I should be totally unworthy of Lord Byron's esteem if I were not to speak the truth without equivocation. Believing that he never will be the object of that strong affection which would make me happy in domestic life. . . .

and so on. She suggested that Byron should see this letter, and assured him of her " perfect silence on the subject."

It was done. She had rejected him. No new experience for her ; yet there was something different about this one. She had said what she need say to Aunt Melbourne ; to her one could not say all that was in one's heart. To M.G. one could ; and two days later to M.G. she did—from Melbourne House, whither she had evidently been summoned for observation under the new light.

" Lady M. showed me all the letters relative to me which she had received from Lord Byron." (She believed in this comprehensive statement ; we are more sceptical.)

> They appear to me expressive not only of the sincerest but of the deepest attachment. In one . . . he says that though he feels the blessing he had once thought of, beyond his reach, he is and fears he shall ever remain attached to me, and that whoever else he may marry he shall always wish to have married me.

Lady Melbourne had made her selection judiciously ! Nothing there of wanting chiefly to call her aunt, or of a mortal aversion to his mamma. And as Annabella read (or listened, as we cannot but think more likely), her feelings began to seem less completely clarified. Musing on what he had said of her, she went on with her letter to M.G.

> Were there no other objection, his *theoretical* idea of my perfection, which could not be fulfilled by the trial, would suffice to make me decline a connexion that must end in his disappointment. I confess that this, and the irreligious nature of his principles are my sole objections ; but you know that I regard the latter too strongly to sacrifice it to the love of Man. I do not fear his passions, for they are united with that generous disinterestedness of character which I *now* think a better security against ill-conduct, than the *systematic* goodness of colder characters. I did not think anything of Genius requisite for the man who would make me a good husband, but I am afraid that *some* genius is requisite to understand a fellow-creature, and a good heart is not the best proof of *penetration*. I think matrimonial unhappiness is often the consequence of one or both the persons having believed that they should be too easily contented.

M.G. should have read a good deal between the lines of this outpouring. " So she wants genius now—and genius is to make her a good husband ! " One of those just opportunities for wickedness ; but neglected, we may be sure, from the sense of

pity which always mingled with Lady Gosford's amusement—
and now more than ever.   Annabella marry Lord Byron !   But
fortunately she had said No.

Whatever M.G. may have read between the lines, it was not
more than the truth.   The Auto-Description is before us :

> The effects upon my feelings were serious—and having put
> it out of my power to act as his friend in the nearest relation-
> ship, I no longer rested content with the prospect of remote
> contingencies.   My state was that of high excitement. . . .   I
> studiously endeavoured . . . to alter the channel of my feelings
> —and fancied I had succeeded ; but I was thrown amongst
> those who had received much more favourable impressions of
> the character than had been placed before me. . . .   I felt that
> I had been uncharitable—

In short, neither the Character nor the Rejection of Lord Byron
had clarified her feelings at all.

Byron took the refusal with high good-humour.   Lady Melbourne begged him not to show any resentment, and he
answered :

> " Cut her ! " my dear Lady M.—Mahomet forbid ! I am sure
> we shall be better friends than before. . . .   She is perfectly
> right in every point of view, and during the slight suspense I
> felt something very like remorse. . . .   Finding I must marry
> . . . I should have preferred a woman of birth and talents. . . .
> My *heart* never had an opportunity of being much interested
> in the business.

All's well that ends well, in fact ; and though originally his
heart had been involved, that was to be forgotten by a tactful
correspondent.

But Lady Melbourne did not give up the game.   Her next
move was to request of Annabella an account of the qualities
she did desire in a husband.

Eagerly Annabella addressed herself to the task.   It was
almost as good as writing a Character—it *was* writing a Character
of Miss Milbanke's potential husband.   But would it not also be
well to sketch the potential wife ?   She made the attempt.
" Defects of temper "—yes, she had them ; but how formidable

they looked in pen and ink ! Could they not be mitigated in a covering letter ?

I am never irritated except when others are so, and then I am too apt to imitate them. . . . I am never sulky, but my spirits are easily depressed, particularly by seeing anybody unhappy.

And now for the husband. Of him she would demand :
(1) Consistent principles of Duty.
(2) Strong and *generous* feelings.
(3) " Genius is not in my opinion *necessary*, though desirable, *if united* with what I have just mentioned."
(4) Freedom from suspicion and from *habitual* ill-humour.
(5) " An equal tenor of affection towards me, not violent attachment."
(6) Fortune enough to keep her as she had been accustomed to be kept.
(7) " Rank is indifferent to me "—but she thought good connections important.
(8) " I do not regard *beauty*, but am influenced by the *manners of a gentleman*, without which I scarcely think that anyone could attract me."

And she added : " I would not enter into a family where there was a strong tendency to insanity."

High comedy here. We have but to imagine Lady Melbourne reading, and making her own discounts—deleting Principles of Duty as merely the sort of thing Annabella was sure to say, and might even imagine she meant ; noticing (as we have not failed to notice) that Beauty and Genius had been considered. Whose beauty, whose genius, but Byron's ! Equal tenor of affection more desired than violent attachment ? Fortunately for Annabella, perhaps ; yet the less propitious of the two where Byron was concerned. Habitual ill-humour—that " *la tante* " could certainly not lay at his door ; and as for the rest about fortune and connexions and the manners of a gentleman, it was the only sensible part of the list. But the girl was on stilts ; time to take her off them. And Lady Melbourne wrote a long letter, referring

to every item on the list—a letter which is among the cleverest she
ever did write, with its subtlety, worldly wisdom, and calculated
bluntness. "The stilts on which you are mounted"—yes ;
she should have it straight from the shoulder ; and as to her
being irritated " only " when others were, was not that the very
time when *not* to be irritated was most advisable ? Especially
with a husband, whether he were Byron or another.

Annabella's answer was exemplary. In manner she did not
entirely discard the stilts, for she could never discard the
dictionary ; but in spirit it humbly accepted her aunt's rebukes.[1]
" Now you will perhaps take off my *stilts*, and allow that I am
only *on tip-toe*. I quite agree with what you say. . . . Most
affectly. yours, A.I.M."

So she was not such a little donkey, after all. She might
do . . . for a devoted nephew.

So far as Annabella was directly concerned, Lady Melbourne did
no more. But she sent Byron his Character (confided to her) to
read. " Much too indulgent," he replied ; " but in some points
very exact." It was now that he invented the nickname of
Princess of Parallelograms—later to be used for ends more
malignant than its present gay denial of his ever having been at
all " enamoured."

Both he and his aunt (as he still called Lady Melbourne) were
absorbed in matters more exciting than a mere girl's rejection of
a proposal. Caroline Lamb was outdoing herself in importunity.
Her letters never ceased ; but there was another confidence
besides for the Whitehall enchantress—a confidence in the best
Byronic vein of ribaldry and lack of decent reticence. Reticence
of any kind was not, perhaps, strongly called for. The new
inamorata was the lovely Lady Oxford, of whom nobody ever
supposed less than the utmost that could be supposed. Byron
was setting off, on October 24 (when Annabella had just sent
her aunt the List of Qualities) for a stay at Lord Oxford's country-
place in Herefordshire. . . . Gradually Lady Melbourne was
fully enlightened, and he added that " all this " was infinitely
more to his taste than the " A. scheme," to which his principal

---

[1] See *In Whig Society*, by Mabell, Countess of Airlie, for these letters in
full, pp. 138-140.

inducement was still A.'s aunt. "*We* are very quiet, and wish to remain so."

That was early in November; but three days later came an end to quiet in the shape of a missive from Caroline to his hostess. This brought on one of the many crises in the ever-renewed battle. It was now that Byron wrote the notorious farewell letter cited in Caroline's novel of *Glenarvon*—a letter which was generally said to have been dictated by Lady Oxford. The seal bore her coronet and initials.[1]

Byron summed up the affair, a good deal less unspeakably, to Lady Melbourne: "I do not mean to deny my attachment—it *was*—and it is not. It was no great compliment, for I could love anything on earth that appeared to wish it; at the same time I do sometimes like to choose for myself."

The turmoil dragged on and on. He made plans for leaving England—among them one for going with the Oxfords to Sicily. All of these fell through; and in July occurred the scene at Lady Heathcote's ball, when Caroline was said to have cut herself purposely with a piece of broken glass. The scandal was immense; all the papers were full of it; and Annabella, who was in London with her parents, must like every one else have read the paragraphs. The contempt she had always felt for Caroline found plenty of nourishment in these. There cannot have been any jealousy by this time; pity—the pity we must feel as we read Caroline's own account of the scene [2]—was for Annabella, judging as she had to by newspapers and gossip only, quite out of the programme. Moreover, she was now resolved to believe nothing but good of Byron. Before this she had been told of his generosity to his cousin Dallas about *Childe Harold*, and recorded it in her diary along with something else she had been told:

[1] As cited in *Glenarvon*, sole text for the words which Byron acknowledged to have been part of the original document, it ran: "Lady Avondale" (Lady Avondale stood for Caroline), "I am no longer your lover; and since you oblige me to confess it, by this truly unfeminine persecution . . . learn that I am attached to another, whose name it would be dishonourable to mention. I shall ever remember with gratitude the many instances I have received of the predilection you have shown in my favour. I shall ever continue your friend, if your ladyship will permit me so to style myself; and, as a first proof of my regard, I offer you this advice: correct your vanity, which is ridiculous; exert your absurd caprices on others; and leave me in peace.—Your most obedient servant,—GLENARVON."

[2] See, among other books, my *Byron*, pp. 161-2 (second edition, 1924).

" Lord Byron never suffers the slightest hint in disrespect to Religion to *pass at* his table."

The Milbankes had come to London in the early part of the season of 1813. She had seen Byron " at a distance " ; then again, " without renewing my acquaintance " ; but at last (turning to the Auto-Description) :

> We met in the following spring in London. I was extremely agitated on seeing him—and offered my hand for the first time. He turned pale as he pressed it. Perhaps—unconscious as I was —the engagement was then formed on my part. We met frequently, but every time I felt more pain—and at last I shunned the occasions.

At the time she confessed nothing like so much as this to the resumed diary, but there are entries in which it is implicit. " At home dead." That makes a picture for us of a girl with brown head bent dejectedly upon the paper, after some of the shunned occasions. And once she broke out more vehemently : " Oh, the misery of being shy amongst those who are too impudent to sympathise with one's sufferings ! " She had not been shy in 1812. We shall read later her own account of her state during that season ; meanwhile one thing is significant—there is never a mention of dancing. She read a great deal, among her books being one called *Pride and Prejudice*, " which is at present the fashionable novel. It is written by a sister of Charlotte Smith's and contains more strength of character than other productions of this kind." [1]

Suitors appeared, but not in flocks as before. In the middle of July she left London for Seaham with her parents ; on the 18th, just before their departure, she wrote to Lady Melbourne : " I am sorry to find that a report very disadvantageous to Lord Byron is in circulation, and as I cannot believe it I wish it may be contradicted." The report was of his harsh treatment of Mr. Claughton, who had bargained to buy Newstead and then found he could not afford to complete the purchase. " It is said ... that Lord B. cruelly takes advantage of the Law to make him

---

[1] That confident announcement she soon found to be premature. In May she wrote to her mother that there were doubts about the authorship. . . . There is an amusing passage here referring to Lady Milbanke's fussiness. " If I should die, Aird " (her maid), " will immediately inform you, and I have bequeathed her 15 new pens for the purpose."

adhere to unfair terms." She asked Lady Melbourne to give Byron a message from her : " However long his absence may be " (he was still supposed to be leaving England) " I shall always have pleasure in hearing that he is happy." She added a good many long words to those simple ones, but they were the heart of the message.

The embarrassment caused to Byron by Claughton's vacillations and final defection is known to every reader of his biography. He now wrote to Lady Melbourne that if anyone was injured it was he, but that he was not fond of defending himself. In a postscript he sent his best acknowledgments to Miss Milbanke, and begged Lady Melbourne to " say what is proper."

That was all *he* said, but he had given Lady Melbourne a free hand. What she said as from him to her niece we do not know —it must have been something more ingratiating ; for at last— on August 22—Annabella took her courage in both hands, her long-suffering pen in one, and wrote to Byron for the first time in her life.

CHAPTER VI

1813

THEIR CORRESPONDENCE

ONE of the longest letters in the world, containing some of the
longest words in the English language—such was Annabella's
first letter to Byron. She often afterwards rivalled it in both
respects ; he competed in length though not in verbosity. But
even Byron, when he wrote to her, was sometimes dictionary-
ridden.

We must assist at this opening of their correspondence ; her
letter is too characteristic to be quite omitted. And indeed her
writings, heavy-handed though most of them are, convey so much
of the truth, or one aspect of the truth, about her that it is a
temptation (in its own kind) to give more of them than their
quality at all justifies. The temptation shall be resisted so far
as is compatible with a portrait of the girl who dared to marry
Byron, the wife who found it impossible to live with him, the
woman who—for all the many activities and interests in her later
life—never ceased to ponder on the enigma of their relations, or
to dwell upon the memory of every happy moment he had
vouchsafed to her young bewilderment.

Here then is her first letter to him, much shortened :

I have received from Lady Melbourne an assurance of the
satisfaction you feel in being remembered with interest by me.
Let me then more fully explain this interest, with the hope that
the consciousness of possessing a friend whom neither Time nor
Absence can estrange may impart some soothing feelings to your
retrospective views. You have remarked the serenity of my
countenance, but mine is not the serenity of one who is a
stranger to care, nor are the prospects of my future years
untroubled. It is my nature to feel long, deeply, and secretly,

and the strongest affections of my heart are without hope. I disclose to you what I conceal even from those who have most claim to my confidence, because it will be the surest basis of that unreserved friendship which I wish to establish between us—because you will not reject my admonitions as the result of cold calculation, when you know that I *can* suffer as you have suffered. Early in our acquaintance, when I was far from supposing myself preferred by you, I studied your character. I felt for you, and I often felt with you. You were, as I conceived, in a desolate situation, surrounded by admirers who could not value you, and by friends to whom you were not dear. You were either flattered or persecuted. How often have I wished that the state of Society would have allowed me to offer you my sentiments without restraint ! . . . My regard for your welfare did not arise from blindness to your errors ; I was interested by the strength & generosity of your feelings, and I honored you for that pure sense of moral rectitude, which could not be perverted, though perhaps tried by the practice of Vice. . . . .

In a letter to Ly Melbourne (after I had informed you of my sentiments) you expressed a determination to render your conduct as conformable to my wishes, as if your attachment had been returned. I now claim that promise, and I do not fear that you will answer " You have no right." I have the right of a constant and considerate zeal for your happiness, and the right which you have given, and will not unreasonably withdraw. I entreat you then to observe more consistently the principles of unwearied benevolence. No longer suffer yourself to be the slave of the moment, nor trust your noble impulses to the chances of Life. Have an object that will permanently occupy your feelings & exercise your reason. Do good. Every human being has a circle of influence more expanded than would be conceived by one who has not systematically tried its extent. But to benefit man you must love him, and you must bear with his infirmities—that forbearance which is recommended as the dictate of selfish prudence, is the more exalted dictate of philanthropy. Feel benevolence and you will inspire it—you *will* do good, for to excite such dispositions is to bless. You have so frequently received the advice of those whose conduct was false to their doctrine that you will naturally doubt the agreement of mine with my principles. I confess they have often but ill accorded—yet imperfect as my practice is, I *have* enjoyed the happiness of giving peace & awakening virtue on occasions which only this habitual direction of my thoughts could have enabled me to seize. Your powers peculiarly qualify you for performing these duties with success, and may you experience the sacred pleasure of having them dwell in your heart ! Will you undertake this task, and will you lay aside the seeming misanthropy which repels the affection of your fellow creatures ?

I have lately had very little information concerning you on which I could depend. On ill reports I never rely, for if I desire to be a Christian, it is more especially in the Charity which thinketh no evil. Need I say that such information from yourself would be received with gratitude ? I request your secrecy as to this communication and its contents. Only my parents are aware of it. In particular I would not have it known to Ly Melbourne. I am indebted to her kindness, but we have little sympathy, and she is perhaps too much accustomed to look for design, to understand the plainness of my intentions. I trust them to your candour. You must be sensible of my great confidence in you, since I mention opinions which I should be very sorry to have repeated. Believe in the sincerity of a regard, which, though it never can change to love, deserves to be considered as more than worldly friendship.

Yours most faithfully

A. I. MILBANKE.

I shall be obliged to you at least to acknowledge the receipt of this letter, that I may not apprehend it has fallen into other hands.

Fortunately, she wrote a very clear hand.

Byron may or may not have read the letter through—he made two allusions to briefness in his answer. But he answered immediately.[1] He would—" briefly, if possible "—advert to last autumn : " my first and *nearest* approach to that altar to which in the state of your feelings I should only have led another victim." He alluded to Mary Chaworth, but not by name, saying that he had then been too young to marry. In all probability his approach to Annabella would be his first and last attempt. " I preferred you to all others . . . it is so still . . . We do not know ourselves—yet I do not think my self-love was much wounded ; on the contrary I feel a kind of pride even in *your rejection*." Then came the gist : " I must be candid with you on the score of Friendship. It is a feeling towards you with which I cannot trust myself. I doubt whether I could help loving you."

[1] This letter appears in full in *Letters and Journals*, iii. 397.

It was to those eight words that she wrote her panting answer.

> I will trouble you no more—only this to express—what I cannot withhold—my heartfelt thanks for your most kind, most indulgent answer. Nothing in your letter can displease me— the recollection of my own may. I ought more to have respected your sorrows, and I cannot forgive myself for having intruded on them from the impulse of an ill-judged kindness. That I may not encrease the error—farewell. I will not regret the friendship which you deem impossible, for the loss is *mine*, as the comfort would have been *mine*.
>
> God bless you.

Brief, this time—the dictionary almost forgotten ; yet how much more she said !

Did she believe that these would be her last words to Byron ? They probably would have been, had he left England as he hoped to do. But he was prevented from going abroad, the Oxfords had sailed for Sicily, it was the end of the season, London was emptying. He had Lady Melbourne to write to and visit (for Caroline Lamb was safely out of the way at Brocket Hall) ; his half-sister Augusta Leigh was staying with him ; but there were idle hours—and very dark hours—in his rooms at Bennet Street, St. James's. Time must be passed, his mind turned to things outside its " feverish, restless " broodings. Writing (and reading) long letters was one means to that end. He respected Annabella's wish that he should not tell her aunt of their correspondence —respected it in his own manner, informing Lady Melbourne on the day he acknowledged the Seaham sermon : " I have to write —first, a soothing answer to C., a sentimental one to X.Y.Z., a sincere one to T. Moore." X.Y.Z. would do for the present, but not for long ; how get any amusement out of anything unless one confided in the Whitehall enchantress ? Meanwhile . . . and on the last day of August he answered Annabella's Farewell and God bless you.

> It is not my wish to draw you into a correspondence—yet I must say a few words on your last letter or rather on my own reply to your first.
>
> Neither Ly. M. nor yourself could possibly be to blame. If anyone was wrong it was myself—and after all she (Ly. M.) merely saved me from a personal repulse. My intention was

too plain to admit of misrepresentation, though under existing —or perhaps any circumstances—it was presumptuous, and certainly precipitate. I never did nor ever can deny that I aspired to the honour which I failed in obtaining. That I never sought to conceal my ill-success the following circumstance will convince you—and may at least afford you a moment's amusement. My equally unlucky friend W. Bankes—whom I have known for many years—paid me a visit one evening last Winter with an aspect so utterly disconsolate that I could not resist enquiring into the cause. After much hesitation on his part and a little guessing on mine, out it came—with tears in his eyes almost—that he had added another name to our unfortunate list. The coincidence appeared to me so ludicrous that not to laugh was impossible, when I told him that a few weeks before a similar proposal had left me in the same situation. In that we were the Heraclitus and Democritus of your suitors, with this exception—that our crying and laughing was excited *not* by the folly of others but our own—or at least mine—for I had not even the commonplace excuse of a shadow of encouragement to console me. Do not suppose because I laughed then that I had no feeling for him or for myself. The coincidence of our common grievance, and not the circumstance itself, provoked my mirth ; and I trust I need not add that want of respect to you made no part of the feelings or expressions of either, nor had I mentioned this at all could it place *him* in an unfavourable point of view. For myself, I must also beg you to believe that whatever might be my momentary levity, your answer to me had been received with respect and admiration rather increased than diminished by the dignified good sense which dictated your decision and appeared in your reply.

There is not the least occasion for any concealment of the rejection of my proposal—it is a subject I have never sought nor shunned. I certainly have nothing to boast of—but it would be meanness on my part to deny it.

I hope I did not accuse Ly. M. of misrepresentation—it certainly was not my intention. I thought my overture was too abrupt ; but in the proposal itself—and indeed in everything else—the fault was and must be mine only.

Your friendship I did not reject—though in speaking of mine I expressed some doubts on the subject of my own feelings. Whatever they may be, I shall merely repeat that if possible they shall be subdued—at all events, silent.

If you regret a single expression in your late 2 letters, they shall be destroyed or returned. Do not imagine that I mistake your kindness—or hope for more. I am too proud of the portion of regard you have bestowed upon me to hazard the loss of it by vain attempts to engage your affection. I am willing to obey you—and if you will mark out the limits of our future correspondence and intercourse they shall not be infringed. Believe me with the most profound respect

ever gratefully yrs.

P.S.—I perceive that I *begin* my letter with saying " I do not wish to draw you into a correspondence " and end by almost soliciting it. Admirably consistent ! but it is human nature, and you will forgive it—if not you can punish.

Before we plunge into the welter of the Byronic side-issues, to say nothing of the correspondence now established, let us take up a point or two in the letters we have read.

First, her confession—to call it so—that she was hopelessly in love with some one else. The Auto-Description has shown us that this was not the truth. She was in love with Byron, and by this time she knew it. Soon she was to regret what she had written, to ask Lady Gosford for advice on the best way of " regaining truth," to give her friend (and herself) such reasons for her rashness as evaded it still further. We can understand her more easily than she could understand herself.

She had opened correspondence with a rejected suitor who had shown no intention of approaching her again. There was only one way to preserve her dignity. Her affections must be engaged, and hopelessly engaged ; for if not hopelessly . . . but there she stopped short, unable to face the corollary which we can face with amusement. No ; as M.G. was to learn, it was " enthusiasm " which had made her guilty of deception. Had she any more idea than we have of what she meant by that ? It was by this vague wordiness that half the self-delusions of her life were caused.

We know, for Byron was to be told, whom she had chosen for her man of straw. The confession is one of the most irresistible of the just opportunities, yet so artless that it lends her a charm seldom found in this correspondence. He was M.M.'s brother, Hugh Montgomery—" who, so far from showing any affection for me, had bestowed it elsewhere." She could idealise, in his absence, her " visionary attachment " ; but once the

unconscious victim materialised, " the illusion could not withstand the presence of its object—for I had not seen him since its
creation—and he was no more to me than he had always been."
She saw him again during the days of Byronic illusion, and " I
could not quite forgive him for having *innocently* been your rival."

But the man of straw had other uses besides that of saving
her dignity. In this first letter, she wanted to show Byron that
she could sympathise with his pain ; for had not she too been
tacitly rejected ? His response to her sympathy might have
been mortifying—since he attributed it to his love for Mary
Chaworth—but for that single sentence : " I doubt whether I
could help loving you." Everything else was forgotten, her
own complacency along with it.

When she said that her parents were " aware of this communication and its contents," we suspect her of another white lie.
Incredible that the homily was handed them to read ! Her
attitude was soon to be commented on to Lady Melbourne (supposed by her to know nothing of the correspondence) in Byron's
authentic vein ; but to Annabella he was on stilts like Annabella
herself. He talked about her dignified good sense—very likely
it pleased her—and his momentary levity ; signed himself " with
the most profound respect," was altogether so solemn that
though it may have been an entertaining change for him, posterity
must congratulate itself that this was not his only correspondence.

An entertaining change—a change, at any rate, of the most
violent sort from what was now absorbing the Byron of whom
Annabella, for all her respectful belief in his Vice, had not the
faintest conception.

For some little time there had been in his letters to Lady Melbourne allusions to his half-sister Augusta Leigh, with whom he
was now reconciled after a semi-estrangement. She was
" abominably married " to a first cousin—" impracticable,
helpless, tiresome, and obstructive," [1] and moreover deeply and
perpetually in debt. Colonel Leigh was neglectful of her, yet he
depended on her for everything which he had to get done when
he *was* at home. She was of the Court-circle as well as of the
most fashionable set in London ; " very attractive, though not

---

[1] *Astarte*, p. 26 (edition of 1921).

a regular beauty," affectionate, childish, "ready to laugh at anything," apparently ingenuous, but full of sophistries and graceful expedients ; her moral sense summed up in the principle that so long as nobody was made unhappy, one might do as one liked. In Byron's adolescence he had been devoted to her, as she to him ; then he had quarrelled with her for very insufficient reason ; now their affection had been restored and he was learning, as it were, to know her again. She was his only near woman-relative, daughter of his father by the first (adulterous) marriage with the Marchioness of Carmarthen—born Amelia d'Arcy, only child and heiress of the last Earl of Holderness, and in her own right Baroness Conyers. She had died in giving birth to Augusta, in 1784.

Augusta, then, was twenty-nine in 1813, when Byron was twenty-four. The June of that year had seen a financial crisis at her home, Six Mile Bottom, near Newmarket (Colonel Leigh was a racing-man) ; and she had come to stay with Byron for an indefinite time. It was just before he parted from Lady Oxford, with whom and her family he had hoped to go to Sicily. Now he thought of going there with Augusta instead. She had consented. Early in August Byron wrote to Lady Melbourne, telling her of this arrangement. She replied in words which reveal what confidences he must already have given her, saying that it would be a fatal step, that he was on the brink of a precipice. "If you do not retreat, you are lost for ever—it is a crime for which there is no salvation in this world, whatever there may be in the next." She said more, and still more earnestly— rebuked him for the "cruelty of depriving of all future peace and happiness a woman who has hitherto, whether deservedly or not, maintained a good reputation." Byron's comment on this was : "Lady Melbourne is a good woman after all, for there are things she will stop at."

He did not go to Sicily, with or without Augusta ; and she left London for the country towards the end of August. He remained in Bennet Street, alone. It was now that Annabella's first letter reached him ; he answered quickly, as we have seen ; then came her Farewell, and that too he answered at once. On the same day he wrote to Lady Melbourne, thanking her for a letter which he described as "kind and *unanswerable*." He was miserably feverish and restless, as he told her on another day, amid many veiled references to a possible sensational upshot. He would go on writing to her (he said) if nothing very particular occurred ; if it did, she would probably hear *of* him, but " of course " not *from* him again. And soon he fled to Cambridge—which meant Newmarket—for " a very short stay."

Lady Melbourne, now thoroughly alarmed, did her utmost to put a stop to this. One way was to stimulate him towards the conquest of another woman, giving him " most minute " instructions to that end. Another was to re-open the question of Annabella. (As yet she knew nothing of their correspondence.) Early in September she sent him the List of Qualities for a Husband to read. He replied that he did not understand it. " I would rather have seen your answer. She seems to have been systematically Clarissa Harlowed into an awkward kind of correctness. . . . She will find exactly what she wants, and then discover it is more dignified than entertaining." [1] He must have smiled as he wrote that amusing prophecy (which events were so glaringly to falsify), for he had had a letter from Annabella the day before. It was pathetically happy, for all its solemnity. She welcomed him as a valuable friend " at some future period, without a painful exertion on your part," and went on : " I said the comfort would be *mine*, for the idea—is it a vain dream ?—of alleviating the bitterness of your despondency if only by the *wish* to do so, would give me real comfort. It is my happiness to feel that in some degree I live for others." Woman's friendship, she thought, was better for consoling and calming the mind than man's was ; but he must not look for this in the circles where she had met him. There *was* a woman she would like him to know, " whose age would prevent embarrassment " ; and after much praise of this paragon (strongly inspired by the dictionary) she launched the name—Joanna Baillie.

Perhaps it is only our frivolity which makes us smile. Annabella had met the great Joanna early in 1812, had seen a good deal of her, and had said farewell " with feelings of reverence and gratitude which will survive the longest separation." . . . Whether Byron smiled or not, this letter put an end to the desired secrecy towards Lady Melbourne. When he next wrote to her there **is**

---

[1] *Correspondence*, i. 177-8, 1922.

this : " Without, as A. says, being in a state of *despondency*, I am much perplexed ; however, that must end one way or the other." He had answered " A." before writing this. Some restiveness about the despondency is plainly perceptible ; indeed, the whole letter is more like him than any he had yet written her.

Agreed—I will write to you occasionally and you shall answer at your leisure and discretion. You must have deemed me very vain and selfish to imagine that your candour could " hurt my feelings " in your correspondence. You told me you declined me as a lover but wished to retain me as a friend. Now as one may meet with a good deal of what is called love in this best of all possible worlds, and very rarely with friendship, I could not find fault—upon calculation at least. I am afraid my first letter was written during some of those moments which have induced your belief in my *general despondency*. Now in common I believe with most of mankind, I have in the course of a very useless and ill-regulated life encountered events which have left a deep *impression*. Perhaps something at the time recalled *this* so forcibly as to make it apparent in my answer ; but I am not conscious of any habitual or at least long continued pressure on my spirits. On the contrary—with the exception of an occasional spasm [1]—I look upon myself as a very facetious personage, and may safely appeal to most of my acquaintance (Lady Melbourne, for instance) in proof of my assertion. Nobody laughs more.

After praise of Joanna Baillie as a dramatist, he went on : " The worst woman that ever existed would have made a *man* of very passable reputation. They are all better than us—and their faults, such as they are, must originate with ourselves." Her " sweeping sentence " about London Society had amused him (he said) when he thought of some of its members. " After all, bad as it is, it has its *agréments*. The great object of life is sensation—to feel that we exist, even though in pain." Then (displaying his facetiousness) :

By the bye, you are a *bard* also—have you quite given up that pursuit ? Is your friend Pratt one of your critics—or merely one of your systematic benevolents ? You were very kind to poor Blackett, which he requited by falling in love—rather presumptuously to be sure, like Metastasio with the Empress Maria Theresa. When you can spare an instant I shall of course

[1] From here to the end is in *Letters and Journals*, iii. 399.

be delighted to hear from or of you—but do not let me encroach a moment on better avocations.

Immediately afterwards he paid his first visit to Aston Hall, the Yorkshire home of Mr. James Wedderburn Webster (an old friend of his) and his wife Lady Frances (Annesley), daughter of the first Earl of Mountnorris and eighth Viscount Valentia. There was nothing very amusing to tell in his Whitehall letters. Lady Frances made no impression worth speaking of : " I had and have other things to reflect upon." He had been trying hard to vanquish his demon, but to very little purpose ; a resource that very seldom failed him had failed him in this instance. " I mean transferring my regards to another. I willingly would, but the feeling that it was an effort spoiled all again ; and *here* I am— *what* I am you know already." Then he goes on :

> The epistles of your mathematician (A. would now be ambiguous) continue ; and the last concludes with a desire that none but papa and mamma should know it. . . . The strictest of St. Ursula's 11,000 what do you call 'ems . . . enters into a clandestine correspondence with a personage generally presumed a great *roué*. . . . This comes of infallibility—not that she ever says anything that might not be said by the town-crier.

Unlike us, Annabella had not relished her first really Byronic letter. It was all disappointing, even annoying ; but every woman, reading it, will know at what words the annoyance became acute. " I shall of course be delighted to hear from or of you." *Of course*—emphasis which, in such a connection, emphatically takes away with one hand what it seems to give with the other ! She took some days to answer, and Byron had left London for Aston Hall before the letter arrived. But he wrote to her from there, wondering why he had not heard— plain proof that he too prized the clandestine correspondence. Back in town from another visit, he found a letter answering his facetious one. She got in a few thrusts in revenge for the " of course," beginning frostily with : " I shall not be repelled by the irritable feelings of self-dissatisfaction which I imagine you sometimes indulge " ; telling him (as she grew more genial) that he might be *gay* but had not convinced her that he was *content*, and giving her reason : " I do not think you good enough to possess the only real peace—that of reflection." But after this she was shrewd enough to administer the salve that suited Byron best of all—a reference to his Pride. " Do you not sometimes laugh when you feel, because you are too proud to accept of Sympathy ? " For facetiousness was beyond endurance, as every woman will agree ; Harold must have the Marble Heart, must laugh his own best self away for all but her. It is good comedy—to see how she laid her snares for him, all (or half) unconsciously, like any woman in the circles she so scorned. " I will believe anything you say, simply and seriously." Not that she put it like that, but that is what she would have written, had not an abstract noun or two lain in wait for her. And then . . . We must not laugh ; then : " May I know your sentiments on Religion ? "

She dwelt on that awhile in her most solemn strain ; but came to earth with a dignified snub about Blacket and Pratt. Best regards from her father and mother. " You understand my wish that the knowledge of our correspondence should still be confined to them."

Was there some second-sight in that ? For by this time every letter of hers was being sent to Lady Melbourne for reading.

Meanwhile Byron had been at Six Mile Bottom. On getting back to Bennet Street, he found this letter. He might be flippant about the " now ambiguous A.," but again he answered at once and at length.[1]

" You don't like my restless doctrines—I should be very sorry if you did ; but I *can't stagnate* nevertheless. If I must sail, let it be on the ocean no matter how stormy—anything but a dull cruise on a level lake." . . . Very true that he was gay but not content ; true also that he never attempted to justify himself—sometimes couldn't and occasionally wouldn't. Besides, how many people would be pained instead of pleased if he proved himself a good sort of country gentleman ? Then comes a passage so Byronic that it must be given in full :

To the charge of Pride I suspect I must plead guilty, because when a boy, and a very young one, it was the constant reproach of schoolfellows and tutors. Since I grew up I have heard less

[1] *Letters and Journals*, iii. 401.

about it—probably because I have now neither schoolfellow nor tutor. It was however originally *de*fensive—for at that time my hand, like Ishmael's, was against every one's, and every one's against mine.

Religion. . . . He had shirked that, as we perceive ; but the moment had come. " I was bred in Scotland among Calvinists the first part of my life—which gave me a dislike to that persuasion " ; then follows an account of the dangerous illness at Patras in 1810 which is familiar to readers of his biography. " I believe doubtless in God, and should be happy to be convinced of much more. . . . The *moral* of Christianity is perfectly beautiful " ; but its finer principles had been anticipated by the Greeks. " Good-night—I have sent you a long prose. I hope your answer will be equal in length ; I am sure it will be more amusing. You write remarkably well—which you won't like to hear, so I shall say no more about it." He signed himself (a fancy which sometimes took him) as " Biron."

He stayed in London till October, when he went again to Aston Hall. During this interval he heard from Annabella—restored to complacency by his appeal to go on with their correspondence. She discussed his " *reputed* character " and must have delighted him when she admitted that by many he was thought of with a kind of vague horror. She spoilt this, perhaps, by adding that her wisest friends believed his mind to be " replete with the best feelings." There is more than one reason why Byron's lips may have twitched as he read that. Religion was treated briefly—she was conscious that her too great seriousness might fatigue him, and apologised for it by anxiety and sorrow about " my most valued friend Miss Montgomery," who was going abroad by medical advice. But—and it seems to say that Byron's " of course " was not wholly forgotten or forgiven—she went on : " By attributing my depression to this cause, I do not seek to invalidate what I once hinted of another impression. Subjected as it is to reason, I need not blush to own it. I *should* blush to be its slave." And all her guileless guile is in the immediately following words : " Once more of your Pride— it is perhaps so mingled with magnanimity that the vice might be mistaken for virtue. The distinction need not be *proved* to *you*."

Byron, then at Aston Hall in the full tide of his much more amusing second visit, wrote to Lady Melbourne of this letter that it was melancholy.   Annabella had just written to her aunt, after having read the enlarged edition of *The Giaour*.   " The description of Love almost makes *me* in love. . . . I consider his acquaintance so desirable that I would incur the risk of being called a Flirt for the sake of enjoying it."   The Whitehall lady-confessor told her entertaining penitent that *she* had had a gay letter from A.—on which he commented : " I wonder who will have her at last. . . . The little demure nonjuror ! "

But now, back at Aston Hall, he was absorbed in Lady Frances Webster : " Still, fair . . . a thorough devotee, and takes prayers morning and evening, besides being measured for a new Bible once a quarter."   Some of his most characteristic letters were written to Lady Melbourne about this affair.[1]   He was at first incredulous of his involuntary conquest, then analytic, then highly sentimental for a while, but always witty and shamelessly unreserved.   It progressed—up to a very maudlin point on both sides ; then ended in smoke.   " She would not go off with me *now*, nor render going off unnecessary " ; and though for some time he feared that the jealous husband had found out and would challenge him to fight, that too (in one sense) ended in smoke—and in a loan from Byron to Webster of £1000.

Lady Frances haunted him intermittently, in memory and her tearful letters.   *The Bride of Abydos* was now written ; and the White Rose rhapsody was undoubtedly inspired by her—despite the other, and justified, attribution to Augusta read into the first part by contemporaries.

From London at the end of October Byron wrote to Lady Melbourne : " My Seaham correspondence has ceased on both sides, and I shall not renew it."   He had not answered Annabella's letter, with its recurrence to the " hopeless " attachment of her heart.

She, with no such distractions as his (and the smart of an unanswered letter), had been wondering and pining in the North. Her seriousness *had* fatigued him—was this the end of their friendship ?   She bore the pangs until November ; then she could hold out no longer.   Of all her letters to him this is the

[1] *Correspondence*, i. pp. 195-219.

starchiest (as Byron said later of her style) ; the wounded feeling to be read between the lines is the only interest it possesses. Never did she use so many long words, tangled constructions, meaningless underlinings. It was all about Religion, Revelation, Reason—on Reason she got in a thrust : " I have not as high an opinion of your powers of Reasoning as of your powers of Imagination. They are rarely united." On mathematics too she was crushing : " At your age, [this science] is not to be commenced." But these touches of human nature are not enough to make the letter a readable one. " I am not exacting an answer. I only request to be informed when my communications become unacceptable, that I may discontinue them." On that resentful note she ended.

Among the minor puzzles about Byron, none is more perplexing than his evident pleasure in this correspondence. For think what we may of this latest homily, *he* thought it worth many pages of his rapid, impossibly punctuated writing. She had written on November 3 ; he began his answer on the 10th, but though finished, it lay on his table for a week. By that time he was " in the very heart " of *The Bride of Abydos*. To Annabella he wrote :

Nov. 10*th* 1813.

A variety of circumstances and movements from place to place—none of which would be very amusing in detail, nor indeed pleasing to any one who (I may flatter myself) is my friend—have hitherto prevented me from answering your two last letters ; but if my daily self-reproach for the omission can be of any atonement, I hope it may prove as satisfactory an apology to you as it has been a " compunctious visiting " to myself.[1]

He touched upon Reason and Mathematics ; again insisted that he was a facetious companion, though she seemed still inclined to believe him a " gloomy personage," and went on :

I am happy so far in the intimate acquaintance of two or three men with whom for ten years of my life I never had one word of difference ; and what is rather strange, their opinions religious, moral, and political are diametrically opposed to mine—so that when I say difference I mean of course *serious*

[1] Part of this letter is in *Letters and Journals*, iii. 404-5.

dispute—coolness—quarrel—or whatever people call it.   Now for a person who began life with that endless source of squabble —satire—I may in this respect think myself fortunate.   My reflections upon this subject qualify me to sympathise with you very sincerely in the departure of your friend Miss Montgomery, the more so as notwithstanding many instances of the contrary I believe the friendship of good women more sincere than that of men, and certainly more tender—at least I never heard of a male intimacy that spoilt a man's dinner, after the age of fifteen—which was when I began to think myself a mighty fine gentleman and to feel ashamed of liking anybody better than one's-self. [1]

He would send her, if she would accept it, a copy of *The Bride of Abydos*.   When would she be in town ?   " You won't take fright when we meet, will you ? and imagine that I am to add to your thousand and one pretendants ?   I have taken exquisite care to prevent the possibility of that."

The gibe at himself in this hidden allusion to the Other A. could explain itself to Annabella in no way but that of his having some " mysterious romance " on hand.   Of its nature she could not have dreamed ; and he went on to allude to a woman who would not be troubled to assume the part of Beatrice to his Benedick.   " I think we understand one another perfectly. If I find my heart less philosophic, I shall keep out of the way, but it has got a new suit of armour, and certainly it stood in need of it."   He had heard that another was added to her list of unacceptables ; she made sad havoc among " us youth."   And then two postscripts :

P.S.—Nov. 17th.   The enclosed was written a week ago & has lain in my desk ever since.   I have had forty thousand plagues to make me forget not *you* but *it* ; and now I might as well burn it—but let it go, & pray forgive ye scrawl & the scribe.

. If you favour me with an answer, any letter addressed here will reach me wherever I may be.

I have a little cousin Eliza Byron coming—no, going to school at Stockton.   Will you notice her ?   It is the prettiest little black-eyed girl of Paradise, and but 7 years old.

---

[1] The rest, except the two postscripts, is in *Letters and Journals*, iii. 407-8, under date November 29—evidently erroneous, as the dates of her letters prove.

After the long silence—this. His heart well-shielded by a new suit of armour, a letter to her forgotten in his desk for a week. . . . It would have to be answered ; but first there must be some outlet for the real Annabella, the Annabella who was in love with him. And to M.G. she began a letter, with an attempt at dispassionate self-analysis ; but soon it was beyond control— to some one she must speak out :

> I do not always succeed when I wish to be *enjouée*. It is not quite my proper character. . . . Every one of my friends has a different influence on my humour. MM makes me romantic ; you make me thoughtful ; HM light-hearted (with a few exceptions) ; Joanna humble ; By— religious ; Miss Raine reasonable ; Miss Doyle sanguine ; Dr. Fenwick diffident, &c. &c. You will be surprised at the production of my piety ; but surely the survey of Heaven-born genius without Heavenly grace must make a Christian clasp the blessing with greater reverence and love, mingled with a sorrow as Christian that it is not shared. Should it ever happen that he & I offer up a heartfelt worship together—I mean in a sacred spot—*my* worship will then be almost worthy of the spirit to whom it ascends. It will glow with all the devout and grateful joy which mortal breast can contain. It is a thought too dear to be indulged—not dear for *his* sake, but for the sake of *man*, my brother man, whoever he be—& for any poor, unknown tenant of this earth I believe I should feel the same. It is not the poet— it is the immortal soul lost or saved ! Now I have written and thought till my tears flow—Could I have your sympathy at this moment, & could I feel it in the pressure of your hand on my heart, I should not experience this bursting feeling. Dearest Mary—receive these evaporations of a soul which does not melt quite in solitude if it flies to communicate its emotion to you.

After that, she felt better able to write to *him*. Next day she summoned all her familiar spirits—self-control, dignity, and the rest ; but not all of them could entirely uphold her. A girl like other girls would take the pen at moments. " I hoped you could " ; " I must find my *just* level." . . . Perhaps he would read between those lines ?

> Pray let me have your new composition—I have received more pleasure from your poetry than from all the Q. E. Ds in Euclid. Though I think Mathematics eminently useful, they

are by no means what I like and admire most, & I have not a friend more skilled in them than yourself. People of methodised feelings are to me very disagreeable, being myself so *un*demonstrative as to prefer, if not always to approve, those generous spirits " who are pleased they know not *why* & care not *wherefore*." I hope I have not appeared to assume either mathematical or any other superiority. Everyone has in some point what another wants, & thus the weakest may afford some aid to the strongest. On *that* principle I thought it not presumptuous to offer mine. . . . Perhaps I *have* occasionally forgotten the humility which should have regulated my opinions, and in giving advice I may have taken occasion to show my own wisdom at my neighbour's expense, but could you read my thoughts—and I hoped you could—you would know that my general feeling is very different. I never meant to engage you in religious controversy—you will remember that I owned myself not qualified for converting—I would only persuade you to take the means of convincing yourself. . . .

I cannot now have the least fear of your entertaining a wish for more of my regard than you possess. By enabling you to form a closer estimate of my character, I was aware that the charm which Distance confers with persons of a warm Imagination would vanish, & that I must find my *just* level. But if I have thus permanently secured your peace (as far as I am concerned) and if I have spared you but a single regret . . . I resign my vanity, & wish the sacrifice could make me your equal in disinterestedness. I look forward to meeting you next spring in London as one of the most agreeable incidents which my residence there can produce. *I* shall not be distressed if the design to captivate should be imputed to *me* (which I think probable) ; but if my father & mother should be rendered uneasy . . . I shall try to avoid the occasions, & shall then frankly tell you why I do so, and what I wish—since you will not unkindly suppose that a doubt of your intentions can actuate me. . . .

Me. de Staël's manners were to my taste disgusting—and as I am not an adorer of Genius *for itself*, I did not seek to know her. The more I see of Authoresses, the more I admire in Joanna Baillie a perfect exception to their *professional* failings. I must repeat *my* wish that you knew her, and if yours has not abated, might not the introduction be easily accomplished ? . . .

I was afraid you had experienced some vexations when Lady Melbourne wrote to me a short time ago that you were not looking well. You will never be allowed to remain at peace. Everyone (I must include myself) seems determined to interfere with your repose. After this reflection my conscience obliges me to conclude.

P.S.—I shall like very much to be the playfellow of your little cousin if I can contrive it, for Stockton is 22 miles from hence, & we never go there except in our journeys to and from London. We will gladly send for her, if she may have leave to spend some holidays here.

Whenever you are inclined to improve me by your criticisms, I will pay the poetical debt which I am to have the pleasure of incurring. Unfortunately Mathematics have sobered my Muse —not myself !

Early in this November Byron began, for the first time in his life, to keep a diary—that journal of 1813-14 which is familiar to all readers of his biography. He recorded most of his doings and hinted darkly at one of his thoughts, the thought which beset him—that of Augusta Leigh. He began poems and destroyed them, abandoned schemes for new works because " the thought always runs through, through . . . yes, through." One night he wrote : " A wife would be my salvation " ; but added : " If I love, I shall be jealous ; and for that reason, I will not be in love."

He did not read between the lines of Annabella's letter, for the diary received this entry :

A very pretty letter from Annabella which I answered. What an odd situation and friendship is ours !—without one spark of love on either side, and produced by circumstances which in general lead to coldness on one side and aversion on the other. She is a very superior woman . . . and yet, withal, very kind, generous, and gentle, with very little pretension.

His answer to her was this :

Nov. 29th, 1813.[1]

No one can *a*ssume or *pre*sume less than you do, though very few with whom I am acquainted possess half your claims to that " Superiority " which you are so fearful of affecting ; nor can I recollect one expression since the commencement of our correspondence which has in any respect diminished my opinion of your talents, my respect for your virtues. My only reason

[1] Part in *Letters and Journals,* iii. 406-7.

for avoiding the discussion of *sacred* topics was the sense of my own ignorance & the fear of saying something that might displease ; but I *have listened* & will listen to you with not merely patience but pleasure.

When we meet—if we do meet—in Spring, you will find me ready to acquiesce in all your notions upon the point merely personal between ourselves. You will act according to circumstances. It would be premature in us both to anticipate reflections which may never be made—& if made at all, are certainly unfounded. You wrong yourself very much in supposing that " the charm " has been broken by our nearer acquaintance. On ye contrary that very intercourse convinces me of the value of what I have lost—or rather never found ; but I will not deny that circumstances have occurred to render it more supportable. You will think me very capricious. . . . It is true that I could not exist without some object of attachment, but I have shown that I am not quite a slave to impulse.

For was he not twenty-six and still unmarried ! Only two women had ever approached his ideal—his " early idol," and " one who had disposed of her heart already." It was too late to look for a third ; he would take the world as he found it. " I can only say that I never was cured of loving anyone but by the conduct of the object herself—change or violence."

I owe you some apology for this disquisition, but the singularity of our situation led me to dwell on this topic, & your friendship will excuse it. I am anxious to be candid with you, though I fear sometimes I am betrayed into impertinences. They say a man never *forgives* a woman who stands in the relation which you do towards me ; but to *forgive* we must first be offended—& I think I cannot recall even a moment of pique at the past to my memory. I have but *two friends* of your sex—yourself and Ly. Melbourne, as different in years as in disposition ; and yet I do not know which I prefer. Believe me a better-*hearted* woman does not exist ; and in talent I never saw her excelled & hardly equalled. Her kindness to me has been uniform, and I fear severely and ungratefully tried at times on my part ; but as it cannot be so again—at least in the same manner—I shall make what atonement I can, if a regard which my own inclination leads me to cultivate can make any amends for my trespass on her patience.

The word *patience* reminds me of ye book I am to send you—it shall be ordered to Seaham to-morrow. I shall be most happy to see anything of your writing ; of what I have already seen you once heard my favourable and sincere opinion.

From this he went on to talk of poetry and poets in a passage well known to Byron students—that in which he compared poetry to " the lava of the imagination whose eruption prevents an earthquake." [1] For himself, " the active and tumultuous departments of existence " were the only experiences he recalled with any satisfaction. He was now talking with a friend of an excursion to Holland. If they went, he would be

> able to compare a Dutch Canal with the Bosphorus. I never saw a Revolution transacting—or at least completed ; but I arrived just after the last Turkish one, & the *effects* were visible, & had all the grandeur of desolation in their aspect. Streets in ashes—immense barracks (of a very fine construction) in ruin —and above all Sultan Selim's favourite gardens round them in all the wildness of luxuriant neglect, his fountains waterless & his kiosks defaced, but still glittering in their decay. They lie between the city & Buyukderé on the hills above the Bosphorus; and the way to them is through a plain with the prettiest name in the world—" the Valley of Sweet Waters." But I am sending a volume, not a letter.

Long enough, had that been all, to satisfy the hungry heart at Seaham. But that was not all. " Circumstances had rendered ' it ' more supportable ; unable to exist without some attachment ; a woman who had disposed of her heart already." She was that woman, and she *had* disposed of her heart—but not to another. How should she answer ? There was one way . . . But there were those circumstances which made it more supportable. Better consult M.G., who had seen a copy of her last letter to him. Even with her, though, one must remember those circumstances ; no more about " bursting feelings." And M.G. read this :

> I received your approbation of my letter to B— by the last post, & also an answer from himself, more satisfactory than any which I have yet received. He expresses every disposition which is desirable on the subject of Religion. There is much

---

[1] In *Letters and Journals*, iii. 405, part of this appears under date of November 10—again erroneous. It would seem that this and the other wrongly dated letter were confused with each other by the editor of *Letters and Journals*.

about himself & me, signifying, but in the handsomest manner, that the wishes which he once entertained of possessing me no longer exist, tho' he is as sensible as ever of the value of my affection as ever (*sic*)—saying " It is true that I could not live without an object of attachment." At the same time he says that there are only two women for whom he has a strong regard & that of these he scarcely knows which to prefer—myself or Ly Melbourne, & that of these he scarcely knows which to prefer (*sic*). He then speaks *very* highly of her heart and talents. His mode of speaking of his heart is very mysterious. I fear he has done something rash from a romantic motive. I *really* must take care of my own heart, since he so positively declares that it is out of his power to requite any attachment.

But it would not do. Twice, in her agitation, she unconsciously repeated herself, and the letter ends on a cry—the one word " Oh ! " dashed recklessly down, and left. . . . Two days later, M.G. heard from her again.

I want your advice most seriously. You know that in my first letter to B— I signified the existence of an attachment in my mind, in order to destroy all his hopes. I acted from enthusiasm. I could have devoted much more to his happiness had it been in my power. To this confession he has three times recurred, & again in his last letter, where he declares he shall never marry —for it is now too late—since the only woman to whom he could trust the happiness of his life *has disposed of her heart to another.*

Now certainly I am fully convinced that I have never done so. I have been in danger of it, in great danger—but that is past—& for ever.

You will not suspect me of any selfish view. I am certain that my heart is purified from *Self* in *this* concern ; but I feel very uneasy at the idea of keeping up a deception, & especially with one who has undoubtedly practised no deception with me. Had the circumstance not been mentioned, I should not have felt it necessary or conscientious to allude to it in any way, but now a continuation of silence is an acquiescence in untruth. If we have been so unfortunate as to forsake the path of Sincerity, it has always been my opinion that the sooner we return to it the better. Not by an explanation, for I will not enter into any detail on the subject. It would be indelicate & improper, yet I think something might be done to alleviate the reproaches of my conscience. It depresses me very much. Wisdom as well as will is requisite to be perfectly true—the wisdom of self-knowledge—in which I have failed. Might I not say to this effect—

"For the sake of that Sincerity which I have invariably desired to practise, I have to regret that in one point a want of wisdom has betrayed me into deception—unintentional deception ; & I think I cannot err in acknowledging the error as soon as I am fully convinced of it. An explanation would be of no advantage to either ; & if any disadvantage should arise from the original fault, it must be to myself—& I deserve it."

I shall be unhappy until I can regain *truth*. Such are the unhappy effects of Imagination. He has never yet *suspected* me, & in this brief recantation I think there is nothing to excite suspicion—certainly not to deserve it. I may improve the *form* a little if you approve the sense.

Nothing can be nobler than the sentiments of his last letter.

One of the just opportunities ; and did not we know the sequel, how tempting to be "wicked" about it ! Still she could half-deceive herself : "I have been in danger of it, in great danger—but that is past, and for ever." (Unless, indeed, she was thinking of Byron. He had given her so clearly to understand that she was superseded !) "Past and for ever." Yes, if *he* was lost to her. But even to M.G. that could not quite be confessed.

Then she heard that he had left England.

He had made another serious attempt to go ; but again it had fallen through, and again he was being pursued by Caroline Lamb. The Lady Frances affair was dragging on too—she lachrymose, he completely cured and bitterly ironic to Lady Melbourne. Her indiscretion was such that once more he feared a challenge from the husband. "In my case it would be so dramatic an end. . . . C. would go wild . . . that *it did not happen about her* . . . and poor —— she would be really uncomfortable. Do you know I am much afraid that that perverse passion was my deepest after all." *The Bride of Abydos* was in the press : "It will for some reasons *interest you* more than anybody."

It is scarcely surprising that the Northern A. had been neglected. Not that she had yet answered his letter about the newly-armoured heart. The problem of how to regain Truth had something to do with her delay, and also with a more tangible reason for it.

She had broken down—had had a severe illness. We need not look far for its origin. But among her Christmas presents was a letter from some one with the news that Lord Byron was still in England.

On St. Stephen's Day she took heart, and wrote to him.

Having heard that you are still in England, another day shall not pass before I account for my silence, which without excuse would have been ungrateful both for your verse and prose. Though I wish to make some observations relative to the subjects on which you have lately touched, I will defer them till there is a greater probability that they will find you. I hope that during your stay abroad you will not deny me the pleasure of hearing from you. Can you foresee the length of your absence? If you should not return till summer I shall have one reason the less for regretting the postponement of our journey to London, which on *my* account will not take place so early as I had expected. Though at present recovered from a severe illness, I remain more unequal than before to the labours of a London life.

Every blessing attend you—is the wish of your faithful friend.

Thus—Truth still unregained—1813 ended for Annabella.

CHAPTER VII

1814

OUT OF THE LABYRINTH

EARLY in the New Year Byron left London, in the snow, for Newstead. He sent Augusta a letter for her husband's eye, telling her that she must join him there, she *must* see the Abbey while still it was his. She obeyed ; and Lady Melbourne wrote to him, strongly disapproving the arrangement, which had as usual been confided to her. It was on Augusta that she threw most blame ; Byron answered : " Pray do not speak so harshly of her to me—the cause of all. . . . The intentions of both were very different, and for some time adhered to . . . In short, I know no name for my conduct."

At some time in the year just ended, Augusta had sent him from Six Mile Bottom a lock of her dark silky hair and had written on the covering paper her name and these words : " Partager tous vos sentimens (*sic*) ne voir que par vos yeux n'agir que par vos conseils, ne vivre que par vous, voila (*sic*) mes voeux, mes projets, et le seul destin qui peut me rendre heureuse." He wrote on the paper containing the hair : " La chevelure of the *One* whom I most loved X." X was the symbol he used for Augusta ; they both, later on, wore " almost constantly " gold brooches with three such signs on each.

But during Byron's stay at Newstead, there was another woman about whom to confide in Lady Melbourne. This was Mrs. Chaworth-Musters, the Mary of his boyish dream. She had written at the end of 1813, asking him to come and see her if he should be in Notts. Her marriage had been miserable ; she was now living apart from her husband, and she was ill—" thin, pale, and gloomy ", as she told him.

He had not welcomed the renewal. " I have no feelings beyond esteem, etc. now to spare " ; but he had a great deal besides to say about it to Lady Melbourne. At Newstead they were snow-bound ; this gave him a pretext for not going to see Mrs. Musters, though she wrote to him almost daily. He never did go : " One day too busy, and another too lazy, and altogether so sluggish on the subject." . . . This three weeks' sojourn was to be one of his most remorseful, and Augusta's most sentimental, recollections when the time came for parting with the Abbey. She could not understand his feeling, and he was bitterly contemptuous of hers.

While they were there, *The Corsair* was published and Byron received a triumphant letter from Murray. "Never in my recollection has any work . . . excited such a ferment." But when the author returned to London on February 6, he found himself in the middle of another ferment, not so agreeable, though it was one reason for *The Corsair's* multitudinous sales. This was the sensation about his *Lines to a Lady Weeping*—an incident at Court on which he had published anonymously and only now acknowledged (by their appearance in the Corsair volume) some verses. It is treated at length in all the Byron biographies ; here no more need be said than that this was the first paling of his star. People were talking adversely of the *Lines*, and they went on to talk adversely of something more serious. Already there had been whispers, started by the publication of *The Bride of Abydos*. Everyone was asking if Mrs. Leigh had read it ; a nephew of hers at Eton was questioned and taunted about the first part, where Selim and Zuleika believe themselves to be brother and sister. Now, with this pretext of the affront to Royalty, Society was beginning to turn the cold shoulder ; the newspapers were in convulsions, as Byron told Lady Melbourne ; and all his defiance was ready. "If stepping across the room would stop them, I would not cross it."

He stayed in London, angered about this and wretched about " *that within*." " It is the misery of my situation to see it as you see it, and to *feel* it as I feel it, on her account, and that of others." Sometimes he talked of marriage, both to his diary and Lady Melbourne ; two or three girls were considered—the sister of Lady Frances Webster among them. The Princess of Parallelograms was once mentioned, but he did not answer her Christmas letter.

" Rage and resistance and redress ; but not despondency or despair." When the *Edinburgh Review* attacked his *English Bards* in 1808, that was Byron's description of his state of mind. He could not have repeated it now. The rage was his ; but so were the despondency and despair which then he could resist and redress. He had long known of something against which there was no resistance, and but an ignoble redress—Augusta's pregnancy by himself. The child would be fathered by her husband ; but Byron, scoff at conscience as he might, had too much of it to feel that as anything but an added wrong. Now arrived the foolish turmoil about his foolish acknowledgment of the *Lines*. Nothing in itself, perhaps ; something when taken with the rest. The world he scorned was scorning him—a difference that defiance could not do away with. " The thought runs through, through—yes, through " ; in his new quarters at the Albany there were hours darker even than those in Bennet Street. " Am I not in reality worse than they make me ? "

Up at Seaham, Annabella was recovering. No answer to her Christmas letter ; but the break-down had been a relief, she had won back some of her fortitude—and we are free to smile when we find her writing instead to Hugh Montgomery. To him she always wrote in a strain so different from the solemnity she used with Byron that, were it not for the issue, we might wonder at her choosing to show never a gleam of fun with him who was so insistently " facetious." But she had made no mistake ; Byron admired her letters, though with Lady Melbourne he might jeer about starch and stilts.

Hugh Montgomery, at any rate, got a sprightly account of home-politics in the New Year of 1814 ; a " fashionable glossary " of somewhat obvious satire on the usual topics of religion, morality, conduct ; and later, when events were making her feel that hope still lived, there was this : " When my Dad and I get tipsy together, our toast is always ' Friends far away.' He keeps quite well—no temptations here.... My mother may prefer my health to a son-in-law." Thus gaily she could tell *him* that she was not going to London that spring.

Byron was told the same news in February, with every long word she could think of. For this letter was most portentous.

The attempt to regain Truth was to be made in it. M.G. had
approved the idea, but not its first embodiment ; so the tentative
paragraph was altered—into something scarcely more intelligible.

> You have understood *me* as least as well as I understood
> myself. Both may have been partly deceived, though unwit-
> tingly by me ; but I have found that Wisdom (often the most
> difficult Wisdom, Self-knowledge) is not less necessary than Will,
> for an absolute adherence to Veracity. How I may in a degree
> have forsaken *that*—and under an ardent zeal for Sincerity—is
> an explanation that cannot benefit either of us. Should any
> disadvantage arise from the original fault, it must be only where
> it is deserved. Let this then suffice—for I cannot by total
> silence acquiesce in that which, if supported when its delusion
> is known to myself, would become a deception.

After comparing his Conrad (in *The Corsair*) to Milton's Lucifer,
and recommending him to read Locke's *Treatise on the Reasonable-
ness of Christianity*, she allowed herself one admission : " Are
you going to leave England ? . . .   I am anxious to know."   And
she enclosed a copy of verses on the snow at Seaham, to him who
had been snowbound at Newstead, with Augusta.

He answered immediately, from the midst of his various
distresses. . . . If the Fates were changing horses (his letter
seems to say), might it not be towards this girl that they would
carry him ?

Fy. 12th, 1814.

> I am just returned to London after a month's absence and
> am indeed sorry to hear that your own will be so much longer—
> and the cause is not of a description to reconcile your friends to
> it entirely, although the benefit you will derive to your health
> will prevent us from regretting anything but the time—if the
> effect is accomplished. All expressions of my good wishes to
> you and for you would be superfluous.
> Mr. Ward postponed our Dutch expedition ; but as I have
> now nearly arranged my domestic concerns—or at least have
> put them in train—and the Newstead business is set at rest in
> my favour, " the world is all before me " and all parts of it as
> much a country to me as it was to Adam—perhaps more so ;
> for Eve as an atonement for tempting him out of one habitation
> might probably assist him in selecting another, & persuade him
> into some " Valley of Sweet Waters " on the banks of Euph-
> rates.

In thanking you for your letter will you allow me to say that there is one sentence I do not understand. As you may have forgotten it I will copy it. . . .

This I believe is word for word from your letter now before me. I do not see in what you have deceived yourself ; & you have certainly never been otherwise than candid with me—and I have endeavoured to act accordingly. In regard to your kind observations on my adoption of my conduct to your wishes—I trust I should have been able to do so even without your suggestion. The moment I sunk into your friend, I tried to regard you in no other light. Our affections are not in our own power ; but it would seem strange indeed because you could not like me that I should repine at the better fortune of another. If I had ever possessed a preference, the case would have been altered—and I might not have been so patient in resigning my pretensions. But you never did—never for an instant—trifle with me nor amuse me with what is called encouragement—a thing, by-the-bye, which men are continually supposing they receive without sufficient grounds ; but of which I am no great judge—as except in this instance I never had an opportunity. When I say " this instance," I mean of course any advance on my part towards that connexion which requires duty as well as attachment ; and I begin to entertain an opinion that though they do not always go together, their separate existence is very precarious. I have lately seen a singular instance of ill-fortune. You have perhaps heard that in my childhood I was extremely intimate with the family of my nearest neighbours—an inheritor of the estate of a very old house and her mother. She is two years older than me ; and consequently at so early a period any proposal on my part was out of the question—although from the continuity of our lands & other circumstances of no great importance, it was supposed that our union was within the probabilities of human life. I never did propose to her, and if I had it would have answered very little purpose—for she married another. From that period we met rarely—and I do not know very well why—but when we did meet, it was with coldness on both sides. To cut short a tale which is growing tedious : eight years have now elapsed, and she is separated from her husband at last after frequent dissensions arising entirely from *his* neglect, and (I fear) injuries still more serious. At eight-and-twenty, still in the prime of life, beautiful (at least she was so), with a large fortune, of an ancient family, unimpeached and unimpeachable in her own conduct—this woman's destiny is bitter. For the first time for many years I heard from her desiring to see me. There could be nothing improper in this request. I was the friend of her youth ; and I have every reason to believe—to be certain—that a being of better principle never breathed. But she was once deep in my heart ; and though she had long ceased to be so, and I had no doubts of her, yet I had many of myself—at least of my own feelings if revived rather than of any consequence that might arise from them ; and as we had not met since I was 21 . . . to be brief, I did not see her. There is the whole history of circumstances to which you may have possibly heard some allusion from those who knew me in the earlier part of my life. I *confide* them to you, & shall dwell upon them no further except to state that they bear no relation whatever to what I hinted at in a former letter as having occurred to prevent my reviving the topic discussed between us—at least with a view to renewal.

I have to ask for an answer, when you have leisure, and to thank you for your description, which brings the scene fully before me. Are you aware of an amplified coincidence of thought with Burns ?

" Or like the snowflake on the river
A moment shines—then melts forever."

The verses are very graceful & pleasing. My opinion of your powers in that way I long ago mentioned to another person—who perhaps transmitted it to you. I am glad you like *The Corsair*, which they tell me is popular. God bless you. Ever yours   B.

P.S.—I am not perhaps an impartial judge of Lady M.—as amongst other obligations I am indebted to her for my acquaintance with yourself ; but she is doubtless in talent a superior—a *supreme* woman—& her heart I know to be of the kindest, in the best sense of the word. Her defects I never could perceive—as her society makes me forget them and everything else for the time. I do love that woman (*filially or fraternally*) better than any being on earth ; & you see that I am therefore unqualified to give an opinion.

He wrote again before her answer reached him :

Febry. 15*th* 1814.

In my letter of ye 12th in answer to your last I omitted to say that I have not for several years looked into the tract of Locke's which you mention—but I have redde (*sic*) it formerly, though I fear to little purpose since it is forgotten—& have always understood *that* and Butler's Analogy to be the best treatises of the kind. Upon the subject of which it treats, I think I have

already said that I have formed no decided opinion ; but I
should regret any *sceptical bigotry* as equally pernicious with the
most credulous intolerance. Of the Scriptures themselves I have
ever been a reader & admirer as compositions, particularly the
Arab-Job—and parts of Isaiah—and the song of Deborah.

Your kind congratulations on the subject of certain prejudices
against me having subsided is a little premature ; for in discussing more agreeable topics, I quite forgot to mention what
you perhaps have seen in some of the journals, viz : a series of
attacks—some good and all hearty—which have been called
forth by the republication & avowal of some lines on the
Princess Charlotte's weeping in 1812—at a time when the
Prince assailed Ld. Lauderdale at a public dinner, soon after
his own abandonment of Grey & Grenville. These still continue,
and rather more violently than ever—except that I think the
destruction of the Custom House has a little interfered with
mine, and Buonaparte's recent advantage has usurped the
column generally devoted to the abuse of a personage who,
however unimportant, appears to be very obnoxious. I have
hitherto been silent, & may probably remain so—unless
something should occur to render it impossible.

You will have received so long a letter from me before this
arrives, that I will not at present intrude upon you further.
Pray take care of yourself, consider how many are interested in
your health and welfare—and reconcile us to your absence by
telling us that you are the better for it.

P.S.—My best respects to Lady Me. and Sir Ralph.

Meanwhile she had made, and despatched, her second attempt
at regaining Truth.

I have twice implied that I suffered from Disappointment.
It was an effort to make such a disclosure, but I thought it could
only have been withheld, when it *might* be beneficial, from
selfish considerations. I resolved to overcome a reluctance that
seemed so ungenerous—to extenuate nothing—to give the
greatest possible force to my confession. In this fever of Sincerity I first made & afterwards repeated the allusion to my
attachment ; yet even then I had doubts which prevented me
from expressing it more fully & distinctly. I had certainly felt
greater interest for the character I attributed to one man (with
whom my personal acquaintance was comparatively slight) than
for any other within my knowledge. In believing him deserving
of happiness, I earnestly wished he might enjoy it ; but he had
never given me any reason to think I could bestow it, nor was

my partiality discovered by himself or any other person.   I
indulged no hope, & had hope been offered, should have rejected
it from regard to the views and wishes of others.   Circumstances
have since made it impossible for me even to dream of Hope. . . .
I have sometimes regretted that lost chance of domestic
happiness—sometimes I have doubted if I should have possessed
the characteristical happiness of married life, that of making
happy—and lately such doubts have, by additional proof, been
converted into a certainty which destroys every wish for the
trial.   You can now judge if I deviated from the language of fact
in representing my own feelings—if my view of them were not
partly delusive—from what I remember of my expressions, I
think so.   Yet as my intention was blameless I reflect upon my
error without pain. . . .   When I *know* Truth I follow it, or
return to it, come what may.

I have time only to add—you may feel secure that your
secret rests with me alone.   My father & mother being perfectly
satisfied as to the general nature of our communication, with
their usual generous confidence, enquire no further.   Your
decision was undoubtedly right and wise, but the story is
melancholy, and must have grieved *you*.

Truth had not been entirely regained, as the Auto-Description
testifies ; but since his heart was so well shielded, she too had to
buckle on some armour.   She had rewarded his confidence about
Mary Chaworth by one as dispassionate about the man of straw
—each should have felt that things had got a little further.

Byron replied :

Feby. 19*th* 1814.

Many thanks for your answer, which has cut the knot—but
I had no right to interrogate you on such a subject ; and had I
been at all aware that my question would have led to any
explanation of feelings to which you do not like to recur, of
course I should have remained in silence and darkness.

Still it is not to be regretted in one point of view on your own
account—as it sets all apprehension of the revival of a subject
already discussed long ago between us, at rest.   It is true that
it was not in any great peril of revival before ; but it is now more
completely " numbered with the things that were " and never
can be again.

Ignorant as I am of the person & the circumstances to whom
and which you allude, I can form no opinion except that if he
has put it out of his power to avail himself of such a disposition
in his favour, he is fortunate in not knowing that it ever existed.

I was rather sorry (though probably *they* would not believe me) for Bankes & Douglas—who are both clever and excellent men, & attached to you ; and as I had contrived to make my own fortune like Sir Francis Wronghead, I confess that (that terrible pronoun *I* being put out of the question) I should have been glad to have seen one of them in a fair way for happiness. But I shall grow impertinent, which will do them no good & me some harm—& so Adieu to the subject.

Since my last letter I believe I have sent another of *omitted* replies to parts of your own, and I must shorten this, or you will think me more tedious than usual.   I am at present a little feverish—I mean mentally—and as usual on the brink of something or other which will probably crush me at last, & cut our correspondence short with everything else.   Till then I must take as much of it as I can get ; & as to my own epistolary offerings, you will only find them too profuse.   Besides these domestic stimulants, I have the further satisfaction of still finding the Pe. Regent's friends & Newspapers in gallant array against me—the latter very loud—the former I don't see.   If I did, our dialogue would probably be very short but more to the purpose.   I am told also that I am " out of Spirits "—which is attributed to the said paragraphs. He must however be a happy man who has nothing deeper to disturb him. Ly. Me. I have not yet seen, but I believe she is well ; & I hope to find her so shortly. Pray how old are you ?   It is a question one may ask safely for some years to come.   I begin to count my own.   A few weeks ago I became six-&-twenty in summers—six hundred in heart— and in head and pursuits about six.

This letter had a curious effect on her.   For some reason she felt it her duty to reprove him.

Had you humbly bowed before the Chastener, that fever of spirit would have been calmed, & this world would have lost its power to make you guilty, even were you still to be overwhelmed by its sorrows.   To signify some calamity impending over you, yet to leave me in painful suspense as to its nature and the possi- bility of averting it, is not quite considerate towards one who so anxiously desires your welfare.   You can *only* wrong me by doubting *that*—by refusing me a participation in your cares.   It might possibly a little decrease their burden to you, & could not grieve me more than the vague conjectures which I am left to form.   If the causes of those attacks of anguish ought to be secret, I will not seek to divine them—but if the secrecy be only *self-imposed*, cannot my prayer dissolve it ?

I was twenty-one last May. My prospects are full of uncertainty, and inspire me with doubts respecting my future peace. On the whole I think myself formed for domestic ties, but I cannot seek them on the principle of Self-love or Expediency. Could my choice have been regulated by such views, perhaps it might not have been deceived in either of your friends. I was early sensible that they could not attach me as I feel I could be attached—and I fear, *must*, since the capacity for affection is destined some time to be concentred. It is now shared amongst some excellent friends, who improve whilst they fill my heart. Joanna is not one of the oldest in point of acquaintance, & I therefore consider myself the more obliged to her. If you have made use of my introduction pray tell me what opinion you conceive of her.

Though Byron answered immediately, he did not immediately answer her lecture. Nor did he go to see Joanna.

I have not availed myself of your kind introduction to Mrs. Baillie, because I hope time or chance will one day bring us into the same society, & then you will do it in person ; & although I wish much to be acquainted with her & have the sincerest admiration of all I see and hear of her—yet—in short I have a strange awkwardness and repugnance in making new acquaintances, & have had ever since I was a child ; & you will easily believe this is not at all diminished by the respect I may entertain for the person to whom I am to undergo presentation. This is constitutional ; & not all I have seen, or all I may see, can or could ever cure it entirely. I conceal it as much as possible—so well, indeed, that many would believe it affectation in me to say this. With *you* I have no such apprehensions in stating the simple truth. I am very glad she likes ye Corsair, because she is one of the very few who can understand the passions & feelings I have endeavoured to describe ; but not even my Vanity can get the better of me in ye respect I mentioned above.

I have troubled you lately with so much scribbling that I feel some remorse in intruding on you again so soon.

His next letter, written before he had another from her, concludes with a postscript which might be translated : " Let us get some life into this correspondence ! "

March 3d. 1814.

In your last you stated that you were about to quit Seaham for a short time. I trust that you have derived benefit—that is better health—from your excursion. I have to regret having perhaps alarmed you by something I said. Writing hastily in one of my late letters, I did not very well—at least I do not—recollect exactly what I said. It was the " hectic of a moment " probably, occasioned by a variety of unpleasant circumstances pressing upon me at the time, arising from follies (or worse) into which I betray myself—& escape I cannot tell how, unless there be such a thing as Fate in this best of all possible worlds.

You allude in your last to the very indignant newspapers—whose assaults I would most willingly encounter every morning for the rest of my life, provided I could exchange for them some of my own reflections & recollections on very different subjects, which assail me much more formidably.

He thanked her very much for her " suggestions on Religion[1]; but it was a source from which he never had—and he believed never could—derive any comfort. " Why I came here, I know not ; where I shall go, it is useless to inquire . . . Why should I be anxious about an atom ? "

I am writing to you with " the night almost at odds with morning," and you are asleep. Perhaps I were better so too—& for fear my letter should prove a commentary on Pope's line, " sleepless himself to give his readers sleep," I will conclude by wishing that you may awake to the most agreeable day-dreams which the " pure in heart " desire and deserve.

P.S.—I was told to-day that you had refused me " a *second* time," so that you see I am supposed to be the most permanent of your plagues, & persevering of your suitors—a kind of successor to Wellesley Long Pole. If this multiplication-table of negatives don't embarrass you, I can assure you it don't disturb me. If it vexed me I could not, & if I thought it would do otherwise than amuse *you*—I certainly *should* not, have mentioned it.

Her reply was of many pages ; but she came to the point at last. " As for the report, it is absurd enough to excite a smile. In avoiding the possibility of being in a situation to refuse, I cannot consider myself as having refused." And though she tried by passages about Mme. de Staël and so on to cover up the hint that she was willing to be proposed to again, Byron read between the lines this time, for he remarked to his Diary : " A letter from

---

[1] In *Letters and Journals*, iii. 408.

Bella, which I answered.   I shall be in love with her again if I don't take care."   His answer should have rejoiced her heart.

March 15th 1814.[1]

To rob you of my conversion some pious person has written & is about to publish a long poem—an " Anti-Byron " which he sent to *Murray*—who (not very fairly) sent it to me ; and I advised him to print it—but some sort of bookselling delicacy won't let him.   However, some one else will.   I thought some parts of the verse very good.   The author's object is to prove that I am the *systematic* reviver of the dogmata of Epicurus, & that I have formed a promising plan for the overthrow of these realms, their laws & religion, by dint of certain rhymes (Runic I suppose) of such marvellous effect that he says they have already had the " most pernicious influence on civil society." Howbeit—with all this persuasion of mine evil intents—what I saw was very decent invective & very grave, no humour nor much personality ; a great deal about Gassendi, Locke &c. and a learned refutation of my supposed doctrines.   The preface is all about the 8 lines (ye Tears)— which have I believe given birth to as many volumes of remarks, answers, epigrams &c. &c.   So you see, like the fly on the wheel in the fable, " what a dust we create."   In addition to these, I do not believe that there be 50 lines of mine in all touching upon religion ; but I have an ill memory, & there may be more.   However, I had no notion of my being so formidable an Encyclopedist, or a Conspirator of such consequence.   Now can anything be more ludicrous than all this ?   Yet it is very true—I mean the Anti-person of whom I am speaking.   He assumes at first setting-out my *Atheism* as an incontrovertible basis, & reasons very wisely upon it.   The real fact is I am none ; but it would be cruel to deprive one who has taken so much pains of so agreeable a supposition—unless he believed that he had con-vinced me of that which I never doubted.   I will send it to you the moment it is out, to shew you what an escape you have had, for there is a long prose passage against *my marrying*—or rather against any one's marrying me—on account of ye presumed philosophy wherewithal I am incessantly to lecture the future Ly. B. and the young Spinozas tutored in the comfortable creed with which I have already inoculated " civil society," & which they are to take instead of the Vaccine.

You do not know how much I wish to see you—for there are so many things *said* in a moment, but tedious upon the tablets.

[1] Five lines from paragraph 2 of this letter are in *Letters and Journals* iii. 409.

Not that I should ever intrude upon your confidence anything
(at least I hope not) you should not hear ; yet there are several
opinions of yours I want to request, & though I have two or
three able & I believe very sincere *male* friends, there is something preferable to me in ye delicacy of a woman's perceptions.
Of this at least I am sure—that I am more liable to be convinced
by their arguments. As for ye *report* I mentioned—*I* care not
how often it is repeated. It would plague me much more to hear
that I was *accepted* by anybody else than rejected by you.

I have passed the bourne of my paper, & must leave Me de
Staël, Miss Rn. and somewhat more of egotism for another
opportunity. You are better—and God knows I am glad of it.
I am interrupted by a visitor, and you won't regret it—and I
must not.

" Rejoiced her heart." Yes ; but again we might think to
discern some unconscious second-sight in her delay to answer
this letter. She did not write again for a month. · In the interval
what had happened ?

Byron had been with Augusta at Six Mile Bottom. " Col. L."
as he gibed to Lady Melbourne, " was in Yorkshire, and I regret
not having seen him of course very much." A week after his
return to London, Augusta's child was born—the Elizabeth
Medora Leigh who was to play so strange a part in the later
story of Annabella's life.

He wrote to Lady Melbourne, after another stay at Newmarket and his first sight of the baby :

> Oh ! but it is " worth while," I can't tell you why, and it is
> not an " ape," and if it is, that must be my fault. . . . But
> positively she and I will grow good and all that, and so we are
> *now* and shall be these three weeks and more too.

His phrase : " It is not an ape " is an evident allusion to the
mediaeval superstition that the child of incest must be a kind of
monster. Again, he wrote to Lady Melbourne : " You—or
rather *I*—have done *my A.* much injustice. . . . *She* was not to
blame, one thousandth part in comparison. She was not aware
of her own peril until it was too late."

It is the cry of Manfred : " I loved her, and destroyed her."

When Annabella wrote again on April 13 the most interesting
passages are her timid question : " Am I mistaken in imagining

that you are disposed to visit us ? " ; and the repetition of her wish (long disregarded) that Lady Melbourne should not know of their correspondence.

Yet—I must account to her for your visit, if purposed. Do you think it necessary to say more than that you have been invited to Seaham whenever you again travel northwards ? My father will kindly express to you that invitation, if you will give us reason to hope it will be accepted. Perhaps these are idle speculations, and then think of them no more.

He instantly told Lady Melbourne, with this corollary : " Circumstances, which I need not recapitulate, may have changed *Aunt's* mind ; I do not say that *Niece's* is changed, but I should laugh if their judgments had changed places." A word from her would put an end to that " or any similar possibility " ; and he concluded with a quotation from Annabella's letter : " If so, think no more of it."

At this time he was in his doctor's hands. " An old complaint, troublesome but not dangerous " ; yet the doctor had put some searching questions about the state of his mind. " He thinks me horribly restless and irritable, and talks about my having lived excessively, ' out of all compass,' some time or other."

Lady Melbourne did not forbid him to go to Seaham ; and he wrote to Annabella :

If I could flatter myself that my visit would not be disagreeable to you nor yours I should very willingly avail myself of Sir Ralph's possible invitation. Distance is no object with me, and time can hardly be misspent in your society ; besides a good deal of mine is generally passed in my own company, so that I could almost hope that I should not be found an intruder upon your studies or amusements. You will do as you please—only let it be *as you* please, & not to gratify any supposed or real wish of mine that you make this sacrifice at the shrine of hospitality.

I quite coincide with you upon religious discussion. It should at all events be treated with some degree of respect—if for no other reason than that it is so easy, so common, and so unfit a subject for would-be witticisms. Upon that score I may have as a scribbler something to answer for (I allude to some notes on some of the things of the last 2 years), but they have been as it were wrung from me by the outcry on the subject—the common effect of contradiction upon human nature. It gave me great pleasure to hear from you again. I thought you unwell or indisposed to correspond with me further. In either case I had no claim to trespass upon your health or patience.

All ye world are for Paris. Italy is my magnet ; but I have no particular wish to be of the vanguard or forlorn hope of foolish travellers, & shall take my time without much regretting a *summer* month or two in this country more or less. Besides I have some previous business to arrange ; for if I do once cross the channel, I know my own loitering disposition well enough to fix no precise period for my return. Buonaparte has fallen ; I regret it, and the restoration of the despicable Bourbons—the triumph of tameness over talent, and the utter wreck of a mind which I thought superior to Fortune. It has utterly confounded and baffled me, and unfolded more than " was dreamt of in my philosophy." It is said the Empress has refused to follow him. This is not well. Men will always fall away from men—but it may generally be observed that no change of Fortune, no degradation of rank or even character, will detach a woman who has truly loved—unless there has been some provocation or misconduct towards herself on the part of the man, or she has preferred another for whom her affection will endure the same. I have brought my politics & paper to a close —and have only room to sign my abdication of both.

She answered :

I *wish* to see you, and am happy to think I shall not wish in vain. . . . Your ode to Buonaparte was read in the company which I have just left. It was thought not perfectly lyrical—of this I cannot judge, but it appeared to me like a spontaneous effusion. . . . I was amazed indeed when his " magic of the mind " melted into air. I rejoice in the hope of peace, yet could not join in the triumphant exultation over his fall—a very serious, if not melancholy contemplation. . . . I cannot make excuse for a silence which cost you a doubt, unless you will accept as such that I did not once conjecture you would feel it any loss. In the disposition whence this arose, our characters may have some analogy ; therefore it will not, I hope, appear incomprehensible or strange.

Before hearing from him again, she wrote to Lady Melbourne and told her of the invitation ; wrote also to Byron, informing him that she had done this. " I think she would be glad to learn it." (In her letter, which he kept, Byron underlined those nine words, and wrote : " WILL SHE ? *Credo di No* ! ") She enclosed some verses of her own : " I like them, because they followed the incident naturally." They were to a friend who disliked her habit of frowning :

> O be it thine to chase the frown
> Which thou can'st never raise,
> When I, with brow in thought bent down,
> Tread Care's perplexing maze.
>
> O be it thine to wake the smile
> Which thou can'st only cloud
> When, with thine own, in tears awhile
> It finds a watery shroud.

His opinion of these lines was not imparted to her—perhaps mercifully.

Unaware of Annabella's having taken so decided a step about his suggested visit, Byron wrote to Lady Melbourne on the subject. He was evidently getting frightened, for his comments are as fractious as the doctor had said that he was. " That eternal Liturgy " ; " If she imagines that I . . . delight in canvassing the creed of St. Athanasius, or prattling of rhyme, I think she will be mistaken." He continued :

> I don't know what to say or do about going. . . . I am not now in love with her ; but I can't at all foresee that I should not be so, if it came " a warm June " (as Falstaff observes) ; and, seriously, I do admire her as a very superior woman, a little encumbered with virtue. . . . I am quite irresolute and undecided. If I were sure of *myself* (not of her) I would go ; but I am not, and never can be.

And next day he wrote :

> Your niece has committed herself perhaps, but it can be of no consequence ; if I pursued & succeeded in that quarter, of course I must give up all other pursuits. . . . My heart always alights on the nearest perch—if it is withdrawn it goes God knows where—but one must like something." [1]

He did not answer Annabella. From his letters to Lady Melbourne, it is evident that he was hearing from Augusta almost every day. Possibly, too, Annabella's decisive action about the invitation had annoyed him. At any rate, nothing passed between him and the Other A. until the middle of May.

[1] *Correspondence*, i. 253.

It was she who resumed the correspondence, in a letter which it surely cost her some struggle to write. But she had a pretext, valid enough for self-deception. They were leaving home for a week—going to Halnaby ; they still hoped they might some time see him. " I am as well as possible, enjoying the chearfulness (*sic*) of health, and satisfaction from causes more interesting to me." A skilfully enigmatic ending ! She posted her letter and waited. But she waited in vain. There was no answer from Byron.

" Prim and pretty as usual." That is his reference to the cry wrung from her a month later.

> Pray write to me—for I have been rendered uneasy by your long silence, and you cannot wish to make me so. Though my conjectures as to the cause—which has much and anxiously occupied my thoughts—have been various, they have never assumed any motive on your part but the best. On mine I do not feel equally confident. I have perhaps been too careless of forms and expressions, having expressed & omitted so injudiciously that it might be impossible to understand my meaning. Or my meaning itself may have been faulty ; and if so, whilst I hope that your kindness is undiminished, I should expect correction from you—it would be received with grateful attention. Lest there should have been any failure in the delivery of my letters, I have written thrice since I had the pleasure of hearing from you—briefly each time, for being prepossessed (too strongly perhaps) with the idea of a better mode of communication, I suppressed much. I have been charged with this correspondence. The direction of letters were, I know, observed once or twice. If you should hear of it, do not suffer yourself to be embarrassed by my injunction of secrecy. . . . Not wishing to attract observation of *any* kind, I should have preferred silence, and still I may not be called upon to break it, if the report dies away ; but I should acknowledge without a blush that I have *sought* your friendship.

Her hint about gossip amused him : " This has naturally given a fillup (*sic*) in my favour which was much wanted." But at the moment he was absorbed in again protecting himself from Caroline Lamb. " She comes at all times, at any time, and the moment the door is open, in she walks. . . . If there is one human being whom I do utterly *detest* and *abhor* it is she." Yet it must have been now that in his rooms at the Albany the following scene took place. We have it on Caroline's testimony only, but later events show that he certainly did confide in her at this time.

> He pressed his lips on mine . . . he said " Poor Caro, if every one hates me, you, I see, will never change—no, not with ill usage." And I said, " Yes, I *am* changed, and shall come near you no more." For then he showed me letters, and told me things I cannot repeat, and all my attachment went. . . . It had an effect upon me not to be conceived.

Nothing at all like this can be gathered from his letters to Lady Melbourne, which are hot with hatred for Caroline. But meeting her at a masked ball in July, he was " pestered " by her questions and guesses. " There is no conjecturing what she may assert or do." If Caroline's story is true, this was disingenuous ; he had then shown her the letters of which she speaks. But even to Lady Melbourne he may have been ashamed to confess his betrayal of the secret.

Was it because Seaham offered an escape from the dual torments that he now began to think seriously of going there ? Towards the end of June he had at last answered Annabella :

> I have delayed writing from day to day, first because you were absent from Seaham, and 2ndly, I wished to fix a time when I might have the pleasure of availing myself of Sir Ralph's very welcome invitation. You may be assured that " my kindness," as you are pleased to call it, *is* " undiminished ; " you have much more cause to apprehend its troublesome progress than conjecture its decay. You make me laugh about " forms & expressions." I will not say that I wish you to be less formal, because I had rather you pleased yourself ; but Me Scudèry herself could not have imagined a more correct correspondent. As to " meanings," I hope you do not think that I have presumed to mistake them ; and if I do not, who else has any business with them except Sir R. and Lady Milbanke—who have permitted our correspondence ?
>
> I shall await your answer and your convenience before I pretend to name any period when I can hope to see you. Believe me, it will give me great satisfaction. I do not find my comparisons very favourable to those in the crowd where I have lately mingled—and this may in some measure augment a regret which is now useless.

You have been " charged with this correspondence." Might I ask by whom ? It is no great matter, unless with those very discerning persons who think that between people of our time of life and in our situation there can be but one topic of discussion. If all this has not alarmed you, let me hear from you again, and at all events believe me

very affectly. & truly yrs.

But for once, something had been happening to *her*. Lady Wentworth, her uncle's wife, was dying ; Lady Milbanke had gone to Kirkby Mallory—the Wentworth estate in Leicestershire—for an indefinite stay. " I cannot think of anything else at this moment. . . . Farewell, dear friend." She wrote that before Byron's tardy letter had reached her. Next day it came, and that day she answered it—able now to think of something else. Of all her letters before their engagement none is more touching than this, when read along with his to Lady Melbourne and those guarded ones to Augusta in which only the mother of Medora could interpret the allusions and the chosen symbol " X."

Here is Annabella's outpouring :

I am made very happy by your letter and the certainty which it affords of your intention to visit us. . . .

The formality and coldness which are, I know, sometimes observable in my manners as well as in my writing, have a source that is painful to myself—therefore pray do not allow me to seem what to you I can never mean to appear. After each time that I met you last year in London. I was vexed by the idea of having been repulsively cold towards you. It would have remained a source of great regret had not the means of removing so false an impression (did you receive it ?) been in my power. I was as anxious then as since to make my real feelings known to you. The recollection of that needless & in part involuntary constraint, only gives me a greater degree of satisfaction in asking you to believe me

Ever affectionately yours

On hearing that Seaham could not offer him immediate sanctuary, Byron fled to Hastings, there to stay through the first ten days of August. His old friend Hodgson, his cousin (and presumptive heir) George Byron, and Augusta were with him. Augusta was match-making for " my dearest B "—had suggested Lady Charlotte Leveson-Gower as a possible wife. Of this girl Byron had already written in his diary : " They say she is *not* pretty. I don't know—everything is pretty that pleases ; but there is an air of *soul* about her—and her colour changes—and there is that shyness of the antelope (which I delight in) in her manner so much that I . . . only looked at anything else when I thought she might perceive and be embarrassed by my scrutiny." [1] So with him, the ground was prepared. Augusta undertook to sound Lady Charlotte, who was devoted to her. The upshot was farcical, as we shall see ; for the present we need only know that this was going on during the late summer and early autumn of 1814.

Annabella got no reply to her self-revealing letter. She had been brooding over Byron's allusion to " a regret which is now useless." How should she convey to him that the regret was not so useless ? She could not tell all the truth, but some Veracity might be regained. She could not wait for a reply—she must write ; and taking the bull by at any rate one of the horns, she began :

> Before we meet, all uncertainty and obscurity should be removed, and the object is too essential to be sacrificed by either to false delicacy. . . . You spoke of " a regret which is now useless."

So far so good. But then the bull escaped from her fingers. Too soon she was talking about the impossibility of return of attachment, acknowledging an affection for him, but an " imperfect " one, which nevertheless might be to him " a bond of peace with himself, with his God." Of late indeed she had not been at all afraid of having it returned too largely ; on the contrary, had shown him some fear of a decrease. " If I have been mistaken—God forbid I should aggravate a regret which I cannot remove ! "

By this time she hardly knew what she wanted him to think, or what she felt herself. " If you love me, make your peace your first object, as it is the first object with me." In other words,

---

[1] And see his letters to Augusta of June 18th and 24th in this year. *Letters and Journals,* iii. 96 and 100.

" Don't come to Seaham unless." . . . She would not look that
" unless " in the face, but even Annabella's pen refused to wander
any farther through obscurities ; the letter turns into a piteous
appeal for help out of the labyrinth. " If I am in any respect
mysterious to you, if you desire any explanation of the past or
present . . . believe that I shall give it most willingly."

Byron instantly responded :

August 1st 1814.

Your letter has only reached me this day from London (where
I shall return in a very short time) ; otherwise it had been
answered immediately.

Allow me to avail myself of your permission to request " an
explanation " which—as I do not recollect the " *ambiguous*
expression " to which you allude in my last letter—is necessary
for me to understand yours. I am the more anxious to receive
it as *this* is my second answer to your letter. The first I have
destroyed ; because on considering yours more attentively, it
appeared to me that I had misunderstood you, and that my
reply would in that case only produce perplexity. Pray then
write to me openly and *harshly*, if you please. If there is anything you wish to know or say, I am ready to answer or listen ;
but whether present or absent—in enmity or charity—you are
the last person I would wish to misunderstand.

My best thanks are due to Sir R. for the invitation which
accompanied your letter. It is however as well that I have
delayed accepting it, as I have not interfered with your Durham
gaieties of the 6th. I hope on my return to London to receive
your reply—I shall be there next week.

ever most affectionately yours

BYRON.

P.S.—I have read your letter once more—and it appears to
me that I must have said something which makes you apprehend
a misunderstanding on my part of your sentiments, and an
intention of renewing a subject already discussed between us.
Of this I am not conscious ; and whatever my regrets or my
regards might have been—or may be—I have not so far lost all
self-command as to betray either to an extent that would render
them troublesome to you ; and my memory is still retentive
enough not to require the repetition that you are attached to
another.

Her reply meant simply : " Try again ! " But the fog of

words hid from her the spectacle of all her boats burning. She might have seen it as she added the postscript.

SEAHAM, *Aug.* 6.

I thank you for the forbearance which made you pause and suspend a judgment of my meaning till it should be elucidated, as I hope it now will, beyond doubt. . . . When I last wrote I feared from some reconsiderations that you might still be in danger of feeling more than friendship towards me ; and if so, that my intercourse which has been governed, especially of late, by a contrary opinion, might have been, or might be, promotive of that tendency. I have not entertained the least apprehension that your self-command would fail in any way that could affect me disadvantageously or disagreeably. . . . I must have smiled, had I not been almost vexed, at your reiterated and most kindly intended assurances to destroy my supposed dread of a renewal, when after your first assurance I should never have doubted that your determination was irremovable. . . . Instead of fancying you likely to conceive my regard greater than it is, I have invariably observed that you did not understand how great it was. You do not appear to know how very little I am inclined to consider my own interests in comparison with yours, nor how much of the former I should, *without a sacrifice*, disregard for the sake of the latter. If *I* am secure from trouble and embarrassment, you seem to think I must be free from anxiety.

My doubt then is—and I ask a solution : Whether you are in *any* danger of that attachment to me which might interfere with your peace of mind ? I am not apt to believe that I inspire such attachment, and in admitting a *possibility* which as your friend it seems that I ought not to neglect, if I err, it is not from vanity. Next, on the supposition of a reply unfavourable to my wishes, I would ask you to consider by what course the danger may be avoided. . . .

Some time ago I had meant to acknowledge clearly, knowing that you would not mistake the motives of my acknowledgment, that I had been deceived (and too willingly, inasmuch as you were concerned) in thinking I had ever formed a decided attachment. The reasons which led me to believe the character of one person suited to my own, have disappeared with opportunities of fuller investigation . . . nothing could now induce me to marry him. You are therefore mistaken if you deem *this* the cause, or any part of the cause, why I am not *even more* affectionately yours.

P.S.—Is not a print published from your portrait ?—and will you send an impression to one who will place on it no common value ?

The Leveson-Gower negotiations were hanging fire. Lady Charlotte's sweetly silly letters to Augusta had begun to disenchant Byron with his antelope. Antelopes and mathematicians—both, it appeared, could be elusive. But *he* had discerned the burning of the boats. As he afterwards told Lady Melbourne, he could see that " Annabella had been bewildering herself sadly." Somebody must speak out—it had better be himself ! And he wrote :

August 10th 1814.

I will answer your question as openly as I can. I did—do—and always shall love you ; and as this feeling is not exactly an act of will, I know no remedy, and at all events should never find one in the sacrifice of your comfort. When our acquaintance commenced, it appeared to me from all that I saw and heard that you were the woman most adapted to render any man (who was neither inveterately foolish nor wicked) happy ; but I was informed that you were attached, if not engaged—and very luckily—to a person for whose success all the females of the family where I received my intelligence were much interested. Before such powerful interest—and your supposed inclinations —I had too much humility or pride to hazard importunity or even attention ; till I at last learned—almost by accident—that I was misinformed as to the engagement. The rest you know ; and I will not trouble you with " a twice told tale," " signifying nothing."

What your own feelings and objections were and are I have not the right and scarcely the wish to enquire. It is enough for me that they exist ; they excite neither astonishment nor displeasure. It would be a very hard case if a woman were obliged to account for her repugnance. You would probably like me if you could ; and as you cannot, I am not quite coxcomb enough to be surprised at a very natural occurrence. You ask me how far my peace is, or may be, affected by those feelings towards you. I do not know—not quite enough to invade yours, or request from your pity what I cannot owe to your affection.

I am interrupted—perhaps it is as well upon such a subject.

He had opened the way out of the labyrinth—and not only that, but had given a quite irresistible grace to the gesture.

" You would probably like me if you could." He never wrote
a more engaging word to a woman. So when her answer arrived,
he naturally felt bewildered himself. Indeed, he felt something
stronger than bewilderment, for his reply was a gust of healthy
anger—and Annabella thoroughly deserved it.

She had written at once in her wordiest manner, but the
essence was that he did not appear to be the person *she* ought to
select as her guide, her support, her example on earth, with a
view to Immortality. She alluded to the George Eden imbroglio
—he had never engaged her heart. Byron was to believe that
for every kindness to himself he was indebted not to her good-
nature and indulgence, but her esteem and affection.

He would scarcely have been human if he had answered this
agreeably ; and he certainly did not.

August 16th 1814.

Very well—now we can talk of something else. Though I do
not think an intimacy which does not extend beyond a few
letters and still fewer interviews in the course of a year could be
particularly injurious to either party, yet as (if I recollect
rightly) you told me that some remarks had been made upon
the subject, it is perhaps as well that even that should end.
This is a point upon which yourself can best determine, and
in which I have nothing to do but to acquiesce. I shall leave
London in a few days, but any letter addressed to me here will
be forwarded, should you deem it proper to answer this.

You have not said anything of your health lately, from which
I infer that it is improved. You have had a good escape from
the last town-winter, which was bustling beyond precedent, and
has I dare say provided invalids for the next ten years.

Pray make my best respects to Sir R. and Lady M. and accept
them for yourself.

She was unlike other girls. That is never more manifest than
in her reception of this letter. She had, it is true, his earlier
confession that he did, and always should, love her ; still, the
impulse of most women would have been to answer, if at all, at
least as curtly as he had. Annabella answered more lengthily
than ever before. She dissected herself from the age of seventeen ; she gave him the irrelevant information that her health
required many hours of sleep and exercise—an unattractive as
well as an irrelevant avowal ! This prevented her from studying

much ; she cared only for philosophy and poetry—but (remembering what was Byron's favourite study) she asked him to recommend her some books of modern history. At present she was reading Sismondi's *Italian Republics*. And she had read *Lara*. Shakespeare alone possessed the same power as Byron had there displayed.

The range of characters you have chosen is most interesting to me, being that through which my imagination has naturally wandered, but amongst models purely imaginary till you gave them life. I have been often startled by finding the creatures of my visions with the colours which, though I could not bestow, I think I am *able* to admire. As one of many traits preconceived by me, I may point out that exultation of Despair, that exhilaration of Misery, which you have embodied. In some early essays of mine, I could show you these and other conceptions, feebly similar to yours, and I do not repent the indulgence of poetical inclinations if it has only enabled me to feel the truth of your touches more exquisitely.

From Newstead Byron, restored to good-humour, answered like a professor. She had used the right bait ; on history he could always abound. Unlike other girls though she was, it is probable that she began by skipping a good deal of his opening paragraph.

August 25th.

You can hardly have a better modern work than Sismondi's, but he has since published another on the Literature of Italy, Spain &c., which I would willingly recommend, though it is not completed and contains only the South as yet. If you have not got it, on my return to London I would gladly forward it. In his Italian Commonwealths there are two characters which interested me much—Eccelin and Giovanni Galeazzo—to say nothing of many others. I am a very bad French scholar, but can read when I like the subject, though I prefer Italian. Davila, Guiccardiani, Robertson, & Hume you know without my telling you are the best " modern Historians ; " and Gibbon is well worth a hundred perusals. Watson's Philip of Spain, and Coxe's Spain and Austria are dry enough ; but there is some advantage to be extracted even from them. Vertot's Revolutions (but *he* writes not history but romance). The best thing of that kind I met by accident at Athens in a Convent Library in old & not " very choice Italian." I forget the title—but it

was a history in some 30 tomes of all Conjurazioni whatsoever
from Catiline's down to Count Fiesco of Lavagna's in Genoa,
and Braganza's in Lisbon. I read it through (having nothing
else to read) & having nothing to compare it withal, thought it
perfection. I have a Tacitus with Latin on one page and Italian
on the other among my books in town. I should think the
original by itself a little severe on a feminine reader, & will send
you that if you would like it. It is a foreign edition.

The only books I brought with me here are a few Novels,
Essayists and Plays—with one classic—and a volume of
Machiavel containing his *Principe* and Life of Castruccio. You
should read Denina's Greece also—and Roscoe's Lorenzo—&
Leo—but I should only bore you with my *shoulds* and sugges-
tions, so there's an end.

You ask me what " my occupations " are ? The " dolce far
niente "—nothing. What my " projects " are ? I have none.
How my health is ? Very well.

I agree with you on the score of " fashionable " life, though I
don't perceive that any other is either better or worse. All
contemplative existence is bad—one should *do* something, since

" All partial evil's universal Good."

Even mischief is remotely productive of advantage to some one
or something in this best of all possible worlds. Now the worst
of civilisation & refinement is that we are reduced to a most
insipid medium between good and harm, and must get very
much out of the beaten track to do either.

It will give me much gratification some day or other to see
the " early essays " you mention, and in the mean time I shall
not like my own the worse for the resemblance.

P.S.—I wrote my last so hurriedly, being on ye eve of leaving
London, that I omitted to mention (with my best thanks and
respects to Sir R.) that I regret it will not be in my power to
proceed to Seaham during the present year. My Northern
expedition (with a son of Sir Jno. Sinclair's to his father's)
during the commencement of which I could have had the
pleasure of joining you for a few days, has been put off ; and I
shall not see Scotland, with which I wished to have renewed my
acquaintance, for some time to come.

" Some day or other " and the postscript—they cannot have
done much to exhilarate her. He was not coming ; not for all
that year.

She took time to answer ; but when she did, reproached him

with grace and dignity. "We had avoided every engagement which might have interfered with that more welcome one." ... To glance aside for a moment, these must have been vexatious days for the parents, more offended than she at Byron's refusal of their invitation, more conscious too of the ambiguous position Annabella had created for herself. They had yielded to her, as they always did ; now they must have regretted it, and hoped that the correspondence would come to an end. She would answer this letter ; else too much hurt feeling might be betrayed —but surely she would tactfully break off ?

Again she answered at even more length than usual ; again she dissected herself ; again she sweetly lectured him. His offer of books was accepted ; she would make another attempt at reading " the whole of Gibbon " ; there was a passage in an unpublished work of Porson's which she would copy for him if he liked. And then—might not one sound a more intimate note?

> I have just been in company where (not a singular occurrence) you were mentioned with great goodwill by those who are personally strangers to you. It is to me a very agreeable circumstance that the persons most attached to *me* are free from prejudice against *you*, though I have not influenced their opinions. I can listen with immovable calmness to the censures which may be passed on my friends, but when any one awakens my sympathy by a sound of kindness, I should find it difficult, if it were necessary, to appear less interested than I am. The date of your letter surprises me—I thought you had sold Newstead. It is time for me, though unwillingly, to bid you farewell.

More revealing than all this was her confession (in a postscript) that she had kept her letter back a day, and now would like to burn it.

> If we could have met, all my apparent inconsistencies would have been dispelled. ... If it be not irksome to you—as I sometimes fear it is—pray write soon. I have no right to ask it—but I *do* ask it, and if I can be justified, *you* will justify me.

Not know the passage from Porson ! Of course he knew it, and would say so at once. But something must again be done to get some life into this business—especially as the other one was even more exasperating. With a Goose (his pet-name for Augusta) as go-between and an Antelope as quarry, that might have been expected ; but it was sillier than he could think of patiently. . . . And now for Porson.   Better begin with Porson.

7th Septr. 1814.

It is Porson's letter to Travis to which you allude and—if I recollect rightly—one of his remarks (the highest praise to be passed on an Historian) is that amidst the immensity of reading through which he had tracked Gibbon, not *one* of his *authorities* was misquoted or perverted even unto a syllable. Perhaps I am wrong in giving this as from P's preface, for years have elapsed since I saw it ; but of the fact as P's opinion—and no one could be a better judge—I am certain.

Porson was slowly extinguishing, while I was a Cantab. I have seen him often—but not in " his happiest hour," for to him that of " social pleasure " could not be so termed. He was always—that is daily—intoxicated to brutality. I hate to think of it, for he was a perfect wonder in powers and attainments.

Newstead is mine again—for the present. Mr. Cn., after many delays in completion, relinquished his purchase. I am sorry for it. He has lost a considerable sum in forfeiture by his temporary inability or imprudence ; but he has evinced a desire to resume or renew his contract with greater punctuality, and in justice to him—though against the advice of lawyers, and the regrets of relations—I shall not hesitate to give him an opportunity of making good his agreement. But I shall expect—indeed I will not endure such trifling for the future.

I am much amused with *your* " sovereign good " being placed in repose. I need not remind you that this was the very essence of the Epicurean philosophy, and that both the Gods (who concerned themselves with nothing on earth) and the Disciples of the illustrious idler, the founder of that once popular sect, defined $\tau\grave{o}$ $\grave{\alpha}\gamma\theta\acute{o}\nu$ to consist in literally doing nothing—and that all agitation was incompatible with pleasure. The truth possibly is that these materialists are so far right ; but to enjoy repose we must be weary—and it is to " the heavy laden " that the invitation to " rest " speaks most eloquent music.

You accuse yourself of " apparent inconsistencies." To me they have not appeared ; on the contrary, your consistency has been the most formidable apparition I have encountered. There seem to me no grounds for complaint on one side nor vindication on the other ; and as to explanations—*they* are always a puzzle. After one or two letters which lately passed between

us, and to which I must request your pardon for recurring we—
at least *I* (to speak for myself)—could hardly have met without
some embarrassment, possibly on both sides, certainly on one.
This has been avoided—and so far is a subject of congratulation.

Your letters are generally answered on the day of their arrival,
so that it can't be very " irksome for me to write soon."

On my return to London, which will not take place immediately, I shall have great pleasure in forwarding the book
offered in my last. The " Agricola " is beautiful. It is a pity
that there are so many objections to a like perusal of Suetonius
also ; whose portraits are but too faithful even in their coarsest
features. You must be partial to Sallust—but after all there
are none like Tacitus, & him you have.

Before he could receive her answer, the other affair had wholly
collapsed. Augusta had written a formal proposal on his behalf
to Lady Charlotte. The reply, " full of alarms," was in effect a
refusal. Byron told Lady Melbourne :

" I then said to X, after consoling her on the subject, that I
would try the next myself, as she did not seem to be in luck." [1]

On September 9, he sat down to try the next. When he had
finished his letter (which we shall shortly see) he showed it to X,
" who on reading it over observed : ' Well, really this is a very
pretty letter ; it is a pity it should not go—I never read a prettier
one.'

" ' Then it *shall* go,' said Byron."

That is Moore's account, given " so far as I could trust my
recollection," from Byron's (destroyed) Memoirs.

The pretty letter was posted immediately it had been read
and approved by X. Meanwhile Annabella had been writing
one to him, and one to Hugh Montgomery. In that to Byron
she fastened on his remark about her consistency, with a touch of
coquetry rare indeed from her.

The " apparition " of my consistency ought not to be
" formidable " to you, since like other apparitions, it may owe
its effect chiefly to the imagination of the spectator, and might
vanish with the light of day. I do not pique myself on its
solidity. . . . I do not recollect my quiescent tenets. Probably
I exalted the blessing of repose at the moment because I did not

[1] *Correspondence*, i. 275. Lady Charlotte Leveson-Gower married the Earl
of Surrey, only son of the Duke of Norfolk.

possess it. In fits of cowardice I envy the Oyster. . . . Interrupted—and I never like to resume.

The letter to Hugh Montgomery gives us the usual side-light on a gayer Annabella, wilful daughter of an adoring father ; but this one, at this moment, has a symbolism so startling that it might be the invention of a novelist.

> The day before yesterday I performed a feat—an humble imitation, however. A man walked from Sunderland here blindfold in three hours, winning his wager in consequence. I betted that if turned blindfold into the field behind the house, I would find my way to the gate at the end. Instead of doing this, I marched directly to the horse-pond, and should have plunged " to endless night," had not Dr. Southey intervened. My adventures will amuse you as told by my father. I regained the path and won at last.

> 1
> Five miles a man did walk for fame
>   Blindfold, a mighty prank !
> Says one, I'd nearly do the same,
>   And that was Miss Milbanke.

> 2
> Away she went as bold as brass
>   And gaily held her course ;
> Nimbly avoiding Jacky Ass
>   And also the pond horse.

> But Dr. Southey by her side
>   Did stand her much in stead,
> Like Pallas when she once did ride
>   At Troy with Diomed.

And so on for two more stanzas. " I think," wrote Annabella to Hugh, " you will admire the ' pond horse ' as a noble inversion." . . .

Byron's renewed proposal was in the post—and she was walking blindfold into danger across the fields of home ! Not often does the trivial event so mimic the event of destiny. The doggerel, the whole incident, have for us an entirely irrelevant pathos. That " honest, red-faced spirit," elated at having turned out his *jeu d'esprit* the very same evening : " Copy the verses for Hugh, Bell ! "—and Bell copies them, as gay as he, with another

kind of elation in her heart ; and on the 14th the pretty letter
reaches her. Here it is :

Septr. 9th 1814.

You were good enough in your last to say that I might write
" soon "—but you did not add " *often.*" I have therefore to
apologise for again intruding on your time—to say nothing of
your patience. There is something I wish to say ; and as I
may not see you for some—perhaps for a long time—I will
endeavour to say it at once. A few weeks ago you asked me a
question which I answered. I have now one to propose—to
which, if improper, I need not add that your declining to reply
to it will be sufficient reproof. It is this. Are the " objections "
to which you alluded insuperable ? or is there any line or
change of conduct which could possibly remove them ? I am
well aware that all such changes are more easy in theory
than practice ; but at the same time there are few things I
would not attempt to obtain your good opinion. At all events
I would willingly know the worst. Still I neither wish you to
promise or pledge yourself to anything ; but merely to learn a
possibility which would not leave you the less a free agent.

When I believed you attached, I had nothing to urge—indeed
I have little now, except that having heard from yourself that
your affections are not engaged, my importunities may appear
not quite so selfish, however unsuccessful. It is not without a
struggle that I address you once more on this subject ; yet I
am not very consistent—for it was to avoid troubling you upon
it that I finally determined to remain an absent friend rather
than become a tiresome guest. If I offend it is better at a
distance.

With the rest of my sentiments you are already acquainted.
If I do not repeat them it is to avoid—or at least not increase
—your displeasure.

Her answer needs no comment.   It was written the same day.

I have your second letter—and am almost too agitated to
write—but you will understand. It would be absurd to suppress
anything—I am and have long been pledged to myself to make
your happiness my first object in life. *If I can* make you happy,
I have no other consideration. I will *trust* to you for all I
should look up to—all I can love. The fear of not realizing your
expectations is the only one I now feel. Convince me—it is all
I wish—that my affection may supply what is wanting in my
character to form your happiness. This is a moment of joy

which I have too much despaired of ever experiencing—I *dared* not believe it possible, and I have painfully supported a determination founded in fact on the belief that you did not wish it removed—that its removal would not be for your good. There has in reality been scarcely a change in my sentiments. More of this I will defer. I wrote by last post—with what different feelings! Let me be grateful for those with which I now acknowledge myself

Most affectely yours.

She was afterwards told by Augusta of this letter's arrival at Newstead. " He received it at dinner—the apothecary was the only person present besides A. . . . His remark to her, as he handed the letter across the table, looking so pale that she thought he was going to faint, was : ' It never rains but it pours.' "

An excuse for this flippancy was provided by Annabella herself. It is one of the moments when we smile—against the grain ; yet cannot but smile. She had sent another letter to the Albany, and accompanied it by a " few lines " from her father. She told Byron this on a sheet added to the Newstead one, saying that she had done it " on the chance of sparing him a moment's suspense." Hobhouse says that the Albany letter was a duplicate ; but this does not seem to be the truth, for she adds on the extra sheet : " I hope you will find in my other letter *all you wish*." And certainly it is difficult, if not impossible, to conceive of a woman who would copy the letter we have just read !

Long afterwards she said of Byron's answer to her acceptance : " I thought that I might now show him all I felt. . . . I wrote just what was in my heart." She did not know what we know of the Newstead interchanges ; his answer could not have failed to move her so to write.

This was it :

Septr. 18*th* 1814.

Your letter has given me a new existence—it was unexpected —I need not say welcome—but *that* is a poor word to express my present feelings—and yet equal to any other—for express them adequately I cannot. I have ever regarded you as one of the first of human beings—not merely from my own observation but that of others—as one whom it was as difficult *not* to love —as scarcely possible to deserve ;—I know your worth—and revere your virtues as I love yourself and if every proof in my power of my full sense of what is due to you will contribute to *your* happiness—I shall have secured my own.——It *is* in your power to render me happy—you have made me so already.——I wish to answer your letter immediately—but am at present scarcely collected enough to do it rationally—I was upon the point of leaving England without hope without fear—almost without feeling—but wished to make one effort to discover— not if I could pretend to your present affections—for to those I had given over all presumption—but whether time—and my most sincere endeavour to adopt any mode of conduct that might lead you to think well of me—might not eventually in securing your approbation awaken your regard.——These hopes are now dearer to me than ever ; dear as they have ever been ;— from the moment I became acquainted my attachment has been increasing & the very follies—give them a harsher name—with which I was beset and bewildered the conduct to which I had recourse for forgetfulness only made recollection more lively & bitter by the comparisons it forced on me in spite of Pride—and of Passions——which might have destroyed but never deceived me.——

I am going to London on some business which once over—I hope to be permitted to visit Seaham ; your father I will answer immediately & in the mean time beg you will present my best thanks and respects to him and Lady Milbanke. Will you write to me ? & permit me to assure you how faithfully I shall ever be

yr. most attached
and obliged Sert.[1]

He meant every word of it. " My heart always alights on the nearest perch."

When he handed Annabella's letter across the dinner-table, the apothecary—watchful of his Lordship's agitation—should have become aware that he was assisting at a dramatic moment.

" It never rains but it pours."

And Mrs. Leigh, when she had read, looked at her brother— surely with unusual emotion ? . . .

" It is the best and prettiest I ever read ! " exclaimed the Other A.

---

[1] In this letter the characteristically wild punctuation is left unchanged, since it well conveys his agitation.

CHAPTER VIII

ENGAGED

OVER at last—the shilly-shallying, the floundering. " I offered my existence to him. The reply was gratifying beyond words to describe—it made me feel inspired with the purest happiness."

At thirty-nine she wrote that, recalling—perhaps re-reading—the letter we have just read. Stilted, as she always was on paper, yet even then with some of the purest happiness revived in it. To Byron at the time she wrote : " I have been very foolish, and if you had not been wiser, we might both still be without hope." She added that a sort of quiet despair had possessed her. But if her despair had been quiet, so had her persistence been. Byron's wisdom was not " without aid."

The comedy in their correspondence can escape no one. It lies on the surface, and part of it in the fact that each was attributing to the other a character which that other was eager to disclaim. If she insisted on his Melancholy, he insisted on her Serenity. " That placid countenance "—she disavowed the placidity, as he disavowed the despondency. But it was no use. Neither would yield the cherished point.

Of the stately saraband which their Platonic letters had kept up, Byron could see the absurdity—as he could all absurdities, even his own. But Annabella, with her narcissistic gaze at an ideal image of herself, was inevitably blind to it. She could no more have perceived than Byron could have helped perceiving. For whatever he might now say—and for a while imagine that he felt—he had long since divined that he had only to ask again. A girl might be something of a puzzle to him whose affairs, since the boyish dream of Mary Chaworth, had mostly been with married women ; but that " Niece's mind had changed " he would have been dense beyond precedent if he had not read through her bewilderment.

114

Now antelope and man of straw had made their final exits. A single figure held Annabella's stage ; Byron's was not so easily cleared. The cast had been large—one pretty super had left it, one White Rose been dismissed in tears ; but still he had to reckon with the leading lady, the woman scorned, and the Goddess of Comedy who had presided over all from Melbourne House. The leading lady, it is true, had shown herself gracefully willing to resign her part. The pretty super had been her favourite understudy, but that was over ; the unknown aspirant from the North would have to do. Augusta Leigh, as we have learnt, thought nothing wrong that did not make anybody unhappy. She was aware that the star-actor would not let her go till the last possible moment ; that did not matter so long as the fiancée did not know. When the fiancée should become the wife, there would be danger to happiness ; but for the present . . . and besides, in the immediate present B. and X. were being good again, and X. was back at Newmarket, laughing with " *il marito* " over the bets against B.'s ever really getting married.

To that extent his stage was emptier. But what of the woman scorned ? Uneasiness about " C." was explicit from the first to Lady Melbourne. " She must do her worst if so disposed." Caroline's worst (if we believe her story about the scene at the Albany) might have been very bad indeed ; but Byron was disturbing himself in vain. She did nothing at all except write him a note of congratulation, on which he commented to Lady Melbourne with the godlike complacency of a male let off a scene. " It becomes her . . . when everyone is disposed to forgive and treat her kindly." He answered Caroline briefly (and, one hopes, less insufferably) in a note which he enclosed to her mother-in-law.

That divinity had not refused her " indispensable " consent to his engagement. Cynical though she was, especially about marriage, Lady Melbourne had a heart, and Byron was dear to it. She believed that he would really (as he promised her) " reform most thoroughly " ; moreover she had had nothing to do with his renewed proposal to her niece, between whom and herself there was very imperfect sympathy. She could not have intervened without betraying his confidence ; there was no other objection to the match. She had remonstrated all along, and most earnestly, against the liaison with Augusta ; had seen that the only hope of ending it was his marriage ; had learnt from him that " X." was of the same opinion. Now he was on the way to that ; Annabella would probably do as well as any other girl. He had always had a perplexing fancy for her : let them try their luck ! And she was naturally sanguine, " fortunately gifted with a fund of good-nature and cheerfulness, and very great spirits." So she had described herself to Byron long before this. Lady Melbourne, then, had written cordially to niece and nephew, and now was hearing from Byron nearly as often as Annabella heard.

Not quite ; for in love-letters he was at first inexhaustible. So was Annabella, but she often got two or three to her one. Byron could create emotion in himself, he was not hypocritical— " what could be imputed to him was the voluntary overcharging or prolongation of a real sentiment." These words, quoted by Lord Lovelace from Hazlitt, are the best explanation of him in the early phase of his engagement. Like her, like all lovers, he was exploring Paradise Regained, certain that there was no such name for it as Fools' Paradise—but ready, as she was not, to acknowledge that only fools, perhaps, know paradise on earth. . . . Meanwhile, they recalled their first meetings, first impressions, they sent each other earlier letters to read in the new light, like any simple souls that ever fell in love.

This kind of correspondence is so monotonous for everyone but the lovers that we shiver on its brink. The letters must— or should—be read ; for much revelation of both natures is in them, much indication too of the causes which worked to divide this pair. They are given here, in order not to interrupt the narrative, in an appendix with as little comment as may be.[1] Byron's have their separate interest, in that they are his love-letters to the girl after whom he had persistently hankered, by whom he had been refused, and on whom he was to pour—so soon !—in other writings such contumely and hatred as none but he would have been capable, in any sense, of expressing. We shall see, as we read them, that for a while at least she could not have questioned his love for her.

Did he question it himself ? His flippancies to Lady Melbourne mean nothing. " I suppose a married man never gets

[1] See Appendix I.

anyone else, does he ? I only ask for information." To the
Goddess of Comedy that and its like were obligatory—not particularly amusing, but one must say something. At the bottom
of it all lay a frankly confessed hope that Annabella would govern
him. He said so more than once, to her as well as to Lady
Melbourne. That placid countenance, with its resolution and
its gravity—surely it answered for the steadfast influence which
could keep him out of mischief ? But she, who from childhood
had struggled with the impetuosity of her character, who had
" struck her head with her hand till she staggered back," who
was " always craving for excitement," lying awake to picture
herself the heroine of some passionate devoted episode—the last
thing she desired was to govern. Like any other girl, she thrilled
to the idea that her lover would govern *her*, and all the more
because her parents never had. Her placid countenance : among
all the guileless snares she had laid for him, that had never been
one. From the first she had tried to undeceive him about her
serenity ; but with her Egerian airs, her long words, lectures,
continual talk of composure and tranquillity, it was impossible
for Byron to suppose that this was a girl of feeling, as he and his
kind understood the words. She *would* govern him, she *would*
be composed and tranquil always ; the Marble Heart would
soften, would find rest . . . and he might be glad, though
henceforth he were to be good.

In the beginning that was what he felt, or believed he felt.
Augusta told Annabella afterwards that during the two days she
stayed at Newstead after the engagement, his temper was better
than she had ever seen it. He had said : " Well, Heaven has been
kinder to me than I deserve." Augusta herself was overjoyed.
No jealousy seems to have troubled her, then or later ; and this
was not because she felt sure of her power over his senses.
Nothing is more extraordinary, in this extraordinary triple
relation, than the sister's attitude. No doubt Byron's marriage
was a relief to her, more or less passively his thrall as she had been
in the affair. She adored him beyond measure ; but with
hardly any reference to the incestuous bond between them,
loving him as though he had never been her lover. Only a
superficial nature could have done this ; and the superficiality
accounts for much that in a different woman would justify Lady

Melbourne's often-expressed view that Augusta was very clever and very wicked. We shall be driven to think much the same of her, as the story develops ; yet the truth does seem to be that she was merely incapable of feeling deeply, and could not understand that others did. Byron called her a fool—how often, she herself confessed she could not count. It is true that she sometimes found her convenience in this foolishness of hers ; nevertheless it *was* hers, she " could not help it " (as we say) although she used it—consciously at times, but quite as often unconsciously. That it was one of her charms for Byron there is no doubt ; perhaps, in her devotion, she played it off for him as guilelessly as she adored him.

Byron triumphantly told Lady Melbourne of her exclamation : " It is the best and prettiest letter I ever read." The Goddess of Comedy, with *her* opinion of Augusta, must surely have frowned, though she can hardly not have smiled as well—wondering, like us, how Mrs. Leigh had come to be such an expert in girls' answers to proposals. But for Byron, reticence in these things was out of the programme ; so his leading lady had every privilege of her state before she withdrew to the smoking-room and the bets at Six Mile Bottom.

Annabella, getting her three love-letters at a time, had one to write which was not a love-letter. This was to Hugh Montgomery, stopping with the Gosfords in Ireland. He was now to be dismissed not only as man of straw but as correspondent. No longer might she write to " handsome young batchelors " ; he was to answer this, but there an end. Hugh was commissioned to tell M.G., to whom her mother was writing.

M.G., one thinks, might fairly have expected to hear the news from Annabella herself. However, she was soon to be the confidante again, was to be told to burn all former, and one at least of immediate, letters. But : " I want letters from you more than ever." " I always have a little tremor as I write A.I.*M*. Don't you see the M. diminishing in magnitude ? " " There are abominable stories in circulation concerning me—we don't care for all the attempts to make us appear wrong and ridiculous." And M.G. was later to receive complaints about the vexing sort of congratulations that were coming in. " Nothing affronts me

so much as a dismal *hope* that I may be happy." Even Joanna
Baillie transgressed in this way ; so did M.M. and her brother,
unconscious object of fictive attachment—and yet Miss Montgomery had in the past (as Byron was to be told) " uniformly,
decidedly, and singly maintained " that Annabella and Byron
were better suited to one another than any two people elsewhere
in the world. " I used to laugh at the opinion, with a very ill
grace." And now M.M. had turned round, and was dismally
hopeful ! This tardy attack of insight in her much-loved friend
weighed on the bride-elect's mind, and set her writing, in October,
a serious defence of her choice to M.G. " I have fixed with mature
judgment on the person most calculated to support me in the
journey to immortality." A girl of twenty-two wrote that !
The assurance is a commonplace of her state ; the way she expressed it must surely be unique. But before M.G. reached this
point in the letter, she had had one of those familiar opportunities
for wickedness. " With regard to myself, though my perils
have not been equally evident to common eyes, I have had
hair-breadth escapes. After having had nearly ' the world
before me where to choose ' "—and then came that confident
assertion.

" Half-a-dozen proposals or so—a small world ! " So Lady
Gosford should have commented ; and very likely she did, feeling,
as often before, that Annabella could be ridiculous. The further
apotheosis of Byron can scarcely have convinced her. Had he
indeed learnt " the nothingness of popular opinion " ? Was he
indeed " secured from the temptations of Vanity " ? Had he
tried and found " the inefficiency of all pleasures—of all ways of
abstraction from self—which are not founded on virtue " ?
Whatever the current ejaculation of disbelief then was, we may
be sure that it broke from M.G.'s lips as she read these passages.
And only the day before yesterday, had there not come that
other letter from Seaham in which it had been easy to divine
some trouble of heart ? For " he " was delaying to come, he was
arranging his affairs " with as much discretion and good sense
as if he had never arranged verses in his life. Nothing can be
more rational and considerate. It pleases me much more than
if in the impetuosity of love. . . . " Poor Bell ! Did she really
expect one to believe that ? Did she believe it herself ?

And in fact this very rational and considerate behaviour was the first little cloud—no bigger than a lawyer's hand—on Bell's blue sky. Very like a lawyer's hand ; and that was all she saw in it. But Lady Melbourne may have recalled Hamlet with Polonius as she watched the many forms that little cloud could take. Lord Wentworth was one of them : " The most important personage of both your houses." She seems to have given Byron a caustic sketch of him. " Infinitely inviting," he had sneered ; " the longer I stay away the better." And then : " I cannot go to Seaham, for I know not how long." This time it was Hanson's (his lawyer's) family affairs. Next : " I feel very odd about *it*, not *her* ; it is nothing but shyness and a hatred of strangers which I never could conquer." But one form which Lady Melbourne thought to perceive in the cloud was eagerly dissipated : " X. never threw obstacles in the way ; on the contrary, she has been more urgent than even you." On the 12th of October : " Well, but I am going, am I not ? What would mine aunt have ? "

Seaham, though it saw only the lawyer's hand, was feeling that the cloud had spread. September gone by in letter-writing ; October going by in letter-writing . . . how large that hand could be ! On the 18th the sky seemed to be clearing. " I am thinking and feeling in the next week," wrote Annabella, " and so are you perhaps." But whatever Byron was thinking and feeling, next week too went by. On the 22nd she wrote : " [The old ones] are growing quite ungovernable. . . . It is odd enough that my task should be to teach *them* patience." Even this failed ; it was not until October's very end that she heard he had started to come to her. That was a Saturday. He was to spend Sunday at Six Mile Bottom with Mrs. Leigh, from whom one had had so kind a letter. How soon afterwards could he arrive ? If he came with the impetuosity of a lover, it might be Monday—at latest (so coming) Tuesday. Papa and Mamma were likewise counting the days ; one could have wished they would not. Mamma was well into one of her fusses ; Papa was looking consciously unconscious that Monday was gone, that Tuesday was gone. . . . *They* did not get a letter from him on the way ; *they* did not know that on leaving Six Mile Bottom he had written to Lady Melbourne : " I am proceeding very slowly. . . . I shall not stay above a week. . . . Don't write till you hear from me there, for I am not sure that I shall go now. . . . I am in very ill-humour."

At Seaham they were thinking : " To-morrow he *must* be here." Perhaps nobody said so ; perhaps it would have been easier to bear if somebody had. But on Wednesday he did indeed arrive ; she saw him again after more than a year of longing.

CHAPTER IX

THE FIRST STAY AT SEAHAM: LETTERS

At last. It might be called the motto of the engagement, marriage, separation (short-lived though the union was) of Annabella and Byron.

At last he had come to her.

" I was sitting in my own room reading, when I heard the carriage." One knows that kind of reading; and the perfect self-possession she attributed to herself during the days of suspense seems to have become slightly imperfect, for she put out the candles before she " deliberated what should be done." In the darkness she made up her mind. She would meet him alone. " He was in the drawing-room, standing by the side of the chimney-piece. He did not move forwards as I approached him, but took my extended hand and kissed it." Neither could speak. . . . After a while he said in a low voice : " It is a long time since we met." She could scarcely answer. " I felt over-powered, and made the excuse of calling my parents to leave the room."

Had any thought of Byron's lameness occurred to her, as she went all the way to meet him ? More probably she forgot all about it. For short distances it was barely perceptible ; yet it was the reason for his immobility—*he* could never forget it, though everyone else could.

The evening was spent in general conversation. " I think he talked of Kean." When they said good-night, he asked her at what time she generally appeared in the morning. About ten, she told him ; and went to bed, " my imagination coloured by hope." She was down early. " But I waited till near twelve." Then, with the first chill in her heart, she went out for a walk ; he would surely be down when she returned. Strolling on the beach,

BYRON

*After the miniature by Holmes, belonging to
Augusta Leigh*

she collected her impressions. Had there been one of personal vanity—" the air with which he played with his large watch chain ? "

There were good—or at any rate exalted—moments.

> . . . I think on the craggy brow
> Where I stood . . . that form is before me now,
> That eye is beholding the waters roll,
> It seems to give them a living soul ;
> That arm by mine is tremblingly prest—
> I cherish the dream, he *shall* be blest !

" Our favourite walk "—so it must have been a short one. Byron could not walk far . . . She wrote those lines three years afterwards, at her old home, gazing out over the sea that spread between them.

Well, in 1814 everyone was fascinated by him. He listened to Sir Ralph's long stories, talked business with Judith, showed an interest in the family solicitor's little boy, was very conformable and dutiful, and hoped he was not a troublesome inmate. " Annabella and I have been much together, and it would not be difficult to prove that we appear much attached." This of course to Lady Melbourne.

Not difficult to prove, perhaps ; but he did not prove it to the person most concerned. He was so " strange, moody, and unaccountable," his treatment of her was " so peculiar," that she came to the conclusion he did not love her, and offered to break off the engagement. " A few days ago," wrote Byron to Lady Melbourne, " she made one scene, not altogether out of C.'s style ; it was too long and too trifling, in fact, for me to describe, but it did me no good." When Annabella Byron was sixty-four, she told Mrs. Beecher-Stowe of that scene. So trifling it was that " he fainted entirely away." [1] She stopped for a moment in her narrative ; and " speaking with great effort " added : " Then I was *sure* he must love me."

---

[1] She told this to Robertson of Brighton also, the close friend of her late years. He took the words down from her lips, and is a witness to be trusted. That cannot be said of Mrs. Beecher-Stowe.

At the time she wrote these verses :

> Let my affection be the bond of peace
> Which bids thy warfare with remembrance cease.
> Blest solely in the blessings I impart,
> I only ask to heal *thy* wounded heart ;
> On the wild Thorn that spreads dark horror there
> To graft the Olive branch, and see it bear—
> Behold that scion from the tree of life
> Expand its blossoms midst a world of strife,
> And hope—*believe*, its fruits will ripely bloom
> With the same sun that brightens o'er thy Tomb,
> The sun of Glory—day-spring from on high—
> To souls " in hope to rise," the seraph of the sky.

Melancholy indeed, as the outcome of a lover's visit ; and though we may suspect that for the Tomb a struggle with rhyme as well as tears was responsible, it is not so easy to account for " blest solely in the blessings I impart." Reading, we remember what she did not know—that he had been in very ill-humour after leaving Six Mile Bottom.

He talked a great deal of Augusta—" with sorrowful tenderness," saying that no one would ever possess so much of his love as she did. " I felt an instant's pain—it was perceptible only to myself " ; and she listened as though to take pattern when he told her that Guss always treated him like a child and spoiled him : " You remind me of her when you are playful." Playful with her parents she could be at all times ; with this moody, almost unknown young man it was more difficult. Her intensity, her self-consciousness, were in full possession ; again she was dwelling too persistently upon the Byronic Legend. Not that he failed to remind her of it. The mournful verses were probably inspired by his saying : " If you had married me two years ago, you would have spared me what I can never get over." She asked what he meant ; he turned it off ; she could only wonder, brood, write of his warfare with remembrance, of the dark horror in his heart ; and make the scene " in C.L.'s style," with its sensational climax.

From Seaham he wrote three times to Lady Melbourne. The very first letter revealed some tension. He liked Sir Ralph, whose stories were long, " but I believe he has told the most of them "; Lady Milbanke he did not like at all. " I don't know why . . . but so it is. She seems to be everybody here."

Annabella is the most silent woman I ever encountered ; which perplexes me extremely. I like them to talk, because then they think less. . . . However, the die is cast ; neither party can secede ; the lawyers are here. . . . I fear she won't govern me ; and if she don't it will not do at all. . . . I have always thought . . . that her supposed after-liking was *imagination*. If so, I shall soon discover it, but mean to . . . behave attentively and well, though I never could love but that which loves.

In another few days he had discovered that " her passions are stronger than we supposed " ; but after a further week he sent Lady Melbourne a long bulletin.

Do you know I have grave doubts if this will be a marriage now ? Her disposition is the very reverse of our imaginings. She is overrun with fine feelings, scruples about herself and her disposition (I suppose, in fact, she means mine), and to crown all, is taken ill once every three days with I know not what. . . . I don't know, but I think it by no means improbable you will see me in town soon. I can only interpret these things one way, and merely want to be certain to make my obeisance and " exit singly." I hear of nothing but " feeling " from morning till night, except from Sir Ralph, with whom I go on to admiration. Ly M., too, is pretty well ; but I am never sure of A. for a moment. The least word, and you know how I rattle on through thick and thin (always, however, avoiding anything I think can offend her favourite notions), if only to prevent me from yawning. The least word, or alteration of tone, has some inference drawn from it. Sometimes we are too much alike, and then again too unlike. This comes of system, and squaring her notions to the devil knows what. For my part I have lately had recourse to the eloquence of *action* . . . and find it succeeds very well, and makes her very quiet ; which gives me some hopes of the efficacy of the " calming process," so renowned in " our philosophy." In fact, and *entre nous*, it is really amusing ; she is like a child in that respect, and quite caressable into kindness and good humour ; though I don't think her temper *bad* at any time, but very *self*-tormenting and anxious, and romantic.

In short it is impossible to foresee how this will end *now*, any more than two years ago ; if this is a break, it shall be her doing, not mine.[1]

[1] *Correspondence*, i. 289-91.

He left Seaham on the 16th, and wrote to Annabella from Boroughbridge.

My Heart—We are thus far separated, but after all one mile is as bad as a thousand—which is a great consolation to one who must travel six hundred before he meets you again. If it will give you any satisfaction, I am as comfortless as a pilgrim with peas in his shoes, and as cold as Charity, Chastity, or any other virtue. On my way to Castle Eden I waylaid the Post & found letters from Hanson, which I annex for the amusement of Lady Milbanke who, having a passion for business, will be glad to see anything that looks like it. I expect to reach Newstead to-morrow, & Augusta the day after. Present to our parents as much of my love as you like to part with, and dispose of the rest as you please.

So he was behaving well, as he had said he would ; though in the gibe at charity and chastity, and the faintly insolent reference to Lady Milbanke, we may discern echoes of the tea-cup storms he had fled from.

In Annabella's letters they are more than echoes. There at any rate she was like other women, fatally prone to such recurrences as women are, or used to be. The visit had been shortened by her wish ; on that count Byron was womanish too, for he " kept it up " to her with maddening iteration.

Putting these remorseful letters to him beside his to Lady Melbourne, we can see what was happening. Instinct was warning them both. He said that her liking was imaginative, and might have said the same of his own. But the difference was that, in Annabella, imagination had no other outlet. She had made of him its very symbol ; if *he* was not all she believed him, love was deception and misery, the world of imagination a world without meaning. Her passions, if stronger than Byron had supposed, were not strong in the sense that he and Lady Melbourne gave to the word ; and it might seem that he had divined this (or should have divined it) when he felt her to be " like a child in that respect." It was not a child he needed, but a woman. He knew that well enough ; but perception had done only half its work when he could put faith in " the calming process renowned in our philosophy." Caresses might reassure the troubled child ; but the woman in the child had heard, like him, the voice of ruthless instinct. She stopped her ears against it when she could. She could not always; and so came the scene when Byron " turned green, and fainted at my feet."

For that there may have been reasons other than the one she naturally fastened on. Either he felt such violent revulsion from a scene " in C.'s style " that it could actually break him down; or he felt a mixture of relief and fear at the sense of liberty regained and of what that liberty would bring with it—the resumption, more uncontrolled than ever, of the liaison with Augusta. His grand resolve to break away from her—was it to end in this? He might resent her resolve " to be good " after his marriage; but we should be unversed indeed in human nature (to say nothing of Byron's) if we could not follow his inconsistency. To be thrown back upon his own will only, to have to face the struggle again, not to be safe, however angry . . . and Byron fainted entirely away, and Annabella was sure that he must love her.

She accepted all the blame for his departure. He called it her prescription for the re-establishment of her spirits; she tried to persuade him, and herself, that it had done its work. But the pitiless voice persisted; and she, her ears stopped against the sternest NO that instinct says to the heart, could only rest her hope on " when we are married "—like many another woman thus fighting with herself.

She wrote to him the night of the day he went; and next day too, and the day after. By that time he was at Six Mile Bottom.

A.I.M. *to* B.

If I do repent you shall not have the satisfaction of knowing it. If our present and I hope last separation should spare you the anxiety which my troubled visage has sometimes communicated, it is enough. When you return my troubles will be ended —or very nearly. The Elders are not in very good humour with me as accessory to your departure, which they regret for their own sake at least.

Are you quite sure that I love you? Why did you doubt it? It is *your* only trespass. As for *my* trespasses I must not think of them—I wish we were married, and then I could do my best, and not quarrel with myself for a thousand things that you would not mind. I expect you will write me a lecture—and it shall be studied *con amore*. I must write to our sister—plead for me with her—and plead for me too with my Lord and master—beseeching him still to " love and cherish " his undutiful wife.

A.I.M. *to* B.

Your scrawl is—no—nothing but yourself can really be welcome to me now. My own dearest, there is not a moment when I would not give my foolish head to see you. I knew it would be so, and think it a salutary chastisement for all my misdemeanours. I *am* in my most sober senses, I assure you. What says our Sister ? It is odd that I can write all my goosishness to *her*, and cannot name you to any of those who have been used to receive my thoughts.

Dad and Mam are quite disconsolate without you. You made yourself agreeable here with so much success that amongst all who have seen you there is not a difference of opinion as to *your* perfection—I am in " dim eclipse." Even Billy Hoar told his wife you were " fascinating." Your interest in his boy must have formed a great part of the charm—lest you should be too vain I tell you so. . . . My mother is reading Hanson's letter, and seems very well pleased therewith.

Will you take me to your heart ? My home " till Death do us part "—and don't turn me out of doors in revenge as you threatened.

A.I.M. *to* B.

My own Byron—I must say goodnight before I go to rest. It is my comfort to think of that kind promise that you would make yourself as happy as possible. The spirit of Self-denial, which has always strangely possessed me, must have tyrannised over me when I agreed to your departure. All my present as well as past reflections convince me that to you I may entrust not only my happiness, but every other interest of most importance—and if I could not—my *feeling* is that I would rather share distress *with* you than escape it without you. My fear was that I should create it by disappointing you—anything but that would have been supportable.

I certainly was not myself during your stay. " Now being gone, I am a—what ?—again." Before you pass sentence on me finally, wait to see *me myself*. *Myself* is by no means the grave, didactic, deplorable person that I have appeared to you. I am only sage under some visitation of anxiety. This I wanted you to understand, and to help me out of that atmosphere of sober sadness in which I was almost suffocated. Those who have seen me *quite* as a domestic animal have had more reason to complain of my nonsense than my sense. It has however always been a long time before I could recover my natural temperament with a new inmate.

What a history of *Myself*! I wish I had as long a one of *thyself*—God bless thee—do not—

I have forgotten what I was going to say—Remember me as Thy wife—

His second letter to her was written from the Other A.'s house. That phrase for Augusta he now used to Annabella, whether with conscious double-meaning or not he probably could not himself have said.

Novr. 20th 1814.

My arrival at the other A's occurred yesterday at odds with the post-time, so that I had not a moment to write to you. Your two letters have been received with those to Augusta— who tells me she has answered them. As I am anxious to meet Hanson & hear further of our arrangements I shall not remain here beyond tomorrow ; if Mr. Hoar has finished his part of the papers &c., I will take care that all the subsequent part is got over as soon as possible. Do not tax yourself to write more frequently or at length than is perfectly agreeable ; but address your next to Albany, where I hope to meet it. How do you go on ? is your health better—and your spirits ? I trust that your prescription for the re-establishment of the last has not failed in effect. Augusta and hers are all in good plight. I am trying to arrange so as that she should meet us somewhere, soon after, or before, our next interview.

My popularity with Hoar is a very unexpected pleasure, but I suppose it is a return in kind for the impression you made upon Hanson. I can assure you that any kind feeling on the part of our papa & mamma is most sincerely reciprocal. To yourself, Dearest, if I were to write for ever I could only come to one conclusion which I may as well make now, & that is that I ever am most entirely and unalterably

your attached B.

P.S.—I don't ask you to consider this as a letter, but merely a memorandum that I am thinking of you now—& loving you ever—my wife. A. sends her hundred loves & regrets very much her absence from S.

A.I.M. *to* B.

Nov. 20, 1814.

I hope for a line from you to-day—I want it very much—not so much as yourself; yet I still think—perhaps only for obstinacy's sake—that just now we are better apart. . . .

Have you prevailed on Mrs. Leigh to return with you? I have nothing to tell you, and only wish that you knew—I will leave you to guess what—

A.I.M. *to* B.

Nov. 22, 1814.

I had a letter yesterday not from thee, dearest, but from our Sister, with welcome contents—but I cannot write till I am inspired by a line from you. . . .

Remember your promise to tell me all your feelings & reflections concerning *us*. Mine are at this moment—not *quite* such as I wish to communicate. I am not very well—but shall be before you receive this—therefore don't think of it.

His next letter was from Cambridge.

My Love—I am detained here on my way to town to vote for a friend who is candidate for a medical professorship, & shall not get away till tomorrow. All your letters addressed to me at A's have been received. They are very kind and delightful—but I can't thank you for them properly with this horrible pen. Thank your mother for hers also, and remember me to papa. I feel as if I had left home—and was gone to school again. Opposite to me at this moment is a friend of mine [1]—I believe in the very act of writing to *his* spouse-elect—& complaining like me of his pen & paper, to say nothing of absence & being obliged to scribble instead of speak. It gives me spirits to hear you have them. Pray *keep* them now they have reappeared. " My last will have made you anxious to hear again—and indeed I am so myself: "this is a sentence which I have borrowed by permission from my neighbouring suitor's epistle to his Ladye. I think it does very well in a dearth of periods of mine own. Your mother talks of Hanson's coming to S. again—will that be necessary? I have stolen another pen—but it is worse than the last—& am writing at an Inn, with noise " around, above, and underneath," with the worst & most intractable of implements—ink like water & sand like sawdust. You shall hear from me tomorrow and from Town, where I shall not

_____
[1] The Rev. Francis Hodgson.

remain longer than you like ; but I don't wish to hurry you, or to plague you with my assiduities—if I can help it.

Don't scold *yourself* any more—I told you before there was no occasion—you have not offended me. I am as happy as hope can make me—and as gay as Love will allow me to be till we meet, and ever my Heart—thine   B.

P.S.—Do write—and—never mind—I have several things to say of no great consequence which I will postpone. In the meantime once more—Sweet Heart—Good morning.

A.I.M. *to* B.

Nov. 23, 1814.

I received your no-letter just after mine with the *naughty* postscript was snatched from my hands to the post—before I had time to reconsider it, or it would probably have been withheld. Such are the evils of absence. I am always thinking after I have written that I have not written what I wished—and then it is irremediable.

My mother is just come in to take me home.[1] Be happy dearest B. and you will make happy
                    Your most affec^te.

A.I.M. *to* B.

WEDNESDAY NIGHT (*Nov.* 23, 1814).

I have returned to this place with added satisfaction from the hope that it may still remain in my father's possession. He has so favourable an opportunity of selling other estates that I think this may be saved. When I first went to Durham I was much distressed by some circumstances which I had learnt concerning his embarrassments—now I see a prospect of removing them.

I have had a proof of " evil " to do honour to your theory— rather too near. My maid has been guilty of conduct that has led to an exposure, and rendered her immediate discharge necessary. I am not so unmercifully virtuous as to feel nothing but indignation—yet I believe she is a hardened sinner, and whatever may be the present inconvenience, I must congratulate myself on the escape. I have often thought since our *good and evil* argument, that our opinions would not differ if we under- stood each other's *standard*. I am never much surprised or disappointed at the bad. In the unfortunate case which has just occurred I had entertained a slight & silent suspicion from

[1] She was on a visit in Durham.

observing an affectation of extreme propriety on some occasions. My former maid, who lived with me five years—until she married—and is much attached, returns to me till I can be permanently provided.

I am very well—subject to some inequalities of spirits, but without *rhyme* or *reason*.

Have you an imperial to your carriage ? It is a necessary appendage to a wife.

My mother sends her love—mine—more than I can say is always yours.

I am writing by twilight—can you read—

B. *to* A.I.M.

Novr. 23rd 1814.

My Love—While I write this letter I have desired my very old & kind friend Mr. Hodgson to send you a note, which I will enclose, as it contains a piece of information that will come better from him than me—and yet not give you less pleasure. I think of setting off for London tomorrow—where I will write again. I am quite confused and bewildered here with the voting and the fuss & the crowd—to say nothing of yesterday's dinner & meeting all one's old acquaintances, the consequence of which is that infallible next-day's headache ever attendant upon sincere Friendship. Here are Hobhouse and our cousin George Lamb—who called on me ; & we have all voted the same way, but they say nevertheless our man won't win—but have many votes howbeit. Today I dine with Clarke the traveller—one of the best and most goodnatured of souls—and uniformly kind to me. When we meet I think and hope I shall make you laugh at the scene I went through—or rather which went through me ; for I was quite unprepared, & am not at the best of times sufficiently master of " the family shyness " to acquit myself otherwise than awkwardly on such an occasion.

Well but—sweet Heart—do write & love me—and regard me as thine

ever & most

P.S.—Love to parents. I have not and am not to see H's note, so I hope it is all very correct.

Hodgson's note was to tell her of the extraordinary ovation Byron had received when he appeared in the Senate House to give his vote. " The young men burst out into the most rapturous applause," though they had been forbidden to make demonstrations of any kind. Annabella was writing to M.G. when it arrived. Her letter had been begun under the cloud which was not like a lawyer's hand, but a lover's frown. " I wish I was married. . . . I am sure we shall be more agreeable after the courtship is ended. We shall assimilate more and more— " And then the post was brought to her—the " smiling post " with a letter from Byron and one in a strange hand, but from Cambridge too, so it must have something to do with him. She read them both, and added an exultant postscript to M.G. before adding one to her already written love-letter, likewise begun under the cloud.

This letter has a peculiar interest. During the separation proceedings in 1816 Byron returned it to her with comments. It had been written on a Thursday night ; when he sent it back to her she received it on a Thursday. Did she think then of her birthday-rhyme ? Some part of the Far-to-go was being traversed even while she wrote ; she had gone many a mile when she re-read her own words.

THURSDAY NIGHT (*November* 24, 1814).

Your letters of somethings or nothings always make me as glad now as they used to make me sorry. Seaham is no longer home to me without you. Make it home when you will—too soon for my wishes it cannot be. Do not regard my up and down spirits ; if I am high and low, I am never hot and cold. You are more likely to be wearied with the constant temperature of my affection than disturbed by its inequalities. Perhaps it is not possible for any thinking person to be in my situation without some anxieties ; mine were of such a nature as to prove —that I cannot find a *good* reason for apprehension. I am not preparing you for a second representation of my dismay—if possible, I will make you forget the first. I am so much happier since I have had reason to believe that my father and mother will be placed in more comfortable circumstances than had appeared probable. For their sake and mine you will be glad too.

No to-London post this morning. I do not expect a letter from you to-day—I can live upon yesterday's for another day at least, so welcome & gladdening was its impression. Your silence is not however a source of disquietude—I think I know what you *could* say, if it be unsaid.

After post—and a smiling post—I thank the Cantabs, and

most of all Mr. Hodgson, whose kindness I shall have pleasure in acknowledging myself. A letter from Newmarket has given me scarcely less pleasure than yours. I shall be too happy—there will be no reverse—whilst you love me there cannot. Remember—I have done with doubts. Since I saw you none have occurred on the subject of our happiness. I *was* indeed a *little* unhappy one day that I wrote from Durham. The cause, in which you had not a share, I have *partly* told you. It is all over.

" There will be no reverse." Above and beneath those words Byron drew a thick black line, and commented : " Prediction fulfilled, February 1816." She had added a postscript : " In a fortnight or very little more—I hope to be yours. Do not stay away from your home. Your return will bring joy to us all."

At the bottom of the sheet Byron wrote these lines of Dante :

> " Or non tu sai com' è fatta la donna
>
> .   .   .   .
>
> Avviluppa promesse—giuramenti ;
> Che tutta spargon poi per l'aria e venti."

And added : " The date of this letter (from the postmark on ye cover) is November 8th 1814." [1]

She was at Mivart's Hotel, Lower Brook Street, in the worst stress of the separation-proceedings, when her letter came back to her. . . .

On November 26 she now wrote :

I wish for you, want you, Byron mine, more every hour. All my confidence has returned—never to sink again, I believe. A confidence in the power of my affection to make me anything, everything that you and I wish. Do I understand you ? you asked. Surely I do, for I would not understand you otherwise —I should fear to love you less were you different from what has made me love you—I won't say " not wisely but too well."

Our parents are very cheerful and well pleased with thoughts of your return. My father says " I must have my hair cut before he comes back." . . . Come, come, come—to my heart.

P.S.—My uncle is in London. . . . He makes himself sick with anxiety about us, so great is his affection for me. I am his

---

[1] The postmark really was November 28th.

dearest object in the world—now—and you cannot conceive how eagerly he enters into everything that affects us, " with all the warmth of youth."

" I have just been engaging a cook," she wrote next day—and wrote no more than that : " A retaliation for your elliptical phrases." The erring lady's-maid had been replaced for the moment, and all these arrangements gave a sense of actuality to the happiness which had formerly grown " too like a dream."

B. to A.I.M.

Novr. 28th 1814.

I sympathise with you in the original sin of your Suivante. It is a sad affair in a well-regulated family ; but I am glad it did not occur in *ours*—that is yours and mine that is to be. I would recommend the next to be as much in years and frightful as possible. There is a deal of confusion in Ld. Portsmouth's & Hanson's [1] family. The brother of Ld. P. wants to lunatize him —or stultify him ; and there is law and all kind of squabble, which of course puts my taking Farleigh out of the question—& I must look out for a residence elsewhere. The settlements are arrived and in progress.

I have hardly yet recovered the bustle and bumpers of Cambridge, but am otherwise in tolerable plight—and quiet enough for London.

On Saturday I saw Kean's Macbeth, a fine but unequal performance. Miss O'Neill I have not seen.

I think Southey's *Roderick* as near perfection as poetry can be—which considering how I dislike that school I wonder at. However, so it is. If he had never written anything else, he might safely stake his fame upon the last of the Goths.

Well—but you are returned to Seaham, which I am glad to hear. All your epistles have been regularly received—and I hope that home and those hot luncheons of salubrious memory have quite re-established you. It is odd—while I am writing in comes a clerical relation of mine, & reminds me that he was the first person who ever mentioned your name to me—several years ago. He tells me that our grandfathers were all in the same house at Westminster school &c. &c., so that you see our coming together is quite in the course of events & vastly natural. The man is talking on—& here is another visitor—so—Good morning—ma Mignonne.

---

[1] Hanson's daughter had married Lord Portsmouth.

B. *to* A.I.M.

Novr. 29th 1814.

Yesterday thine Unc. Ld. W. called ; but I was seized with a fit of the *shys* and not at home. But I am going today to return his visit—which is the greatest bore in the world ; but however as I ought I must—and there's an end. I have forwarded your epistle to Mrs. Joanna—I was very glad to see *not*—Southcote.

I am very sorry for the dereliction of your handmaiden—as I said before ; but you could not act otherwise as the case appears. I hope your next selection will be more fortunate. Your letters are very kind, my love. As to the doubts—never mind. You see I have said nothing about them. My naval cousin George has just bore down—and his tongue is running nine knots an hour—so that I must for the present merely add

ever thine,   B.

P.S.—Love to Mamma and Sir R., with whom like his friend Kien Long " I hope to smoke an amazing long pipe."

Writing before she received this acknowledgment of Lord Wentworth's courtesy, she told him that Halnaby was ready to receive them instead of Farleigh.

Tell me the latest, not the earliest, day that you think to arrive here, for my Philosophy likes not " hope deferred." It did me no good before, though *during* those weeks of suspense and renewed disappointments, I would not yield to anxiety for a moment. The *consequences* have made it felt. Now they are surmounted, and I am in every respect well.

To see you at this moment—it is not well to think of it—I grow impatient and forget everything else in the world. If to be loved—wholly, only for yourself, be happiness to you, do you not possess it in the greatest degree ? Believe it—" nothing doubting."

B. *to* A.I.M.

Decr. 1st 1814.

Ld. Portsmouth and his brother have gone to Law about intellects ; and it would be no proof of mine were I to take Farleigh as a tenant until it is ascertained unto whom the brains and buildings actually belong. Of course I must look round for another mansion. Hanson hath gotten the papers and is dealing upon them. I have seen your Uncle Ld. Wentworth—he called —and I returned his visitation.

It would be difficult under these circumstances for me to fix any precise time for my return, as I wish to hear or see more of or from Claughton and his intents about Newstead, and we have not heard from him since the letters I enclosed to you for Lady Milbanke.

I am asked to dine at Whitehall today, but I fear I can't go, for there is a house and a debate among the Lords this evening of some importance—which it may be well to hear.

W.L. and his moiety are not in town, but all the rest, I believe.

Hobhouse is in London & will probably return with me when the time is fixed. So thou hast engaged a Cook for us—I will trust your taste.

I will write tomorrow, and if possible name the day or at least the week when we may meet.

P.S.—Love to our parents.

A.I.M. *to* B.

Dec. 2.

I have pitied the martyrdom of your shyness as much as I admired the " glorious effort." Lord W. wrote that day immediately after your visit, saying " it left the most favourable impression." He only regretted that you did not speak louder —*i.e.* he is rather deaf. . . . His trepidations lest you should not like him amuse me—they are just like what your " Sweetheart " might have been supposed to feel at an earlier period. He desires me to persuade you that he is not " an old stick of a Courtier " &c. &c.

A good journey to you—not chilled, as your last was by the thought of being welcomed by a stranger. There is a weddingcake in preparation which " makes Ossa like a wart."

And then—another postponement ! And another allusion to her having dismissed him from Seaham. And still no cordial word about Lord Wentworth.

B. *to* A.I.M.

Decr. 3d. 1814.

The papers will require about ten days, and I hope also either to see or hear from Clau. in that time. The moment they are ready, I will set out—oh, by the way, I must not forget the licence and all that. I will have it special—if you please—because I think it will be quieter to be married in a room, and mamma will lend us a cushion each to kneel upon. I fear I must trouble your father to lend us Halnaby for a month, as this explosion among the senses of the Portsmouth family has set me off about another house, as I would rather dwell among the reported sane. And so—thou lovest me very much. We will love a great deal more yet though I hope. I am glad you miss me—because *that* is not *my* fault, and I bear my own penance patiently in the malicious hope that you may wish I had remained at S. I told you in my last that I had seen your Unc. W. I thought he looked very well.

I am cut off from Melbourne House for the present, becáuse that family firebrand—Ly. C.—has this day returned to Whitehall ; and now I shan't see Ly. M. again for some time, which I regret.

Write—continue to love and to consider me as thine *most*

B.

P.S.—Make all the duties and remembrances for me to all yours.

A.I.M. *to* B.

Dec. 4, 1814.

I begin to think that after the great cake is baked, and the epithalamium composed, with all other prologues to the performance, the part of Spouse, like that of Hamlet, will be omitted " by particular desire." Really you don't know how sorry I am that you should be detained. Of the causes of delay Hanson's is the only one which I can conceive that we cannot annihilate. I shall be making a visit to the Albany some day, if you stay there much longer. I do all I can to be as patient as you wish I should, during this last separation—reading a good deal, and observing such other discipline as may keep me in my right mind. After this experience of absence I shall not very willingly part with you again for a shorter time. At least I have learned that I cannot enjoy anything without you—these long blank days !

Goodnight—Love—and believe me in all truth
Thine

B. *to* A.I.M.

Decr. 5*th* 1814.

I am glad that Unc. was gracious—I said nothing to you about my fuss lest he should not ; but it is all very well. " The Cake ! " I must try and be ready before it is baked. Hanson is urged & will be ready in ten days. By the blessing of Hymen, his Godship has given up the white ribbon knots & fooleries which he was heretofore wont to inflict upon his votaries—or rather on their lacqueys. I am told that Nobody has them now—so don't let us be out of fashion. I am sure I wish we had been married these two years ; but never mind—I have great hopes that we shall love each other all our lives as much as if we had never married at all. I hear all our cousins are getting ready their presents, *C* among the rest—umph !—" *timeo Danaos et dona ferentes.*" You know you are a blue—so I may quote Latin to you sans pedantry, and if you can't translate—I will in my next. I think I see your indignation at this disparaging proposition.

To amuse thee I send an extract from the Mg. Herald. You see they have not done with us yet—" two such interesting persons " (as Mrs. Locke, do you know her ? called us to some-body the other day). Well—but I won't tell you all the conjectures &c. my journey has given rise to. Ly. M. says it has set all the talkers in tattle—and all is contradiction and mystery. She did not half like my coming away—that was no fault of mine—but we will make up for the past.

A.I.M. to B.

December 5, 1814.

Your malice shall be gratified by knowing that I wish for you only as often as I think of you.

" So you love me very much." If you said so with faith, how can I thank you enough ? Shall I tell you a secret ? I don't like to have my love but half-believed, since, being wholly yours, it is to me my first *virtue*—that of which I am proudest. What else can I do for you but love you. . . . You have not under-stood me in this, but *do* understand me, and though I may have exaggerated the principle of not professing, you must not there-fore conclude that " nothing can come of nothing." Oh, if you could know—well, I won't despair, as I have done, that you *will* know, and shall wait in patience, not in pride. I believe you are the only man who ever really loved one that had not flattered him—on the contrary—one that has censured with the tongue when she approved with the heart. A very common practice of mine. . . .

It is vexatious that you should be banished from Whitehall again. I think Lady Melbourne might visit *you*, if you can't visit her. You may tell her I shall not be jealous if she takes possession of your apartments.

A.I.M. *to* B.

December 6 1814.

You tell me to write. I like nothing so well as to give you my thoughts, but I should tire you with their sameness if I were always to utter those most present. Ever since our correspondence began, a long time, I have had to contend against an inclination to say or signify " I love you "—and to go in quest of foreign subjects. I have burnt more letters than I have written to you for that offence. And when you were here I so often appeared " the most silent woman in the world " because I could not think of anything else. . . . It must be my comfort to think that I succeeded wonderfully well in my desired object —not to appear to more advantage before than after matrimony —but rather than you should continue to see me so very unloveable, I would have sent you to my father's friend, Kien Long. Though I would not be presumptuously confident, I think I have now assured myself against a relapse. Will you prove your confidence in this assurance by returning before the papers are completed ? They do not want an escort, and you have not mentioned any other business to detain you. Take away a few of these wearisome, restless days to *me*, if not to *you*, and let me *see* that you love me. Dearest Love, if you don't come soon, the snow is beginning, and will keep you at a distance. I am very ingenious in finding reasons for the annihilation of " time and space." *Wish* at least to return, if you do not.

B. *to* A.I.M.

Decr. 7*th* 1814.

I yet hope to be ready before the overture has done being played, and at any rate will only wait for the papers. Of this temporary separation I can only re-echo your own words— with this addition, that though perhaps of my deserving it was not of my desiring.

Moore is in town. I was so glad to see him again that I am afraid I was rather too " exquisite in my drinking " at dinner yesterday—for I find my head in a whirlwind and my fingers bitten by the abominable parrot this morning. The latter accident I did not discover when it happened. " I' faith I must have taken too much Canaries," but I won't do so again—for I am never improved by it. " The Cake," dearest—I am in such agitation about it—if it should be spoiled or mouldy—or— Don't let them put too many eggs & butter in it, or it will certainly circulate an indigestion amongst all our acquaintances. I believe I told thee that I rejoiced in Unc's approbation—of which I rather desponded—but 'tis all very well. I have only time to scrawl myself in the midst of fifty interruptions—and in despite of them all

ever thine

A.I.M. to B.

Dec. 7, 1814.

Dearest—" *I* will make up for the past." Talk and tattle are very harmless and would not depend on your *locality*. The good people will be tired of conjectures in time—in a very short time, I should think, when we confute the greater part of them.

We have always meant that " the happy nuptials " should be as obscure and ignoble as possible, whether fashionable or not ; so you need not fear any " outward and visible signs "—my father's epithalamium excepted—to which I suppose you will not object, unless from some poetical jealousy. The *Morning Herald* makes very pretty verses for me, but I am rather offended that my " poetic spark " should be represented as *borrowed*. What do you think I have been doing last ? Playing a rubber of whist for the amusement of the old gamesters. . . . Farewell —I will not wish you any prosperity till you are on the road— not " to ruin."

B. to A.I.M.

Decr. 8th 1814.

Bella—my love—Clau's answer has at last arrived and will *not* do. His proposition is inadmissible, as it not only involves reduction of price but delay in payment. I have ordered the flattest of all possible negatives in reply, and there's an end. One is at least out of suspense with him—but it is vexatious enough in our circumstances. I shall have it sold to some other purchaser, from whom at all events—whether we obtain more or less I can have the whole sum paid down. He wanted me to take £92,000, instead of £114,000 remaining after his present forfeiture (I *will not*)—and even that by slow degrees. The fact is, I take it, he either has not the money—or thinks me to be under such engagements as to give him an advantage, whether he is right or wrong. I have done with him.

Now dearest, I will not add one word as from myself or my own wishes, but leave it to you and yours to determine how far this may—will—or ought to cause any further delay in our

marriage. I have lost no time in apprizing you of the circumstances—which I allow to be as disagreeable & inconvenient as
could have been contrived or imagined.

Your love is *not* but *half*-believed ; it is too comfortable a
creed for me to embrace by halves—I am convinced of it—as
of my own.

Then there was a little incident which rejoiced her heart,
untroubled by superstition. In Sunderland it was reported that
the wedding had taken place, and the bells were rung in her
honour. " This mistake I rather enjoy." (Byron did not enjoy
it, as we shall see.) " The wedding-cake," she went on, " is all
the better for keeping. Don't stay away out of complaisance
to it." She wrote the same day to Augusta :

After post yesterday—" I am sure you have a letter from
Mrs. Leigh, you look so pleased," said my mother, and she was
not wrong. . . . As you like to hear of the hearts that B. has
won, I might give you a list of all who met him here. I am as
jealous as possible, and begin to fear that even my own father
and mother will soon prefer their son to their daughter. I am
sure he does not know how much they like him—that *incurable
diffidence* ! Everybody who approaches him must think he is
made to be loved—but he will not know it himself. Do you
think he will ever find it out ? I hope *you* are not such an
infidel as to your qualifications for being loved, and that you
believe they are felt by
Yours most affectely.[1]

Byron's letter about Claughton now arrived, to dash her hopes
again. She made a grand effort not to be plaintive.

[1] In after years she went over her early letters from Augusta—not
in a malicious but a wondering spirit. Reading them with her sadder
knowledge, she could not but find many a trace of duplicity. The expressions
of adoration for " B." are interspersed with what it is impossible not to
interpret as feline amenities, to say nothing of the deliberate insincerities
about money-matters, and the many references to their love for Newstead.
These cannot have been written quite without intention, whether designed
or not for Byron's reading. But in fact (though Augusta did not know it)
his feeling for the Abbey had undergone a violent revulsion. In a note by
Annabella to one of Augusta's letters we read : " He was always enraged
by the efforts she made to dissuade him from selling Newstead—calling her
a fool. He said once : ' *She* ought to know better.' In London . . . he
exclaimed : ' My intellect, my existence, depend on the sale of that place.'
He told me that the very reason which made him love it before he married,
made him hate it now."

Dec. 10.

Byron, my own, there shall not be any delay to our marriage on account of these circumstances if you are sure you can reconcile yourself to the privations necessarily attendant on so limited an income. *I* can be as happy with little as with much, provided that little be not exceeded, and debt incurred. Of debt I have so great a horror that I should cheerfully make any exertions to avoid it. You are not perhaps aware of the small establishment which our present means can support, yet I think it may be rendered perfectly comfortable (which to me is luxury) if we live for comfort, not for *style*—if we do not sacrifice to the absurd pride of *keeping up our situation*. . . . As far as I know your taste, I don't think the present restrictions to our expenditure would interfere with your happiness. We can only keep one carriage, and one house—if it be within a day's journey from London we may in a great degree unite the advantages of Town & Country, we may receive that quiet kind of society which I think we both prefer. . . . I love retirement—how much more shall I love it with the person who is dearest to me and the few associates whom he may select or approve ! . . . I shall never desire anything beyond what your fortune can supply. If your opinions differ, tell me—you know I *will* look to you as the guide—though you would rather let me tumble into a " pond horse," than show me the right road. It is certainly the extreme of perverseness in a woman not to take her own way when offered.

My father and mother express and feel the greatest desire to see me yours. If Hanson should not fulfil within the promised ten days, I shall begin to think he means to keep you for another Miss Hanson. When Lord Portsmouth's name so often escaped from his lips, Hoar longed to quote from Blue Beard—

> " Tis a very fine thing to be father-in-law
> To a very magnificent three-tailed-Bashaw."

My father called me in this morning (it is to be a profound secret, particularly to you) to " minister to his *Muse* diseased." A stanza of the Epithalamium was deranged, and I was obliged to prescribe—a new rhyme.

How happy I shall be when you return—Pray—no—I need not ask you—

And next day :

If you give your consent to our immediate marriage we have only to gain Hanson's. All my discomposures have arisen from

the uncertainty of our situation—it is trying to me, I own—I should be a different being if it were at an end. Of this I meant to say no more till I should have had your answer to my last letter. . . . *I* never wished to escape from time, as time, before. When, when—well— patience. " You see what a philosopher I am ! " If I lack wisdom, I lack not love, and am in all truth
Thine

And the day after :

I have just received Hoar's answer to my information. He says " I rejoice to think that I have prepared the Drafts of the Marriage Settlements on the cautious plan which I have adopted. I have done them *without any reference* to the projected sale to Mr. Claughton, which I was well aware might end in talk, and I have therefore vested the Newstead Estates in the Trustees for the purpose of Sale *generally*, and *so they must stand.* In consequence of this plan there need not be the least delay in the marriage, as you have made up your mind to submit to the difference of yearly income until a Sale actually take place." He adds afterwards that Mr. Hanson should be *urged* to have the *Ingrosments* (*sic*) instantly perfected, and sent or brought into the country in their present form, without a day's further delay—for which there can be no reasonable ground, or even pretext.

Everything rests with you—I can't say any more than that which is known to you.

Amusing there is the country-solicitor's attitude towards the London one ! Hoar, as afterwards appeared, had no very high opinion of Hanson. He must have enjoyed writing that letter to his client.

When Byron wrote, it is unpleasant to find him still harping on the Mildmay-Rosebery affair, to which he had compared his own with Augusta in a letter to Lady Melbourne.

Decr. 12*th* 1814.

I must needs say that your bells are in a pestilent hurry—a little like their prototypes of Bow. " Turn again Whittington —Lord-Mayor of London." I am very glad that I was out of hearing—deuce take them.

The papers will I suppose be finished in this week or the next —undoubtedly my remaining in London will tend to hasten Hans.

I have not seen Lady Melbourne save at a distance, since the return of Medea & her dragons to Whitehall—but I found myself very unexpectedly opposite the whole party at *Macbeth* on Saturday night. However there was a " great gulph "—the whole pit—between us, and a host of fiddlers. I believe she is going on very well—but know nothing about her.

I feel a little anxious about your answer to my last letter—& must conclude this. I shall probably write tomorrow if only to repeat how affectionately I ever am Dearest

Thine

P.S.—I perceive in the *Mg. Chronicle* report—that Sir H. Mildmay in one of his amatory epistles compared himself to *Childe Harold*. Conceive a *dandy* in despair moralizing—or *im*moralizing—(like the melancholy Jacques) into such a simile !

Then, after a flying word from her (" Good-morrow, dearest. To-day you will have my letter of ' no delay ' ") came this from him :

I waited an entire day and night in the hope or rather intention of sending thee a most heroic answer—but it won't do. The truth is, my Love, you have made me vain enough to believe that you would marry me if I had not a " denier "—and I am very sure I would *you*, if you never *were* to have one.

The sale of Nd. would have liquidated all my debts and left us an immediate surplus sufficient for most of our present exigencies and even wishes. As it is " I am cabined—cribbed " —at least for the present. I should not have cared for the limitation of income so much as the *debts*. They have however been lessened during the last year ; and would perhaps have been done away, were it not that there were others whom it was in some instances my duty—and in others my inclination—to assist. But even this would not have signified, had my purchaser kept to his bargain ; though, poor devil, I can't blame him, since his forfeiture is heavy enough.

In short you know pretty nearly as well as I do how we are situated. Things must come round in the end, for even if N. & R. are both sold at a loss, they will at least leave us clear, and your settlement secured into the bargain. Well—" to marry or not " that's the question—or will you wait ? Perhaps the clouds may disperse in a month or two. Do as you please.

I scrawl in the greatest hurry, and half in the dark—and I am not sorry to quit this matter-of-fact terrestrial topic—but love me and regard me as from my heart of hearts truly thine.

At last she spoke out—a little :

I think, dearest B, thou art happier since the letter of yesterday. Thine came to-day, saying " this week *or the next*." I don't wish to encrease *your* vexation of spirit, made manifest in the hideous D's—but the continuation of these unnecessary delays creates vexation of spirit to my father and mother. . . . You and I do not mind appearances much, but we must allow them to have more weight with those who are not under the influence of our particular feelings.

After all, suppose tomorrow's post should tell me that *the* ring is to wait—well—neither it nor I should change.

Wife or not—always thine.

B. *to* A.I.M.

Decr. 16*th* 1814.

The parchments *are* ready, which I did not know till yesterday ; but I must also compose an epistle to his Grace of Canterbury for the licence. I prefer it, because we can be married at any hour in any place without fuss or publicity. When I obtain it, I will write and fix the day of my arrival—which however can hardly take place before the end of next week or the beginning of the one after it.

I find that Claughton still wishes to treat, although we have rejected his late proposition ; but I have declined answering till I hear from another quarter, where Hans. has been authorized to offer the purchase or sale, or whatever it is or ought to be called.

It would undoubtedly have been better in many points of view to have had this arranged before our marriage—provided no very great delay occurred in the discussion. But—be it as it is.

I forwarded your letter to Lady Melbourne, but have not seen her for some time.

A.I.M. *to* B.

December 16, 1814.

Let us marry then as soon as the writings are done, and we will disperse " the clouds." I feel nothing but sunshine in the thought of being thine—thy wife. You have made me most happy. If you had sent the " heroic " reply which you meditated—I won't tell you what mischief you might have done ; so I do hope that without more *ifs* and *Heroics* you will end this questionable state forthwith. You still leave your own wishes in sublime mystery—to try my powers of Divination ?

We have gone on too long with the magnanimity-s that might keep us at a distance for ever ; and if you won't, I must take the responsibility of speaking plain—only—don't let me marry you against your will. If assured that I shall not, I desire with all my heart to give myself to you.

We can have Halnaby as long as we like ; therefore do not precipitately determine our future residence—at least not till we have met. When will you come ? Your absence is as unwelcome as possible to everybody.

A part of your letter—if I do not misunderstand it, makes me regret that I have mentioned to Mrs. Leigh anything of your present difficulties. So far from wishing undone that share of them which either your " duty " or " inclination " may have created, I regret that your means of bestowing so well will not be greater.

A.I.M. *to* B.

Dec. 17, 1814.

My only anxiety is to learn that you are coming. Then I am sure we should not find any of these obstacles. If difficulties should continue for a short time, they will be very pretty amusement after we are one. Till we are—the molehills are mountains. Are you aware that in the settlements a provision is made for the payment of debts and other present exigencies before the sale of Newstead ? A power being given of raising £20,000 on the Estate by a temporary Mortgage for that purpose—which Mortgage may be made with effect *immediately after the marriage.* Here is a good reason for doing what we wish, and should probably do without any.

Surely the writings will be done before you receive this. What can I say to hasten your journey ? I am scolded every day for your absence, besides feeling it *most* myself. I wish I could retaliate upon you—instead of which, were you but with me, my own Byron, you would know how much I am

Your   ANNABELLA.

B. *to* A.I.M.

Decr. 18*th* 1814.

I have written to the Archbishop and hope to set off on Saturday next. It is proper to add one thing—Ld. Portsmouth's lunatic business comes on on Thursday. If the affair is in the first instance quashed (as is probable) by the Chancellor —there's an end ; but if not, a further trial will come on next week in which my evidence will be required, as I was present at his marriage—but let us hope that the first will decide on his Lordship's intellects. However—even in case of my being subpoenaed to be in Court next week—I will come down if you wish it ; but I shall find it most difficult to quit you again so soon after our marriage—which on obtaining his Grace's fiat may take place on any morning or evening in your drawing-room. The papers are ready and I have desired Hans. to send them off to Hoar, and the signing & sealing may be settled as soon after my arrival as you please. Dearest—all my anxieties have been principally on your account—but if you are satisfied it is enough. I shall have you and Hope—which are as much as mortal man can require. Clau. is very unwilling to relinquish all hopes of the purchase—but of this more when we meet.

Ld. Melbourne called on me yesterday, but I have not seen Aunt M. for many days.

" My wishes "—they are too like your own to bear repetition.

B. *to* A.I.M.

Decr. 20th 1814.

There's the Archbishop's answer for you—and now we have only to get the licence, and become *one* forthwith. I hope papa and Mamma will be kept in good humour by his Holiness's gratulation, and am vastly sorry that you were scolded for my absence, of which you are perfectly innocent—as you must recollect with what zeal you opposed my departure. As I must set out to settle divers concerns and see after this same passport to our union, excuse my Laconism and believe me much more diffusely and attachedly ever thine.

A.I.M. *to* B.

Dec. 20.

If *you* think there would have been some convenience in having Newstead sold before our marriage, I wish it had been so—but as it must be a long business, and the settlements are adapted to that contingency, it really appears to me that the previous sale is of little importance compared with other considerations. But I feel that these *pros* and *cons* have been already too much discussed between *us*. . . . . I have one request to make for *myself*. If you conceive or feel there is *any* cause which can render you dissatisfied, or less satisfied, with your intended return next week—that you will prefer it to all I have said in favour of that measure. Your letters leave something for conjecture. We shall have the more to talk of—and—if

I don't forget it all as usual in your presence, I have many things to ask and hear. But it is useless to think of them before, so I will try and go to sleep.

P.S.—Why should I not own to some conjectures which, if the mere workings of imagination, I am not too proud to submit to censure—if not, it is for *my* good they should be confirmed. I will then ask—Are you less confident than you were in the happiness of our marriage ? *You will never deceive me*—to that promise I trust—entirely and exclusively.

A.I.M. *to* B.

Dec. 21.

" Saturday." The hope, though not quite expectation, rejoices me—but do not come to part again after we are married. Then I could bear still worse to be far from you.

However, I will hope with you that no more delays of any sort will be found. Feel no " anxieties on my account "—I cannot imagine any circumstances in which *for my own sake* I would not be your wife.

I have heard from a person who has been with some relations of Claughton's, that he is far from having the means of making the purchase good. It is a subject of which I always think with regrets that I must not indulge, lest I should join in tormenting you on your inflexible determination. As I shall not inherit any place where I should ever wish to reside, I could have adopted as an additional happiness every association that more particularly attracted you to one spot.

Dad says, " Fly swiftly ye moments till Comus return "—and my Mother stitches with much more alacrity since your mention of Saturday. Dearest—you and happiness will come together, and I cannot wish you a better *compagnon de voyage*—but I hope Mr. Hobhouse will be *bodkin*.

And again the same day :

Was I not a little in the heroics yesterday ? I cannot play that part two days together. If we do not marry under cir-cumstances that might afterwards cause you to wish it had been delayed, I care little what they are. I am in hopes that the expediency of a definite postponement, which would not be liable to the same objection as a protraction from week to week, will be best determined *when you come.* At least we all think so, in part because we all wish that time were arrived. I shall accede to whatever is thought best, and propose nothing myself.

. . . Opposition of every sort has always been an exertion to me, and made from principle solely—whether right or wrong. Very unfeminine !

In the present instance I think I may indulge myself, and leave the decision to be made for me.

Mrs. Leigh seems very sorry that she cannot accompany you ; but the obstacles are not to be removed by wishes, or mine would have some share in the effect.

Forgive my heroics in consideration that they are first cousins to yours—their best apology to myself.

P.S.—For fear you should forget me I present myself in rather a rough shape, but I had no instrument of operation but the wrong end of a quill.

B. *to* A.I.M.

Decr. 22nd, 1814.

I am to have the licence tomorrow, & am just returned from my first visit to Doctors' Commons (and my last too, I presume) where I have been swearing my way to you. The deeds are to be sent off to Hoar, and it will not be amiss if the said Hoar be ready at S. (or to arrive there) to get through the reading and signing and sealing—& then we can be married on any afternoon —or morning if you prefer it. Our passport comprehends all time and any place.

It is my hope to set off on Saturday. I believe Hobhouse accompanies me. I have your letter sans date—with doubts in itself, and questions in the postscript—thereby approving the ancient adage that the important part of a Lady's epistle is generally comprized in that appendix. " Any cause " and " less confident ! " A pretty pair of queries—" happiness " &c. With regard to the last, it would be presumptuous enough to feel too certain of uninterrupted felicity, inasmuch as that depends not altogether on persons but things, and there are little incidents in the shape of disease—misfortune—and disappointment—which few grow old without encountering by way of episode.

I do not see any good purpose to which questions of this kind are to lead—nor can they be answered otherwise than by time and events. You can still decide upon your own wishes and conduct before we meet, and apprize me of the result at our interview. Only make sure of your own sentiments—mine are

yours ever

B. *to* A.I.M.

Decr. 23rd 1814.

If we meet let it be to marry. Had I remained at S. it had probably been over by this time. With regard to our being under the same roof and *not* married—I think past experience has shown us the awkwardness of that situation. I can conceive nothing above purgatory more uncomfortable.

If a postponement is determined upon, it had better have been decided at a distance. I shall however set out tomorrow, but stop one day at Newmarket.

Hobhouse, I believe, accompanies me—which I rejoice at ; for if we don't marry, I should not like a 2d journey back quite alone, and remaining at S. might only revive a scene like the former—and to that I confess myself unequal.

The profile—it is like ; but I think more like the *Sphinx*. I am puzzling myself to imagine how you could have taken it unless opposite a mirror—or two mirrors—or—or—how ?

After all the transparent pretexts for delay, these two letters might well have broken her down—have been her salvation. It was Christmas-time. If she looked back to the Christmas of last year, when their correspondence had seemed at an end, can she have felt much happier than then ? We do not know. From Annabella Milbanke we have no more letters.

CHAPTER X

MARRIED

SHE could not answer those letters—could not for two reasons. The second must have been a welcome one. "No word can reach him now." For Christmas Day was to be spent with the Other A. ; the day after he would resume his journey.

At Seaham they cannot have spent a Merry Christmas. Touching to think of the Epithalamium. Despite the pride of authorship, Sir Ralph may have felt an impulse to tear it in a hundred pieces. Poor Bell, with a wan little Christmas smile, and Judy of course making herself ill with anxiety and anger ! Byron was a fascinating fellow, but . . . had they done well by their girl ? No help for it now ; they could only hope for the best.

And Judith Milbanke ! More clear-sighted, far more touchy, with resentments that Sir Ralph made little of,[1] and probably conscious of Byron's very qualified liking for her . . . Judith can of late have had few happy moments. Sympathy repelled by Annabella's pride, fear, resolution—that nature which was " like Proof-Spirits, not fit for common use " ; anxious eyes that sought the obstinately " placid countenance " ; fond hands that might not minister to pain . . . oh, if they could but put an end to the whole thing, send him packing when at last he should come, show him that Miss Milbanke was not to be condescended to by anyone, Lord Byron or another !

These parents, with their fine sense of rank and its obligations, their quiet pride, instinctive dignity, were confronted not only by the Byronic enigma but by the peculiar obnoxiousness of London in its most infuriating form. Ignorant scorn for

---

[1] " Neither before or *since* Marriage has he made any present to Lady B., not even the *common one* of a diamond Hoop ring. . . ."

From a statement made in 1816 by Lady Noel (as Lady Milbanke then was).

any life but London life—this they were up against, and be sure they knew it. What matter that country-cousins should eat their hearts out in suspense and mortification? Wedding-bells at Sunderland (deuce take them), a wedding-song concocted by Papa, a wedding-cake by Mamma—mental and physical indigestion; how dull it was, and Christmas would only make it duller. No; we delay to start, and having started, we dally on the way. At Six Mile Bottom, though the husband will be prevalent and "minced-pye" on the menu, there is at least the Other A., the other Mignonne with her other name of Medora and the "likeness to B. which makes her very good-humoured." [1]

Of the night at Six Mile Bottom Seaham anger took small account. He had to spend it somewhere—why not with his sister? There was enough to be angry about, as the posts came in. Letters from him—yes. But what was in the letters? Placid countenances can grow paler. . . . It cannot have been a Merry Christmas.

He wrote from Six Mile Bottom. Not much of a Christmas greeting:

Decr. 25th 1814.

I am thus far on my way and as warm as Love can make one with the thermometer below God knows what. Tomorrow I proceed northward, and if the Snow don't come down impassably hope to reach S. in tolerable time. The licence is in my portfolio. It is a droll composition, but enables us to marry in the house —so pray let us. I am sure we shall both catch cold kneeling anywhere else, to say nothing of being without a cushion.

Hobhouse *is* "bodkin," and takes up rather more room than "Happiness," who I believe won't join us till the last stage. We have heard of a treasure of a maid for you, who is I believe past the usual age of indiscretion, though there is no saying where that ends. Col. L. is opposite to me, making so many complaints of illness and calls for medicine that my attention is called off, and the rest of my letter will be like a prescription if I don't leave off. A. is looking very well, and just as usual in every respect—so that better can't be in my estimation. She writes to you with this.

P.S.—My love to Ly. Me. & papa. I hope they will acquit me "of these my crimes supposed," since I went at last like

[1] From a letter of Augusta's to him on December 14 of this year.

Lord Grizzle " in hurry post-haste for a licence—in hurry, ding-dong, I come back," with some apprehension of finding you, like Huncamunca, already " married to Tom Thumb." I wish you much merriment and minced pye—it is Xmas day.

Hobhouse had left London with him, but had not gone to Six Mile Bottom. They met again on the 26th, and set out for Seaham. " Never was lover less in haste." " The bridegroom more and more *less* impatient. . . . Indifference—almost aversion." Some malicious pleasure—pleasure of the intimate bachelor-friend, soon to take second place—seems to inform those entries in the best man's diary. Byron confessed that he was not in love, but felt " that regard which is the surest guarantee of continued affection and matrimonial felicity." [1] He had suggested waiting a year or so, he considering himself engaged. His affairs were again involved ; " it was fair to give the Milbankes every opportunity of delay." But the suggestion had been declined. During his present stay at Six Mile Bottom he had written a letter in which he drew back from the engagement ; Augusta had dissuaded him from sending it ; [2] here he was, then, on the road. Amid these confidences bridegroom and best man fared on, through the winter weather, for four days. They reached Seaham on December 30, at eight o'clock in the evening.

Servants, not the family, received them. They were shown to their rooms, feeling no doubt a trifle hangdog in face of this tacit rebuke. Hobhouse was first to come downstairs, and was taken to the library. There he was standing alone, when Miss Milbanke came to him, " and with great frankness took me by the hand at once. Presently Sir Ralph tottered in "—nervous perhaps, and (even he) somewhat cool in his welcome. Lady Milbanke had gone to her room. " Our delay the cause," wrote Hobhouse in his journal. " Indeed, I looked foolish in trying to find an excuse for it."

The two in the library waited—no sound of another step on the stairs. Those shattering letter , the long winter-day of

[1] This passage, so flagrantly contradicted by events, was nevertheless written by Hobhouse in 1816 during the separation proceedings. He was then concerned to show Byron in the best possible light.

[2] Byron told Annabella this during the bridal visit to Six Mile Bottom, adding to Augusta : " So you see it is all your fault." (Lady Byron's Narrative.)

suspense, Mamma's gesture of resentment (we can admire it, but for the girl it must have been bitter), " the mystery—the darkening—the vain attempts to clear it away," and now at last the knowledge that at any moment she might hear his step, his voice . . . not even Annabella's self-control could withstand all this. " Miss Milbanke heard Byron coming out of his room. She ran to meet him—threw her arms round his neck, and burst into tears. This she did *not before us.*"

The best man had meanwhile been scrutinising her.

> Rather dowdy-looking, and wears a long and high dress (as Byron had observed), though her feet and ankles are excellent. The lower part of her face is bad, the upper expressive but not handsome, yet she gains by inspection. . . . Of my friend she seemed dotingly fond, gazing with delight on his bold and animated countenance.

He adds that this was " regulated with the most entire decorum." She was silent and modest before the guests, but very sensible and quiet ; frank and open with Hobhouse, with no little airs or affectations. On the whole, he thought she inspired an interest which it was easy to mistake for love. That was the first evening's report. Later he wrote : " The young lady most attractive " ; and on the wedding-day he confesses that she had made a conquest of him.

So the house-party, which included Billy Hoar and the Rev. Thomas Noel (an illegitimate son of Lord Wentworth's) who was to marry the couple, shook down together. They must have got over the tension of that tardy arrival, for there was " a little jollity " next day on signing the settlements, and after dinner (at six o'clock) a mock-marriage, which one questions if the bride-elect found amusing. Hobhouse represented her, and was given away by Billy Hoar. " I talked and talked," says Hobhouse ; Byron talked too, for Hobhouse recalls some of his stories. They shook hands for the New Year—1814, with all its stress, was over.

Hopes have a way of reviving when the Old Year carries out its burden. Joy-bells that have nothing to do with weddings make us forget the chimes of Sunderland, about which we had been so snubbed.   We take a turn on the beach with our best man, who talks a great deal, and most affectionately, of Mrs. Leigh. Dinner is not quite so jolly, " but fair, considering," says the now sympathetic Hobhouse to his journal.   Byron comes to his room :   " Well, Hob, this is our last night.   To-morrow I shall be Annabella's "—recording which words, Hob mysteriously adds, *Absit omen*.

The wedding-day dawns.   Hobhouse is early ready, " in full dress with white gloves."   Byron too is early up and dressed. At breakfast Lady Milbanke is so nervous that she cannot make tea ;   Miss Milbanke does not appear.   At half-past ten the breakfast-party separates ;   Byron and Hobhouse go to Byron's room.   At twenty minutes to eleven, they emerge and walk upstairs to the drawing-room.   Kneeling-mats—the much de- siderated cushions take that austere form—are there arranged ; and after a few moments Miss Milbanke comes in, "attended by her governess, the respectable Mrs. Clermont."   She wears " a muslin gown trimmed with lace at the bottom, with a white muslin curricle jacket—very plain indeed, with nothing on her head."

At eleven o'clock they are married.

Hobhouse and the Vicar of Seaham, Mr. Wallace, sign the register.   Then they shake hands and kiss all round ;   Lady Milbanke and Mrs. Clermont are much affected.   The bride hastily leaves the room, but soon returns to sign her name. Her eyes are full of tears as she looks at her father and mother ; " and thus she completed her conquest—her innocent conquest."

In Hobhouse's longer account of the wedding we read that Miss Milbanke was firm as a rock, and during the whole ceremony looked steadily at Byron.   " Byron . . . when he came to the words ' With all my worldly goods I thee endow,' looked at me with a half smile."   This quarrels badly with two other accounts —that in *The Dream* (written in July 1816) [1] and Moore's remem-

---

[1] " And he stood calm and quiet, and he spoke
    The fitting vows, but heard not his own words,
    And all things reeled around him ;   he could see

   .   .   .   .

    The day, the hour, the sunshine, and the shade,

   .   .   .   .

    And her who was his destiny. . . ."

(By her who was his destiny is meant Mary Chaworth, whom he had been " too sluggish " to visit in 1813.)

brance of Byron's narrative in the destroyed Memoirs. He there
described himself as having a mist before his eyes, and wakening
with a start to find that he was—married. But Hobhouse's one
little detail carries more conviction than all this Byronism.

The bride, " looking steadily " at the bridegroom—what was in
her heart ? Long afterwards she wrote (for her grandchildren
after her death) a description of that morning's feelings. Too
much had happened in between for the analysis to be wholly
convincing ; it could not but have been coloured by the issue.
Some words, however, are true to the moment's experience :
" Love and faith on one side."

Of a wedding-breakfast we hear nothing. The mountainous
cake, the Epithalamium—both are ignored in Byron's letter to
Lady Melbourne, written next day from Halnaby.

> So there's an end of that matter, and the beginning of many
> others. Bell has gone through all the ceremonies with great
> fortitude, and I am much as usual, and your dutiful nephew. . . .
> Lady M. was a little hysterical and fine-feeling ; and the
> kneeling was rather tedious and the cushions hard ; but upon
> the whole it did vastly well.

The bride, having gone to change her dress, reappeared in what
Hobhouse calls a " slate-coloured " satin pelisse.[1] The bride-

---

[1] Both wedding-dress and pelisse are preserved at Ockham Park, where
I have seen them. The white Indian-muslin petticoat and over-dress are
delicately embroidered in tambour-work ; the hem of the petticoat and
the detachable cuffs of the over-dress have edges of rose-coloured and pale-
green flower-embroidery ; the hem of the petticoat would have shown
between the fronts of the over-dress. For so small a woman the gown is
longer than those illustrated in *La Belle Assemblée*. It shows no signs of
wear, nor does the little fragile pair of white lace gloves—not mittens—
which lies with the gown.
The " slate-coloured " pelisse is really of the softest imaginable shade of
dove colour, and has no " trimming of white fur "—attributed to it by
Hobhouse. In this the signs of wear are noticeable ; the hem is slightly
soiled all round. Charming detail in stitchery is a feature of the pelisse,
which is of the finest, most pliant satin. She must have had a warmer
wrap in the carriage for the drive of 40 miles on a snowy January day !
With the wedding-garment is preserved a small piece of embroidery-
work, half-finished—such a piece as might form the vest of a gown.
It is of bright flowers in contrasting colours, very finely worked on a
black ground. The stitchery is faultless. Probably the occupation of her
many solitary hours at Halnaby, it puts the last touch to our sense of these
speaking relics.

groom was calm and as usual; the best man felt as if he had buried a friend. These two took a sentimental farewell of each other: "Byron was unwilling to leave my hand, and I had hold of his out of the window as the carriage drove off."

Into the carriage Hobhouse had put his wedding-present—a complete collection of Byron's works in yellow morocco. And into that yellow morocco atmosphere it was his to hand the bride.

"I wish you every happiness."

"If I am not happy, it will be my own fault."

Her eyes looked earnestly into his; he drew aside for Byron to enter. The two men, clinging to one another's hands, obscured the bride from Ralph and Judith Milbanke's view; the carriage turned; they watched it down the drive. Seaham was home no more for the barley-sugar daughter.

CHAPTER XI

THE HONEYMOON

" Did I not behave well ? " asked Lady Milbanke of Hobhouse, when the carriage had disappeared.

Half-a-dozen men had fired muskets in front of the house when the wedding was over ; the bells of Seaham Church were still pealing. Lady Milbanke *had* behaved well ; now it was time for the best man to remove himself, and let her behave as badly as she wanted to. He left Seaham at twelve o'clock and stopped at Sunderland of the offending chimes. There, the same evening, he dined with Billy Hoar, and Sir Ralph and Lady Milbanke were among the guests—" a sort of wedding-dinner."

At Halnaby too there was a sort of wedding-dinner. Let us look in upon it, after the long day of emotion and fatigue.

When Byron's hand was perforce detached from that of his best man, and the carriage passed through the gates of Seaham House, there was a brief interval of silence. The road to York-shire stretched before the honeymoon couple. Utterly alone with her bridegroom at last,[1] the bride sat no doubt a little timidly beside him whose face was so unlike a bridegroom's in its lowering defiance. She had seen that look before, but now it was more paralysing. Soon the silence was broken, not by any word from him, but by " a wild sort of singing." He did not speak until they were coming into Durham. There, as they entered, joy-bells rang out for Miss Milbanke's wedding-day—the one-time Member's daughter, well-known in the city ; her bridal carriage had been

---

[1] Both Annabella and Hobhouse emphatically contradict the story, told by Byron to Medwin, of there having been a lady's maid in the carriage. Byron may have confused occasions. The maid *was* with her mistress on a later transit—that to Six Mile Bottom after their return-visit to Seaham.

eagerly watched for. Then Byron spoke. " Ringing for our happiness, I suppose ? "

Savage sarcasm in the tone, aversion in the look, a shudder dramatically violent ; and soon he turned on her ferociously— she wrote afterwards of the ferocity she recognised too well from the wedding-journey :

" It *must* come to a separation ! You should have married me when I first proposed."

That was the note of all the day. " She might have saved him once ; now it was too late. Enough for him that she was his wife for him to hate her—now ; when he first offered himself, she had it all in her power. Now she would find that she had married a devil." She sat beside him, listening to that reiterated " now," seeing indeed the look of hatred on his face. Why did she not stop the carriage and return to her father's protection ? So her friend Lady Anne Barnard (who had known her from childhood) asked when in 1816 the story was told her ; so we ask to-day, although we have her answer. " Because I had not a conception he was in earnest. He laughed it over when he saw me appear hurt." Yet she had had some warning. As she listened, did an incident of his first visit come back to memory— the day when

> after some affectionate expressions on my part, he said in a low voice with a look of the most fixed malevolence : " I will be even with you yet." When I asked what he meant, he turned it off, and expressed every feeling of tenderness.

It must have come back to her ; but again, hearing him " turn it off," she would not believe he was in earnest. . . . He did not long laugh it over. They came to the inn at Rushyford (she remembered every station of her cross) and there he said : " I wonder how much longer I shall be able to keep up the part I have been playing ! " Stunned into passivity perhaps, she did not make the obvious retort that he seemed to have dropped it already ; and he went on to tell her how he detested her mother, how discontented he was with the settlements and her small fortune, " speaking of me as if I were a beggar." But she was passive still—it exasperated him. What worse could he think of ? Nothing worse, unless he invented ; so Byron proceeded to

HALNABY HALL

From the lithograph drawn by Frederick Peake in the
possession of Lady Milbanke

invent, and did not hesitate to slander the Lady Melbourne whom he so genuinely admired.[1] He told her that her aunt and he had plotted to avenge her refusal of him—" it was something to outwit a woman like you, who had declined so many men " ; but even so, it was only in a moment of pique against another girl that he had renewed his offer. Then he had longed to break the engagement, but they had told him that as a man of honour he was bound to fulfil it. Now he had fulfilled it, now she was in his power ; " and I shall make you feel it."

Thus, through the gathering darkness, they drove on to Halnaby for their honeymoon.

They reached it the same evening. The butler (who was her maid's husband) was on the steps to receive them. Many years afterwards he told Harriet Martineau of the arrival. The bride got out of the carriage " with a face and attitude of despair. The bridegroom did not hand her out, but walked away. She came up the steps with a countenance and frame agonised and listless. . . . He longed to offer his arm to the young, lonely creature." [2]

After the wedding-dinner, toasted at Sunderland by two hopeful hearts, Byron asked her " with every appearance of aversion " whether she meant to sleep in the same bed with him. " I hate sleeping with any woman, but you may if you choose." Wounding enough, but insult was added. Provided a woman was young, one was as good as another. . . . A girl of twenty-two, she listened—was to listen later, between the fire-lit crimson curtains, to his cry : " Good God, I am surely in Hell ! " Now that we can add it to the rest, it ceases to be—as hitherto we may have thought it—merely a very poor joke in the Byronic manner.

She woke to that on her wedding-night ; but it was next morning that " perhaps the deadliest chill fell on my heart." She waited till he came downstairs, then went to him in the library. " He met me repellently, and uttered words of blighting irony : ' It is too late now. It is done, and cannot be undone.' I told

---

[1] Her letters to him after his marriage leave no possible doubt that this was invention.

[2] *Biographical Sketches*, " Lady Noel Byron." From the fourth edition, 1876. The Sketches were first published in octavo form in 1868. Lady Byron died in 1860 ; but the essay on her was, from internal evidence, written during her life-time.

him I did not repent, and tried to inspire a hope which was almost extinguished in my own heart."

That morning Byron received a letter from Augusta which addressed him as " Dearest, first, and best of human beings," and went on to describe her agitation at the hour of his wedding : " As the sea trembles when the earth quakes." It excited in him " a kind of fierce and exulting transport " ; he read the metaphor admiringly to Annabella, then the opening words. " What do you think of them ? " he asked her.

What did she think of them ? Surely, despite the ignorance so soon to be dispelled, what we think—that the moment for such extreme effusion was strangely chosen. The incident, odious for us who know the truth, was then perhaps no more than an added pang for her (he had already made her a little jealous of his sister) ; but this letter, sent to arrive when it did, does give colour to Lady Melbourne's view that Augusta was very clever and very wicked. To recall herself in that fashion on that morning—she could not have been more mischievous. She must have known it ; and the sisterly colour which might seem to account for her ardour, adds baseness to the rest.

Of what this meant, Annabella was to have many an indication during the three weeks at Halnaby. A few days later, she was reading Dryden's *Don Sebastian*, which treats of incest, and happened to ask Byron a question. He said angrily : " Where did you hear that ? "

I looked up and saw that he was holding over me the dagger which he usually wore. I replied, " Oh, only from this book." I was not afraid—I was persuaded he only did it to terrify me. He put the dagger down and said (I am sure I say it without a feeling of vanity) " If anything could make me believe in heaven, it is the expression of your countenance at this moment."

So even at Halnaby there was one of the moments to which she afterwards looked back so poignantly. " Even now I feel that the remembrance of bitterness may wear out, but the remembrance of those few softer moments will to the end remain—' as springs in deserts found.' "

And indeed what pair of human beings could spend three weeks together without some kind of normal intercourse ? Though she never afterwards could speak of her honeymoon without a shudder, though even Hobhouse admitted that " her Ladyship seemed always dismayed when she spoke of her residence at Halnaby " [1]—they must have laughed, have given one another the pet-names, " Pippin " and " Duck," which later became such public property. Annabella's narratives of the brief period they spent together as man and wife were written for the lawyers, explaining her resolution not to return to Byron, and showing that it was not only his relation with Augusta which caused her to form it. Her object was to prove that—as she afterwards expressed it—" *I* could have been of no good to him." That conviction had been the cause of her anguish, far more than the torture he inflicted on her. Writing with such an aim, to dwell on the better moments was beside the mark ; but in her talks with Robertson in 1850 there is many a reminiscence of the " springs in deserts found "—though of Halnaby she could not even then speak without the dismay to which Hobhouse testified. Halnaby was her initiation ; after Halnaby, there was at worst no " amazement " for the girl on whose ears that ominous word in the marriage-service had so recently fallen.

But the better moments came—and went. The pet-names do not appear in their correspondence before marriage ; they appear in almost every one of the few letters after marriage, and before separation. " Pippin " for Bell's round rosy face ; " Duck "—perhaps as a corollary to " Goose," Byron's pet-name for Augusta ! And she copied for him those Hebrew Melodies which he wrote at Halnaby ; they read books together, and discussed them ; Scott's *Lord of the Isles* was sent to Byron by Murray. It they did not only discuss, for he pointed out to her, " with a miserable smile," the description of the wayward bridegroom :

> " She watched, yet feared to meet, his glance,
> And he shunned hers, till when by chance
> They met, the point of foeman's lance
> Had given a milder pang."

Some show of decency, besides, he surely must have made before the servants—all (except his own valet Fletcher) in her father's

---

[1] So much so that throughout her later life she was always disturbed in spirit when snow was falling, as it had been during the drive to Halnaby and the first few days there.

employment. The lady's-maid, it is true, saw much of her mistress's unhappiness. Her companionship was necessary to a bride who was left alone most of the day, or sent out of the room with : " I don't want you. I hope we are not always to be to-gether—that won't do for me, I assure you." Mrs. Minns, who had known her from childhood, was so alarmed by Byron's savage behaviour that she implored Annabella to write to her father. The wife even contemplated returning to her parents ; but changed her mind both about this and telling them of her distress, and made Mrs. Minns promise not to say a word on the subject. " I bitterly reproached myself for betraying a husband's confidence." This refers to a day on which she had broken down in the maid's presence, and cried : " I am sure there has been something dreadful between him and his sister ! "

Though that was what Byron sought to drive upon her by every device of allusion and comparison, she " determined with equal force of will " that she would not believe it. For a time she thought that he might have had an affair with a girl whom he afterwards discovered to be his natural sister—probable enough, from his father's libertine character ; but soon she had to recog-nise that if she believed in his hints at all, she must connect them with Augusta. Since her day, we have learnt that those who practise this and other perversities are given to hovering round the subject with people whom they suppose to be ignorant—a form of psychic vanity, in the scientific view. Of such psychology little was then known ; there can seldom have been a more striking example of it than Byron was. His *fanfaronnade des vices* arose from this. He would be exceptional at any cost to himself or those involved. Thus the dagger-scene at Halnaby was only one of many designed to force on the girl who was alone with him —and innocent indeed, if not so crass in her innocence as he scornfully supposed—the suspicion which, as she afterwards wrote to Augusta, " has nearly driven me to madness *from the first week of my marriage.*"

Secluded from all but him, " the intensity of his sufferings absorbed my feelings in his, almost to self-forgetfulness." The disclosure that she had been married without love, the frequent threats of suicide, the " vindictive exultation over my defenceless state " ; his walks in the gallery at night with dagger drawn, his morbid dread of some mysterious deadly avenger, his hints at being a murderer, and then the speeches wild or cruel or charged with the incestuous significance he harped upon. . . .

"I was a villain to marry you. I could convince you of it in three words."

"I am more accursed in my marriage than in any other act of my life."

"If you had married me two years ago, you would have saved me from what I can never get over."

"I will live with you, *if I can*, until I have got an heir—then I shall leave you."

"I only want a woman to laugh, and don't care what she is besides. I can make Augusta laugh at anything. No one makes me happy but Augusta."

These were her daily bread. Or there would be a set scene of fury, as on the night when he brought out her letters before and during the engagement, and read some passages, dwelling especially on one where she had said that she wished to be the means of reconciling him to himself. Again he reproached her bitterly for delaying to accept him ; his rage was so extreme that she thought he would have struck her. Her first impulse was to disarm him by affection :

He was sitting by the fire and had his red portfolio by him. I found myself on my knees with my arms round his neck, and said : "You forget we *are* married." This calmed him, and he said he had worked himself up to the feelings of that past time—but his revenge seemed only to subside, not to cease.

And then again a gleam of something like tenderness. One night, after he had been roaming the gallery as usual, armed with dagger and pistol, he came to her exhausted and piteously haggard. "Seeking to allay his misery," she moved her head until it rested on his breast. He said, more gently than usual but with piercing bitterness : "You should have a softer pillow than my heart."

"I wonder which will break first, yours or mine," she answered —in "the only words of despair he ever heard me utter."

Then she implored him to tell her what was preying on his mind. He said he would, if it were not another's secret—adding instantly the old reproach about her delay in accepting him.

For a moment he still seemed about to confide in her, but said :
" No. I want to sleep now. Ask me in the morning—I will
tell you then."

After breakfast she reminded him. He tried to evade ; she
urged him—his eyes filled with tears, he got up from the sofa
where he was sitting " with pistol and dagger as usual beside
him," stood before the fire—and now over his face came the
" terrible blackness " she knew too well.

" You shall know my secret if you will ; but if I tell you, you
shall be made miserable throughout your life—I will be another
Falkland to you." This reference to Godwin's *Caleb Williams*
was frequent with him ; she had read the book and understood
its meaning. . . . Seeing that in this mood her efforts would be
worse than useless, she said no more—then or afterwards—on
the subject. Her reward was that on their leaving Halnaby he
said, with a suspicious glance : " I think you now know pretty
well what subjects to avoid." She might avoid them, but he
did not. Over and over again there were the raging fits, the
despairing fits, the reference to some abnormal, unforgivable sin.
He even read aloud Lady Melbourne's letter, in which she had
said that he and another were on the brink of a precipice. " I
took her advice *in part*—would that I had taken it altogether ! "

Remorse—the spectacular remorse, half-genuine, half-his-
trionic, of Byron, that the world was one day to hear wailing
through *Manfred* ! This girl was being practised on, so to speak.
That it was sterile, however sincere, the sequel at Six Mile Bottom
will show.

Such allusions, reproaches, threats were not all the bride had
to listen to. Another regalement was a story of his having
attempted to seduce Lady Oxford's thirteen-year old daughter
(the Ianthe of *Childe Harold*), and of his having nearly stabbed
Lady Oxford herself, on a night when she came to his room and
waked him suddenly. Briefly, he did everything he could think
of to insult, enrage, or terrify her into " running back to your
father like the spoiled child you are." Long afterwards she
summed up her experience in these words :

He required of a woman's attachment—to use an expressive
Scotch phrase—not *heart to heart*, but *heart at his feet*—and mine
was laid before him. But this was not enough. I must have

prostrated every sacred duty—*even the duty of a wife,* and have gratified his pride by the very guilt which would eventually have disgraced himself, whilst I was to thank him for subverting my only power and protection—Innocence. . . .   There is *no* vice with which he has not endeavoured to familiarise me."

She persevered, hoping to gain his love by devotion and sacrifice ; she could even, " for so dear a hope, command some cheerfulness " now and then.   One victory she did achieve— over his morbid silence about the lame foot.   He was reading an article by Darwin on Diseased Volition (a semi-anticipation of Freud) and pointed out to her a passage upon the patient's making a mystery of the diseased association, " which if he could be persuaded to divulge, the effect would cease."   Acting upon this hint from Darwin, and from him, she led him to speak of his infirmity.   He came to talk familiarly of his " little foot " (as he called it) and said that some allowance must surely be made to him on the Day of Judgment, that he had often wished to revenge himself on Heaven for it.   She found, too, that he was nervous about his health ; he often came to her for encouragement and solace.   " I would feel his pulse gravely, and then laugh away his fears."   The alarms of his vanity touched her heart more whimsically—his horror at a grey hair, a blemished tooth.

These were her consolations—to be able, to be permitted, now and then to console him.   But then again the hope would be withered by his " sterile pity " ; the " Poor thing ! " he would sometimes utter, while tears suffused his eyes and " freezing there, gave the appearance of more icy hardness.   If he had not felt, I might have hoped to move him.   But he pitied, and was inexorable."

Sometimes she took refuge in the thought that he *was* mad, as he sought to convince her that he was or might become.   He said one day (referring to the List of Qualities for a Husband which in the past we have smiled to read) : " You were deter- mined that you would not marry a man in whose family there was derangement.   You have done very well indeed—my mater- nal grandfather shot himself, a cousin on the Gordon side was insane and set fire to a house."   On his " black days," when he shut himself away in frenzied gloom, she remembered these things, scarce knowing whether to hope or fear that it actually was a phase of madness.

Was it ? Difficult to believe that it was not ; such savagery seems to pass the border-line.   Yet at Halnaby he was writing the Hebrew Melodies ; from there he wrote to Lady Melbourne and others in his usual strain.   Remorse was the pretext for all. We need not wholly scorn him for its quality ; with all that real contrition signifies Byron's nature was incapable of reckoning. For him the word sufficed.   Almost we might say that remorse stood for a dream, with its scenic effects, its dark enhancing mystery ; nothing else was Byronic enough to continue the Legend.   Sincere in his often-expressed scorn for that legend, he yet through most of his life reinforced it, and no less sincerely than he scorned it.   The vanity of suffering—we all in some measure possess it ; Byron possessed it to extremity.   Only so was it possible that he should thus torture his bride and himself, yet still be accountable for his conduct.   *He* was a prey to re- morse ; anybody else concerned was negligible, except as another kind of prey.

The girl he had to do with was doomed to a part which perhaps no other girl that ever lived would have played just as she did. If he was the enigma of his age, she is the enigma of ours ; and a good deal more perplexingly.   However profound her love for him, there seems to be " no sense," as we say, in her extreme abjection of conduct—for in spirit she was far from abject.   She had her definite aim, her definite, if " almost extinguished," hope of at once saving him from himself and reconciling him to himself.   Shut her eyes as she might and did to what he perpetually held before them, again she could not shut her ears to the voice of instinct, telling her that there could be but one explanation of these things.   Now and then, indeed, she told herself that he was only "playing Petruchio" to the spoiled child that (as he told her) Lady Melbourne had said she was.   But then " something too like reality " would disperse that hope with its companion hope.   To be an unloved wife—that she accepted, saying that the misfortune of their marriage was worse for him than for her, that she would try to lessen it by making no claim on his affection and cheerfully taking the place of his friend only.

" Then if I were unfaithful you would not resent it ? " was his reply to this.

" I have been taught to believe that a wife had better not notice deviations which are more likely to be repented of, if her own conduct continues kind and constant."

" Then you would *let* me be unfaithful ? "

" No—that is a different thing. Even as your friend I should love you too well to *let* you do what would injure yourself."

He answered angrily and sarcastically ; then continued : " A woman cannot love a man for himself who does not love him in his crimes. . . . No other love is worthy the name. "

She would not assent to this, and he said : " I thought you had been more *malleable*," in a tone which she " could never forget."

Yet (as she told Robertson in 1850) she never ceased to consider that a wife was not justified in separating from her husband by any discovery she might make of sins committed before marriage—" not for the deepest in the catalogue of human law— not for anything but the will to go on sinning."

There was nothing but exasperation for Byron in these views. He wanted her to be jealous—" I would give nothing for a woman who was not jealous "—because he wanted to torture her. To revenge himself upon her was part of the remorse for what he had done to the Other A. ; Annabella must suffer because Augusta had suffered. Augusta had relinquished him to this unloved wife —the wife was to pay for the sacrifice that had been made her. He had married to escape from that misery of fear and shame— yes ; but in the doggerel of the notorious verses :

" We repent—we abjure—we will break from our chain,
We must part—we must fly to—unite it again ! "

So, if Annabella would not be jealous, she must expiate her crime of being his wife in other ways. . . . The " madness of the heart " indeed—but no other madness was Byron's.

Soon she too had to realise that. He was not deranged ; he knew very well what he was doing. Now what should *she* do ?

It amazes us to learn. She suggested that they should ask Augusta to come to them at Halnaby. " I hoped to please him." He was pleased, but, " Poor Gussy won't be able to come."

Poor Gussy was not able to come. She was " very grateful for Annabella's kindness, and hoped to deserve it more than she could *yet*." She wrote almost daily to the bride, and the bride wrote cheerfully to her—nearly always, not quite always. " Those half-jests in which misery is so fertile " : so she described her letters afterwards ; but there was one in which jest played no part. The long hours of loneliness—was it they that wrung from her the cry which, did we not read it in her own hand, we could scarcely credit ?   " Augusta—will you be my *only* friend ? "

Inexplicable ; though we do not forget that she had resolved to disbelieve in what was driving her " almost to madness," nor forget either that she was determined not to let her parents know of her unhappiness. But she had friends—was M.G. forgotten ?   Not forgotten ; pride and loyalty forbade. Moreover, Lady Gosford did not know him. No one knew him as Augusta did ; " no one could make him happy but Augusta "—might she not help Annabella to make him happy too ?   Perhaps it is not so inexplicable.

That was the honeymoon. Three weeks of it ; then they left Halnaby for Seaham.

All this time she had been writing gaily to her parents and her uncle. That she did of her own accord ; other letters about her happiness were exacted from her by Byron. " I did write some." But to Dad and Mam it was at her own heart's bidding that she wrote cheerfully. Now she was to be with them. Sad complication of feelings—returning to the home that was her home no more, with what solace in the thought of sheltering love, what fear lest she should fail in her part of happy bride !

She did not fail. The sense of protection, of escape from bewilderment and desolation, may well have helped her really to be happier. " A gleam of hope." Afterwards she summed up the beginning of their stay at Seaham in those words, and " He seemed more kind." [1]   Certainly there were brighter moments. In the evenings they played games or wrote *bouts-rimés*. These

---

[1] It was during this visit that Annabella cut from Byron's head the lock of hair which, carefully preserved by their posterity, serves now to prove that his hair curled naturally—despite Scrope Davies's anecdote of the morning curl-papers.

have been preserved; emotions not commonly associated with *bouts-rimés* belong to the folded scraps of paper. And one night they dressed up. Incredible, though fully attested, is the incident of Byron's snatching off his mother-in-law's wig! Did Judith suffer that good-humouredly? Apparently she did; and Annabella could make an act of oblivion for the Halnaby revilings of her mother. She was at home, though it was home no longer; he was "more kind"; she could remember and forget—remember that she was a girl of twenty-two, forget that she was a wife unloved, a "curse."

But Byron soon got bored; and if Annabella read him the letters she still almost daily received from Augusta, he was well assisted to that state. They are on the surface charming, yet it is impossible to evade an impression of malice in her comments on the Seaham amusements, and on how many of Annabella's happy moments she was able to bestow on Guss. "Not even I can know him better than you do"; "I am glad you are at Seaham. B. will be more at his ease than in his character of 'the worst of lovers'"; "Here comes *Medora*" (underlined); "I am so glad he is spoiled at Seaham, because he would have it no one could spoil him but *me*"; "Only think of B. playing drafts! I never should have suspected him, though I don't exactly know why"; "He has now so many occupations—walking, dining, playing drafts with Mamma . . . but I am vain enough to think he does not forget Guss."

Guileless in appearance; but Guss was not so guileless as all that. Did Annabella see through the ingenuousness? Possibly not, though by this time she had taught herself to "depart from veracity" in her own letters. But she was resolute to put away from her the Halnaby horror: "Look on't again I dare not." Only on one evening did the spectre hover. It was when they were writing the *bouts-rimés*; some accidental coincidence came into the verses. "You must send those to Guss," said Byron. She said she would distinguish his and hers by crosses. He turned pale: "For God's sake don't—it would frighten her to death. . . . I never wrote anything about *love* to Guss," he added vehemently. He would not write to her himself, and seemed angry and ashamed when Annabella urged him to it; yet at Halnaby he had written letters to her

which he had burnt. . . . But except on this evening Annabella
was firm in self-discipline : " I *would not* entertain those suspicions.
It was odious to believe that my thoughts might sully a relation
so dear and sacred."

There was a dramatic incident early in their stay.   Annabella
relates it thus : [1]

> He was in the habit of sitting up writing till near one in the
> morning.   Having been annoyed by a large fire in the small
> room when he was thus occupied, he threw a quantity of water
> on the coals, and some kind of gas was produced by which he
> was nearly suffocated.   When he came into the bedroom, he
> staggered, and was in a state of stupor.   I did not then know
> the cause, but lost no time in taking him to an open window,
> using Eau de Cologne &c to revive him.   As soon as he recovered
> his consciousness, the idea that he was dying presented itself
> to his imagination, and he broke forth into the wildest ravings
> of despair, saying that he knew he was going to Hell, but that
> he would defy his Maker to the last, with other expressions of
> a revengeful nature. . . .   Afterwards, recovering, he became
> softened, and said " I have tried everything—I will try virtue,
> I think.   Perhaps I shall go to Heaven, holding by the hem of
> your garment."

Sometimes, " but very rarely," he showed the same kind of
gratitude for small attentions—if she fetched a book for him or
got up at night to bring his lemonade.   " You are a good kind
Pip—a good-natured Pip—the best wife in the world."   The
smallest momentary pleasure she could give him consoled her :
" His misery was usually of so harsh a temper. . . .   He inflicted
misery, but I felt that he suffered more than he inflicted."

And there was, too, what she afterwards called his " child-side."

> A state of being, for brief intervals, resembling that of a
> guileless playful child—it was more than acting.   He would then
> speak of himself, as little children do, in the third person, as
> " B," and forget entirely all that belonged to later years—a
> blessed suspension of memory ; but after a few minutes it often
> happened that some careless word of his own would strike some
> painful chord, and then the man's mind returned with all its
> wretchedness.   He would say " B's a fool "—" Yes, he *is* a fool,"
> bitterly—or " poor B—*poor* B "—with the feelings of hopeless
> self-abandonment expressed in the lines " There's not a joy the

[1] Byron also told it to Lady Melbourne.   *Correspondence*, i. 301-2.

world can give " etc. But no verse of his could make an appeal half so touching as those artless, scarcely conscious utterances.

"Therefore they are here, whatever it costs." Writing to Robertson in 1850, in an attempt to give the other side of the picture, she added those words.

> Little it seems, and yet
>   Maybe of all
> The last they shall forget,
>   Or dare recall.

In these lines by a modern versifier the poignancy of such memories as hers of Byron's " child-side " seems to be summed-up.

Byron wrote from Seaham to Moore and Lady Melbourne— to " *ma tante* " not now confidentially, for she learnt nothing of the black days at Halnaby, and little of the ennui at Seaham. The tone is quite superficial ; flippant as usual, but (for Byron) reticent. " Bell does as she likes, and don't bore me."

Moore got the reversal. Sir Ralph had been making a speech at Durham, " and not only at Durham but here, several times after dinner. He is now, I believe, making it to himself (I left him in the middle)." " I must go to tea—damn tea ; I wish it was Kinnaird's brandy." The boredom culminated in a plan of going at once to Italy, with or without Moore, but anyhow without his wife. This did not come off ; or rather, did eventually come off under altered circumstances—and without either wife or friend.

They left Seaham on March 9 for a bridal visit to Six Mile Bottom. Byron suggested that he should go alone, leaving Annabella with her parents. She would not consent to this, and he flew into a terrible rage—the ferocity which was now familiar to her. As they were getting into the carriage, Lady Milbanke called to him : " Take care of Annabella." Again he was infuriated ; again she drove away, alone with him and her deeper knowledge of the road which lay before her—Thursday's Child, who still had so far to go. Courage did not fail her. On this journey she contrived—as she had been too stunned to do on the earlier one—" to get him ' less disagreeable,' as Augusta would say."

CHAPTER XII

SIX MILE BOTTOM

AUGUSTA had betrayed much unwillingness to receive Byron alone. Her house was small and inconvenient; she was half-expecting her aunt, Miss Sophia Byron, and if this happened she " would not have a hole " ; Colonel Leigh was vacillating about a Northern shooting-party, and if he went she would be able to put up the bridal pair . . . but—" in short I am *utterly distracted*, and can settle nothing until I know." This kind of thing went on for days.

Then the situation cleared up. Miss Byron did not come, Colonel Leigh did go, and she could manage. So husband and wife set out on the much longer drive than that to Halnaby—for, leaving Seaham on March 9, they did not reach Newmarket until the 12th.

Byron started in a bad temper. " What on earth does your mother mean by telling me to take care of you ? I suppose you can take care of yourself ! " But Annabella smoothed him down as they drove on, and she could laugh at the explanation he gave of his fractiousness : " I feel as if I were just going to be married " —a pleasantry doubtless as hackneyed then as now.

At Wandsford, the last stopping-place, she had her reward. " He spoke the kindest words I could ever have wished to hear." It was at night ; he said : " You married me to make me happy, didn't you ? " She does not give her reply, but it is easily imagined. He went on : " Well then, you do make me happy." He spoke " with passionate affection. I was silent, and he did not see but felt the tears of joy which rose from my heart. Then again he seemed to pity me for some impending, inevitable misery."

They were driving up to the house when he said : " You

AUGUSTA LEIGH

After the miniature by Holmes

stay in the carriage; I will go in and prepare Guss." She acquiesced, and he went in. But Mrs. Leigh was not downstairs, and Byron returned, " in great perturbation," to hand out his wife.

The two women had seen one another, but had not been introduced, at a party in 1813. Augusta was very far from being the " Dowdy-Goody " described by some of Byron's partisans, when to make her so was part of their case. She was, as Holmes's miniature of fifteen years later still showed (Holmes, of whom Byron said that he did " inveterate " likenesses), a distinctly attractive woman ; and looking at Hayter's pencil sketch of her in 1812, the last epithet one would apply to the high-bred features and gracefully-turned neck is dowdy. . . . Now, with her fine silky dark-brown hair in little curls above the un-expectedly serious face, brown-eyed and oval, she would have come rustling in a long narrow robe (approved by *La Belle Assemblée*) down the stairs to welcome the little bride and " my dearest B." She greeted Annabella warmly, but did not kiss her—Annabella noticed that, and so did Byron. Turning to B. she must have trembled, for the blackness of his countenance was terrific. " He accounted for it by a letter about Newstead which he had just opened."

The women went upstairs. " I expressed my happiness at being under her roof, and kissed her. She went down and told him what had passed. He afterwards reproached her mysteriously, as if to vex her, for not having kissed me at first."

Guss was enraptured with her sister-in-law. " I think I never saw or heard or read of a more perfect being in mortal mould than she appears to be." So she wrote to Byron's and her friend, Hodgson. But though at first she thought that Byron seemed happy, that impression wore off ; and she told Hodgson that his nerves and spirits were very far from what she wished them. The disingenuousness and " spurious piety " which were among her unlikable traits are marked in this second letter. It is true that she could not even have hinted at what the fortnight forced on her as well as on the bride.

The note was struck at once. Byron came to his wife's room that night in a savage state ; " Now I have *her*, you will find I can do without *you*—in all ways."

He was savage because this was not true. Augusta then, and always after the marriage, refused herself to him. But such a prologue to their stay obliged Annabella to look the Halnaby episodes in the face. Even now, though, " I could not bear to admit things to myself." And the less because Augusta's kindness throughout the fortnight was unfailing—" she seemed to have no other view but that of mitigating his cruelty to me." There could be little mitigation, however, for the sister herself was victimised. " She seemed fearful of every word he uttered, and fearful of checking him." He spoke to her with such gross indelicacy that in after-days, when it was necessary for Annabella to set down some details of the visit for the lawyers, she could not bring herself to write the words except in " Beeby's shorthand "—a precursor of Pitman's, very similar in principle. His pleasure was, as he expressed it, to work them both well. If the wife was trampled on, so was the sister. " She submitted to his affection, but never seemed gratified by the signs of passion which were so marked that she must have been conscious of them."

One detail, though, tells badly against all Augusta's kindnesses —her constant wearing of one of " the two gold brooches, containing his hair and hers, with three crosses on them," which Byron received from a London jeweller two or three days after their arrival. The other brooch was worn by him ; he said to Augusta in Annabella's presence : " If she knew what these mean ! Do you remember our signs at Newstead ? " Then with a sigh or sneer : " Well, Guss, I am a reformed man, ain't I ? "

Every night the bride was insulted into retiring early. " We don't want *you*, my charmer." Sometimes, indeed, she " could not have remained without bursting into tears. A sense of desolation came upon me. I sustained his insults without seeming to comprehend them." For his purpose was avowed ; and Augusta afterwards confessed that he had tried to renew the incestuous relation. In after-years Annabella became convinced that she *had* refused ; but at the time she could achieve no more than the attitude of trust in her, for Byron's speech and behaviour " would have brought conviction to any other person."

Very many years afterwards, Annabella made a draft for the memoir she thought of leaving for her grandchildren to read.

She never went further than this synopsis. Of the stay at Six Mile Bottom she wrote :

> Confirmation forced on her by documents and testimony of her having been a dupe and a victim. A feeling on her part of immeasurable horror and pity. Brain in danger. . . . Practical errors and unintelligible conduct, all with outward calmness and gentleness—seen through by him. Insult—evidently studied —disregarded in conduct, but sinking into the heart to wither its very life. . . . A sense of Inevitability—who quarrels with death ?

" Don't touch me ! "—in a voice of " raging detestation." **One** night she woke to hear that cry, for some movement had brought her nearer to him.

She could not bear it, and got up.

" Where are you going ? "

" To my own room," she answered. . . . " There I wept myself into some peace."

It is difficult, as one reads the wife's narrative, to believe in the regained innocence of the sister's relations with Byron. He would greet her in the morning with such allusions as (in Annabella's words) " sometimes made Augusta ready to sink "— personalities of the implied situation, compliments on Guss's " inflammable temperament " and so on ; but he ranged further still when Medora was the topic. One evening the three were looking at some portraits of him. It must have been one of the hours of respite which, as at Halnaby, were granted the bride ; for she was able to say : " I should like to have him painted when he is looking at Medora." (Recording this, she added : " The tenderness of his expression then I thought quite lovely "). She spoke without a thought of any underlying significance, yet could not but be struck by Byron's extraordinary emotion as he heard. " I did not at the time know why." But before they left the house, she knew why.

" You know," he said another night, before both women, " you know that is my child "—pointing to Medora and going on to calculate the time of Colonel Leigh's absence from home in the year of her birth, so as to prove she could not possibly be the husband's child. Not much wonder that Augusta seemed fearful of every word he uttered and sometimes ready to sink. Once or twice she spoke to Annabella, almost as if desirous to confide in her. " You are kind to me because you do not know me " ; " He can never respect *me* " ; and to Byron, on his calling her his best friend : " Oh, I fear I have been your worst." The two women went for walks together, and one day Annabella spoke of Byron's feelings for herself. " She gave me little encouragement to think he loved me." Nevertheless his malice towards the sister, the insults he heaped upon her, established (as the wife afterwards confessed) " a sort of tacit understanding between us." Strange outcome of such a martyrdom, though she was able to persuade herself of Augusta's equal martyrdom— had she not learnt at Halnaby what Byron's malignity towards a woman could be ? But no degree of incredulity could make the visit endurable. During the terrible two weeks she wrote in her diary that cry of the Psalmist : " My heart is withered away, so that I forget to eat my bread." Had there been nothing worse behind Byron's cruelties, they would have themselves sufficed to wither any woman's heart. The letters about his intrigues before marriage, which he made Augusta read to her (" and all the time *you* thought I was dying for you ! ") ; others written during the engagement in a tone of aversion from marrying her ; perpetual inveighing against the accomplished fact as the cause of all his wretchedness—" Cursed fool that I was ! " sometimes followed by a sarcastic apology : " I mean nothing personal " . . . these alone would explain Annabella's summary of the fortnight. " What I suffered during our stay at S.M.B. was indescribable."

At last came the day of escape—March 28. Byron was reluctant to go, but Augusta " evidently wished for our departure." So they drove away, he looking back and waving passionately as long as he could see her, then sinking down beside the Other A., with a dark look and the question : " What do you think of her ? "

Annabella, as she left " the scene of such deep horrors," tried to shake off its associations. She told herself that it all had come of Byron's morbid desire to create a sensation, and torment her into the bargain ; that it had " escaped Augusta's penetration " —but as she told herself that, she found her own penetration refusing to accept it. Then she took refuge in the idea that it

might have been " some unrepeated *hour*, not systematic guilt."
She took everything into account—his cruel temper with women ;
his denigration of himself, designed for theatrical effect ; her own
unloved state, Augusta's long affection—the "sacred relation "
which she feared to sully by her thoughts, sedulously induced by
him though they might be.   But it was in vain.   Tell herself
what she might, her " opinion " (as she afterwards owned) " had
scarcely varied."   Conscientious as always, she pondered further.
She must be careful to distinguish between opinion and judgment.
" I had become familiarized with these horrible ideas before I
was sufficiently convinced of their foundation to act upon them
without injustice.   This may serve to account for my toleration."

And now she had left that scene for her first married home.
She resolved to forget the hours when she had been so miserable
at night that

> I could not go to my restless bed till near the time of his
> leaving A, and I trembled as I heard his terrible step.   He swore
> at Fletcher as he was undressing with a degree of rage that
> seemed to threaten his life, and every night he came to my room
> in the same mood, except once or twice, when I heard the
> freezing sound of heartless professions—more intolerable than
> his uncontrolled abhorrence.

Their own home.   It could not be worse ; it might be better.
And in her heart there was another hope, if hope she could dare
to think it.   But since he wanted an heir, since that was the
avowed reason for his marrying. . . .   " I mean to live, like a worm
of the earth, to propagate my kind, and then I shall put an end
to my existence."   Only his way of talking—had he not told her
" not to mind my words, and then we may get along very well " ?
Suppose it were a daughter—how tenderly he had looked at
Medora ; and as for what he had said about the child being his,
those were some of the words she was not to mind.   Even a
daughter might please him. . . .

They drove on to London.

CHAPTER XIII

1815-16
LONDON : BIRTH OF ADA

THEIR destination was No. 13 Piccadilly Terrace, facing south over the Green Park.[1] The house belonged to the widowed Duchess of Devonshire, who was living in France ; Hobhouse had taken it for them at a rental of £700 a year.

Thirteen—and Byron was immensely superstitious. Already at Halnaby there had been omens. Annabella had tied on her wedding-ring with a bit of black ribbon ; his horrified exclamation had made her undo the ribbon, whereupon the ring fell into the fireplace, and he was horrified again. The ring was itself unpropitious ; it had been his mother's for her wedding to Captain Jack Byron—a union which took place on the Thirteenth of May, and was nearly as disastrous as that of her son. She had lost it many years before in the grounds of Newstead ; a gardener had found it and brought it to his master on the day that Annabella's letter of acceptance arrived. Byron had at once resolved " to be wedded with this very ring." Truly it seems that for these people, at any rate, it was foolhardy to defy augury.

He may have had forebodings when he accepted Number Thirteen ; what Annabella had were more like certainties. But she banished them with all her " self-compulsion," and again, as on the journey to Six Mile Bottom, she had her reward. " For

---

[1] It was one-half of " Old Q.'s " house which in his lifetime (he died in 1810) had been 138-9. The house was afterwards divided, and in 1889 this part was destroyed (Wheatley, *Old and New London*, v. iii : " Piccadilly "). Behind the site lies Hamilton Gardens, where there is a seated statue of Byron with his dog. It is on the plinth of this statue that the yearly tribute of a wreath of Gloire de Dijon roses is laid on April 19—his death-day—under the bequest of Mrs. Rose Mary Crawshay, " until the time that his name shall be inscribed in the Poets' Corner of Westminster Abbey."

ten days he was kinder than I had ever seen him." They arrived
on March 31—a Friday, Byron's most dreaded day ; on April 7
Augusta was to come to them. That seems to reduce the
ten days to a week, for this prologue to her visit can hardly be
reckoned among kindnesses : " You are a fool for letting her
come to the house, and you'll find it will make a great difference
to *you* in all ways."

Nothing very novel ; but ten days of kindness may have made
it freshly distressing. Not that the wife had not reckoned with
the Newmarket scenes when she sent her invitation. She
afterwards summed up her ponderings :

> It was hopeless to keep them apart—it was not hopeless, in
> my opinion, to keep them innocent. I felt myself the guardian
> of these two beings, *indeed* " on the brink of a precipice ; " and
> in this I sought to forget my own miserable and most humiliat-
> ing condition.

He met Augusta " with lowering looks of disgust and hatred " ;
then changed, and the Six Mile Bottom amenities began again
for wife and sister. No need to dwell upon them ; more
interesting is Annabella's confession, years afterwards, to
Robertson.

> I must not (having so far spoken of myself as to imply that
> I preserved, generally, self-possession and forbearance) omit to
> state that my feelings were once—in London—so worked up
> by the continual excitement of horrible ideas . . . that in a
> moment when one of them became to my imagination *a fact*—
> I turned round to use a deadly weapon lying by—not against
> him, but against one whose treachery seemed at that instant
> revealed. . . . There are moments of one's past life before
> which one stands in awe.

Elsewhere she wrote : " There were moments when I could
have plunged a dagger in her heart, but she never saw them. . . .
I resisted suspicion to the utmost. . . . I was almost mad—and
to prevent myself indulging the passion of revenge, I was obliged
to substitute another—that of romantic forgiveness."

Little more than a year afterwards, wife and sister were writing
to one another as explicitly as the written word permitted of
Augusta's visits to Piccadilly before the birth of Ada.

Augusta wrote in July, 1816 :

" Had I even entertained the slightest suspicions of any
' *doubts* ' of yours—I never could or would have entered your
house—perhaps I did wrong as it was to do so, but I was under
delusion. . . . I *endeavoured* to do right. . . . Dearest A. *I have
not wronged you, I have not abused your generosity . . . intentionally* I have never injured you."

Annabella answered :

You will now remember some things by which I intimated
that I knew more than you thought, and I almost offered
myself to your confidence. . . . As you do not, and never have
attempted to, deceive me about *previous facts*—of which my
conviction is unalterable—I rely more on your simple assertion
of " never wronged me " intentionally—*I believe it implicitly.*
. . . Dearest Augusta, you will think, perhaps justly, that I
erred in encouraging you myself—but my situation was most
extraordinary. I could not till a late period bear to admit
things to myself . . . and you were to me the kindest friend and
comforter. . . . Let the past be *understood* now, to be buried
in future.

Augusta's reply was long and incoherent.

Many a time I should have felt it a consolation to have
confided unreservedly in you—but concealment appeared a
duty under the circumstances, and you know I am of a sanguine
disposition, and to the very last had hopes of better for you—
and him. . . . I always replied to arguments, " *If you knew all,
you would think differently.*"

" It is my unalterable belief that she never meant to do me
harm." So Annabella summed up, in 1817.

Nevertheless, this first visit was brought to an end by Lady
Byron's expressed wish. It was a time of other anxieties and
sorrow for her. Very soon after the instalment at Piccadilly,
Lord Wentworth fell mortally ill. She left No. 13 for Kirkby
Mallory, to be with him until her mother could arrive from
Seaham. She was there three nights, and afterwards wrote : " I
felt that death-bed a relief from the horrors of an incestuous

household." Lady Milbanke arrived in London on April 13 or 14 ; Byron immediately wrote to his wife :

> Dearest—Now your mother is come I won't have you worried any longer—more particularly in your present situation which is rendered very precarious by what you have already gone through.
>
> Pray, come home.

She went home ; her uncle died on the 17th. She was still fighting against her convictions (Augusta was " always so devotedly kind to me "), but the situation as treated by Byron was beyond her endurance. She bore it until the end of June, more than two months ; then she spoke resolutely though not explicitly, and Augusta left at once—but not before, incensed by Byron's cruelty to his wife, she had herself threatened him with departure.

Byron's letter of recall had relit the hopes which were almost extinguished. Whether he was softened by the prospect of an immediate legacy from Lord Wentworth, or whether Augusta's absence mitigated his remorse with its moods of savagery, there was now some ordinary ease and cheerfulness between the pair. Annabella wrote of this period afterwards :

> When he would converse familiarly . . . there was a sort of conventional language of nonsense between us, relieving his fears of *sermons* and *sentiments*. He would give play to his imagination, and suddenly deliver the deepest reflections, then shrink from them into frolic and levity. The transitions had all the grace of genius, and formed its greatest charm to me. They were as the foam that might float on the waters of bitterness."

She quotes a couplet of his, which has not before seen the light. A Mr. Weekes had made an offer for Newstead ; it seemed hopeful for a time, and Byron wrote :

> 'Twere strange indeed could I expect
>   From Fortune in her freaks,
> What *months* and *years* could not effect
>   Should now be done by *Weeks* !

That, and their equally feeble witticisms on the names of various public men, were reported to Sir Ralph. Annabella wrote in her old vein of fond impertinence, finishing often with the pretty phrase of " Loves and Graces " which was her special property in endings. " Yours most confectionately " was another, when food was the topic—as it often was. In her capricious state of health she would take violent fancies for certain things to eat, such as the goose-pie of which we have read on an earlier page. " A favourite dish of B.'s—*I* may devour it all at one meal, for I am afflicted with a raging appetite and rapid power of digestion." But when the goose-pie arrived, it was " highly approved and gratefully acknowledged by B.'s voracious stomach." So, despite his whim of hating to see a woman eat, they evidently did dine together sometimes, and she tells of her serving a turbot so badly one evening that " I was told I performed with paternal skill." For the most part, though, her meals after Augusta's departure were solitary. " No greengages or fruit-pies," she wrote ; " my abstinence could not be greater if I lived at the Pulteney Hotel.[1] . . . *Tout va bien*, except the pocket, which is in a confirmed atrophy."

Lord Wentworth had left no legacy to his niece. The Kirkby Mallory estate and £7000 a year went to Lady Milbanke—who was to resume her maiden-name of Noel—for her life ; only on her death would Lady Byron be enriched. This made no difference to Byron's creditors. They instantly came down on him ; duns and threatened executions were soon added to Annabella's experience of married life. The parents (Sir Ralph too assumed the Noel name) could not give any help, for Sir Ralph had long been in great difficulties, and Kirkby Mallory " ate itself up," as Lady Noel —taking the estate in hand with all her energy—soon discovered. So the Noels were nearly as hard put to it as the Byrons were ; Sir Ralph was at this time let in, by a man for whom he was surety, to the tune of £1500 ; the Durham Bank failed ; there was " no money anywhere." Annabella consulted lawyers and friends about raising mortgages for her father and her husband ; but the settlements proved " an insuperable bar."

She could face all this with cheerfulness and energy, once her household ceased to be incestuous. In the matter of health her pregnancy was little trouble to her ; Dad and Mam got anecdotes

[1] This was at 105 Piccadilly, and was of the highest fashion. The Emperor of Russia had stayed there in 1814.

about her bigness and its inconveniences—how she had been caught between two posts in Hyde Park and extricated herself with difficulty, how writing gave her the fidgets because she had not yet had the table " cut like a shaving-dish." Though her mourning kept them in some seclusion, they did go out now and then, and received visitors. On June 20 Sir James Bland Burges, Lady Noel's brother-in-law, called with the news of Waterloo, and came in for the sensation of Byron's famous cry : " Well, I'm damned sorry for it ! " [1]   The same day young George Ticknor, the enquiring American diarist, paid the first of several calls. He wrote of Annabella that she was pretty, not beautiful —for " the prevalent expression of her countenance was that of ingenuousness " ; and when three days later he saw her alone :

> She did not seem so pretty to me as she did the other day, but what she may have lost in regular beauty she made up in variety and expression of countenance. She is diffident—she is very young . . . but is obviously possessed of talent, and did not talk at all for display. For the quarter of an hour during which I was with her, she talked upon a considerable variety of subjects—America, of which she seemed to know considerable, of France, and Greece, with something of her husband's visit there—and spoke of all with a justness and a light good-humour that would have struck me even in one of whom I had heard nothing.

Then he saw her with Mrs. Siddons and contrasted the masculine power of the older woman with Lady Byron, " all grace and delicacy " ; next night, sitting with her husband and parents in Byron's box at Drury Lane, he thought her more interesting than he had yet seen her.

Among her wedding-visits was one to Caroline Lamb. She went with her mother, and found Mrs. Musters there. " She asked after B. Such a wicked-looking cat I never saw. Somebody else looked quite virtuous beside her." So she wrote, in a style very unlike her, to Augusta of all people— a curious instance of retrospective jealousy expressing itself to a much more formidable rival. But she had to express it

---

[1] This attitude towards Napoleon was a Whig convention ; the Whigs used to toast him at dinner-parties. But Byron was still more ardent. He loved to point out—when he took the Noel name in 1822—that he and Napoleon signed with the same initials : N.B.

to somebody. To pay a visit to one forerunner in her husband's affections, and come upon yet another—it was an exasperating ordeal for the bride who knew herself unloved ; and Guss was always so kind, there was something about Guss which disarmed her ! What it was she never to the end understood.

Her feeling for Augusta was more than sincere ; it was, like that which she had felt for other women in her girlhood, impassioned : " These—passions, I must call them." Throughout her life Annabella was strongly attracted by other women ; she was much more of a woman's woman than a man's. To none, however, was the attraction so strong as to Augusta. Jealousy was present —it can never really have died ; but so was the paradox of retrospective jealousy which lends a peculiar glamour to the one who came first. Explicable enough by longing for all that may be learnt of a past in which the successor has had no share, that element here was powerful indeed. The circumstance which made the liaison most horrible to imagination was precisely the circumstance which worked most irresistibly upon it. How much Augusta knew of him—she who had alone befriended his unhappy adolescence, the origin (in Annabella's ponderings) of all that had since gone wrong ! So, amid bewilderments, sudden fierce resentments, the girl who still was fighting her more than suspicion found herself turning to the sister, protected by the sister ; and under all was the hope that, whatever might have been, here was the one who understood him and would impart her understanding. " Augusta, will you be my *only* friend ? "

They who in 1869 sought to disprove Augusta's charm were surely insincere. Charm she must have had, no matter how susceptible Annabella to the attraction of her fellow-women. The childishness, effusiveness, incoherence, levity of Byron's sister had their counterparts in him with his " child-side," those transitions of mood which had " all the grace of genius." With genius added they made, not indeed for happiness but for in-fatuation ; and infatuation, despite the issue, was what ruled Annabella Byron in her relations to both. Act as she might, her heart was irrevocably theirs till their deaths, and afterwards.

At the end of August Byron went to Six Mile Bottom for a short visit, after having been " perfectly ferocious " to his wife for four days. " As he was starting, he asked my forgiveness, half-earnestly, half-jestingly—but a kind word from him was then too precious to be rigorously examined."

She had been very much alone with him ; her parents were at Kirkby, most of her friends out of town. " No human being to take care of me, except Mrs. Clermont, and she was not in the house." Yet as with relief we read the letters exchanged during his absence, it is once more evident that they had their better moments. Normal husbands and wives write no more affectionately than they did. Here is Byron's first note, from Epping on the way :

> Dearest Pip—The learned Fletcher with his wonted accuracy having forgotten something, I must beg you to forward it. On my dressing table are *two phials labelled " drops,"* containing certain liquids of I know not what pharmacopoly—(*but white and clear, so you can't mistake, I hope*). *One* of these I want in my materia medica. Pray send it carefully packed to me at Goose's per coach on receiving this—and believe me
> ever most lovingly thine
> B.
> (not *Frac.*)

" Not *frac* " we may take to be a further apology for the four days. She had already written :

> Darling Duck—I feel as if B. loved *himself*, which does me more good than anything else, and makes young Pip jump.
>
> You would laugh to see, and still more to hear, the effects of your absence in the house. Tearing up carpets, deluging staircases, knocking, rubbing, brushing !—by all these I was early awakened, for Mrs. Mew seems convinced that my ears and other senses have departed with you. She no longer flies like a sylph on tiptoe, but like a troop of dragoons at full gallop. The old proverb—" When the Cat's away, the Mice will play." *They* shall have their holiday, but I can't fancy it mine. Indeed, indeed, *nau* B. is a thousand times better than *no* B.
>
> I dare not write any more for fear you should be frightened at the length, and not read at all ; so I shall give the rest to Goose.

I hope you call out " Pip, pip, pip," now and then—I think
I hear you ; but I won't grow lemoncholy. . . .   A-da.
(*Thursday*) *Aug.* 31.

I have just got post—with dear good B's mandate, which
shall be obeyed, and *I* am rather obliged to Fletcher for his
forgetfulness.

Sir J. Burges returned.

Byron replied :

Dearest Pip—I am very glad that Sir James has at last found
his way back.   He may now transfer his attention from his son's
leg to your mother's *leg*acy—which seemed in some peril of
amputation also in his absence.

Goose left a mousetrap in the apartment allotted to me, the
consequence of which is that from the very convenient place of
its application I have nearly lost a toe. . . .   All the children
here look shockingly—quite green—& Goose being as red as
ever, you have no idea what a piece of patchwork might be made
of the family faces.

Has Hanson marched for N ?   Goose is taking a quill from
her wing to scribble to you—so—yrs. always most conjugally
B.

A-da—

The " A-da " here and in her note, if it was not an allusion to
the name chosen for a daughter, must have been one of the
nonsense-words of which Annabella speaks in the passage quoted.

These letters should have made his absence a bright interlude
for her, despite the activities of Mrs. Mew—or Mule ; for this is
clearly Byron's " gaunt and witch-like " housemaid at Bennet
Street and the Albany, of whom Moore writes.   She had been
the aversion of his visitors, and they all rejoiced in the thought
that she would be left behind when he moved into Piccadilly.
But she was not ; and when Byron was asked why he carried her
about with him, " his only answer was : ' The poor old devil was
so kind to me.' "

He returned from Six Mile Bottom in a few days, " most kind
to me, but offended with Augusta "—who told Annabella that he
had been very disconsolate without her.   The wife was, as she
wrote to her father, " marvellous happy at the expiration of my
widowhood."   Augusta had offended him by taking the part of
Annabella's parents against his abuse of them.   But his kindness

was transient ; in four days he was " frac " again, speaking
vindictively of Guss and declaring that he would break both
their hearts.

Meanwhile the parents were doing everything they could to
raise money. These anxieties were as yet all they knew about
their daughter's trials. That seems to imply some denseness on
the mother's part, at any rate. But there were so many
anxieties ; money scarce, Kirkby mismanaged . . . better not
enquire too closely into anything else that might prove disturbing.
On one matter, though, Annabella did confess to uneasiness.
Two days after Byron's return she wrote to Sir Ralph :

> Drury Lane opens on Saturday—I don't much like the
> concern, and I believe it is the general sentiment, as far as
> regards B's share of it. Lady Hardwicke told me it was only
> fit for *a six and eight penny man*—and it seems to involve a
> species of business & attendance which I did not at all foresee.
> In short, it is the vocation of an *Acting* Manager—to superintend
> the candle-snuffers, lecture the performers, &c &c. It is no easy
> matter to get rid of it now, but I think it will produce unpleasant
> consequences, in opinion at least. It is one reason for which I
> think it would be advantageous to leave Town. Of that I know
> nothing. The more one sees of this world, the more difficult it
> must appear to judge what is really best, when there are in
> everything such *pros* and *cons* as Reason can hardly balance.
> A short time must settle our plans.

She was right in her forebodings. The Drury Lane management,
one of the great subjects of scandal later on, was at the time
a source of continual wretchedness, and even danger to her
health. Byron used his position to wound and insult her, adding
to his boastings of the many mistresses he had there the still
bitterer affront of declaring them to be " as much to vex Augusta
as you "—for Augusta returned to Piccadilly in November.

Between August and October things grew steadily worse. For
days he would not speak to his wife. The well-known anecdote
of her asking, on entering his study : " Am I in your way ? " and
his replying " Damnably," was only one of many such sayings ;
yet we find this from Annabella to her mother in September :

> I wish I could see the practicability of our going to Kirkby—
> but I do not. The moment B. were to leave town, for a per-

manency, some measures that are now suspended would immediately ensue. He is in great anxiety about me and would have me go by myself—which I *will not*. As long as I am with him I am comparatively comfortable, and the anxiety of absence under such circumstances would far overbalance any little good that a change of air might do. In short, it is my *summum malum* at present—and of these things I think no one can judge for another.

The suspended measures were threatened executions in the house. Later in the year she wrote that she should very much lament the seizure of the books ; otherwise, for herself she did not greatly care, " but I care very much to see him *in agony*." He was in agony about other things besides these, for she gives an extraordinary account of his sleepless nights, haunted again by the Halnaby fears of some dire vengeance.

Once between 3 and 4 a.m. he fancied a step on the stairs, and lay afraid to stir, suffering so much that I said I would get up and see. He let me, though I was within three or four months of my confinement—but I am convinced it was because he thought *himself* the only one against whom harm was intended. Had I thought of other danger, I believe I should have rejoiced to die for him for whom I despaired to live. I reassured him on my return, and he ceased to persecute me that night.

Now and again he spoke to her with the " sterile pity " she had learnt to know at Halnaby. " Well, poor thing, you are easily pleased, to be sure "—when she was glad in the scarce hours he bestowed on her ; " I believe you feel towards me as a mother to her child, happy when it is out of mischief " ; " If any woman could have rendered marriage endurable to me, you would " ; " I believe you will go on loving me till I beat you." (To this she afterwards added : " Why did he not ? "—but erased the words.)   " If I had known you since I was five years old, I might have been happy."   Such kind moments she could never forget : " I dwell on them even now too fondly."   One day she said with a smile (" prophetic only of future tears ") that she believed he would love her yet.   He replied with the old reproach : " It is too late now.   If you had taken me two years ago. . . . But it is my destiny to ruin all I come near."

The hopes built upon her coming motherhood were shaken

when he announced that so soon as she was delivered he meant
to go abroad ; " because a woman always loves her child better
than her husband." She might have rejoiced at his seeming to
set value on her love, but the speech had been well-designed to
take with one hand what it gave with the other ; and, " I
answered with agony : ' You will make me hate my child if you
say so ! ' "

The maternal instinct was not, in Annabella, of the primal
kind to which infancy makes strong appeal. In childhood,
as we have seen, she had never cared for a doll ; now it was
chiefly for Byron's sake, and in the hope of reconciling him,
that she had looked forward to maternity. He need not have
been afraid of this woman's loving her child better than her
husband—not only because she loved him so intensely, but because the protective impulse in her was always awakened by the
maturer being. Not an anecdote of her childhood and girlhood
but reveals this trait—Sophy Curzon's, Harriet Bland's love-
stories ; the early verses on Dermody ; the deep attachment to
M.M. and M.G. (both ill-fated); and, for the cardinal proof, Byron
and Augusta—with, long afterwards, the daughter of that incest.

A letter from her mother in September must have made coming
events feel very actual.

As it seems finally settled that you are to be confined in Town,
I very *highly approve* of your engaging Mr. le Mann, in preference
to any of the fashionable Accoucheurs as really it is not a business of *fashion* but of *Nature,* and I believe le Mann very
clever. . . . Indeed, my dear, it is rare that any difficulty
occurs, and I have no doubt but that you will get thro' without
more than the necessary sufferings ; at your age *they* are seldom
very severe, and especially to those who, like you, have been
in the habit of using exercise from your Child-hood and not led
a sedentary life ; and I trust and believe that the first cry of a
fine Child will cause you to forget them, as the Sweet Sound of
yours did me, tho' from my Age (40) I suffered long and much.
I well remember the *surprise* excited by my chusing to stay in
the Country and have Bainbridge, instead of going to London
and having *Denman* or some other *fine* man ; but I have heard
Stories of them all, which then *did* and still convinces me, they
are not more skilful than others, and not *half so attentive.* Croft,

the fashionable Man for a long time, people continued to place confidence in, even after he became *deranged* ; I believe he is *now insane*, at least he has been quite so—but independent of his professional Character, he was a very *vile Man*, and owed his celebrity to attending the Duchess of Devonshire, and keeping her *Secrets*. A great man of the present day is indebted for his introduction to the fashionable World from attending *Moll Raffle* abroad, for which the Marquis of Wellesley gave him an immense sum and his Patronage. But at all Events, *you* are the only Person who ought to decide on this business, and where *you place confidence* will be the only proper choice. . . . Pray let little *Pip* have handsome Apparel, as well as *Mamma*, and order Bonter to send the *Bill to me*, as I shall have pleasure in decorating the little Byron.

She was still dining out ; and sent Sir Ralph an account of a " banquet " at Holland House :

—which amused me for as long a time as I can possibly *laugh* at the Varnish of Vice. Lady H., I am told, wears a sort of *aimabilité* in my presence, which is as little consistent with her general habits as with her Nature. She evidently does not know what to make of me, and handles me as fearfully as if I were a Hedgehog. . . . The Manager is as flourishing as the Magpie [1] whereof Renown is rife—only we have been having a conjugal dissertation or disputation on the merits of *Punch*, at which I don't want you to be an Assistant, as I am sure you would be my Adversary either theoretically or practically.

How carefully she hid her sorrow from her parents could not be better proved than by this gay allusion to punch, contrasted with some verses written that September on Byron's return from a " Kinnaird dinner." She sent them a year afterwards to a friend :

> She listens yet to hear his voice—
>   Is that his coming tread
> Which used to make her heart rejoice ?
>   Such power, alas ! is fled.
>
> But still her cheek will flush and fade,
>   For still those sounds are dear ;
> And all she feels is still betrayed
>   When bursts the silent tear.

[1] This was a melodrama produced at Drury Lane on September 12 1815.

Too soon that withered heart of Love
　　Must wear one lifeless hue—
The winter of Despair above
　　Shall weep no drop of dew !

But again we get the other aspect in a letter to her mother :

... The Parrot made another attack upon my toe, but without either injuring or alarming me.   However, when I mentioned the circumstance to B., thinking it would amuse him, he left the room—and informed me when he came back that he had thrown Parrot and Cage out of the window down the Airy (I don't know how to spell it), and I feared I had been too well revenged.   But the Bird came down quite safe and did not lay (*sic*) in a trance like Satan, but called out " Johnny ! " B's idea was that he should have a winged child.   He is vastly entertained with the thought of making you a Grandmamma. Indeed it is the only prospect that cheers him, amidst the very distressing circumstance to which we must look forward. . . . It seems a labyrinth of difficulties.   I wish that *such* distresses were as comparatively unimportant to others as to me.
I am very well to-day—delighting in the frosty air.

October 7.—Don't mind the Blue Devil sentence.   Every thing that I care most about is well.

To look into her heart, as we are now enabled to do, may truly be said to keep sympathies on the jump ; for in these days she was reading Leigh Hunt's *Rimini*, and copied a passage of twenty lines on the character of Giovanni—evidently because it was to her as a portrait of another difficult husband :

" He kept no reckoning with his sweets and sours ;
　He'd hold a sullen countenance for hours,
　And then, if pleased to cheer himself a space,
　Look for immediate rapture in your face. . . .
　And all the joy he took in her sweet ways,
　The pride he felt when she excited praise—
　In short, the enjoyment of his own good pleasure
　Was thanks enough, and passion beyond measure."

A letter to her father on the same day that saw *Rimini* copied :

What a dinner yesterday !   The recollection almost prevented me eating a better one at home to-day.   There was Salmon which had every appearance of having been kept *since* it was *in*

Season—for it is now *out*. Raw Rabbits-Wool of Mutton, Eggs as addled as Sir James's head. All these miseries were to me trifling in comparison with the quartette of Miss Bs, relieved only by Lady Anne Barnard & Major Something (a nephew of Sir James's) who had been in Canada, and walked across the room in some wonderful snow-shoes. The Misses were determined to talk, and poetically too, either in honour of Papa or their Guest; and B. was attacked by ecstasies about " autumnal tints " in Scotland, which he cruelly answered by raptures about whiskey. In short, they *yelped* and he *snapped*.

But with that letter we bid farewell to cheerfulness. The next is to Augusta, only a week later; and once more we see how her parents were kept in the dark about everything but money-troubles.

My head is better; and I wish to make a few observations respecting the nature of my greatest fears for B.—and I think I daily understand the case better. His misfortune is an habitual *passion for Excitement*, which is always found in ardent temperaments, where the pursuits are not in some degree organised. It is the Ennui of a monotonous existence that drives the best-hearted people of this description to the most dangerous paths, and makes them often seem to act from bad motives, when in fact they are only flying from internal suffering by any external stimulus. The love of tormenting arises chiefly from this Source. Drinking, Gaming &c are all of the same origin. How far it may depend on body or mind it is difficult to ascertain. I am inclined to think that a vitiated stomach, particularly if arising from habits of excess, is a chief cause of the sensation of Ennui; and that change of Scene, air, & exercise are more efficient to its removal than any efforts of Reason. As for seeking a cure in worldly dissipation, it is adding to the evil. I know in what it must end if it encreases; and with such apprehensions, will you wonder if I am sometimes almost heart-broken before my time? My dear, dear A., do give me every opinion of yours on this, & don't mistrust your own judgment. I will not blindly adopt it. Such were my waking reflections last night.

Next day, to the same:

Everything is explained by a Bailiff sleeping last night in the house. From the old quarter . . . God knows what I suffered yesterday, & am suffering from B's distraction, which is of the *very worst* kind. He leaves the house, telling me he will at once abandon himself to every sort of desperation, speaks to me only to upbraid me with having married him when he wished not, and says he is therefore acquitted of all principle towards me, and I must consider myself *only* to be answerable for the vicious courses to which his despair will drive him. The going out of the house & the drinking are the most fatal. He was really quite frantic yesterday—said he did not care for any consequences to me, and it seemed impossible to tell if his feelings towards you or me were the most completely reversed ; for as I have told you, he loves or hates us together. . . . Things never were so serious—I don't mean the circumstances, for they must mend, but his feelings.

You shall hear again to-morrow, but I hope for no better. Don't be unhappy about *me*—and perhaps you will see less cause than I do to be so about *him*.

P.S.—I have waited till the last in hopes of some change, but all is inexorable pride and hardness. O Augusta, will it ever change for me ? I scarcely know what I say. Tho' I have been making the best of things till yesterday, when self-deception became impossible—I have thought that since last Saturday (on which he sat drinking with Kinnaird's party till ½ past four in the morning), his *head* has never been right—and he will add, I fear, more and more to the cause.

Next day :

B. relented last night, for he returned earlier from the play, and I took the opportunity of attacking him, which I had scarcely had before, as he had never been in my company throughout the day for much more than an hour. He was kind to me again, but still rather odd. However, I am very thankful after my fit of despair, imparted to you—cruelly, I fear. He does not think I know the circumstance of our unwelcome guest. I wish George B. or some man friend of common-sense were in the way to laugh B. out of his excessive horrors on this subject, which he seems to regard as if no mortal had ever experienced anything so shocking ; and *we* can do less, because he thinks that women don't enter into those sublime grievances. They are quite the subject of his *romance* at present.

After post

I must tell you that you are " Augusta " again to B.—for you were " Mrs. Leigh " during the paroxysm, & I expected you would soon be " The Honorable." I ought to have laughed at this ; but I took it as another misery, fancying that *I* was in some way the cause of such an alteration.   And now for my peace and comfort, dearest A., let me express my earnest desire that whatever you may see or hear towards me, you will never think it an act of friendship for me to risk B's displeasure.   I suspect you of any *disinterested folly* of this kind.   But in the first place, under any circumstances, I should be more *grieved* if he & you were to differ ; and in the second (which may have more weight with you) I don't think it could do *me* any good to have *my part taken*.   So remember.

I am afraid *this* bailiff is a sad brute, & will proceed to very great inconvenience.   I have written to my Mother on the sub-fect, who if she can, will certainly send me some money—but my father has been as nearly in Gaol as possible.

Again—and finally ; for Augusta came to No. 13 four days afterwards :

Don't be afraid for my carcase—it will do very well.   Of the rest I scarcely know what to think—I have many fears.

Let me see you the middle of next week—at latest.

Hobhouse is come—I have great reason to think to arrange a plan for going abroad.   My heart aches—it has been severely tried—but I won't say more on paper—

You will do good, I think—if any can be done—

My dearest A.—I feel all your kindness—

Lady Noel also was to be in London for the confinement. Annabella wrote of the arrangements to Sir Ralph : " I suppose my Mam will choose to come and fidget while I squall. . . . I daresay we shall all be very agreeable."   Was there a gleam of irony about her lips as she wrote the concluding words ?   There must certainly have been some fear in her heart—could the truth now escape Mam's sharp eyes ?

Augusta arrived on November 15.   For a time Byron was chilling to her ; then (as on her first visit) he resumed the old insults to both, varied by the boastings which were " as much to vex Augusta as you."   The sister's dilemma was observed by the wife with curiously indulgent detachment.   " She dared not avoid opportunities of a dangerous nature, lest the cause should be surmised.   She may appear to have courted them. . . . I was wretched, but I thought her more so."   One evening Augusta came very near confession. " Her remorse almost overpowered her. She said : ' Ah, you don't know *what* a fool I have been about him.' The bitterness of her look as she threw her hair back from her forehead with trembling hand wrung my heart. I kissed that forehead, and left the room."

Both women took refuge in the thought that his mind was temporarily deranged—little wonder, when we read of his locking a door against the wife because, as he said, he was about to renew incestuous intercourse with the sister. The servants were so alarmed for their mistress's personal safety that Fletcher, and the nurse now installed for the confinement, used without orders to take steps for her protection every night. Mrs. Clermont too was—at Byron's own suggestion—staying in the house, her room being next to Annabella's ; and she and Augusta anxiously guarded the wife.

> This I knew at the time, for there could be no concealment, on account of the overtly menacing words and acts. However, my *new* duty imposed all possible self-control, and life had then lost some of its value to me—not that I wished to die. Nothing was done, however, to interfere with him ostensibly, and I saw him alone.

Here are some of his words on the occasions when she saw him. Three hours before her labour began, he told her that he hoped she would perish in it, that the child would not live ; and that if it did, he cursed it. She had already contemplated leaving the house, but had decided to postpone the decision till her baby was born. " I might die, and be spared having to make it." During the separation-proceedings, she drew up a paper of questions to be put to Augusta and George Byron—whom Augusta, in her fears for Annabella's safety, had implored to come and stay in the house. Among these questions was one referring to the speech quoted above : " Did he not say this, amid expressions of abhorrence ? . . . Did not Augusta sit up late with him every night during the confinement, avowedly to prevent an act of outrage towards me ? Was it not felt by them all that, after the child was born, I was not safe for a moment alone with him ? "

A daughter was born on Sunday, December 10—amid the flinging about of furniture and soda-water bottles in the room

immediately below, by the expectant father. This might be
looked upon as Byron's way of relieving the agitation of normal
husbands, were it not for some incidents immediately after his
wife's delivery. He sent her a message to say that Lady Noel,
who was dangerously ill at Mivart's Hotel, had died—an event
to which in the earlier hours of labour he had said that he was
eagerly looking forward. Then he was summoned to the mother's
room. He entered saying : " The child *was* born dead, wasn't
it ? "

Annabella told this to Lady Anne Barnard ; Byron denied it
to his friends, saying : " *She* will not say so, though God knows,
poor thing ! it seems now she would say anything ; but no—
she would not say that."

She did say it ; but even on her testimony it is difficult to
believe.

On December 20, while Annabella was still confined to her
room, the baptismal registration—not the christening [1]—took
place.

The names given were Augusta Ada ; for some time the baby
was called Augusta Junior.

On a day in this December Byron said, while they were looking
for a family likeness in the child : " I wonder where it was
begotten. If it was at Newmarket, no wonder if it should be like
Augusta."

[1] When in November 1816 (nearly a year afterwards) the christening was
celebrated, Lady Noel and Lady Tamworth (Sophy Curzon) were the
godmothers. Augusta was to have been one of them, but this was not
adhered to. She was not told of the change, but heard of it and wrote to
enquire, " apparently without receiving any answer." (*Astarte*, p. 67).

CHAPTER XIV

THE SEPARATION

ONE of Goethe's many remarks about Byron was that if he had invented the Separation-drama, he could scarcely have found a subject more appropriate to his genius.

It might almost be said that Byron did invent it. The first act, "Honeymoon," stated the elements—remorse, pseudo-insanity, cruelty, all working to a climax: *Make the wife run back to her father like the spoilt child she is.* The second act was mere development; for the third he had arranged a surprise. Now there was to have been no wish on the husband's part that the wife should run back. She was to be sent back, indeed; but the husband . . . he was to sob in the newspapers:

> " Fare thee well ! and if for ever,
>   Still for ever, *fare thee well* :
> Even though unforgiving, never
>   'Gainst thee shall my heart rebel.
>
> Would that breast were bared before thee
>   Where thy head so oft hath lain,
> While that placid sleep came o'er thee
>   Which thou ne'er canst know again." . . .

We have learnt something about that placid sleep at Halnaby, Six Mile Bottom, and Piccadilly. Never to know it again might scarcely have seemed a calamity; yet there were to be sobs at Kirkby Mallory too—sobs not included in the part of Unforgiving Wife. The Sister (whose part was so sympathetically conceived) was to remain in the deserted home, tending the deserted dramatist and reading, unknown to him, the piteous cries that came from Leicestershire : " Oh, that I were in London, if in the coal-hold ! " . . . " A little more crazy still " . . . " I am not fit to have the management of myself, not to be left alone." ... " I gallopped yesterday ... and felt something like good spirits while I was in danger of fracturing my sconce." ... " I dare not *feel* anything now." In this, at any rate, Annabella was like other women.

The Lovelace Papers take us behind the scenes, not only when Byron had rung up the curtain on his third act, but while he was still considering its composition. The central female figure saw little of the dramatist at this time ; *her* part was to be improvised by herself, as in the old Italian comedies.

She was, as she told her mother, " giving suck " while she wrote her letters. " Oh dear ! she pinches me. . . . I talk of it for your satisfaction, not my own, and shall be very glad when you have it under your eye." Her father heard that she was " bleached most beautifully. Dear me, how pretty I look in that glass ! " A little later the parents were warned that the Byron family might suddenly descend on them at Kirkby, and that Byron had spoken of Sir Ralph as the good old man, " at which you'll be affronted." Lady Melbourne wrote congratulations and was told of Augusta's kindness and attention, which Annabella " could never forget." Some intention there ; for she had been thoroughly enlightened about Whitehall's intimate knowledge of Byron's affairs. Pride or consideration for Augusta —who shall say which prompted the tribute ?

The answer to her aunt was written on January 4. Two days later there was brought to her ladyship's room a note from his lordship.

When you are disposed to leave London it would be convenient that a day should be fixed, & (if possible) not a very remote one for that purpose. Of my opinion on that subject you are sufficiently in possession ; & of the circumstances which have led to it, as also to my plans—or rather intentions, for the future. When in the country I will write to you more fully. As Lady Noel has asked you to Kirkby, there you can be for the present—unless you prefer Seaham.

As the dismissal of the present establishment is of importance to me, the sooner you can fix on the day the better ; though of course your convenience & inclination shall be first consulted.

The child will of course accompany you. There is a more easy and safer carriage than the chariot (unless you prefer it) which I mentioned before. On that you can do as you please.

The curtain was up on Act III.

Bailiffs were in the house, the dismissal of the establishment certainly was of importance ; yet it is not surprising that " her ladyship was much offended by this note." [1] The first to be sent away, she might have expected a word or two of kindness ; however, the dramatist next day received a note in *his* room.

I shall obey your wishes, and fix the earliest day that circumstances will admit for leaving London.

Not bad for an improvisation—as unforgiving as dramatist's heart could desire.

But this heroine and some other members of the cast were being Pirandellian in their independence of the author. They were doing all sorts of things that he had not included—consulting doctors and lawyers, drawing up statements, getting tutored in the playing of their parts. Wife, sister, and cousin-heir . . . could he have guessed it, the dramatist was in danger of being hissed when the play should be produced. So far, however, the third act had every appearance of proceeding as he had designed. January 15 was to be the day of departure for the Unforgiving Wife. She interpolated a farewell-interview—not arranged for, but he found that he could work it in. She could be received with a cold stare, followed by the words, ironically and mockingly delivered : " When shall we three meet again ? "—their new-born child the third. It would sound cruel ; but the hero, rent by remorse, *was* (in this part of the act) to sound cruel. And by God ! this Wife had a gift for impromptu. Could she have found a more excruciating reply than " In Heaven "—spoken with all the tranquillity that . . . that did not indeed belong to a spoilt child, but did to a heroine of melodrama. Now this should be the end—they should part on this. He would send her no message before she left the house next day ; would stay in his room, hearing the boxes brought down, her step on the stairs, and (rent by remorse) would not stir from his chair. Effective !

[1] Lord Broughton (Hobhouse), *Recollections of a Long Life*, ii. 215.

Had she paused an instant outside his door ? Poor thing—
but no ! Effective moments for her were not in the scheme.

> Yet, oh yet, thyself deceive not—
> Love may sink by slow decay,
> But by sudden wrench, believe not,
> Hearts can thus be torn away.
>
> Still thine own its life retaineth—
> Still must mine, tho' bleeding, beat ;
> And the undying thought which paineth
> Is—that we no more may meet.

Those lines were in his part, not hers. And now the hall-door
had clanged ; she was gone.

.   .   .   .

I fell into a sound sleep on the last night, as I believe is often
surprisingly the case in such cases of deep sorrow. Next
morning I woke exhausted. I went downstairs—the carriage
was at the door. I passed his room. There was a large mat on
which his Newfoundland dog used to lie. For a moment I was
tempted to throw myself on it, and wait at all hazards, but it
was only a moment—and I passed on. That was our parting.

Augusta remained at No. 13. Dr. Baillie (Joanna's brother),
consulted on the state of Byron's mind, had said that he ought
not to be left alone with any young woman. But when Captain
Byron came to stay in the house, these fears were removed ;
moreover, Augusta declared that she was afraid Byron would do
away with himself if left without a woman to look after him.
Annabella yielded, though she did not believe in any such
probability.

Another thing Dr. Baillie had said, in advising the wife's
absence " as an experiment," was that she must avoid all but
light and soothing topics in her correspondence with her husband.
In obedience to this counsel, she wrote the two letters long afterwards produced by Moore in his Life of Byron, to prove that she
had had no thought of a separation when she left London and had
been persuaded, if not coerced, into that step by her parents.
The first was written on the way, from Woburn.

THE KITCHEN-ENTRANCE AT KIRKBY MALLORY HALL

Dearest B.—The Child is quite well, and the best of Travellers. I hope you are *good*, and remember my medical prayers & injunctions. Don't give yourself up to the abominable trade of versifying—nor to brandy—nor to anything or anybody that is not *Lawful & right*.

Let me hear of *your* obedience at Kirkby—though *I* disobey in writing to you.

Ada's love to you with mine.

Pip.

Hobhouse took seriously the "abominable trade of versifying," and gave a wordy explanation of its probable origin—the effect of composition on Byron's health and spirits. This he did "in justice to her ladyship." It is one of the many instances of his denseness; for the phrase surely sounds (so Sir John Fox remarks in his *Byron Mystery*) as if Byron had used it about himself. . . . Next day, or the day after, from Kirkby Mallory:

Dearest Duck,—We got here quite well last night, and were ushered into the kitchen instead of the drawing-room, by a mistake that might have been agreeable enough to hungry people. Of this and other incidents Dad wants to write you a jocose account, & both he & Mam long to have the family party completed. Such . . . .! and such a *sitting*-room or *sulking*-room all to yourself. If I were not always looking about for B., I should be a great deal better already for country air. *Miss* finds her provisions increased, & fattens thereon. It is a good thing she can't understand all the flattery bestowed upon her, "Little Angel." Love to the good Goose, & everybody's love to you both from hence.

Ever thy most loving

PIPPIN . . . PIP . . . IP.[1]

She very soon realised her mistake : " I must have been mad to write the Kirkby letter." She also, however, defended it on the grounds that her own feeling naturally prompted the kindest expressions ; and that she could not bear the last words to do injustice to a heart which suffering had not detached. " When

---

[1] Her defence of these letters (which may be read in the Byron biographies) was, in effect, to quote Dr. Baillie's advice. Moore inserted it as an appendix to the second volume of his book ; and it was privately circulated by her. This was in 1830. Her sole purpose was to refute the " injurious charges " against her parents.

all is explained," she added in a letter (which was never sent) to an old friend, " they form the strongest proof of attachment. The distraction of my mind . . . was beyond all that I had ever imagined. There were moments when resignation yielded to frenzy."

Though in her letter to Byron she could so gaily hold forth the sanitary arrangements as an inducement to visit Kirkby, her aspect had shocked Sir Ralph and Lady Noel into distress which they did not conceal. She yielded at last—at last they learnt part of the truth. If Byron was to be considered sane, nothing on earth could make her return to him. . . . There was still the hope that he was not entirely sane, and in that hope they consented to invite him to Kirkby. But on the 18th Annabella heard that nothing like lunacy had been discovered by Dr. le Mann. There was great instability of temper, " but I think that may be easily overcome."

So the poor hope had vanished. There was nothing for it but separation. The parents' invitation was withheld from post, and Lady Noel went to London, taking with her a statement from Annabella to be shown to Sir Samuel Romilly.[1] Nothing was to be done without the wife's sanction.

" You cannot think how severe my father is, much more than my mother," she wrote to Augusta, with whom she was in daily correspondence. Her letters can be read elsewhere,[2] but must be touched on here. They show that the two had come very near an explanation during this last stay of Augusta's. " No, if all the world had told me you were doing me an injury, I *ought not* to have believed it. . . . I *have* wronged you, and you have never wronged me. . . . It makes me feel I have no *claim* to what you *give*." " It is my greatest comfort that you are in Piccadilly."

These, too, were long afterwards brought up against her ; and these in a more harmful sense. It was sought to show by them that " the most degraded of street-walkers in the Haymarket was a worthier character than Lady Byron "[3]—if she had known what

---

[1] He was distinguished for his humanity and liberality. In 1819, on his wife's death, he committed suicide by cutting his throat. Byron wrote of this with savage exultation.

[2] *Letters and Journals*, iii. 296-99.

[3] From an article in *Blackwood* (1869) by a barrister named Paget.

she had known, and written and acted as she did! She knew nothing at that time—it was all " wretched doubts " and strong impressions. (This also was to be part of the indictment against her ; they were determined to have it both ways.) True that Byron had always spoken to her of Augusta as his mistress ; true that he had avowed his intention to renew the intercourse if Augusta would permit—but by this time Annabella had taken the measure of his " *fanfaronnade des vices.*" What Byron said was not evidence. But there were Augusta's admissions " when in a state of despair and distraction " (over his cruel treatment of them both) " which were of the most unequivocal nature, unless she had expressly named the subject of her remorse and horror." Annabella sincerely believed that from the first night at Six Mile Bottom the sister had refused to renew that intercourse ; moreover Augusta had shown her such kindness and affection as she could never think of without emotion. And besides, " we had suffered together, and for each other." From Augusta, too, she could hear the sort of details about Byron's health and behaviour which Captain Byron would, manlike, never think of giving. In them there might be something to justify belief in his temporary madness—the one hope for their continued union. For unless he was deranged, his wife could but irritate him afresh. " *I certainly can do no good,*" she wrote, out of her anguished experience of his " abhorrence."

Soon she had again to realise, as Augusta did not or would not, that he was not deranged, that her resolution to leave him must be adhered to. " I never must see him again—I shall wish otherwise when I am less sane, but let me be preserved from it by every means." Of her mother in London Annabella wrote to Mrs. Clermont : " She will break my heart if she takes up the thing in *bitterness* against him." Judith Noel, as we know, was hot-headed and impulsive. Her daughter trembled as she thought of her. Nothing was to be done—but might not much be written, said, set in motion ? These fears were not concealed. Lady Noel answered affectionately—but carried the war into Annabella's camp.

My Dearest Child—It appears to me by your letters that the first thing to be attended to in the present instant is the state of *your own mind,* for I too plainly perceive that your agitation and unhappiness (which I do not wonder at) bring on apprehensions of evils which, bad as things are, *do not* or *ever can exist*. Let me entreat you therefore to endeavour to *calm* your mind, and not see *imaginary Bugbears*—when so many *real* ones exist. *Be sure of this*, that nothing worse can happen than what has taken place, and it is great comfort to me to find Sir Samuel, Heywood, and Doyle—all unanimous as to the *first step* to be taken, namely Sir Ralph writing to Lord B.—of which letter I am to form a Copy and then subject it to Sir Samuel's *correction*. Now as this letter can only be written when I get back, and is the first thing to be done, you perceive no *Measure* can be taken till we have met. . . . As to your fears that I should be cajoled by sweet words, I can only say " Old birds are not caught by chaff." . . . I assure you I am *very sane*, my brains are particularly clear. . . . This moment I have your letter—recollect that you will see me before anything is done. . . . Both G.B. and Augusta declare your life would not be safe with him. . . . I have heard of no soft words about you, therefore suppose none are used.

After this, Annabella gave her written consent to such measures as might be necessary for a separation. On the day she wrote, her mother had, by Romilly's advice, seen Dr. Lushington, D.C.L., " a civilian." Of him Lady Noel reported :

I would not but have seen Lushington for the world—he seems the most *gentlemanlike*, clear-headed and clever man I ever met with ; and agrees with all others that a proposal should be sent by your Father for a *quiet adjustment*. . . . But observe that he insists on Lord B's not being allowed to remain *an instant* at Kirkby should he go there, and he says *you* must not see him on any account—and that your father should remain in the room with you. If you see him voluntarily or he is suffered to remain, you are wholly in his power, and he may apply to the Spiritual Court for a restoration of *Conjugal Rights*, as they term it, & oblige you to return. Neither must you answer any letter he writes. He was surprised to find *I* had given this advice before I left Kirkby—he said it was the best possible.

A note of triumph there, for she knew how the two at home regarded her. " You all seem to have so little idea of my prudence that I get quite frightened. . . . I shall not *act* till I see you. I made that promise before I left Kirkby and you might have relied on it. I am half-angry that you do not. . . . Keep yourself as quiet and sane as you can. Miss Doyle, Clermont, and I set out on Saturday and shall be with you Sunday."

Meanwhile Augusta had been sending frequent bulletins from Piccadilly. This was one of them.

B. stayed at home yesterday evening—no brandy and took his medicines. He was well the beginning of the evening but towards the end grew *fractious*, and in reply to a question from George . . . of when he thought of going to Kirkby, he said, after a vacant stare : " I go there ? Not at all ! I've no thought of it if I can help it." From that moment he talked all sorts of strange things—fell on me as usual—abused my spouse, my children—in short all as you know, and have heard before.

He talked of you quite coolly and of his intention of going into a lodging by himself . . . in short, looked black and gloomy, nobody could tell why or wherefore, the rest of the night. One of the things he said was . . . that he considered himself " the greatest man existing." G. said laughing, " except Bonaparte." The answer was, " God, I don't know that I do except even him." I was struck previously with a wildness in his eye.

She was still clinging to the thought of temporary insanity. In her interviews with Lady Noel she stressed this note, but could not deny that he was perfectly competent to transact business—" indeed, particularly *acute*." Annabella impressed upon her mother that Augusta had been one of the truest of friends to her, and added :

" I hope you regard her, and *seem* to regard her, as such, for I very much fear that she may be supposed the cause of separation by many, and it would be a cruel injustice."

It was the first hint she had given of that complication.

On January 28, Lady Noel returned to Kirkby. Annabella wrote to Augusta of the arrival.

I as nearly fainted as possible when she first came, and looked paler than usual when I meant to look better. I don't know that my heart has done beating yet. Your letter yesterday has given me the feeling more like comfort than I have experienced for long. Your kindness must always be more to me than that of any other now. Of myself I can only say that I feel well enough to go through my present duties, and that is all I wish.

I am content. There are subjects I am more inclined to speak of than myself—but I have resolved not to do so unnecessarily, and alas ! I have nothing to suggest which can alleviate their pressure on you, my dearest Augusta. I am advised not to enclose.

A letter from Sir Ralph to Byron, proposing a separation, was now sent, but was intercepted and returned by Augusta, in the hope of delaying the final decision. This made Lady Noel very angry. She drafted two letters to Mrs. Leigh (whether either was sent remains uncertain), in the second of which she said :

Wonder not that I write *strongly*. Who could see that suffering angel sinking under such unmanly and despicable treatment, and not feel ? . . . Oh, my God, how was my poor child sacrificed—not only to a *wicked* but an *unmanly* creature !"

She wrote later to Mrs. Clermont telling her " what the Dowager Duchess of Leeds " (Augusta's aunt by her mother's first marriage) " said to Mrs. Leigh—that she *ought* to quit Lord B.'s house, and *so she ought*, but she is a fool, and perhaps her brother's having left *her* all he has to dispose of may make her shy of offending him." [1]

At this time her dislike of Lady Melbourne found vivid expression. Letters to Sir Ralph, when in his turn he went to London, spoke of her as " a very Devil ; " she even retailed one of Byron's grossest slanders about the woman whom nevertheless he sincerely loved and admired. It was a lie so evident that only Lady Noel could have believed it, but on the subject of her sister-in-law she was then beside herself. She had taken it into her head that Lady Melbourne had poisoned Byron's mind against Annabella, because the birth of this daughter had disinherited a favourite nephew. They are at once comic and pathetic—her frequent complaints that Sir Ralph will not answer her remarks about " the Viscountess."

I am rather inclined to believe you have *shrunk* from exposing *this wretch*. . . . The only unhappiness you have ever caused me has been seeing the sway she has at times had over you.

But Sir Ralph continued to lie low, even when he was urged to read *Liaisons Dangereuses* because " the Viscountess is exactly

---

[1] On July 29, 1815, Byron had signed a will entirely in Augusta's favour. This was known to Lady Byron at the time.

depicted in La Marquise." Perhaps it was this which brought on erysipelas in Lady Noel's head, and obliged her to wear a night-cap at dinner because she could not endure the pressure of her wig—the wig which Byron had snatched off during the second part of the honeymoon, at Seaham. The spice of comedy which life never fails to throw in, lay naturally in Judith Noel's part ; between Viscountess and erysipelas, vacillating daughter and pusillanimous husband, she abounded in her own sense. Though so newly installed in her new estates, with plenty to do and see after, and plenty of money-worries too, the difficulty of " keeping my mother quiet " is well shown in the diatribes against Lady Melbourne. There is nothing whatever to indicate that the aunt was secretly hostile to Annabella, and at this time Lady Noel knew nothing of the incest gossip.

Augusta's interception of Sir Ralph's letter availed her little. He now went up to London ; another letter, dated February 2, was delivered to Byron by hand. It informed him that Lady Byron's parents could not feel themselves justified in permitting her return to his house. He was called upon to appoint a professional friend to confer with one of Sir Ralph's on the terms of separation.

Byron at once told Augusta to write to his wife and ask if this had been done by her wish. The answer came without delay. " It has."

I will only recall to Lord Byron's mind his avowed and insurmountable aversion to the married state, and the desire and determination he has expressed ever since the commencement to free himself from that bondage, as finding it quite insupportable. . . . He has too painfully convinced me that all attempts to contribute to his happiness were wholly useless, and most unwelcome to him.

But Byron also wrote to her himself.

I have received a letter from your father proposing a separation between us, to which I cannot give an answer without being more acquainted with your own thoughts & wishes—& from *yourself*. To vague and general charges & exaggerated statements from others I can give no reply : it is to *you* that I look, & with *you* that I can communicate on this subject. When

I permit the interference of relatives, it will be as a courtesy to them—& not the admission of a right.

I feel naturally at a loss how to address you, ignorant as I am how far the letter I have received has received your sanction ; & in the circumstances into which this precipitation has forced me, whatever I might say would be liable to misconstruction. I am really ignorant to what part of Sir Ralph's letter alludes. Will you explain ?

To conclude—I shall eventually abide by your decision ; but I request you most earnestly to weigh well the probable consequences—& to pause before you pronounce.

Whatever may occur, it is but justice to you to say that you are exempt from all fault whatever, & that neither now nor at any time have I the slightest imputation of any description to charge upon you.

I cannot sign myself otherwise than
                                yours ever most affectionately . . .

Forbidden to answer him directly, she wrote to Augusta, begging her not to withhold the earlier letter. Augusta, however, did withhold it ; and Byron wrote again to Annabella, enclosing the letter to Mrs. Fletcher, his valet's wife. She was bidden to deliver it with her own hands.

Dearest Bell—No answer from you yet—perhaps it is as well —but do recollect that all is at stake—the present—the future & even the colouring of the past. The whole of my errors—or what harsher name you choose to give them—you know ; but I loved you, & will not part from you without your *own* most express & *expressed* refusal to return to or receive me. Only say the word—that you are still mine at heart—and " Kate !— I will buckler thee against a million."

The instruction to Mrs. Fletcher, implying that Byron did not regard his wife as a free agent, caused natural indignation and distress at Kirkby, best exhibited in Lady Noel's report to Sir Ralph.

I enclose a copy of a letter which has terribly agitated Annabella, tho' it has not *shaken her determination.* Her answer will go to Lushington for his approbation. *If he approves* he will send it—if not *suppress* it, and advise her how to answer. All these things are *terrible.*

Annabella thinks it was written from the mere impulse of a *moment's* tenderness and remorse—which has at *moments* been exemplified before, tho' never attended by following good conduct.

I confess that may partly be the case ; but at the same time, he is very anxious that his character should not be entirely blasted, and perhaps pecuniary motives may help to influence. ... If his revenge was so deep and bitter for the first refusal, what would it *now become*, for what has passed, were she daring enough to risk it ? But thank God ! she is not.

She has just shown me a copy of her answer, which she wishes to send *by the Post* that he may not imagine it is from the *dictate* of anyone. I *think & hope* it can do no harm— but she is in *such a state*, I *dare* not oppose her wishes. Her agitation is such I could not answer for the consequences—nor am I much better *myself*.

She told Miss Doyle yesterday that just such a letter *would come*, and felt quite relieved when the letters were brought in— and as *she thought*, none from him. Therefore the blow was the greater, as it took her by surprise.

Wednesday Morn.—We had a sad day of it yesterday. I had neither time or strength to copy the letter to Ld B. last night, as she had not settled *what* it should be till near eleven o'clock.

This was what it was.

Wednesday, February 7 1816.

If I had not written to Mrs. Leigh what I deemed a sufficient answer to the contents of your first letter, I should not have deferred the still more painful task of addressing yourself. Your second letter, received yesterday, seems to require from me this exertion. I am surprised at the manner in which that letter was delivered to me, since my correspondence, as well as my determination, is free. I have indeed placed myself under the protection of my parents, but I act on my own conviction— independently—as they do on theirs. You know what I have suffered, and would have sacrificed to avoid this extremity—and the strong proofs of duty & attachment I have given by a persevering endurance of the most trying inflictions. After seriously & dispassionately reviewing the misery that I have experienced almost without interval from the day of my marriage, I have finally determined on the measure of a separation—which my father was authorised to communicate to you, and to carry into effect.

It is unhappily your disposition to consider what you *have* as worthless—what you have *lost* as invaluable. But remember that you declared yourself most miserable when I was yours.

Every expression of feeling, sincerely as it might be made, would here be misplaced.

Dr. Lushington approved this letter. Byron answered it thus :

February 8*th* (*Thursday*) 1816.

All I can say seems useless—and all I could say might be no less unavailing ; yet I still cling to the wreck of my hopes, before they sink for ever. Were you then *never* happy with me ? did you never at any time or times express yourself so ? have no marks of affection, of the warmest and most reciprocal attachment, passed between us ? or did in fact hardly a day go down without some such on one side and generally on both ? Do not mistake me.

I have not denied my state of mind—but you know its causes ; & were these deviations from calmness never followed by acknowledgement & repentance ? Was not the last which occurred more particularly so ? & had I not—had we not— the days before and on the day when we parted, every reason to believe that we loved each other—that we were to meet again ? Were not your letters kind ? had I not acknowledged to you all my faults and follies, & assured you that some had not—& would not be repeated ? I do not require these questions to be answered to me—but to your own heart.

The day before I received your father's letter I had fixed a day for rejoining you. If I did not write lately, Augusta did ; and as you had been my proxy in correspondence with her, so did I imagine she might be the same for me to you.

Upon your letter to me this day—I surely may remark that its expressions imply a treatment which I am incapable of inflicting, & you of imputing to me—if aware of their latitude, & the extent of the inferences to be drawn from them. This is not just— but I have no reproaches—nor the wish to find cause for them.

Will you see me, when & where you please—in whose presence you please ? The interview shall pledge you to nothing, and I will say and do nothing to agitate either. It is torture to correspond thus, & there are things to be settled and said which cannot be written.

You say " It is my disposition to deem what *I have worthless*." Did I deem *you* so ? did I ever so express myself to you—or of you—to others ? You are much changed within these twenty days, or you would never have thus poisoned your own better feelings—and trampled upon mine.

ever yours most truly and affectionately

(Scribbled signature)

One passage in that letter she knew—and we know—to be untrue. " On the day when we parted." . . . They had not even seen one another. It had been written with a purpose, easily divined. But for all that, she did not easily resist the appeal. Let us grant that it would have been the end of estrangement—and the beginning of fresh miseries—for almost every imaginable woman. Like Mme. de Staël when she read the Farewell verses, most of us must feel that " *Je n'aurais pu m'y tenir un instant.*" So Annabella felt at first. Mrs. Fletcher at this time wrote to her husband that Lady Byron was in agony, " rolling on the floor in a paroxysm of grief." It took her some days before she could steel herself. On the 11th she wrote, for Lushington to see and approve :

I have determined, *if possible,* not to indulge the language of feeling in addressing you, as it would only be injurious in our present relative situations. I wish you had spared me by a similar conduct.

By means of our authorized friends, those points which require conversational discussion can be settled ; and whatever may now appear to you inconsistent, satisfactorily explained.

But reading Byron's letter again—we can guess how often and how mournfully—she could not rest content with that inflexible curtness. Two days afterwards she wrote another letter, likewise (we must suppose) approved by Lushington :

On reconsidering your last letter to me, and your second to my father, I find some allusions which I will not leave to be answered by others, because the explanation may be less disagreeable to you from myself.

My letters of Jany 15th & 16th. It can be fully and clearly proved that I left your house under the persuasion of your having a complaint of so dangerous a nature that any agitation might bring on a fatal crisis. My entreaties, before I quitted you, that you would take medical advice—repeated in my letter of Jan. 15th—must convince you of such an impression on my mind. My absence, if it had not been rendered necessary by other causes, was *medically* recommended on that ground, as removing an object of irritation. I should have acted inconsistently with my unchanged affection for you, or indeed with the common principles of humanity, by urging my wrongs at that moment. From subsequent accounts, I found that those particular apprehensions which I & others had entertained, were groundless. Till they were ascertained to be so, it was my wish & intention to induce you to come to this place, where, at every hazard, I would have devoted myself to the alleviation of *your* sufferings, and should not then have reminded you of *my own*, as believing you, from physical causes, not to be *accountable* for them. My parents, under the same impression communicated by me, felt the kindest anxiety to promote my wishes and your recovery, by receiving you here. Of all this, my letter of Jan. 16 is a testimony.

If for these reasons (to which others were perhaps added) I did not remonstrate at the time of leaving your house, you cannot forget that I had before warned you, earnestly and affectionately, of the unhappy and irreparable consequences which must ensue from your conduct, both to yourself and me— that to those representations you had replied by a determination to be wicked, though it should break my heart.

What then had I to expect ? I cannot attribute your "state of mind" to any cause so much as that *total* dereliction of principle which, *since* our marriage, you have professed and gloried in. Your acknowledgements have not been accompanied by any intentions of amendment.

I have *consistently* fulfilled my duty as your wife. It was too dear to be abandoned till it became hopeless. Now my resolution cannot be changed.

Her resolution was assailed not only by Byron, but by Hobhouse and Hodgson. Hobhouse had early intervened in an eloquent letter (which was rather too much like a homily to a rebellious wife) begging that he might see her and recalling her farewell words on the wedding-day : " If I am not happy, it will be my own fault." She had not forgotten them ; what she had forgotten was that she had ever liked Hobhouse. Clearly she had come to regard him as a bad influence on Byron ; there are references to him and Douglas Kinnaird in later letters—" the Piccadilly crew " —which show deep resentment and distrust. He too had by this time forgotten her " innocent conquest " on the wedding-day ; antagonism had grown up between them, no less manifest in his allusions to her than in hers to him. . . . She now declined, in a freezing note, to see him or discuss the matter with him in any way. He wrote again, this time designating Sir Ralph's letter to Byron as a revolting proposition, wondering what pleasure she could derive from her present attitude, and adding : " Your sole

to her." [1] Her feeling had never been more than suspicion of a renewal of incest, after their marriage ; but Lushington realised that she could not return to Byron without in fact condoning incest ; she could not exclude Mrs. Leigh from her brother's house without exposing the whole situation to the world ; and that she was resolved not to do, for Augusta's and Byron's sake, and in another sense, her child's. As soon as Lushington learnt all the facts, he made his declaration that re-union was impossible.

Before anything could result from this interview, the old rumours about Augusta and Byron had been strongly revived. Augusta's intimate friend, Mrs. George Villiers, wrote to Lady Byron concerning them ; and on February 29 was answered :

I consider your letter as a very kind proof of the justice you do to my feelings, which are by no means so absorbed in my own distresses as to forget those of others who perhaps suffer still more.

I deeply regret the reports which have been circulated relative to the causes of separation between Lord Byron & myself, and none can occasion me more sorrow than that which you mention as reflecting on Mrs. Leigh's character—but as I can *positively* assert that *not one* of the many reports now current have been sanctioned or encouraged by me, my family, or my friends, I cannot consider myself in any degree responsible for them.

During my residence under the same roof with Mrs Leigh, *all* my friends have heard me express the most grateful and affectionate sense of her good offices towards me ; and before I left the house I wrote of her or spoke of her in those terms, to every one who was intimate with me.

In the present state of circumstances you must be aware that a publication of the *real* grounds of difference between Lord B. and myself would be extremely improper—and in conformity with the advice I have received, I *must* abstain from any further disclosure. It is very painful to me to be obliged, in consequence, to appear less confidential than I wish towards you. . . . I must ask your indulgence for this answer. You do not know the *extreme* perplexities & miseries of my present circumstances, or I should feel secure of it. [2]

---

[1] *The Byron Mystery*, by Sir John Fox (1924), pp. 57, 60.

[2] This letter was published in the *Quarterly Review*, January 1870, wrongly dated. There is no record of it in Lady Byron's or Mrs. Villiers's papers. Lord Lovelace thought that Mrs. Villiers handed it over to Mrs. Leigh, and that its publication must have been the act of Mrs. Leigh's descendants.

She had not declared the reports to be false. Mrs. Villiers was shrewd enough to read that between the guarded lines, and for a time was indignant with her. The gossip (fomented by Augusta's continued stay at Piccadilly) grew more and more wide-spread. Now it was not only at fashionable parties, but in the theatres, the streets, that high and low were telling the story—not a new story, but made immensely more exciting by the introduction of a wife who had put herself under her father's protection.

The play was not going quite as the dramatist had intended. Those improvisations had upset him, even while he had not realised their extent ; now they were making him sob in his room, though he kept a brave face to lawyer and publisher and acquaintances. With Moore, as usual, he took a sincerer line, writing that he had never been in a situation so completely uprooting of present pleasure or rational hope for the future.

> I say this, because I think so, and feel it. But I shall not sink under it. . . . I have made up my mind. . . . I had a few weeks ago some things to say that would have made you laugh ; but they tell me now that I must not laugh, and so I have been very serious—and am.

Later, Moore was to receive the well-known tribute to Annabella :

> I do not believe—and I must say it, in the very dregs of all this bitter business—that there ever was a better, or even a brighter, a kinder, a more amiable and agreeable being than Lady Byron. I never had, nor can have, any reproach to make her, while with me. Where there is blame, it belongs to myself, and if I cannot redeem, I must bear it.

It was the least he could say ; but let us grant that not all would have said it so nobly. . . . He had brought the catastrophe on himself, as he brought most of his catastrophes, never dreaming that it would take such proportions. To " make you run back to your father, like the spoilt child you are "—that was one thing (and a thing in which he had not entirely failed, for as Lady Noel wrote to Annabella : " You are vexed because it is the *ton* to speak of you as a *spoilt child* ") ; but that the world should get hold of other matters, however assisted by his own loquacity, was what Byron had not foreseen when he rang up the curtain on Act III.

And now, amid all his legal letters, literary letters, friendly letters, came a succession of (at first) quasi-anonymous love-letters. The first was from one " E. Trefusis," describing herself as an utter stranger, saying that she placed her happiness in his hands, and asking him if—should she confess the love she had borne him many years—he would betray her, or be silent as the grave ? He did not answer. Then " E. Trefusis " turned into a less alarming " G.C.B." All " G.C.B." wanted was an interview in the utmost privacy, on a certain Sunday evening. He answered this, acquiescently but stiffly. . . . To make a foolish and familiar story short, the writer of both these letters was soon revealed as Claire Clairmont, Mary Godwin's step-sister, later to be Shelley's sister-in-law, and later still the mother of Byron's acknowledged daughter, Allegra. Her importunities far transcended Caroline Lamb's comparative refinements in the sort. Byron resisted, but she had her way in the end—a mistress accepted through sheer inability to withstand bombardment (" my heart always alights on the nearest perch ") and soon wearied of. But her lovely singing did enchant him. He wrote for her " There be none of Beauty's daughters "—one of his best short poems.

The austerest of us could scarcely be very hard upon Byron for this interlude. He did what he was pestered into doing, and when he found that this verbose adorer—whom, without any noticeable success, he often begged to " write shorter "—was gifted with a beautiful singing voice, it is not much wonder that he yielded to the charm of at any rate her music, coming to make him momentarily forget the money-worries, separation-worries, worse than worries about Augusta, and all the calamitous consequences of that play which was developing so disconcertingly. In after-days, indeed, he was to show Claire Clairmont what he showed most women—cruelty and scorn ; but in these weeks we cannot refuse him some sympathy, as we read her letters and reflect upon the desolation he had wrought for himself.

Of this imbroglio nothing was then known to the Noel party, nor apparently to the lawyers and friends on both sides. The Drury Lane actresses were freely assigned to Byron by everyone ;

that was an old story, important only because he had boasted of
it so insultingly to his wife. Other things that just then occupied
his mind were to have much wider reverberations. These were the
Farewell verses and the *Sketch*—the latter an attack on Mrs.
Clermont. He wrote them both in this March, and commissioned
Murray to print them "*for private distribution.*" But somebody
was indiscreet, and on April 14 they were published by the
Champion, a Tory paper. The turmoil they created was frantic—
more frantic even than that about the Weeping Lines in 1814 ;
it was made into a party matter, while the Noel side, though
scornfully silent, was outraged equally by "the degrading tribute
to the world's opinion" in the *Farewell*, and the abuse, "black-
guard beyond belief," of Mrs. Clermont. The latter lines were
indeed a disgrace to Byron. Had there even been any truth in the
basenesses of which he accused her—and there was none—such a
gross attack had nothing to excuse it, even to his most devoted
allies. Whether he was angered by the publication or not, there
is nothing in the documents to show.

By this time he had consented to sign a deed of amicable separation, but not until it had been distinctly notified to him that if he
persisted in refusing "recourse must be had to legal measures." [1]
On the same day that the two sets of verses appeared—Easter
Sunday, April 14—Byron said good-bye to Augusta, who some
time before had left Piccadilly for her apartments in St. James's
Palace. (She was bedchamber-woman to the Queen.) But earlier
than this Lady Jersey, the great social leader, had given the famous
party at which Augusta was cut by some people,[2] and Byron was
cut by every one except Miss Mercer Elphinstone. After that

---

[1] "Lady Byron . . . was prepared, if necessary, to bring a suit in the
ecclesiastical court on the ordinary grounds, which, as the law then stood,
would have entitled her to a separation *a mensa et thoro*. She did not seek
for freedom to marry again, so that the question whether she could have
established a case for divorce by Act of Parliament remained undecided."
(*Lady Noel Byron and the Leighs.* Privately printed, 1881.)

[2] Mrs. George Lamb was among them. She had written to Annabella,
saying that she "could almost pity" Augusta. Annabella had replied :
"I am glad that you think of *her* with the feelings of pity which prevail
in my mind, and surely if in *mine* there must be some cause for them.
I never was nor ever can be so *mercilessly* virtuous as to admit *no* excuse
for even the worst of errors."

he gave up the fight, consented to sign the deed of separation, and made arrangements for leaving England.

He wrote to his wife on that Easter Sunday—a letter which was for the first time accurately printed in *Astarte*, having been previously taken from a copy made from memory by Hobhouse.

" More last words "—not many—and such as you will attend to. Answer I do not expect—nor does it import—but you will hear me. I have just parted from Augusta—almost the last being you had left me to part with—& the only unshattered tie of my existence. Wherever I go—& I am going far—you & I can never meet again in this world—nor in the next. Let this content or atone. If any accident occurs to me—be kind to *her* —if she is then nothing—to her children.

Some time ago I informed you that with the knowledge that any child of ours was already provided for by other & better means, I had made my will in favour of her & her children—as prior to my marriage. This was not done in anger [1] to you for we had not then differed—& even this is useless during your life by the settlements. I say therefore be kind to her and hers— for never has she acted or spoken otherwise towards you. She has ever been your friend—this may seem valueless to one who has now so many—be kind to her however—& recollect that though it may be advantage to you to have lost your husband, it is sorrow to her to have the waters now, or the earth hereafter, between her & her brother.

She is gone. I need hardly add that of this request she knows nothing. Your late compliances have not been so extensive as to render this an encroachment. I repeat it (for deep resentments have but half recollections) that you once did promise me thus much. Do not forget it, nor deem it cancelled ; it was not a vow.

Mr. Wharton has sent me a letter with one question & two pieces of intelligence. To the question I answer that the carriage is yours ; & as it has only carried us to Halnaby—& London—& you to Kirkby—I hope it will take you many a more propitious journey.

The receipts can remain, unless troublesome ; if so, they can be sent to Augusta, & through her I would also hear of my little daughter. My address will be left for Mrs. Leigh. The ring is of no lapidary value, but it contains the hair of a king and an ancestor, which I should wish to preserve to Miss Byron.

[1] In the MS. letter " anger " is effaced, and " prejudice " substituted.

To a subsequent letter of Mr. Wharton's I have to reply that it is the "law's delay" not mine, & that when he & Mr. H. have adjusted the tenor of the bond I am ready to sign.

Annabella left London next day with her father. She did not answer Byron's letter, probably being forbidden to have any communication with him at this stage.

Since her interview with Lushington, she had not again wavered. The struggle, as she had said, was past ; she had placed herself in her lawyer's hands, and was ready to obey his instructions. But her misery was overwhelming. Soon after that decisive interview, her mother wrote to her :

> I neither do or can expect that you should not feel, and deeply feel—but I have sometimes thought (and that not only lately) that your mind is too *high-wrought*—too much so for this world ; only the grander objects engage your thoughts. Your character is like *Proof-Spirits*—not fit for common use. I could almost wish the tone of it lowered nearer the level of us every day people. . . . I have not slept on a bed of roses through my life—I have had afflictions and serious ones, though none so severe as the present. But in my sixty-fifth year I have endeavoured to rally, and *shall* rally, if *you* do so. Now, my love, here is a Sunday's sermon for you, and here it shall end.

Impossible to find a better phrase than that of " Proof Spirits " for Annabella Byron's character. The mother's insight had, as we see, early perceived the danger of that absorption in " grander objects." Had Lady Noel at this time known of the resolution to befriend Augusta, what confirmation it would have brought to her fears ! When later she did learn all, she warned Annabella in arresting words : " *Once more*, take care of X. If I know anything of human nature, she *does* and *must* hate you."

During Annabella's stay in London, she had met Augusta two or three times. Augusta wrote of one meeting to Hodgson :

> I never can describe Lady Byron's appearance to you but by comparing it to what I should imagine a being of another world. She is positively reduced to a skeleton, pale as *ashes*, a deep hollow tone of voice and a *calm* in her manner quite super-natural. She received *me* kindly, but that really appeared the only SURVIVING feeling—all else was *death-like* calm. I can never forget it, never !

They spoke only once of the subject uppermost in both their minds, when Augusta alluded to the reports about herself, " with the pride of innocence ! "—as long afterwards Annabella wrote, indignantly recalling it. She felt bound to befriend Augusta, yet was conscious of how much explanation her conduct needed now, and would possibly need still more in the future. So vital did Lushington also consider this point that on March 14 he— together with her friends Mr. Robert Wilmot and Colonel Doyle[1] —had induced her to draw up a document setting forth her reasons for the continued intercourse with " Mrs. L." (only the initial was used). These were, that suspicions were all she had to go upon " though they impressed her forcibly ; " that she could take no middle course unless she definitely charged Mrs. L. with the offence . . . in short, as we have read. She declared that she had not set the rumours in motion, nor ratified them ; she could not clear her own mind of suspicion, but was keenly desirous of harming in no way Mrs. L.'s reputation. She had been told that nothing could so well shield Mrs. L. as a resumption of friendliness ; therefore she consented to that resumption.

In effect, the document was drawn up in order that " if circumstances should compel Lady Byron to prefer the charge, she should be at full liberty to do so without being prejudiced by her present conduct."

On one contingency only would she have preferred " the charge" —namely, if her child were taken from her and placed under the care of Mrs. Leigh. This fear had become an obsession ; she had even, while at Kirkby, imagined that the baby might be kidnapped. Whatever her affection and pity for Augusta, she could not have contemplated that guardianship without a sense of outrage. Moreover, at the end of March she had had an interview with Caroline Lamb which had, as she wrote to Lushington, " changed her strong impression into *absolute* conviction." (Incidentally, this affords proof that Caroline's story of the scene in 1814 was not invention.) On March 26, the day before that interview, Annabella had by her own wish seen Augusta at Mivart's Hotel. Their conversation is nowhere recorded ; one result of it was to make Byron send his wife testimonies from Lord Holland, Rogers,

[1] Afterwards Sir R. Wilmot Horton and Sir Francis Hastings Doyle. Mr. Wilmot, who married an heiress, was Byron's second cousin.

and Douglas Kinnaird that " he had never spoken of her with disrespect, with unkindness, or defending himself at *her* expense." He had appealed to them [1] to testify that they had heard him say " that when there was a right or wrong, she had the *right*."

This, as a consequence of her interview with Augusta, made Annabella uneasy. She returned the testimonies as quite unnecessary—" I had not accused him of so speaking of me ; " and added : " I am anxious to acquit you of all misrepresentation, and myself of having supposed it. . . . I cannot give you pain without feeling yet more myself." But mistrust had inevitably been sown in her mind. She reproached herself ; she resumed (some time afterwards) the most intimate correspondence ; none the less, remembrance of that episode persisted, and accounts for many things yet in the future. Her mother's warning : " If I know anything of human nature, she *does* and *must* hate you " . . . that was the kind of knowledge which Annabella most shrank from believing in, yet the words must often have occurred to her in years to come.

By Sunday, April 21, all vacillation was over.   On that day Byron—on the next, Annabella—signed the deed of separation. They had not seen one another since she left Piccadilly ; they never saw one another again.

[1] See Byron's letter to Rogers of March 25, 1816 (*Letters and Journals*, iii. 275-6).

CHAPTER XV

REACTION

At Kirkby, in the shattering reaction, she looked back on love and faith. Bitter enough, but less bitter than to hear Mam's denunciations of both Byrons, especially Augusta. Clermont, from London, had tried to calm these down: "Even for Lady Byron's life I believe we have to thank Mrs. Leigh." No use! "I may be *Goosish* about her, but I firmly believe she is fit company for Mrs. Fletcher." Mrs. Fletcher, snake in the grass, signer of an affidavit: "Has heard Lady Byron say she would go back to Lord Byron, but they would not let her."... Those terrible hours of frenzy in February —had one indeed said that? Not impossible; but if one did, it was a lie.

Yet one may not claim parents' protection, and then sulk because they are hot in one's defence. Happy in their marriage, how should these understand? If Mam would only be silent! Silence is what we long for; solitary hours of grief, remembrance, self-justification, self-accusation. How soon it had been extinguished (so soon that there self-accusation could find no place), that presumptuous hope of reconciling him to himself, of dispersing the famous gloom! But was there not something a wife might have been which would not have proved "no good?" Years would not be too long for pondering on that; and instead we have to listen while his pet-name for Guss is sneeringly used against him and her, while epithets are showered upon them—for in March Lady Noel had heard the gossip, had written to Sir Ralph from London: "I *now* know what was the report said to be so shocking—it was that the Brother and Sister *forgot they were so*...." Ever since then it has been terrible. Soon one will have to break free —go off somewhere by one's-self with Ada, now no longer Augusta Junior, now "A-da," with its other poignant echoes. Scarcely a word that does not in some way recall him ! Yes ; one will go, and meanwhile be good—as he used to say.

In London Byron's few friends gathered round him, as yet with no reaction to endure. They had still to get him out of No. 13, out of England. When a man is groaned at in the theatre, the streets, his friends will inevitably be furious with everyone but him. They would not be much good if it were otherwise ; and indeed posterity would not be much good if it could look on Byron with anything but pity as he and his play were hissed off the stage. Whatever we have felt while it was developing, at the close our hearts are melted ; like Hobhouse we hear him sobbing in his room, and for the moment forget how often, driven from him by his cruelty and " abhorrence," his wife had sobbed in hers.

He was not mad ; he was only Byron—poor Byron who at this very time declared that he considered himself the greatest man existing. George had laughed : " What about Bonaparte ? " He had hesitated . . . but, " God—I don't know that I do except even him." She who listened thought to see a wildness in his eye— Augusta, Goose, " my sister, my sweet sister," recounting the scene to her who, for all his abhorrence, was far better able to understand it. *She* knew that Byron was not thinking of his fame, of the poetry that was " not my vocation ; " that it was from something " which was in his nature more than in theirs who did not ridicule or deny the Divine," that this belief in his greatness was drawn. Her understanding had been " no good," it never would be any good. He would not have her near him ; there was something in her to which he could not respond.

What was it ? Not only the wifehood which was so vast an error. " She ought never to have married him "—of course not, as one has agreed a hundred times with those who think that an explanation of the disaster. Let us grant further that she did, in the derisive sense of the phrase, " marry him." But Byron had been determined to marry—if not this girl, then another. Had it been another—say, the lovely Antelope who wrote silly-sweet letters and fled from him in the end ? She too would have suffered, but not as Annabella suffered. No other woman ever did call forth that special kind of cruelty from Byron.

It was the quiet strength in her, meeting the violent strength in him, which made the disaster of their marriage. " Like Proof-Spirits, not fit for common use ; " and common use—not only in the contemptuous sense—was what Byron wanted of women. He wanted chiefly, for this common use, what Annabella could not give to anything ; we call it the light touch. " I only want a woman to laugh." So he had told her during the honeymoon ; and she, accustomed to parental adoration of her impertinences, was sure that she did know how to laugh. But jokes about fleas and lice, *bouts-rimés*, dressing-up, time-honoured harmless double-ententes on legs and sanitary arrangements—he was inured to women who laughed at more far-reaching ribaldries than these. Lady Melbourne, Caroline Lamb, Augusta : *they* had the light touch, and not for common use alone—for life as it was lived in the circles which had given Annabella so much " pain." Pain ! One did not talk about pain, except in verse. Things were taken for granted. Adultery was a matter of course ; incest not quite that, but even incest was a topic on which one could now and then be facetious with the Goddess of Comedy at Whitehall—or, more bitterly, with her whom it most affected. And here one was, married to a woman who took such things so seriously that one had to retaliate by bringing them home to her. Then there had been " sentiment and sermons ; " sobs too ; yet always something in her that he could not get at.

Inward strength—but that was the Byron prerogative. He had wanted to be governed, still wanted to be ; that kind of strength was outward, a prop on which it would be comfortable to lean and " be good." And that kind of strength she would not use ; he was left to do as he liked in the things he did not like at all, but never could help doing. That was all marriage had done for him !

Yet no ; not all. True, she was not directly to blame for one change wrought by marriage—the change in Augusta. Guss had always said it must be so, no matter who the girl might be ; and he had agreed with her, had become engaged agreeing with her ; and then had found that he should not be able to bear it. But Guss did not mean it—Guss mean anything seriously ! Not, at any rate, so seriously that B. could not persuade her out of it. And then had come the night at " S.M.B." on the way to that first Seaham visit. Then he had found that Guss *could* withstand him ; had been " in very ill-humour " when he left her house.

Had he not tried to frighten the girl off ? had he not muttered " I will be even with you for this "—then felt ashamed of himself, and invented some lie to account for it ? She had taken the warning, though—had offered to set him free. What had possessed him to make a fool of himself by fainting ? For then there had been the little attentions, the fond alarm—and a man whose heart always alighted on the nearest perch returning to consciousness to find a woman bending over him with eyes that were dim with glad reassurance. (" Then I was *sure* he must love me.") Fatal, that going-off ; and it had only made him angrier within. He had wanted to be good ; but like that saint (Augustine, was it ?) " not yet."

Long before the wedding he had known that it was hopeless. The trial-stay had, really, proved it to them both. What had made him go through to the end ? Without being fatuous, one knew what had made *her*—she was in love with him. In love, as she understood being in love ; not as he did. Her seriousness, her intensity : " nothing but *feeling* from morning till night. . . ." Something had come over him as they drove away together—and then those accursed Durham bells had finished him, exulting over Lord Byron married !

Halnaby . . . three weeks of it ; then Seaham with its ennui ; then S.M.B., Guss and her resolution, Annabella and her sobs one night. But despite the sobs, that inward strength. One saw through it ; she guessed the truth—but the exasperation of her fortitude, sitting there between Guss and Mignonne ! How could he help flinging it at her that Mignonne was his child ? Guss had not liked it ; but the secret would be safe with Bell. . . . Then Piccadilly. This marriage was accursed, he was accursed ; let them live in accursed Number Thirteen. Their child was already conceived ; he had married for that too, and now (like the other achieved object of marriage) it only made things worse. It put hatred and malice in his heart. At first he had managed to behave well ; then all the money-worries, and the old stick of an uncle dying without a legacy to her who was supposed to be the apple of his eye (but one had been defrauded all round about money-matters) ; then Augusta's arrival, and Drury Lane and its complaisant hussies, and his liver tormenting him as usual but worse than usual, and the pompous preparations for the confinement, women and nurses wherever one looked—how could a man contain himself? How could he help throwing furniture and bottles about, and inventing savage speeches, and behaving as though he were mad? *Was* he not mad? The doctors would not say so, and in their sense he was not; but " the madness of the heart "—the madness which no one had ever known but himself— that was his kind, and it was far more agonising than what doctors prosed about.[1]

Once the child is born, they must part. He can bear it no longer. " Make her run back to her father "—like the spoilt child she is? If only she was! Precisely because she is not, she must go. Go with her strength, her cheerfulness, gentleness, faith, hope, love— but go. She makes him cruel, and he is not cruel. . . .

> Because my nature was averse from life,
> And yet not cruel.

He cannot bear it—this cruelty that is not his. The things he has said to her since her delivery—some day he will not be able to believe he has said them. Send her away, then; write and order her to go. Bid her a derisive good-bye—coming to him, unsummoned, with their child in her arms. " When shall we three meet again? . . ." " In Heaven." He who is doomed, no matter what he does or is, to Hell—she knows he believes that, and she talks of Heaven!

Gone—gone. Now he can think again, can feel again. Was it so horrible when she was here—was she so difficult to live with? And here is a letter from her. Angry? " Dearest Duck "—and the wonderful water-closet at Kirkby! Not angry any more, though she had been angry. " Pippin: " she liked that name. " If I were not always looking about for B." . . . Let him do and say what he will, she will never be estranged. Poor thing—little round-faced wife and mother; poor Pippin, poor Bell! Some day, most likely, he will want her back.

---

[1] In that January of 1816, Annabella had written in the sort of diary she kept at Kirkby: " Remorse for ill-using me—irritating to further ill-usage. . . . As if I were *Conscience*. . . . I made the irritation more raging. . . . Had he thought himself worthy of me, he would have been kind. I write this in a moment of illumination. *I know this to be truth*. . . . I was humble and devoted in vain—I was the more rejected; but could I resent while I must pity? "

A letter from Sir Ralph, delivered by hand. What can this
be ?   " Lady Byron's parents . . . not justified in permitting her
return to Lord Byron's house . . . terms of separation " . . . And
her letter from Kirkby ?   This is the old woman's doing ! But no.
Bell has answered Augusta's question, written at his behest :
" Has this been done by your wish ? "   Laconically : " It has."
Unlike her ; fond of long words as she is—but there is more.
" He has too painfully convinced me " . . . But, again, her
letter from Kirkby ! He must write to her himself. Once, twice,
thrice—the answer to the third as resolute as those to the first and
second, and " explaining " the Dearest Duck one. So she had
been consulting doctors and lawyers before he told her to go—she
and the rest of them. And he who had been thinking of her since,
wondering if he would not want her back some day ! Oh, unforgiving wife. . . .

> All my faults perchance thou knowest,
>   All my madness—none can know ;
> All my hopes—where'er thou goest—
>   Wither, yet with *thee* they go.

Tears falling thick on the paper as we make the fair copy. (Not
fall as we were composing ? Of course not. Every poet knows
that. One has to see how it goes before one really feels a poem.)
Moore shall read this before we send it to Murray for printing—
privately, of course. It *is* a poem ; some day the world may read
it too, and learn how Lord Byron suffered. Not yet ; private
circulation only. Moore will talk, perhaps, and the rest of those
who are to see it—and see this other too, on which no tears shall
fall ; but might not one think to see the paper blaze with the fury
that is flung upon it ?

" Born in the garret, in the kitchen bred "—the woman
Clermont, " festering in the infamy of years." . . . . Can we find
words that are blasting enough ?

Scenes every day—Hobhouse and Scrope Davies drawing up
charges for the Unforgiving Wife to disavow, then Davies declaring
that these things had better not be put on record ; Wilmot telling
Hob about the gossip, saying " If you find I have misrepresented,
I give you leave to pull my nose ; " Hob coming next day and
finding " the whole house in a rumpus " because again one has

refused to negotiate, and Wilmot is furious, and a duel seems imminent. But the duel, like that other duel, ends in smoke ... only we have done with Cousin Wilmot for ever. On March 22, amid "the hardest frost known for years," an earthquake at Newstead. The omen! It was bound to come; and now that at last we have a sign from Heaven or Hell, we throw up the game.

Their cards are too strong. Go into court? We may threaten, but into court we cannot go. "Augusta." There, in one word, is their case. They would not cite it, but that is their case. They know that we know it.

Hob is more portentous than ever, these last few days; says it is his duty to declare that he has changed his opinion. But Hob will not change, though his opinion may. Men do not change; that is for women—for wives. Sisters ... not sisters.

> Then let the ties of baffled love
> Be broken—thine will never break. ...

Stanzas to Augusta—yes, we will head the verses so and send them to Murray, like the others. ... But what has Murray been doing? For behold! a letter from Caroline Lamb:

> Byron, hear me. ... I do implore you for God's sake not to publish them. ... You will draw ruin on your own head and hers if at this moment you show these. ... If you could hear all that is said. ... Believe one who would perhaps die to save you. ...

One does not answer *her*, of course; but Murray shall be written to. " Really you must not show anything of mine to Lady C.L. You do not know what mischief you do by this." Nevertheless ... " I wish more particularly the *last* not to be circulated, at present. (You know which I mean, those to A.) "

A man can pull himself together for that sort of thing; it helps him to forget that play and author have been hissed off the stage. And when letters are done, arrangements made, and a travelling-carriage has been bought—it costs £500, though we are bankrupt —there are still the farewell visits to distract the mind. The faithful Hob, the faithful Scrope, are coming to Dover; but Rogers and Kinnaird arrive, make their good-byes, and go ... go back to the familiar life that was amusing, after all. The house is empty now, and we must face reaction black and pitiless. But

must we ? There is a way of escape. And on that 20th of
April, the night before he signs the separation-papers, Claire
Clairmont comes to him, unloved, but with her magic voice to sing
above the earthquake.

Newstead and Byron. Newstead is not down. Sing, sing—
" like music on the waters." The waters of Babylon . . . that
Hebrew melody ; Bell copied it. The waters of ruin and eclipse.

.   .   .   .

On the 23rd he left London for Dover. There, while waiting
to embark for Ostend, he went with Hobhouse and Davies to visit
the grave of Charles Churchill—" he who blazed, the Comet of a
Season." It was being re-turfed after long neglect ; he talked
with the sexton ; then in a sudden impulse (Hob's diary has
preserved it for us) : " Byron lay down in the grave."

CHAPTER XVI

THE CORRESPONDENCE WITH MRS. VILLIERS

SOME one else had been writing verses, not so fluent, by no means so moving. These would never stir a great poet of another nation to translate them.[1] *On a Mother being told she was an Unnatural One*—dated December 15, 1815. Five days after Ada's birth! The lines can scarcely have been written then ; but in feeling they belong to those days. The mother begs her child's forgiveness for " the heart withheld from thee ; " she dares not cherish the issue of this marriage, now that she is " resolving to be free." Dated also in 1815 is *A Contemplation of the Future* :

> No, no—it will not break—this heart
>   Will labour still to beat ;
> Tho' now as free from pause or start
>   As in its winding-sheet
> The heavy pulse moves changeless on,
> The ebb and flow of Hope are gone.

Her morbidity had fastened on the sense of baffled maternal love, for an unfinished effort of March 1, 1816, reiterates the theme :

> And heart-wrung I could almost hate
>   The thing I may not love,
> And ask, while shuddering o'er its fate,
>   If pity dwelt above.

And after Byron's Farewell had appeared, with all the newspaper turmoil attendant on it, her own Farewell was wrung from her. There is nothing here to make a Corinne exclaim : " *Je n'aurais pu m'y tenir un instant ;* " tears did not fall on this fair copy, sent to nobody for private or public circulation ; but the title does

---

[1] Heine translated Byron's *Farewell*.

arrest us. *On the Words " Fare thee well, by thee Forsaken."* Those
are not Byron's words. It reveals her self-accusation, the thought
which pursued her : " I might have been something that would
not have been ' no good.' "

It was now that her correspondence with Augusta's friend, the
Hon. Mrs. Villiers, began. Annabella had gone to see her before
leaving London, and a " partial explanation " had taken place
between them. Mrs. Villiers *had* declared that Lady Byron ought
publicly to discredit the rumours against Mrs. Leigh ; but as a
result of this interview, she urgently advised that Augusta should
be told what Annabella had learnt from Byron's lips.

From Kirkby Annabella wrote, defending herself on both
counts of silence. As to discrediting the rumours, she could not
sanction unjust imputations against her friends, " and obliquely
against myself," of being wholly to blame for the catastrophe.
Other things she would do, and had done, to protect Augusta's
reputation ; but not that. Of her reluctance to speak out to
Augusta she wrote :

> I doubt if any woman would forgive to another such an
> avowal. I have sometimes thought that a tacit understanding
> existed between us. . . . It is scarcely possible she could on
> various occasions have supposed me unconscious, and I do
> not conceive that his words to me in private could make a
> change in her feelings, if what passed in her presence did not."

Mrs. Villiers was then seeing Augusta frequently, and the
reports were discussed between them. One of Augusta's arguments was that if Lady Byron had ever heard the rumours, or if
she had not treated them " with the contempt they deserved,"
would she have invited Byron's sister to Piccadilly ? There was
force in this ; Mrs. Villiers asked Annabella to explain the invitation. The answer was that there had been no certainty, only
" wretched doubts," rejected as long as possible. Moreover, she
had believed that Byron's inclinations were then " most averse "
from his sister ; and feeling that any human being's presence in
the house would be the means of saving herself and her child, she
had turned to Augusta as the one person she had to look to.
Nevertheless, before allowing her to come (for she had many times

offered it), Annabella had urged her to reflect on possible consequences.

It then came out that Augusta had at the time represented things quite differently to Mrs. Villiers. " *Your* urgent requests to *her*." Annabella's warnings had never been mentioned ; and " I now find," wrote Mrs. Villiers, " that I have been made accessory to her doing the very things she ought most to have avoided "—meaning that she had been led to advise Augusta's going to Piccadilly. As the correspondence went on, Annabella yielded to Mrs. Villiers' urgency. "A full and immediate communication" of how completely Byron had betrayed his sister to his wife she still thought inadvisable, one reason being that Augusta was far advanced in pregnancy ; but she did feel that the situation had become impossible, for Augusta had lately " pursued a line of conduct very detrimental to me, countenancing the accusation of ' unforgiving.' . . . and giving me the unmeaning praise of ' perfection,' which never creates sympathy ; representing him with all the interest of repentant error and blighted affection—perfectly incompatible with what she has herself acknowledged of his conduct—even since we parted. . . . I had rather she had openly attacked me."

But the cardinal reason was the old fear for her child's security. " I might legally compromise it, by affording her the means of forming an artificial defence "—in the event of the wife's having to protest against the sister's guardianship. Therefore a middle course seemed best—to disclose only so much as would make Augusta conscious of the forbearance shown to her, " without compelling her to the utterly degrading confession of her own guilt."

Accordingly, she wrote the following letter to Augusta :

Monday June 3rd 1816.

Before your Confinement I would not risk agitating you, but having the satisfaction of knowing you are recovered, I will no longer conceal from yourself that there are reasons founded on such circumstances in your conduct as (though thoroughly convinced they have existed) I am most anxious to bury in silence, which indispensably impose on me the duty of *limiting* my intercourse with you.

I should more deeply lament this . . . if your feelings towards me could give me the power of doing you any good—but you have not disguised your resentment against those who have befriended me, and have countenanced the arts which have been employed to injure me. Can I then longer believe those professions of affection, and even of exclusive zeal for *my* welfare, which I have been most reluctant to mistrust ? And on *this* ground my conduct, if known, would be amply and obviously justified to the world. I shall still not regret having loved and trusted you so entirely. May the blessing of a merciful God be with you & those nearest you. I am truly interested in the welfare of your children, and should your present unhappy dispositions be seriously changed, you will not then be deceived in considering me as one who will afford every service and consolation of your most faithful friend.

A. I. BYRON.

KIRKBY *June* 3, 1816.

I attest this to be a true copy of a letter from Lady Byron to Mrs. Leigh, sent according to date.

RALPH NOEL.

KIRKBY MALLORY
　June 3rd, 1816.

She told Mrs. Villiers that this had been done. " By avoiding all ambiguity of meaning," she added, " I have precluded the occasion for future explanation . . . yet have said everything that could soften the blow—everything that I truly feel."

Avoidance of ambiguity is certainly not a feature of her letter. Only to one who well understood the state of affairs would it have been comprehensible. Augusta's answer shows that she did understand ; there is little attempt to evade the issue.

SIX MILE BOTTOM
June 6th 1816.

As I always mistrust the first impulses of my feelings, & did not wish to write under the influence of such as your letter could not fail to produce, I would not answer it by return of post. I cannot say that I am *wholly surprised* at its contents. Your silence towards me during so long an interval, and when all *obvious* necessity for it must have ceased, formed so decided a contrast to your former kindness to me—and to what *my Conscience tells me my conduct towards you deserved from you*—that it could not but require some explanation. I have often thought of—though not determined—to ask it—when my health, strength, & spirits would allow me. If my feelings have been wounded by your silence, how much more deeply they must now be so by your expressions I *need* not—*cannot* say. To general accusations I must answer in general terms—and if I were on my death Bed I could affirm as I *now* do that I have uniformly considered you and consulted your happiness before and above any thing in this world. No sister ever could have the claims upon me that *you* had—I felt it—& acted up to the feeling to the best of my judgment. We are all perhaps too much inclined to magnify our trials, yet I think I may venture to pronounce my situation to *have been & to be still one* of extraordinary difficulty. I have been assured that the tide of public opinion has been so turned against my Brother that the least appearance of coolness on your part towards me would injure me most seriously—& I am therefore for the sake of my children compelled to accept from your compassion the " limited intercourse " which is all you can grant to one whom you pronounce no longer worthy of your esteem or affection ! But the time may come when your present convictions and opinions will change—in the interim I feel how hopeless would be every attempt to defend myself. The only person whose testimony could avail me in proving how strictly and invariably I have done my duty by you—I have heard from your own lips you consider unworthy of belief. On the particular points of accusation—1st, my not having disguised my resentment to those who befriended you—I know nothing but the change of manner to Miss Doyle, which was discussed between us ye last time I saw you—and 2nd, my having countenanced the acts which were employed to injure you.—Really you must have been cruelly misinformed, and *I* cruelly injured ; I ask not however by whom —for I feel I *scarcely* could forgive them. Before you judge and condemn me on the first point, you ought to consider that *I* as well as *you* may have had provocation—that it was impossible, hearing and seeing all I did, I should not be under the influence of *some* degree of irritation—not against those who would befriend YOU but whom I often thought condemned OTHERS *too severely*. I will not however say more at present than that you need not indeed regret having loved & trusted me so entirely— & the *sincerity of my affection for you & exclusive zeal for your welfare* ALL to whom I ever spoke of you—and who witnessed my conduct—can fully *prove*. I would not dwell a moment on having done what was only my *duty* and *inclinatiou*, but in *self-defence*.

My " present unhappy disposition "— ! I have indeed in *outward* causes sufficient to make anyone *wretched*, but inward peace which none can take away. It never occurred to me you could act but on the strictest sense of duty—therefore I'm convinced you do so now towards me.

God bless you—for every mark of kindness which you have bestowed on me and mine, of which neither time or circumstance can efface the recollection.

Of this Annabella wrote to Mrs. Villiers that it was perhaps the best letter Augusta could have written. Almost pleadingly she then asked if it might not be " mutually advisable " for her to write occasionally, without mentioning that subject, to Mrs. Leigh.

There is no point in Annabella's behaviour which has met, and meets, with more condemnation than what is variously called her " gloating over the incest " in these letters, and the " spiritual blackmail " which she and Mrs. Villiers held over Augusta. Let it be granted that no one who has read the correspondence can fail to wish that it had never taken place. But is it not asking too much of that " perfection which never creates sympathy " to demand that the wife should not have dwelt with some one on the circumstance which had ruined her hope and her life ? To her parents she could not speak out ; their feeling against Byron and Augusta was too violent. Was she to dismiss it all from her thoughts—to behave as if nothing had happened ? Mrs. Villiers had the attraction of being Augusta's friend ; she would want to think the best, as Annabella wanted to think the best, of her. That was the original motive. It became obscured in both ; nevertheless it was there. The girl who had written a Character of Lord Byron to clear up her feelings about him as a possible husband, was now the wife insulted and abhorred, to whom the sister's hold upon his heart had been so fatal. Yet to that sister she perhaps owed " even her life," and certainly much kindness and active protection. Here, then, was an opportunity for the analysis she loved to practise. She could never be at rest until she knew why, or thought she knew why ; and now, in the reaction that was seldom allowed to be quiescent, she would have been something more, or less, than human if she had not yielded to the urgency. But there was besides that other urgency of Mrs. Villiers' affection for Byron's sister. She too felt the charm of that gossamer irresponsibility, dulcet silliness, laughing through the sordid tragi-comedy that marriage had been to the wife of Colonel Leigh, laughing too above the abyss that meant her social ruin— laughing, yet shuddering, pushing her dark hair from her brow with hands that trembled . . . and for all that adoring " B," suffering B's insults to flow over her, and ruffling her feathers only at the yet grosser insults to his wife.

In that spirit of yearning indulgence Annabella began her correspondence with Augusta's friend. Too soon the other urgency prevailed. Between them, they could analyse her! And with analysis was always blent the spiritual pride that was Annabella's most dangerous defect.

There was nothing of spiritual pride in Thérèse [1] Villiers. Her indulgence was wide as heart could have desired—wider than Annabella's heart did desire, as future years were to show. It was not merely that of affection for Augusta. She was a woman of the world, " of a strong and ardent nature, but also a woman of the world." Many things that Annabella shrank from, Mrs. Villiers could philosophically accept. But not incest. She saved herself from condemning Augusta by regarding her as Byron's victim ; and when in September 1816 confession had been made to her, she wrote to the sister that her " horror, detestation, and execration of Lord Byron exceeded all expression." " Lady Byron," she continued, " is your guardian angel." Reporting this in their renewed correspondence, Augusta added : " And I am sure you are so."

Thus doubly apotheosised, Annabella tried to keep her head ; and did keep it in a surprising degree. Long-winded she must ever be, only seldom striking out one of the phrases which, in her letters as in her mother's, ring through the verbosity and feeble emphasis like a bronze bell. To Colonel Doyle in 1817 she wrote in an almost humorous spirit of detachment :

> My natural feelings sometimes create a sort of scepticism as to my ever having been injured by anybody. . . . The harm- lessness of my life, which indeed I think its chief, though not brilliant, quality, may account for my difficulty in thinking myself an object of persecution.

[1] As she always chose to spell her given name, Theresa. She had been named after the Empress Maria Theresa—oftener called Marie- Thérèse,

So dispassionate a mood was naturally rare. But from the first she had striven for something like it, as when she wrote to Lady Anne Barnard—one of the occasions when the bronze bell sounded:

It is not necessary to think ill of his heart in general—it is sufficient that to me it was hard and impenetrable, that my own must have been broken before his could have been touched. . . . As long as I live, my chief difficulty will probably be not to remember him too kindly.

Moving indeed, in the far distant future, to find how true this premonition had been, and find as well how the sense of humiliation and outrage in that year of marriage keeps breaking through, to prove her—as so often—a creature more " human " than has been supposed. She was flesh and blood like the rest of us—could suffer and resent, if also suffer and forgive. The alternation was constant. With Robertson in 1850 she would soar to unearthly altitudes of magnanimity on one page of a letter ; on the next, would tell with unflinching realism some anecdote of Byron's savage cruelty. . . . Now, in 1816, with Mrs. Villiers it was on Augusta that she concentrated all her powers—and they were formidable !—of wire-drawn analysis. Was Augusta conscious of guilt, repentant, sincere ? Her kindness and affectionateness were freely granted. But what was their value ? How deep did they go ? Interminable was the never-to-be answered questioning. For at the end, when they met after long and bitter estrangement, the enigma was not merely unsolved but more insoluble than ever. Still bitterer estrangement followed ; then to Augusta's death-bed Annabella sent that " old word of affection," the *Dearest Augusta* which called forth from the dying woman a scarcely-audible answer : " . . . my greatest consolation."

To a feeling like this, must all expression be denied to the one who most suffered in it ? Augusta kept home, husband (such as he was) and place in the world ; Annabella lost all three—and with them the affection which, but for Augusta, Byron might have come to feel for her. To take it on the most trivial ground, the situation was interesting—and the wife is the one to whom all interest in it is forbidden !

The other accusation of " spiritual blackmail " is an example of the facile phrase that seems to answer a difficult question.

Those who use it forget, or do not know, that Augusta flung herself upon these two for help and counsel—upon Annabella in abjection so complete as to implore her for advice on answering Byron's (at first) passionate reproaches and appeals to the love between them. Again, let us call the situation merely interesting. Here was the rejected wife, there the desired sister. Shudder though she might, the wife must feel the poignancy in such a drama. And only with Mrs. Villiers could the mere woman, not the mere guardian-angel, speak *her* part. . . . When all is said, repugnance persists. But it is vain to condemn human nature. It too persists against all our self-judgments. It drove Annabella to Mrs. Villiers; and Mrs. Villiers, Augusta's friend, " a strong and ardent nature, but also a woman of the world," felt that, responded to it, and—being human too—enjoyed herself a good deal while she did.

CHAPTER XVII

LOWESTOFT: AUGUSTA

IN Ely and Peterborough, on the 8th of June, 1816, there were
little crowds outside the successive inns at which a four-horse
carriage waited. A young lady travelling with a baby of about
six months old and a lady's maid—nothing remarkable in that;
but it had somehow got about that lady and baby were Lord
Byron's wife and daughter. The presence of such notorious
personages was exciting, and so these little crowds had assembled.
Lady Byron—small, still, dignified, but pale and tired-looking
—seemed to resent the staring, to feel herself the object of
intrusive curiosity; Ely and Peterborough, however, stared but
the harder for that. Bury, when the carriage stopped there, was
more enterprising. Into the lady's hand was thrust a copy of Lord
Byron's touching Farewell to England and his daughter; and
still less did she seem to like that. But when she should read the
Farewell, even *her* Unforgiving Heart must surely melt.

The Bury people did not know how that heart had been taught
to steel itself against his lordship's beautiful laments.[1] " Vastly
domestic, as if he were the best father and husband in the world."
Could they have read that comment, perhaps Lady Byron would
have been hissed at Bury, as Lord Byron had been in London.

She had got away at last—ill, sleepless, " headachy "—from
Kirkby and the reaction; was on her way to Lowestoft in
Suffolk, spelling it (as they all do) Lowestoffe. Ada was with her,
and Merle the lady's maid, and a footman.

By this time the Sole Daughter was " stouter and stronger than
any boy or girl of a year old that I ever saw, and so good-humoured
that it will be a very agreeable companion." Again the neuter

---

[1] This was not one of them. All the poems in that pamphlet were
scornfully repudiated by Byron in a letter to Murray.

pronoun ; but there is reassurance in the normal young mother's conviction that " it " surpassed all other babies of either sex. And it wrote its grandmamma a fictive letter about the incidents at Ely, Peterborough, and Bury : " Mamma said we were *Lionesses*—pray what does she mean ? "

They stopped two days on the road—at Worlingham, the Sparrows' place ; and there, for the first time in three years, M.G. and Annabella met again. They were both in the same plight, for to live with Lord Gosford had proved as impossible as to live with Lord Byron. But for very different reasons. Lord Gosford had become converted, was thrall to his formidable sister, Lady Olivia Sparrow, a great light among the Evangelicals. " It is the devil," wrote Annabella to her parents. M.G. was to flee from the devil to Lowestoft, and live next door to the " small house, but neat and clean," in full view of the sea, which Annabella had taken there. . . . So there was something to look forward to, and with full conscientiousness it was recognised. That her spirits were willing to revive is comically testified by the re-entry of the Mutton theme. " Divine mutton ! I am sure it wore the Golden Fleece." Comical too is her helplessness. The distracted ménage at Piccadilly had evidently taught her nothing, for she daily asked her mother's advice about beer-money, maids' laundry, and the right weight for the divine joints.

Of her " little establishment " at Lowestoft she wrote to her old friend, Anne Hoar : " It consists of my maid, the nurse, footman, and a maid hired here of all works. These creatures eat a great deal of beef and mutton, so that we live *altogether* for about £3 10s. a week. What do you think of it ? House rent is 4 guineas, inclusive of all wants ; and washing with extras, makes the sum up to £10 a week, which you see is beyond the limit of £500 per annum—but I don't know how to retrench. I eat *nothing* but meat, eggs, and biscuits—neither bread, butter, milk, tea, or strong drink."

They were neither of them very well, these " sick and hunted deer of the herd "—Mrs. Norton's bitter phrase (born of experience) for a separated wife ; and for Annabella's ills we are nowadays inclined to blame a diet composed of meat and eggs. But people were then devoutly carnivorous ; even Ada was sucking beef and mutton in a bag, and—perhaps as a consequence—showing " a touch of her Mam's *sauvagerie.*" There were long walks and some sailing—the latter much enjoyed. " It equalises my circulation and unloads my stomach ; " but sea-sickness was proudly repudiated.

Repercussions of the catastrophe had not been entirely escaped. Clermont was at Kirkby, and would not let Lady Noel talk about Ada, " who she says she is *determined* not to care about." And gossip about Byron kept filtering through—how he was shunned abroad " both by English and *Natives*, despite the Viscountess's warm recommendations ; " how Hobhouse and Scrope Davies (" a blesséd set ! ") were going out to him ; how he had a page again—the page being by Lord and Lady Darlington reported (to Colonel Leigh !) to have been said to be Augusta. " And their informant could not be persuaded it was not so," wrote Guss to Annabella from Six Mile Bottom. . . . Or it would be heard that Caroline Lamb had been to a party at Anglesea House, where no one would speak to her. Notorious personages, all of them ; even the sea could not drown Byronism.

Nor Gosfordism. The fierce convert had pursued his wife to Lowestoft, and was " pushing her into confessing her errors to Lady O. and begging pardon." He extended his ministrations to the other hunted deer : " Because I go to church very regularly and sometimes talk pye-house " (this to Sir Ralph), " Lord G. takes to himself the merit of having converted me." He at any rate got her to one of his Methodist meetings, whereupon it was at once reported in London that she was in the constant habit of attending them. " But I am not very likely to turn saint just now."

Nevertheless, it was now that she began to show the tendency —so strong in later life—towards what she calls " pye-house." She had always been serious-minded enough, but she had been a fashionable young lady too, able to be mordantly satirical about a City ball when she attended one. Now the good works at Seaham among her father's tenants were extended to the poor of Lowestoft, especially " her " fishermen's wives. She made friends with a clergyman's family at Pakeford near by, and visited with them among the deserving cottagers. The clergyman was the Rev. John William Cunningham, Vicar of Harrow since 1811 and author of an enormously popular Evangelical tract, *The Velvet Cushion*, published in 1814, and by this time boasting ten editions ; he was a member, too, of the famous Clapham Common sect, of which Thackeray has a satiric picture in *The Newcomes* : " The rich old ladies with their circle of flatterers, their hothouse grapes and their hothouse piety." But to Annabella the Clapham Common atmosphere proved just then so congenial that she went to stay with the Cunninghams from Lowestoft, telling Sir Ralph that his letters were " too shocking " to be sent on to her there.

She wrote daily and cheerfully, but briefly, to her parents ; almost daily, but neither cheerfully nor briefly to Mrs. Villiers and Augusta, pouring out the feelings which were the absorbing element in her life. As with Byron himself, " the thought ran through, through—yes, through." Even to Anne Hoar, after that prosaic beginning, she found herself dilating on the agonised past, and at such length and with such detail that she never sent the letter, but preserved it as containing memoranda. " I cannot *retain* resentment," she had written ; " in this case I never felt it."

She repeated that in a letter to Mrs. Villiers. " I am *not* unhappy ; it is impossible to have given up the heart devotedly and on principle without feeling for the being who has possessed it under every circumstance." On the same day she wrote to Augusta. It was in this letter that she spoke of " the thought which *from the first week of my marriage* has nearly driven me to madness." But : " Do not suppose I wish to exact any confession."

In this she deceived herself, as she had done before in lesser things. Gradually, under the pressure of these correspondences, a precisely opposite wish was growing in her. Augusta's letters could not have failed to foster it. They were in her most maddening style of what Byron was soon to call " d——d crinkum-crankum ; " all underlinings and dashes, breakings-off and goings-on, pious commonplaces mingled with extravagant self-accusations (" I am the one *much* the most to blame, and *quite* inexcusable ") cries to her guardian-angel—and then this : " I have said but little of *him*, my dearest A., fearing you might mistake the *nature* of my feelings. I am certain they are, and have ever been, such as you could not disapprove."

That was too much. Annabella broke out to Mrs. Villiers—now more sceptical than herself of Augusta's penitence, after some meetings of which the wife had already heard. Mrs. Villiers' account of these, though published at length in *Astarte*, must find some place here.

She came sooner than she expected, being ordered to come up for the Regent's fête. She wrote to me the preceding day to prepare her dress for her, & therefore when we first met (an interview which I own *I* dreaded beyond measure) our whole conversation turned on *Gauzes & Sattins*—but I was foolishly dissatisfied—I thought her looking quite stout & well (which by the bye she still does) & perfectly cool and easy, having apparently nothing on her mind but what there was abundance of ostensible cause for. This rather provoked me. . . . Yesterday, for the first time, she dined here, & was here between 4 and 5 hours, & I must say that in my life I never saw any thing equal to her dejection—her absence—her whole mind evidently preoccupied and engrossed—& apparently insensible of being in society. Mr. V., who really exerted himself & commanded himself much better than I expected to shew her as much kindness as before, tells me that while I was called out of the room to speak to a person, he could not extract an answer—even a monosyllable from her—except when he joked about the predicted destruction of the world to-day & said (à propos to some arrangements which the boys wanted to make) " We need not give ourselves any trouble about it, for the world will be at an end to-morrow & that will put an end to all our cares "—she quite exclaimed before the boys, the servants, &c., " I don't know what *you* may all be, but I'm sure *I'm* not prepared for the next world, so I hope this will last." This looks well for her mind—if this feeling is well kept up I hope every thing from it *with time*—but do not think me brutal or even unkind if I tell you the work is not done yet.

A week later Mrs. Villiers had again written : " Since my last letter to you I have seen upon her table a thick unsealed letter addressed by her to him. . . . Be her penitence what it may, in *you* she is bound to confide implicitly, and *to* you she is bound to obey implicitly."

Well, well ! Counsels of perfection are easy to draw up, whatever the imperfection of surreptitious glances at letters on a hostess's writing-table. But Annabella was able to reassure

Mrs. Villiers ; Augusta had told her about the letter to " him."
Yet now—here was this boast about the nature of her feelings.
Disconcerting ! And it was quoted with an exclamation-mark
and : " On this I shall animadvert very severely. . . . Upon
such principles what may not be justified ? "

That letter is an epitome of Annabella's vacillations between
tenderness and severity—typical as they are of her attitude
towards Augusta from first to last. Sometimes she yielded so
completely to tenderness that she could write : " To principles and
feelings like yours, the sacrifices you made must have been
entirely sacrifices. . . . I hope I understand you as well as any
human being can another. . . . I think there is a similarity between our characters." Delusion could go no farther than that ;
but even delusion jibbed when the nature of Augusta's feelings
was offered for approval.

She wrote to her—and did not animadvert so severely as she
had promised.

> Associations most prejudicial to a good influence from you
> have subsisted too deeply and too habitually in his mind. . . .
> *Our* visit to S.M.B.—even the very first night of it—will make
> you sensible of this. . . . His feelings towards you have varied.
> . . . Sometimes he has spoken of you with compassion—some-
> times with bitter scorn—and sometimes with dispositions still
> more reprehensible. The only time when I believe he was really
> on the brink of suicide was on an occasion relating to his remorse
> about you. . . . Till you realise that he has in reality been your
> worst friend—indeed *not* your friend—you cannot altogether
> think rightly. . . . Forgive him, desire his welfare—but resign
> the pernicious hope of being his friend more nearly—do not
> think me cruel. . . . You will not be offended when I say that
> I think his mind too *powerful* for you—I could not feel secure
> that he would not bewilder you on any subject. . . . Alas, my
> dear A. you do not, I believe, know him.

She went on to advise about correspondence with Byron.
Augusta was to avoid " all phrases or *marks* " which might recall
wrong ideas to his mind, " and let me also warn you against the
levity and nonsense which he likes for the worst reason, because
it prevents him from reflecting seriously. . . . Perhaps I have gone
too far in using the privilege you allow me. But I will hope not
to be quite useless to one I love so well."

Augusta's half-abject, half-defensive answers decided Annabella to go to London at the end of August, " as I agree with you [Mrs. Villiers] in thinking an interview particularly desirable." Augusta promised to remain in town ; Annabella then arranged to come to rooms between Knightsbridge and Green Street on August 31. Mrs. Villiers expressed great relief at the prospect, and added : " I am *now* very *sanguine* about her, and have the greatest hopes that your approaching interview will complete her reformation—I might almost say, salvation."

This is what has been called their spiritual blackmail. The pressure put upon her may too easily be seen in that light. A " conscious innocence " which called upon her guardian-angel to approve the nature of her feelings could not but outrage the wife's sense of what they had meant for her own feelings ; yet in Augusta it did represent an aspect of the truth. Hers was a sort of perverted innocence, born of superficiality. And more —there can be no doubt that Guss would have been glad to love her dearest B. as a brother only. She told Annabella afterwards that from the time he was sixteen, he had been a source of misery to her " on that account." But he was B. ; she could refuse him nothing—his mind was, as Annabella wrote, too powerful for Guss. Her wretched husband was no help to her—it was she who had to help him ; her life was one perpetual scene of distraction between his debts and his fecklessness, and her incessant pregnancies ; Byron was greatly generous to her with money—and besides, they could amuse each other as no one else could, could laugh and then (his phrase, that Annabella too would often quote !) " put finger in eye " over a melting poem. If he demanded more of her, demanded all of her, did it very much matter " so long as nobody was hurt ? " *She* would have been happier without a brother-lover, but B. would have it so, and B. must have his way. . . . That was " the nature of her feelings ; " she was as honestly convinced as Guss could be about anything that they were, and always had been, such as Annabella could not disapprove. Muddled as she was about most things, the conviction did not seem to her a strange one. She never could get it expressed as she felt it—little wonder ; but when she tried, the truth (as she saw it) was in her words.

The other two, it is argued, should have been able to divine this.

A second counsel of perfection—and especially as they had Augusta's flimsy little personality to contend with! Coming up to London to talk about " Gauzes and Sattins," looking as well as she had ever looked, waiting (a favourite trick of hers) till other people were in the room before she would touch a thorny subject with her friends—Thérèse Villiers knew her subterfuges, evasions, " flights into illness " (as modern psychology has it) by heart. They could irritate her, as we have seen ; none the less she had written to Annabella in July : " I think I am justified in saying *very* confidently that her mind *was* purity and innocence itself, and now her eyes are really opened as to the enormity she has been led into, her former feelings and principles will, I really hope and believe, return with double force." Mrs. Villiers flinched from this position as the weeks went on, was inclined to accept Annabella's ruthless phrase of " a kind of moral idiocy from birth "—but then Annabella in her turn would hover back to indulgent tenderness. So it went on between them, till finally they resolved on an interview—whether with the conscious aim of obtaining a verbal confession, we may be sure that neither the one nor the other could have told.

On August 31 Annabella went up to London, taking rooms at 1 Lower Seymour Street for a fortnight. Augusta was in her apartments in St. James's Palace. A meeting, followed by several others, took place immediately. At one of these Augusta " made full confession of the previous connection—any subsequent to my marriage being stoutly denied." Afterwards, in 1817, Annabella wrote of these interviews in two of the statements by which, as she hoped, posterity would judge her behaviour more kindly than contemporary opinion had been given the opportunity to do. Augusta (she recorded) had acknowledged that the verses, " I speak not, I trace not, I breathe not thy name," were addressed to her ; she declared that she had never had any idea of Annabella's suspicions until the summer of 1815 (" when I evidently wished she would leave us "), but had often told Byron that he said such things before his wife as would have led any other woman to suspect. He had reassured her, saying that Annabella was entirely unconscious, " and she seems to have acted on the principle that what could be concealed from me was no injury." She denied that during the separation-proceedings Byron had ever

addressed any criminal proposals to her ; and said that she had
never seen remorse towards her in him but once—" the night
before they last parted, previous to his going abroad."

No analysis could so well convey the insensibility of Augusta's
nature as does a note on the day after one of these interviews.

> I am so sorry for your bad night—& for your *idea* of my
> *uncomfortableness*—which is however quite a *fancy of your own*
> —but I daresay I *looked* something or other which made you
> fancy. Pray have a good night & write me a 2d post note to
> say when I am likely to see you again, & tell me you are no
> longer sorry. I assure you I only feel & felt pleasure &
> comfort in seeing you &c., ALL at least that I am now capable
> of feeling.

And now again we are conscious of that repugnance for the
exchanges between Annabella and Augusta's friend. Confession
had been made to the person most concerned ; but it was not
enough. To Mrs. Villiers too confession must be made. In vain
we ask ourselves why. They gave themselves reasons which
convinced themselves ; they believed in their purely good
intentions of " bringing her to realise the horror of the crime "—
but even if these were convincing to us, what can be said of this
from Mrs. Villiers, unrebuked by Annabella ?

> I should on my part only make the condition of being asked
> no questions as to the sources of my information, though I
> would assure her, and with truth, that it came from quarters
> unconnected with *you*. . . . She *never must* know of any
> communication of yours.

The lie which is half a truth was never more flagrantly shown in
its power to delude the teller. And it deluded as well the clearer-
sighted conscience of Annabella. She acquiesced ; she passed on
the half-truth to Augusta in these words : " Mrs. Villiers . . . had
received detailed information *which originated with Lord B. from
an authority she could not doubt.*" Both women were salving their
consciences—a little uneasy after all !—by telling themselves that
they meant " Lady G." (whom Lord Lovelace, in *Astarte*, conjectures to have been Lady Granville), and Lady G. was to be the
stalking-horse for their own motive—believed in, let it be repeated,
by both, so deep was the sophistry they had induced in themselves

... the motive of preventing Mrs. Villiers from " precipitating you into greater dangers by her imprudent and ignorant zeal."

They were self-deluded—true ; but analysis, if it takes us some way towards condonation, takes us also nearer than we could wish to the underlying truth. One hesitates to write : " Desire to prolong the sensation ; " yet those words are more indulgent than another word which suggests itself—the German *Schadenfreude*, of which " pleasure in another's wretchedness " is a coarse, yet the only, translation. For such pleasure it was not—this laying of Augusta on the rack of a second confession. It was the unconscious cruelty in human nature, asserting itself in both because their hold over another was too powerful for their human nature to use generously. Magnanimity is one thing—and a very dangerous thing for the mortal who displays it ; in generosity no danger lies. Had it been generosity which Annabella was displaying, not even one confession would have been wrested from Augusta.

Well ! she was only magnanimous, and she had been sorely injured. Augusta was laid upon the second rack, and wrote :

Dearest A.—I scarcely know what to say except that I will be with you early to-morrow—& that I am grateful to you & to Mrs. V.—I don't think I *can* see her—& yet I wish you not to say so—and in fact I can't just now say *what* I wish. If you have the lines, keep them.[1] God bless you.

The ordeal was arranged—Annabella writing in the meantime to Mrs. Villiers, part of her letter " under A's inspection," a postscript added when she was alone. " The humblest sense of her own situation. . . . She has shown me of her own accord *his* letters to her—having only suppressed them because of the bitterness towards me ; they are *absolute love-letters*, and she wants to know how she can stop them."

We shall return to these letters of Byron's. She who wanted to know how she could stop them must nevertheless—being human

---

[1] " The lines " were Byron's *Epistle to Augusta*. They had just been sent by him to Murray ; Mrs. Leigh was to say whether they should be published or not. After months of vacillation (see *Letters and Journals*, iii. 366-7 for her letters to Murray on the subject) she finally wrote to Byron that the *Epistle* must be withheld, and it did not see the light until 1830.

Annabella wrote to her after the confession : " I have read the lines to you, and think they ought not to be seen by anyone."

like the other two—have had other feelings about them besides that one. That one was sincere; but here was B. showing her that outcasts could be lovable and loving! Was Geneva any crueller than London, where a single confession was not enough—where one was told (wisely and kindly, no doubt) that B. had betrayed one to woman after woman? The revelation had been overwhelming; in her revulsion she had exclaimed: "I will never write to him again!" But this had not been encouraged—"violent resolutions had better not be taken." It was hard to know what they really wanted, except that one must confess to Thérèse also.

And then, confession made again, the penitent escaped to Six Mile Bottom and from there wrote to "Dearest A."

> I shall be glad that you see Mrs. V. again. I have a *very* great dread of *her* thinking me a perfect *stone*, and perhaps she will believe *you* that I am not. I feel I can't undeceive her, for the more anxious I am, the less I am able. Towards *another* person she is *very* violent in her expressions of resentment—and it is I daresay very natural, but I think it better not to say a word in answer—though in fact I am the one *much* the most to blame—and *quite* inexcusable.

And at the end: "Do not show the letter I sent you to Mrs. V. I should think it wrong to any but you—my Guardian Angel!"

All our pity, during that fortnight, is Augusta's. They were breaking a butterfly on a wheel. Shallow, insensitive though she was, the torment of divided feelings—common to them all—was for her beyond comparison the keenest. The other two had no humiliation, no pain at B's betrayal, no "absolute love-letters" to wring their hearts. Secure on their pinnacles of virtue, with each other to expand to; and the culprit at Six Mile Bottom with not only B's troubles to face but her husband's: "I found things better in some ways than I expected—the *Spirits* better than they have been for some time, but without any particular reason, for *affairs* are the same—so of course *durability* can't be expected." Then follows the Darlington gossip about the page at Geneva.

On the day she wrote this, Byron was writing to her from Ouchy :

I have recently broken through my resolution of not speaking to you of Lady B.—but do not on that account name her to me. It is a relief—a partial relief—to me to talk of her sometimes to you—but it would be none to hear of her. *Of* her you are to judge for yourself, but do not altogether forget that she has destroyed your brother. Whatever my faults might or may have been, *She* was not the person marked out by providence to be their avenger. One day or another her conduct will recoil on her own head ; *not* through *me*, for my feelings towards her are not those of Vengeance, but—mark—if she does not end miserably *tôt ou tard*. She may think—talk—or act as she will, and by any process of cold reasoning and a jargon of " duty & acting for the best " &c., &c., impose upon her own feelings and those of others for a time—but woe unto her—the wretchedness she has brought upon the man to whom she has been everything evil [*except in one respect (effaced)*] will flow back into its fountain. I may thank the strength of my constitution that has enabled me to bear all this, but those who bear the longest and the most do not suffer the least. I do not think a human being could endure more mental torture than that woman has directly & indirectly inflicted upon me—within the present year. . . .[1]

Scrope has by this time arrived with my little presents for you & yours and Ada. I still hope to be able to see you next Spring, perhaps you & one or two of the children could be spared some time next year for a little tour *here* or in France with me of a month or two. I think I could make it pleasing to you, & it should be no expense to L. or yourself. Pray think of this hint. . . . I would return from any distance at any time to see you, and come to England for you ; and when you consider the chances against our—but I won't relapse into the dismals and anticipate long absences.

The great obstacle would be that you are so admirably yoked —and necessary as a housekeeper—and a letter-writer—& a place-hunter to that very helpless gentleman your cousin, that I suppose the usual self-love of an elderly person would interfere between you & any scheme of recreation or relaxation, for however short a period.

What a fool I was to marry—and *you* not so very wise, my dear. We might have lived so single and so happy—as old maids and bachelors ; I shall never find any one like you—nor

[1] This letter is given in full in *Astarte*.

you (vain as it may seem) like me. We are just formed to pass
our lives together, and therefore—we—at least I am—by a
crowd of circumstances removed from the only being who could
ever have loved me, or whom I can unmixedly feel attached to.

Had you been a Nun, and I a Monk—that we might have
talked through a grate instead of across the sea—No matter—
my voice and my heart are

ever thine. . . .

This, like the rest of his letters, was shown or sent to Annabella.
Perhaps Augusta, too, had her *Schadenfreude* ! It was bitter for
the wife to read such words, of either kind. Already she had seen
that uncontrolled handwriting flung across the ocean in this cry :

> Do not be uneasy, and do not " hate yourself." If you hate
> either, let it be *me*—but do not—it would kill me. We are the
> last persons in the world who ought or could cease to love one
> another. . . . I always loved you better than any earthly
> existence, and I always shall, unless I go mad.

And then the X and B.

Differently, but not less poignantly, must Annabella's heart
have ached to read of the presents Scrope Davies was bringing to
England, " expressly for you to divide among yourself and the
children, including also your niece Ada, for whom I selected a
ball . . . and moreover a Chrystal necklace, and anything else you
may like to add for her—the love ! " But the heartache was
again to alter as the wife read on :

> And so Lady B. has been " kind to you," you tell me—" very
> kind "—umph—it is as well she should be kind to some of us,
> and I am glad she has the heart & the discernment to be still
> *your* friend ; you were ever so to her. I heard the other day
> that she was very unwell. I was shocked enough—& sorry
> enough, God knows, but never mind ; H. tells me however that
> she is *not* ill ; that she *had* been indisposed, but is better and
> well to do. This is a relief. As for me I am in good health, &
> fair though very unequal spirits ; but for all that, she—or rather
> the separation—has broken my heart. I feel as if an Elephant
> had trodden on it. I am convinced I shall never get over it—
> but I try. I had enough before I knew her and more than
> enough, but time & agitation had done something for me ; but
> this last wreck has affected me very differently. If it were
> *acutely* it would not signify ; but it is not that—I breathe lead.

While the storm lasted and you were all pitying and comforting me with condemnation in Piccadilly, it was bad enough & violent enough, but it's worse now ; I have neither strength nor spirits nor inclination to carry me through anything which will clear my brain or lighten my heart. . . . H. has told me all the strange stories in circulation of me and mine—not true . . . and as to all these " mistresses "—Lord help me, I have had but one. Now don't scold—but what could I do ?

Follows the well-known account of the Claire Clairmont business, to be read elsewhere.[1] That could be smiled at with lips that may have quivered for all their scorn ; but what was this, in yet another letter ?

You know, I suppose, that Lady Bn. *secretly opened my letter-trunks before she left Town, and that she has also been* (*during* or since the separation) in *correspondence with* that self-avowed libeller and strumpet [*erased*] [2] wife. This you may depend upon, though I did not know it till recently. Upon such conduct I am utterly at a loss to make a single comment—beyond every expression of astonishment. I am past indignation. . . .

This country is altogether the Paradise of Wilderness. I wish you were in it with me, and every one else out of it. Love me, A.

Augusta wrote, sending that letter :

Do tell me if I can do anything about *you,* for I can't tell you the grief it is to me his having such ideas—*IF he really has them.* I *sometimes,* indeed *often,* think it a *real* madness, and you know how I have been doomed to witness this *perverted* way of seeing things—*not only* in *him*—thinking real friends enemies—right— *wrong*—and so on. . . .

About the trunks—Could I not say something true to con-tradict such a vile calumny ! Do advise me—and consider yourself as what I consider *most.*

Annabella's reply was contemptuous of both accusations : they were made to discredit her testimony ; she had not seen " C.L.," had not written her a single line since the separation beyond " that note of which you know, merely declining her visit." [3]

---

[1] *Letters and Journals,* iii. 347-8.   [2] " Wm. Lamb's."

[3] This had been on September 7. She would not receive Caroline, but was ready to see William Lamb, if desired. There is no record of any interview with him.

Conscience, it seems, can do other things besides making cowards of us all; and it did some of them to each of these three women. Self-delusion, self-complacency, cruelty, it induced in two; in Augusta—besides the cowardice—treachery towards her dearest B. Had she fiercely refused to show his letters, our pity for her would be a good deal purer. That part of the counsel of perfection she followed with an abject fidelity which we could almost feel to be redeemed by *Schadenfreude*.

CHAPTER XVIII

1816-17

TAKING UP LIFE AGAIN

During the London fortnight Lady Byron gave a dinner-party " of duty and expediency," her guests being Mrs. George Byron, Mrs. Villiers, and Augusta—for whom the confessional interviews can scarcely have been more excruciating. Byron was evidently told by someone of the renewed intercourse, for there now came a letter from Brougham, written on his behalf to attempt reconciliation. The parents suspected a plot, urged Annabella to be cautious—it was in this connection that Lady Noel launched her warning : " Once more take care of X.—if I know anything of human nature she does and must hate you." That was incredible to the guardian angel ; but though her answer to Brougham began with a moving confession of difficulty and pain in refusing the overture, it soon took a sterner tone : " Some *necessary* intercourse which I have had with Mrs. L. since I came to town has doubtless been employed disadvantageously to me by Lord Byron's friends, as a mark of intended reconciliation ; but the ends I have in view were too important to be sacrificed to any transient and false impressions." Of this letter she wrote to her father : " The *manner* is such as to prevent any idea of my hard-heartedness." Brougham had given his own opinion—it went " very unequivocally " against Byron.

This was not Byron's first attempt at reunion. Already in August Mme. de Staël—whom he often visited at Coppet— had persuaded him to write to a friend in England. He had written, and sent her the letter to do what she liked with : " But it will be useless. It contains, however, the truth of my feelings and wishes on that subject, and as they have been doubted I am willing to put them to the proof." [1] Whether this letter was

[1] See *L. & J.*, iii. 343.

sent remains uncertain. Mme. de Staël did intervene through Lady Romilly, sending Annabella a message to say that she "suspended judgment." A very formal and intentionally enigmatic reply was received : "Lord Byron is well aware that my determination *ought not* to be changed."

He had been deeply angered. It was immediately afterwards that he wrote the *Lines on Hearing that Lady Byron was Ill*, though they were not published until after his death. "The significant eye that learns to lie in silence " ; " the moral Clytemnestra of thy lord "—these phrases mark his resentment ; Clytemnestra became almost a synonym for her in his letters to friends. Yet he now made this second attempt, to be again repulsed. . . . In 1823 he sent Lady Blessington one of his many withheld letters to his wife, in which he had said :

> I considered our re-union as not impossible for more than a year after the separation—but then I gave up the hope entirely and for ever. . . . For my part, I am violent but not malignant. . . . To you, who are colder and more concentrated, I would just hint that you may sometimes mistake the depth of a cold anger for dignity, and a worse feeling for duty. . . . I have ceased to reflect on any but two points—that you are the mother of my child, and that we shall never meet again. I think if you also consider the two corresponding points with reference to myself, it will be better for all three.

That letter was never sent ; but in the last year of his life Byron once more approached his wife, with a request for her portrait. It was done through a friend of Lady Blessington's who had come to Genoa, and whom he knew to be an intimate of Annabella's also—Hugh Montgomery, the one-time "innocent rival " who had been fabled to possess her hopeless love ! [1]

The two points she was to have been called upon to consider had never left her thoughts. When in the April of 1816 she had written that the struggle was over, it was to nothing less than anguish that she referred. Read this letter to her in

---

[1] Colonel Montgomery wrote to Annabella that Byron talked " kindly and nobly of her." But he added that Augusta's hair was worn in a large brooch, and in a bracelet on his left arm. From this letter she first heard of the Greek plans (May, 1823).

the February before the separation : " My heart and mind were so full of the dreadful suffering I had witnessed at Kirkby that I have told a friend, thinking I was doing but mere justice to the unexampled gentleness, goodness, and wise forbearance of the perfectest of human beings.

Your faithful and most tenderly affectionate

S. SARAH SIDDONS."

Little wonder that she shrank from re-opening the chapter. Knowing Byron as she knew him, hope could never revive in her heart. All their incompatibility was plain to her now ; and to it were added the knowledge of his feeling for Augusta and of Augusta's blindness to its persistent nature. The sister's super-ficial view that " B." could be good though she were constantly to be in his company—this made a hopelessness the more. No. There was nothing to be retrieved for Annabella, or for Byron, in their re-union ; she knew that all too well. " ' Heart at his feet '—and mine was laid before him." As he had trampled on it then—at Halnaby, Six Mile Bottom, Piccadilly—he would trample on it again. She had given him her best ; he had " abhorred " it ; would abhor it always, once they should be together.

But to the extent the chapter *had* been re-opened, the re-open-ing broke her down once more. She went from London to her new friends, the Cunninghams, at Harrow. It was too much for her. " I shall feel relieved at going to-morrow," she wrote to Mrs. Villiers, " not being in a company state. And besides it requires more exertion to keep up the character of a saint—at least you who know what a sinner I am will think so." Though she says nothing of the Byronic associations with Harrow, they must have been in her thoughts—when she passed the school, looked at the famous view of London, saw " his " elm-tree golden with September.

After this visit she went home, looking ill and disappointing her parents. Soon after her arrival she came across an old MS. book of 1810, and wrote on one of the many blank pages :

After what an interval do I resume this volume ! What a volume of human nature has since been opened to me ! . . .

The objects which at present most occupy my mind will best mark my character, which on referring to the preceding pages, must, I think, be little changed. I have sacrificed self-justification in a great measure to A.'s salvation—or the hope of it ; and am now considering it more than anything else—to save her from the dangers around. I do believe her sincerely penitent—I have *found* her so—and my truest friend ; I feel that whatever the world might judge, I owe her more friendship than I have shown—that in some respects I have been actuated by personal considerations, or distant fears for my child, to regard her welfare less than otherwise I should—and than in any case I ought.

All this I am now determined to compensate for—if possible.

She was never to free herself from that coil. At this time she was still writing perpetually to "A," who was still sending her Byron's letters ; and the third canto of *Childe Harold* was selling in thousands. It opens with the apostrophe to "Ada ! sole daughter of my house and heart," which closes on the lines :

> " Yet though dull hate as duty should be taught,
> I know that thou wilt love me . . . "

It was published on November 18 ; but before that everybody concerned knew all about it. Annabella wrote to Mrs. Villiers on October 24 :

The volume containing those lines was exhibited at Mme. de Staël's without restriction. . . . Some will say, " If there had been any truth in the report, he never could have written such lines." We must therefore hope the best. I did not tell you the particulars of his proposal to her to go abroad . . . but as she has herself owned the direct nature of [it], I may add that it appeared to me of the most insidious nature.

Her situation was made still more painful by the fact that her friends, including Lushington, Doyle, and her mother, wished that Augusta *would* " flee to Byron in exile." [1] In their view, that would put an end to false and intolerable relations, and the victory would remain with the wife. " But," continues Lord Lovelace, " she dreamed of miracles, of Augusta purified from sin " ; moreover, Mrs. Villiers was pressing her hard to be kind,

[1] *Astarte*, p. 63.

win Augusta's confidence, save her from ruin. She persevered in her chosen course, and (though Lord Lovelace does not speak of it) we do not forget that a voice more powerful than any other had pleaded with her " to be kind." She could not think that that would be to snatch the victory for herself.

But nothing could save Augusta from the persecution-by-poetry. The sensation caused by the third *Harold* was naught to the " pucker " (as Byron called it) when in June 1817 *Manfred* was published. The Incantation which forms part of it was intended for his wife :

> Though thy slumber may be deep,
> Yet thy spirit shall not sleep :
>
> .   .   .   .
>
> Thou art wrapt as with a shroud,
> Thou art gathered in a cloud ;
> And for ever shalt thou dwell
> In the spirit of this spell.

More prophetic words were never written. He did not mean them as we in our knowledge can read them—yet to say that may be foolishness. They escaped from his anger to his imagination. She dwelt in the spirit of that spell to the end of her long, active life, which was so sublimated yet so " gathered in a cloud."

Of the stanzas to Ada she wrote to Lady Anne Barnard :

> It is said that hatred of him will be taught as a lesson to his child.   I might appeal to all who have ever heard me speak of him, and still more to my own heart, to witness that there has been no moment when I have remembered injury otherwise than affectionately and sorrowfully.

And that is borne out by some words to Mrs. Villiers on the same subject : " Don't be afraid to send me any histories of my hard-heartedness, for I am just now so soft-hearted that I think they may impart a little of their imagined qualities, and be of some service."

The long agonised year of 1816 came to a close for her at Kirkby. Ada was christened on November 1, the godmothers being Lady Noel and Lady Tamworth (Sophy Curzon). On that very day Byron was writing to his wife. Somebody had told him that she meant to pass the winter abroad. Instantly he sent Augusta a letter " to be despatched with all speed," insisting upon a promise that the child should never leave England. Annabella's reply was to Augusta : " Lady Byron has never had any intention of quitting England." [1]

On December 10 fell Ada's first birthday. Annabella wrote to Mrs. Villiers on the last day of the year, sending her some lines she had composed and saying : " It has occurred to me that they might be misunderstood, as if they expressed a wish that she were with her father, such as she is ; when on the contrary, I consider her as *fatherless*."

> Thine is the smile and thine the bloom
>   Where hope might fancy ripened charms ;
> But mine is dyed in Memory's gloom—
>   Thou art not in a Father's arms !
>
>   .   .   .   .   .   .
>
> And there I would have loved thee most,
>   And there have owned thou wert so dear
> That though my worldly all were lost,
>   I still had felt my life is *here* !
>
>   .   .   .   .   .   .
>
> Thou fatherless [2]—who mayst not rest
>   Save in one frail and shattered bark,
> A lonely Mother's offered breast—
>   May Heaven provide a surer ark.
>
>   .   .   .   .   .   .

[1] This did not satisfy Byron. He wrote to Hanson, bidding him take steps to prevent the possibility. The trouble lasted until well into 1817. Then, at the beginning of March, Byron received from Hanson the following document :

KIRKBY MALLORY, *January* 30, 1817.

There never has existed, nor does there exist, the remotest intention of removing Miss Byron out of the Kingdom.

ANNE ISABELLA BYRON.
RALPH NOEL.

But under Sir Ralph's signature were the words : *Without the leave of the Chancellor*. A bill in Chancery, making Ada a ward of the Court, had been filed against Byron during the separation-proceedings—no hint being given him of the step. We shall see what he wrote to his wife in that March.

[2] In the copy sent to Mrs. Villiers this line runs :
    " Thou Dove ! who mayst not find a rest " . . .

Nor think me frozen, if for thee
  No earthly wish now claims a part ;
Too dear such wish—too vain to me—
  Thou art not near a Father's heart !

Anniversary of her last day of hopeful girlhood, New Year was a date even more marked for her than for most people. Now it was rung in for the second time since that Seaham wedding, of which all that survived for the world was her marriage-name and her child—*their* child, as the coming months were to drive upon her. What else dwelt with her was of the inner life. True to herself, she paid a New Year tribute to conscience. It was a written summary of duties, headed (with all her unconscious humour) " Mems : Duty to B. ; duty to A. L."

> *Duty to B.*—Not only to decline occasions of hostility to him, whenever it is possible without compromising the real interests of my daughter, but to exert myself in order to prevent his involving himself in difficulties, the event of which would probably be to raise me somewhat in the general estimation, and to ruin him yet more.
>
> At the same time, to employ every means, unattended by these consequences, of taking all power out of his hands—as I should take away a knife from my child. The instrument would only be used to the hurt of the bearer & others.
>
> To arm myself against him in every possible manner, so as to obtain a perfect sense of Security . . . the necessity of caution producing, on the contrary, a temper of Suspicion which injures the perfection of Forgiveness, and prevents a comprehensive wisdom, by making little things too important.
>
> *Duty to A.L.*—It is my unalterable belief that she has never meant to do me harm, and that she has often incurred personal vexations to fulfil her conception of acting as my friend. Moreover, she has placed confidence in me—I cannot prove its motives to have been altogether selfish, nor altogether sincere —but I am not to presume the *evil* only.
>
> It is in her power to give the most important evidence against Lord B., & in case of a contest respecting my maternal guardianship, I consider her bound to afford it to the utmost—excepting only the confession of her guilt. Were she to refuse what I conceive to be just, I should think myself at liberty to proceed against her personally—but in no other case.

Ada inspired a New Year copy of verses.   Now that she could walk alone, could " understand what she was told to do," her appeal was strengthening.   There was something in her for the mind, and so the heart was readier.

ON SEEING A FLOWER SHELTERED FROM THE STORM BY AN OAK

(The Mother—to her Child)

I, like this tree which spreads its shelter wide,
" The pelting of the pitiless storm " would bide
To save the blossom of the flower below—
And oh, my flower ! if from the cup of woe
Pour'd on my head, some lonely drop should fall,
Escap'd the love that would have spar'd thee all—
May it on thine descend, a softening dew,
And add but tenderer grace—a lovelier hue !

Taking up life once more after disaster—it is a painful process, slow in results ; the step gained one day seems lost the next.   So it was with Annabella.   Early in the New Year she stayed with Sophy Tamworth, and wrote " happy " in her diary ; then she went on to the Wilmots at Catton.   There was a fellow-guest who sang beautifully, and she wrote to Mrs. Villiers :

> She sang two or three airs in a way that touched me, but as I was not shut up in a band-box, where I wished myself, I could not *put finger in eye* without being suspected of giving a scene, and I had much rather keep my flinty character.

Put finger in eye.   She was hearing another voice than the singer's when she wrote those words ; and soon Augusta submitted a letter from the inventor of that silly-sweet phrase.   It was chiefly concerned with the stanzas to Ada (" which I hoped would give *you* pleasure at least "), but his daughter figured in another connection :

> I wrote to you the other day about Ada.   If the *answer* is still refused I shall take *legal measures* to enforce it, and have ordered H. to do so.   *Remember I* do not seek this, I wish it not, but I require an explicit promise that Ada shall on no consideration quit the country, whether the mother does or no,

and by all that is most sacred, there is no measure which I will not take to prevent it, failing in a reply to my just demand. So say—and so I will do.   They will end by driving me mad, I wonder they have not already.

The document quoted on page 262 was then drawn up, and sent by Hanson.

Soon afterwards Lady Byron left home for London.   She felt that she must return South, " in order to *circulate* my real character.   I should afterwards sink into retirement more comfortably when I had left a part of the world longing for me."   A social campaign, in a word ;   she marked its nature by seeing little of Augusta.   At the same time she wrote to Colonel Doyle :

> My conduct toward her may appear to you more extraordinary when I acknowledge that I have hardly ever had a doubt of her turning upon me as an enemy, whenever she could, by that plausible sophistry in which she excels as much as he does, acquit her conscience of particular obligations. . . .   I believe she never takes a step towards evil without making a pseudo-conscience the authority for it.   The true conscience and the false one are as like as twins.   For my own conduct, I think it as well to pay forgiveness *by advance*—and besides I cannot act upon unconfirmed suspicions of the future.   My views on the past you know.

Here she added, as her view of the past, the passage quoted in Chapter XVI.

But peace was not yet to be established by any campaign of hers.   She stayed only a few weeks in London ;   then returned to encounter indignation about Walter Scott's review (in the *Quarterly*) of the new *Harold*.   The Wilmots had written " in a passion," her parents were in a passion too ;   of herself she wrote :

> I confess it has not had that effect upon my phlegmatic constitution, and I have been sending a message through a friend to Walter Scott—the forbearance of which may touch him—if he has a heart.

Scott soon showed that he had a heart.   On March 6 Annabella wrote the following to Mrs. Villiers :

> . . . I have had a communication from Walter Scott as long as a marriage settlement, whereby he makes over to me his

esteem and admiration in such terms as it becometh me not to repeat ; and to say the truth it is quite incomprehensible to me—though I feel certain of his sincerity—since he persists in reasoning from such false premises as appear to me inevitably damnatory of my conduct. . . . To any person who knew the nature of the case even as to my personal treatment, his letter would appear that of a lunatic. . . . But it is really *very* kind towards me, and I must not quarrel with people for not being able to see, when the film has so lately fallen from my own eyes. Nothing short of taking Lord B. " for better for worse " would, I think, cure Walter Scott. The principal insane ideas are—that Lord B. is not *quite* a Joseph, but that he *is* the soul of honour & generosity ; that he never told even a white lie, nor made himself whiter in any way than he truly is ; that he did think me a little too good, and was in a passion, which frightened me, and my friends still worse ; & then was rather too proud to beg pardon, which we were too much *affronted* to grant ; that he showed a disregard of money which was foolish, to be sure, but poets will be romantic sometimes—though in Mr. Scott I know no instance of it except this partiality. All these ideas are not expressed, but I think directly implied. I have sent a rejoinder—through the same friend—& have named Mr. Wilmot & Capn. Byron . . . as persons of judgment & integrity who had personal opportunities of investigating Lord B.'s conduct & motives towards me, as well as mine towards him ; and they were *therefore* concerned when it was supposed that . . . from the provocation of a transient estrangement, I could have been induced . . . to leave a husband whose . . . " inborn generosity " must surely preclude the idea of treating a woman with studied cruelty, & of sacrificing her to vindictive pride & selfish calculations. I added that *I* could not uphold the character of such a wife ; but as I had never consented to give any currency to the knowledge of my deepest wrongs, I was far from complaining of the consequences of this *voluntary* reserve.

I flatter myself this is rather sharp *for me*. I shall become a shrew after I have engaged a few more reviewers. I did not touch upon the Remorse—because when a confidence cannot be made it is an ungenerous policy to give a hint.

So it had all begun again. There is a letter from Lady Noel to Hugh Montgomery, about this time, in which she speaks of Annabella's illness. " She is upset from a certain quarter, but she is a philosopher and heroine. I myself am neither, and even

A. is *mortal*.   Ada is all that could be wished, but I cannot look
at her without a pang, considering what may be her future fate,
and into what hands she may fall.   Quiet suits me best," adds
poor Judith, who like her daughter was denied it—for besides the
domestic trials she, as a landed proprietor, was suffering from the
terrible distress in the country.   It was the time of the Luddite
riots—the stocking-weavers of the North were in revolt : " Pray
have some feeling of compassion," she wrote to William Frend,
" for us unfortunate people." [1]

Annabella soon came again to the end of her tether.   She
wrote to Mrs. Villiers : " It is essential to the comfort of all
parties that my Mother and I should have separate establish-
ments."   There was no sort of quarrel ; " only a great difference
in the lives we lead."   A house had been taken at Frognal,
Hampstead, and there she was going on the 1st of April.   Meanwhile she was composing the story of her life for Ada, so that
" her youthful imagination shall not be led astray by the poetical
colouring of circumstances."   For Byron was still raving through
the post about his daughter.   On learning of the Chancery proceedings, he had written to Annabella, passionately, eloquently,
with poignant reproach ; again one of those letters which we
marvel that she could have wholly ignored.   But she knew him
as we cannot know him. . . .   " I am not humble enough to
be vindictive "—that fine phrase, used (but less admirably
worded) in his *Lament of Tasso*, first sounded here.   He went
on :

> If you think to reconcile yourself to yourself by accumulating
> harshness against me, you are mistaken ; you are not happy,
> nor even tranquil, nor will you ever be so. . . .   You will smile
> at this piece of prophesy—do so, but recollect it ; it is justified
> by all human experience.[2]

She did not answer.

Then came a letter from him to Augusta.

> I desire to repeat what I have said—& say.   I have forgiven
> everything up to this—but this I will never forgive ; & no

---

[1] Father of Mrs. Augustus De Morgan.   He was a very distinguished
University Professor, and a Unitarian ; she was the mother of William
De Morgan.

[2] *Letters and Journals*, iv. 66-68, and (partly) in my *Byron*.

consideration on earth shall now prevail on me to look upon her as otherwise than my worst enemy. I curse her from the bottom of my heart, & in the bitterness of my Soul ; & I only hope she may one day feel what she has made me suffer. They will break my heart or drive me mad, one day or the other ; but she is a Wretch and will end ill. She was born to be my destruction & has become so. Ten thousand curses be upon her & her father & mother's family now & for ever.

When this reached England in the middle of April, Annabella was established in the Hampstead house. She had written to her father on the way from St. Albans, where she had gone over the Cathedral. " My ambition is to go to the top of the Tower, and I hope to *look down* on Brocket Hall. . . . I was amusing myself on the road to-day with translating some religious phrases into fashionable language. You shall have a few specimens.

To commune with one's own heart.	To meditate upon a love-letter.
To have one's Conversation in Heaven.	To keep one's carriage waiting at Holland House.
To be unspotted from the world.	To visit no persons of Christian Morals.
To be a doer of the word.	To keep an assignation.
To love our Neighbour as ourselves.	To give him a Ticket for Almack's.
Signs of Grace.	The Devonshire drawl—and *Con amore* waltz.
To attend the established worship.	To follow the lion of the day.
To let our light shine *before men*.	To be a coquette.
To let not one's right hand know what one's left hand doeth.	To keep one's husband out of one's secrets.

So it was in the old scornful spirit that she began her social campaign. Rigorous selection was to rule it—M. G. and the Miss Baillies, Mrs. Villiers, the Doyles, Mrs. George Byron, the Siddonses. A new friend, Lady Ormonde, soon figures in her diary—unhappy, of course, for that was the irresistible attraction. Hers was a " piteous case "—she loved a man who had no affection for her ; there was a gross and cruel misunderstanding ;

" her mental conflicts are like my own." And M. G. was still being persecuted : " I had my usual misery of hearing her depreciated in every possible way ... She has been injured equally with the world and the pious by the insidious misrepresentations of one of the deepest villains that ever existed."

However, they all dined with each other continually, Lady Byron's larder being supplemented from Kirkby : " I hope the *Prog* for your dinner arrived, safe and *sweet*." Sir Ralph took charge of the wine, giving her *carte-blanche* at his merchant's ; but when the Romillys were to dine with her he felt so anxious that he ordered a few bottles of his own choice to be delivered at once, even suggesting that she should send in for them so as to be sure of their being in time. . . . All this was part of her campaign " to wipe off the stain of methodistical gloom which at present disfigures the alabaster skin of my reputation. It is surprising how prevalent the report is." But before April was over Lady Noel heard that Lady Byron was considered too cheerful. " People seem to think you ought to be like Niobe, all tears."

The sick and hunted deer was learning her lesson. She begged her mother to come to her, but Lady Noel demurred : " I might perchance see those than whom I would rather see the Devil." And soon a little storm blew up between them. Annabella was " entreated " to tell the truth about her health ; the omission of Dr. Lushington from a dinner-party was thought regrettable— these urgencies evidently caused some loss of temper, for the mother's next letter begins : " So, my dear, you are very angry with me—but you must allow for the anxieties of love." Written on May 16, this reached Annabella on her twenty-fifth birthday and made her burst into tears. She wrote remorsefully ; on the 21st Lady Noel too burst into tears—and the sky cleared.

A little later she decided to go North, and visit Seaham for some necessary papers. As travelling-companion she took a new acquaintance—who was to become a life-long friend—Miss Frances Carr,[1] " of the most amiable, accommodating and affectionate temper. . . . She has *no sorrows*, and I believe a little contrast with my own peculiar form of thinking may be advantageous to me after the broken-hearted people to whom I am accustomed."

---

[1] Miss Carr was Dr. Lushington's sister-in-law.

Before she started there came a letter from Byron to Augusta, announcing the birth of Allegra, his daughter by Claire Clairmont :

> I am puzzled how to dispose of this new production. . . . They tell me it is very pretty, with blue eyes and dark (*sic*) hair ; and though I never was attached nor pretended attachment to the mother, still, in case of the eternal war and alienation which I foresee about . . . Ada, it may be as well to have something to repose a hope upon.

Later they heard that the new production was much more like Lady Byron than her mother : " Very blue eyes, and that singular forehead, fair (*sic*) curly hair, and a devil of a spirit— but that is Papa's." He was then at Venice ; Augusta had been writing him melancholy letters, but he told her that his sympathies were in suspense, for :

> I can't make out whether your disorder is a broken heart or the earache—or whether it is *you* that have been ill or the children—or what your melancholy & mysterious apprehensions tend to, or refer to, whether to Caroline Lamb's novels —Mrs. Clermont's evidence—Lady Byron's magnanimity—or any other piece of imposture ; I know nothing of what you are in the doldrums about at present. I should think all that could affect *you* must have been over long ago ; & as for me— leave me to take care of myself. I may be ill or well—in high or low spirits—in quick or obtuse state of feelings—like anybody else, but I can battle my way through. . . . Sooner or later time & Nemesis will give me the ascendant—& then " let them look to their bond."

And a little later :

> I repeat to you again and again that it would be much better at once to explain your mysteries than to go on with this absurd obscure hinting mode of writing. What do you mean ? what is there known or can be known which *you & I* do not know much better ? & what concealment can you have from me ? *I* never shrank—and it was on your account principally that I gave way at all—for I thought they would endeavour to drag you into it—although they had no business with anything previous to my marriage with that infernal fiend, whose destruction I shall yet see. Do you suppose that I will turn aside till they are trodden under foot ? do you suppose that I can breathe till they are uprooted ? Do you believe that time will

alter them or me? that I have suffered in vain—that I am reconciled to the sting of the scorpion & the venom of the serpent which stung me in my slumber?——If I did not believe —that Time & Nemesis—& circumstances would requite me for the delay—I would ere this have righted myself. But " let them look to their bond "——

This letter was punctuated with long and vehement dashes of the pen, as in all those where Byron expressed anger. His wife saw them all.

It was now—on June 16—that *Manfred* was published. Mrs. Villiers wrote: " It is too barefaced for her friends to attempt to deny the allusion. All that appeared to me practicable I have done with her own family, who have all spoke (*sic*) to me about it. . . . Did you see the newspaper of June 23rd? There is a long critique of *Manfred*—the allusions to Augusta dreadfully clear. Lady Chichester[1] brought it to me!" Augusta wrote to Annabella for advice about her own comments; she replied: " You can only speak of *Manfred* . . . with the most decided expressions of your disapprobation. He practically gives you away, and implies you were guilty *after* marriage."

Again the whole miserable business was upon her. She might go South, but it followed her—North, but it followed her. From the north she wrote to Mrs. Villiers that she was now taking a different line about Augusta. Hitherto she had been supposed the blind victim of a most artful woman; " therefore I make no mystery of having known his cruel designs towards her. The kindness I am known to feel for her removes every impression of her having been the accomplice. I did not see the newspaper. What does the Queen think, I wonder?"

A few days afterwards she went to Seaham, for the first time since she had driven away with Byron to the " scene of such deep horrors " at Six Mile Bottom. No place was so dear to her, or ever was to be so dear. She had had no home but this; what home with her parents now meant was too full of bitterness. And gazing out over " the unplumbed, salt, estranging sea " that rolled before her, and between her and the only lover she had loved or was to love, she wrote—at twenty-five— her elegy on the hope that had borne her through the wedding-

[1] Augusta's half-sister, by her mother's first marriage.

day, the honeymoon, the stay at Newmarket, her pregnancy ;
and now at last was dead.[1]

ON SEAHAM—1817

There is a spot—be my mansion there
When I've seen the end of earthly care !
I fain would endear its beauties wild
To thy softly-opening heart, my child !
I would lead thy blithesome footsteps o'er
The sparkling sands of my native shore,
And see thee mount the rocky isle
Where visions of peril seem to smile,
As the waves foam'd round my childhood's throne,
And I fearlessly joy'd to be thus alone !
But tho' 'tis not Memory's powers that fail,
I see those moments as thro' a veil ;
The veil of sorrow hath passed between
And dimmed the hues of the distant scene ;
And the beach where Hope's unchidden rover,
So joyfully has bounded over,
Shall never shew her traces again,
The tides of grief have made them in vain !
Ada ! wilt thou by affection's law,
My thoughts from the darken'd past withdraw—
Teach me to live in that future day
When those hands shall wipe those tears away
Which flow, as I think on the craggy brow
Where I stood . . . that form is before me now !
That eye is beholding the waters roll,
It seems to give them a living soul ;
That arm by mine is tremblingly prest,
I cherish the dream, he *shall* be blest !
O yet—tho' the phantom melt in air,
The heart's devotion may *not* despair !

.   .   .   .

Again must I break from the magic bond,
Which Memory fastens with links too fond ?
Had I been happy I might have wept,
The resisting nerve of my soul had slept ;
But I must not soften beneath the spell,
Nor pause o'er the spot where the tear-drop fell !

[1] In a MS. diary of Frances Carr's, kept during this tour, we read that as
they drew near Seaham, Miss Carr's admiration of the scenery was interrupted by the overwhelming distress of Lady Byron—"her suffocating sobs."

While in the North she crossed the Border, and from Edinburgh wrote to Walter Scott, apparently proposing herself as a visitor. He answered instantly :

August 14, 1817.

I have just received the honor of your Ladyship's letter and hasten to say with what pleasure we will receive you at Abbotsford and accompany you to Melrose or to any other scene in this neighbourhood which may possess any interest. Mrs. Scott desires me to add more apologies than I am able to express for the very humble stile (*sic*) of accommodation which we are able to offer, as great part of this cottage is at present in the act of being rebuilt. But I have always found my house like the fairy-tent, capable of being stretched to any dimension to receive those we wish to see, & have only the hope that the goodness which promises us a visit so agreeable will overlook the inconvenience of a garret-bedroom in consideration of the warmest welcome we can give. There is no chance of our being engaged on any day, but if your Ladyship will honor me with a line to say when you leave Edinburgh, I will take care to be absent on no rambling excursion.

Permit me to add that few things will give us more pleasure than the honour of receiving Lady Byron.

P.S.—The people at Bankhouse know the way to this place, but pray do not permit them to try the ford, which is sometimes dangerous—the bridge is about three miles round but much more safe. . . . I am afraid your Ladyship must have found Edinburgh very empty, for the inhabitants migrate like wild geese about this time of year.

She recorded her impressions in her diary, and in a letter to Mrs. Villiers. In her diary she wrote :

Walter Scott appeared to me to have a pride in acting the Selkirk Laird. His manners are unpolished, but I think not unaffected . . . too studied a contrast with the " man of letters." His love of the country is the very opposite of Cowper's. In the country Man is more of a lord . . . supreme over the activities of those sports from which Cowper turned with disgust. He talked of Cowper coldly. Told stories about Burns.

To Mrs. Villiers she wrote at the end of August, on her way to Scarborough—much better in health, " which was singularly affected by my return to those spots of happier memory." Of her one-night visit to Abbotsford she gave a very insipid account, though it could scarcely have been more romantically all it should be. "Scott accompanied me along the Yarrow, Ettrick, and Tweed.... My curiosity was in many respects gratified, and I hope not without giving some pleasure at the same time."

Scott was much more enthusiastic about her, in a letter to Joanna Baillie. It may be read in Lockhart's Life, but one or two passages come aptly here. "Her visit gave me a most lawyer-like fit of the bile. I have lived too long to be surprised at any instance of human caprice, but still it vexes me.... I can safely say, my heart ached for her all the time we were together; there was so much patience and decent resignation to a situation which must have pressed on her thoughts, that to me she was one of the most interesting creatures I had seen for a score of years. I am sure I should not have felt such strong kindness towards her had she been at the height of her fortune, and in the full enjoyment of all the brilliant prospects to which she seemed destined."

Back at Kirkby in October, she confided to her diary: "I feel as if in a desert—and do not like passing through the dark alone.... Two months ago the reality of Solitude did not give me these sensations." For some time she had been feeling, in her own concerns, "a sort of awful suspension"; now, on October 27, she recorded: "A blight in the evening. Received from Dr. Lushington the copy of a paper written by Lord B. Date Venice, Aug. 9, 1817. I could not read—heart-heavy."

This is the paper known as the La Mira document. It was written during a visit from "Monk" Lewis to Byron at his Venetian villa. Lewis had reported one of Brougham's indiscretions, and Byron "in a state of the greatest agitation" had drawn up the paper. Some considerable time afterwards Augusta wrote to Annabella of the incident, reported to her by Hobhouse. Byron had "called upon Hobhouse to prove that he [Byron] had done everything to induce you to come *into Court* !!" Hobhouse had tried to persuade him not to give the paper to Lewis . . . " *in vain*, and an hour after it was gone B. expressed regret he had written and given it." [1]

But the blight passed away; the paper was not circulated even privately; soon afterwards she was well and happy with M. G. at Kirkby, reading Cicero and admiring his rejection of Expediency, " his assertion of the duties we owe to our Natures." This produced a further Reflection: " The virtues . . . of the chivalrous cast have had more fascination for my youth than those of justice and veracity. *Le dévouement* was all in all— hence errors." Ada was flourishing and promising; there was no news of Byron, except that the forthcoming canto of *Harold* was to have less of personal affairs. " I am afraid I shall at last be suffered to drop into obscurity ! "

But that fresh re-opening of the chapter was not to be until the spring of 1818. The chief Byronic event of 1817 was the sale, early in December, of Newstead for £94,500. It was bought by Colonel Wildman, who had been at Harrow with Byron.

Annabella remained at Kirkby, her social campaign abandoned; but she was more resigned. On Ada's second birthday she measured her " progressive renovation " by the difference between her feelings now and those on the first birthday. " My heart uncloses to the kindly influence of her smiles." She wrote to Hugh Montgomery on the last day of the old year. Her father's affairs were improving, she told him; of her own : " Nothing but the danger of my own safety or my child's welfare would induce me to revive accusations of any kind."

---

[1] It was found among Lewis's papers after his death, and first published in *The Academy*, October 9, 1869. Lewis evidently suppressed it because he was conscious of its essential untruth.

CHAPTER XIX

1818-24

BEFORE THE END; THE END

THE New Year's first incident was Lady Byron's sponsorship of Mrs. Leigh's newborn daughter, Emily. Symbolic of forgiveness on both sides—for Augusta now knew that she had been supplanted as Ada's godmother—it marked as well a lapse in Byron's correspondence with X. There was another " awful suspension " —soon to be broken ; but meanwhile Annabella could read the new novels, *Northanger Abbey* and *Persuasion* (recommended by Augusta), and contrast that kind of real life with the kind she had learnt to know better.

Then—early in May—came the news of Lady Melbourne's death. " It *did* move me." Annabella had written to Mrs. George Lamb on hearing of her aunt's mortal illness, but the letter had come too late. " She had been for a long time unable to receive any message. Hobhouse," continued Mrs. Lamb, " wrote yesterday a most disgusting letter, asking for Lord B.'s letters—really one of the most unfeeling I ever read, saying he was desired by Lord B. to apply the moment of Lady M.'s demise, and no expression of sorrow or kindness to the family. I always had the worst possible opinion of that man, but I can believe that they are all in a great fright. I do not know that she kept any ; indeed the probability is that they were all burnt." [1]

It was like ploughing up frost-bound fields ; and soon afterwards Murray sent an advance-copy of the new *Harold*. She read the imprecation, supposed to be spoken in the Colosseum :

> . . . Let me not have worn
> This iron in my soul in vain—shall *they* not mourn ?

[1] Posterity knows that they were not burnt, since the publication in 1922 of what have come to be called the Melbourne Letters.

—with the two lines which prophesied his immortality of personal rather than poetic fame :

> But I have that within me that shall tire
> Torture and Time, and breathe when I expire.

She feigned indifference at first. " The passage was probably intended to make a great impression on *me*. Whilst I am so free from disordered brains, this will at least be postponed." It was not long postponed. A day or two later she was " well, but very *weak.* . . . The new canto is beautiful indeed " ; and referring to some recent reproaches from Augusta about her friends' continued defence of her, she wrote : " Now though *I* have ever been desirous of an act of oblivion, how is it possible that it can be carried into effect when Lord B. continually revives that discussion, and gives impressions concerning it through a medium much more powerful than I can command ? Surely this must appear to any dispassionate person ? "

It was a sting, just then, to get excited letters from both the Montgomerys about having seen Byron in Venice. " Extremely fat . . . bloated and heavy " ; " His face is much more like a full moon than ever *yours* was." Broad comedy, when tragedy was in her heart—yet was there not tragedy here too ? did she not know how distressful this fatness was to him ? . . . " The wounds with which I was wounded in the house of my friends " ; and restlessness awoke in her again, she fled from Kirkby again —fled to the lost lovely Abbey, never seen by her while yet it was his. Impulse most comprehensible ; one of the many which prove her the hot-hearted creature of her own self-knowledge, that even those who knew her best could fail to see. He was bloated and heavy, was he ? If he was, it was another pang for both ; she would soothe it by a pilgrimage to the place where Byronic romance still lingered (still lingers !)—to the home he had loved and lost, that might have been her own home.

On May 22 we have this, written at Mansfield, close to the Abbey :

Just come from Newstead. The sunshine, the blue lakes, the re-appearing foliage of the remaining woods, the yellow gorse over the wild wastes gave a cheerful effect to the surrounding scenes. My feelings were altogether those of gratification. In becoming familiarised with the scene I seemed to contemplate the portrait of a friend.

I entered the hall—and saw the Dog; then walked into the dining-room—not used by Ld. B. as such. He was wont to exercise there. His fencing-sword and single-sticks—beneath the table on which they stood, a stone coffin, containing the four sculls which he used to have set before him, till (as he told me himself) he fancied them animated.

I saw the old flags which he used to hang up on the " Castle walls " on his birthday. The apartments which he inhabited were in every respect the same—he might have walked in. They looked not deserted. The Woman who had lived in his service regretted that the property was transferred. He should have lived there, particularly after he was married—but his Lady had never come there, and " she, poor thing! is not likely to come there now," compassionately & mysteriously. She said that he was " very fond of Mrs. L——, very loving to her indeed," as if this were the only part of his character on which she could dwell with commendation, for she drew a very unfavourable comparison between him and G. B. in regard to charity. Ld. B. " never gave a thought that way." Old Murray. . . . The parapets & steps where he sat—the leads where he walked. His room—where I was rooted having involuntarily returned. . . .

And then, after that strangely stilted record where the few phrases at the end alone break through to her sense of the moment, some verses :

> I pass'd the portal, trod the twice-worn stone
> Where thou would'st meditative sit alone ;
> I thanked the careless guide who left me free—
> She knew not how it touched, each word of thee !
> When the heart-pressure is unshar'd, unguess'd,
> Its very agony may be suppress'd ;
> Aye—till the sufferer shall begin to doubt
> If feeling live, so fix'd his frame throughout.
> That hall of ancient festival and state
> To thy lone tread return'd its echoes late,
> But never shall again :—the walls are bare,
> The vastness has an aspect of despair. . . .
>
>   Strange—what I next beheld, still passing on,
> I know not !—from my mind the forms are gone,
> And leave a chasm, ev'n such that it might seem
> I but retrace the picture of a dream.

Yet I remember when beside the bed
Which pillowed last that too reposeless head,
I stood—so undeserted look'd the scene
As there at eve its habitants had been.
Struck by that thought, and rooted to the ground,
Instinctively I listen'd, look'd around,
Whilst banish'd passion rush'd to claim again
Its throne, all vacant in my breast till then ;
And pardon'd be the wish, when thus deceiv'd,
To perish, ere of hope again bereav'd !

And then again, as if to link his loss more closely still with her own, another stay in Seaham. And from Seaham to the Cunninghams at Harrow : " I *will* not have reports spread to Lord Byron's injury ! "

They had been spreading such reports—or she had been told so. Mr. Cunningham " explained " ; she consented to forgive him ; but Clapham Common was not yet her spiritual home— nor indeed was ever to be. The rebellious fibre in her could not accept the Velvet Cushion as a medium of repose.

She stayed at Seaham until September. One day she heard some beautiful pianoforte-playing. " It seems as if by incantation the visions of earlier days reappear, without their power to deceive—no longer embodied in hope. To feel that we *can* feel has its charm, when we have sometimes thought that all the surface of the heart was torpid—and that sorrow had come down upon us with the ice, as well as the weight, of the avalanche. . . . I do not feel confident that I view myself with reference to my actual situation—but I shall do so—shall disperse those mists of error in which I have long been involved." And again, of the Fourth Canto : " May not each of the children of passion feel that he understands so much more intimately than all the other multitude that to him the revelation is really private ? So I have felt."

The new *Harold* had done its work.

She did not know what her mother was doing at this very time. Among the Lovelace Papers is a letter to the Prince Regent, written by Lady Noel on September 14, 1818. It " begs His Royal Highness's consideration of the relief it would afford Sir Ralph and Lady Noel to be enabled to call their insulted and injured daughter by another title than that of Byron, viz. by the title of Wentworth, Lady Noel waiving her claim."

If the letter was sent, nothing resulted from it. She bore Byron's name as long as she lived, refusing, when it fell to her, the title of Baroness Wentworth. It is unlikely that she ever knew of this suggestion ; but the incident is notable as a sign of the anger which ever and again seethed up at Kirkby, and made life there too difficult for Judith Noel's daughter. Sir Ralph was in the background as usual—the solace of that pseudo-home for her tormented spirit.

Not long was the new *Harold's* work left undisturbed. For some time she had been writing less to Augusta : " There is a sort of stagnation," she had written to Mrs. Villiers ; to write for writing's sake was wearisome. But now the stagnation gave place to a fresh annoyance : " The strange interest she feels about Lady F. W. [Lady Frances Webster], for whom she wishes apparently to engage my sympathy, but I have been very cold and dry on the subject. I believe Lady F. W. to be as far as possible from the simple character which I am told she appears —and what can be her object in seeking Augusta but to keep up a guilty connection ? " [1] She went on :

> Whilst A. remains in London I must be elsewhere. Ada's intellect is so far advanced beyond her age that she is already capable of receiving impressions that might influence her—to what extent I cannot say—and without supposing that A. would mean to injure me, her delusion might tempt her to put ideas into Ada's mind that might take root there—something of " poor Papa," &c. My apprehensions may be exaggerated—but I have an insurmountable repugnance to Ada's being in her company, and at the same time, though I might do it consistently with what I have always told her on that subject, I cannot bear to distance her for that reason. So I must avoid the alternative. . . . Ada loves me as well as I

---

[1] Byron remarked in 1821, in a letter to Murray : " All my loves make a point of calling on Mrs. Leigh. The year before last, I think, Lady F.W-W. marched in upon her. . . . It is a very odd fancy that they all take to her." In 1818 he knew of this intercourse, for there is a letter bidding Augusta see that one from him to Lady Frances is safely delivered. Webster was then proposing that he and his wife should come to live at Venice.

wish, and better than I expected, for I had a strange prepossession that she would never be fond of me. Lord B. remains
at Venice with his other daughter. I have had an intimation
through Augusta that he was writing his life for publication,
and she did not seem alarmed ! I think it better not to speak
of it till it prove the fact.

She had already written of this to Colonel Doyle :

The worst consequence, to my feelings, would be the opposition between my own views and those of some of my friends.
I am sick, quite sick, of taking my own part. I never did it
but as an act of duty towards Ada, and the pains which on that
principle I have taken . . . have been the most laborious and
vexatious of my life. May I not, on such an occasion as I now
contemplate, let things take their course ?

But, perturbed by the possibility, she wrote the following
passage under the heading of Reminiscences in a MS. book
of 1818 :

In explaining the tenor of my own conduct, I do not attempt
to maintain the defensibility of every part of it. At the time
of my quitting, my mind was certainly possessed by passion ;
and was prevailed upon in his favour by what could not have
been of any weight in the scale of reason. Of this he was
probably aware, and made use of it accordingly. I clung to
an hypothesis repeatedly overthrown—that there was some
secret good at the bottom of his heart—though such motives
were never evidenced ; and such delusion will always be liable
to return. It then embarrassed my conduct. . . . To wound
him by a word was intolerable to me—perhaps I may never be
able to perform the duty of making such a statement without
experiencing afterwards all the pangs of Conscience. This was
my weakness throughout ; it is A.'s to a still greater degree—
and I can feel for it.

1819 was not Byronically disturbed until June. Annabella
was then at Tunbridge Wells with Ada, again feeling as if a crisis
were approaching. She had seen Augusta in London, and
thought her " repressed and oppressed." " And certainly,"
wrote Augusta, " the sight of dear Ada contributed in a great
degree to *unnerve* me." But this letter revealed what had really

been weighing on her mind. She had spoken to Annabella of one from Byron, but had not shown it : now she enclosed it— " for I have endeavoured in vain, in *thought and deed*, to reply to it. . . . He is surely to be considered a *Maniac*." She apologised for sending it—" many would condemn the act as an *insult*, but it is your advice and superior judgment that is wished for."

Byron's letter was that in which he said : [1]

I have never ceased nor can cease to feel for a moment that perfect & boundless attachment which bound and binds me to you—which renders me utterly incapable of *real* love for any other human being—for what could they be to me after *you* ? My own XXXX we may have been very wrong—but I repent of nothing except that cursed marriage—& your refusing to continue to love me as you had loved me. I can neither forget nor *quite forgive* you for that precious piece of reformation— but I can never be other than I have been—and whenever I love anything it is because it reminds me in some way or other of yourself. . . . It is heart-breaking to think of our long Separation—and I am sure more than punishment enough for all our sins. Dante is more humane in his " Hell " for he places his unfortunate lovers (Francesca of Rimini & Paolo, whose case fell a good deal short of *ours*—though sufficiently naughty) in company—and though they suffer—it is at least together. If ever I return to England, it will be to see you— and recollect that in all time—& place—and feelings—I have never ceased to be the same to you in heart. Circumstances may have ruffled my manner & hardened my spirit—you may have seen me harsh & exasperated with all things around me ; grieved & tortured with *your new resolution*—& the soon after persecution of that infamous fiend who drove me from my Country & conspired against my life by endeavouring to deprive me of all that could render it precious—but remember that even then *you* were the sole object that ever cost me a tear, and *what tears* ! do you remember our *parting* ?

Annabella wrote that she could not possibly mistake Augusta's motive ; the letter told her nothing new. She could not agree that it was " mere raving " ; perceived the danger of not burning it but returned it as a proof, which might in a possible future be valuable to Augusta, that there had been no renewal of incest

---

[1] It is given in full in *Astarte*, Chapter IV., together with Annabella's correspondence about it with Augusta.

after Byron's marriage. She could not definitely advise about answering. Augusta might either say that after this she considered it her duty to break off all correspondence with him, or she might take no notice of it. " Tell me what you do, though I feel sure that the gentler expedient will appear to you the best. We must act consistently with *our own* opinions."

Augusta wrote twice in reply—the usual labyrinth of vacillations. She *did* lean to the gentler expedient, but " decision was never my forte." Providence might graciously interpose. Situated as she was, if she once gave way to despair she could never shake it off, and she hoped that it was not presumptuous to *trust* in that Power who alone could shield and protect.

There is no further reply from Annabella; how Augusta wrote to Byron is not recorded. He wrote to her again in July—there are no reproaches, nor any more raving. But there is a message to Annabella. " If you see my spouse, do pray tell her I wish to marry again, and as probably she may wish the same, is there no way in *Scotland*, without compromising her immaculacy? cannot it be done by the husband solely? " His liaison with Teresa Guiccioli had recently begun. Of it he wrote to his friend Hoppner : " I should like to know who has been carried off—except poor dear *me*. I have been more ravished myself than anybody since the Trojan war."

The stagnation was well over. Early in July appeared the first part of *Don Juan*. " The impression was not so disagreeable as I expected," wrote Annabella.

In the first place I am very much relieved to find that there is not anything which I can be expected to notice. As for myself, I do not think that my sins are in the pharisaical or pedantic line, and I am very sure that he does not think they are, but avails himself of the prejudices which some may entertain against me, to give a plausible colouring to his accusations. I must however confess that the quizzing in one or two passages was so good as to make me smile at myself— therefore others are heartily welcome to laugh. . . . I do not feel inclined to continue the perusal. It is always a task to me now to read his works, in which, through all the levity, I discern enough to awaken very painful feelings.

Not long afterwards she received a letter from Byron.[1] His pretext was some German verses which had been sent him, with the " ardent wish " that they could reach Lady Byron.

> Perhaps it may not offend you, however it may surprise, that the good people on the frontiers of Denmark have taken an interest in your domestic Affairs, which have now, I think, nearly made the tour of Europe, and have been discussed in most of its languages, to as little purpose as in our own. . . . I will not close this sheet without a few words more. Fletcher has complained to me of your declining to give his wife a character, on account of your " doubts of her veracity in some circumstances a short time before she left you." If your doubts allude to her testimony on your case during the then discussion, you *must* or at least ought to be the best judge how far she spoke truth or not ; *I* can only say that she never had directly or indirectly, through me or mine, the slightest inducement to the contrary, nor am I indeed perfectly aware of what her Evidence was, never having seen her nor communicated with her at that period or since. I presume that you will weigh well your justice before you deprive the woman of the means of obtaining her bread. No one can be more fully aware than I am of the utter inefficacy of any words of mine to you on this or on any other subject, but I have discharged my duty to Truth in stating the above, and now do yours.

He went on to write one of his longest letters, telling her of the places he had visited lately, and of Ravenna in which he then was. He prattled about Francesca di Rimini, his own Parisina and Ugo ; and perceiving how he had abounded, remarked, " In writing to you at all, I may as well write much as little." He inquired about Ada : " I have not heard of her for many months. . . . You must let her be taught Italian . . . and pray let her be musical, if she has a turn that way. I presume that Italian being a language of mine will not prevent you recollecting my request." She was to let Augusta know if she received the letter : " I want no other answer." He would like to have a picture of " Miss Byron," as soon as she could sit to Holmes or any other painter.

We know Annabella well enough now to know how all this must have moved her. But she merely sent the desired message

[1] In full in *Astarte*, 291-3.

through Augusta, his response to which we shall see. In the meantime a great scare descended upon those at home. Letters from Byron to Murray and Augusta in December announced his immediate return ; he expected to be in or near England by the New Year.

On hearing this, Augusta wrote to Annabella : " Luckily (or *un*luckily perhaps) I do not die easily—or I think this stroke would about finish me. However, my trust is in Providence."

Annabella answered at once. " It can scarcely be doubted that you are his principal object in England." She foresaw the most serious consequences from Augusta's having any kind of intercourse with him. His power over her was two-fold—personal and pecuniary ; he was known to have made his will in favour of her and her children. But she added : " You would not act consistently unless you acted from *Conviction*. You would take half-measures, which must end in your ruin. Anxious as I feel to support and comfort you . . . I could not hope to do so by an attempt to impose my own opinions." Like Augusta, she was desirous to consult his welfare now and in the future. " If my reasons convince you, they become *yours* ; if not, I have no wish to enforce them." At the same time she wrote to Mrs. Villiers : " It is impossible for me at this crisis to let her rush into destruction without a warning."

But though Byron had made all preparations and even fixed the day of his departure, the third woman in the case intervened. Teresa Guiccioli fell ill, with her accustomed skill in so doing at useful moments, and he was summoned to Ravenna. The Return-Scare was over. He wrote to Murray : " Let my sister be informed that I am not coming. I have not the courage to tell her so myself, at least as yet."

Augusta, overwhelmed as she had been by the prospect, had finally made up her mind to receive him if he did return. " I trust I may be spared the trial—I scarcely know of any greater that could befall me." Here she showed the courage lacking in her conduct about his letters ; for even after they knew that he was not coming, she wrote to Annabella, laying her reasons before her. Their basis was deep affection, wholly apart from lawless love. But she had also to think of her position before the world, and " *most of all*, my husband. What reasons could

I give for not seeing him?" And from her instinctive knowledge of her brother—from her affinity with him—she wrote
convincingly:

> I never have, I cannot now believe as you do in the *depth and
> strength* of what is manifested by fits and starts—when there is
> nothing else. . . . Then, dearest A., I do not feel that I could
> *without one effort* relinquish the hope of making some impres-
> sion on his better feelings. . . . Do you think there is one
> person in England who would, who *could* say to him what *I*
> might? . . . What a mercy it has ceased! My own opinion
> is that he will *never* come. . . . Pray do not hate me for what
> I have written, and do answer me—for I scarcely ever feel
> confidence in my own opinions.

Again she has all our sympathy. Impossible that she should
refuse to see him; instinct spoke there, and—whatever his
conduct might have been, had he come—spoke rightly. She
would have been inhuman had she refused.

And for the first time, in her answer, Annabella *was* inhuman.
Phrases of kindness were used, phrases of dispassionateness:
" I do not consider you bound to me in any way"; but the
letter is repellent in its rigorous refusal of sympathy, its sledge-
hammer reiteration of Byron's " viciousness " and " wickedness "
as regarded Augusta—a stupid letter, in short, as all inhuman
letters must be. She took up Augusta's words " when there is
nothing else " (which so unmistakably mean " no other affair
of the heart ") as referring to their physical intercourse: " Is
experience nothing? Did you not before indulge this delusion? "
and finally, despite the declared dispassionateness, there was
this: " Should I, by your reception of him, be obliged to relinquish my intercourse with you, I shall do so in such manner as
shall be least prejudicial to your interests. I shall most earnestly
wish that the results of your conduct may tend to establish your
peace instead of aggravating your remorse . . . "—but, herself
dissatisfied, she added a postscript: " I may have failed in
expressing my deep interest in your happiness, but I trust you
will believe it."

Once more, though I have called this letter inhuman, human
nature can be pleaded to account for it. She must have known
that Byron would make some attempt to see her; his so recent

letter, telling her so many little details of his daily life, answered
for that. And suppose they met ? Not only would the whole
unhappy question be re-opened, her parents be agitated, the
lawyers be vocal, again ; but herself would look into his face—
herself whom his letters had cursed, his latest poem mocked !
How different would be his meeting with Augusta, the " one soft
breast," the Astarte of *Manfred*. . . . No. If these two were
to be together, such bitterness must possess her that there would
be an end to forgiveness, " kindness to Augusta," searchings of
heart, self-accusation. Nothing would survive but resentment,
rancour—jealousy. For all her self-knowledge she did not
know that that was why, but that *was* why, her letter to the sister
about his return was the one unkind, the one stupid letter she
wrote in the tormented years immediately following the separation.

Its effect, however, was to make Augusta yield. She wrote
very coldly to Byron about seeing him if he returned. It should
be only in the presence of other people ; not at his house, or hers.
He answered angrily : " You say nothing in favour of my return.
Very well—I will stay where I am—and you will never see me
more."

But in the meantime Annabella's dissatisfaction had grown.
She wrote to Mrs. Villiers that while reluctant to give her own
impressions, she would like to hear Mrs. Villiers's opinion of the
facts ; and though he did not come, the bitterness lasted. From
that time until 1824 there was much less intercourse between her
and Augusta.

The Return-Scare over, a fresh one began. With the New
Year of 1820 came a letter from Byron to his wife. It began by
answering her message about Ada's portrait.[1] Anything would
be welcome, at any time she chose. " I have been taught waiting, if not patience." The wretchedness of the past should be
sufficient for them both ; now they might be gentle. " This
time five years I was on my way to our funeral marriage." After
this gentleness he told her that only three hours ago (" in society
where I ought not to think of you ") the principal person con-

[1] This letter in full in *Astarte*.

cerned had said to him : " *Tu pensi di tua moglie.*" The conjecture was so right that he had started, asked why she thought so. " Because you are so serious—and she is the woman whom I believe *tu ami più ed ami sempre.*" . . . But the " object of his writing " was to come. It was to offer for her reading his Memoir, written up to the summer of 1816. The part she occupied was long and minute ; he had stated the truth, but there were two ways of looking at it. She would find nothing to flatter her, nothing to lead her to the most remote supposition that they could ever have been, or be, happy together. But he wanted her to see what he looked upon her to have been, and depicted her as being. If she detected what was false, or could answer what was charged, she was to mark the passage—her mark should not be erased. And now she had had the option.

Her first impulse was to draft a long letter, declining because she considered the present or future circulation of the Memoir wholly unjustifiable, and would not even indirectly appear to sanction it. " If you truly state our domestic circumstances, I can only express my astonishment that *you* should wish to expose them." She had submitted to some injustice, would still submit ; " but there must be a limit to forbearance, and that limit is fixed, absolutely fixed, in my own mind."

This letter was not sent. After a good deal of correspondence with Colonel Doyle and Dr. Lushington, it was decided that she should write only these words :

KIRKBY MALLORY,
March 10th, 1820.

I received your letter of January 1st offering to my perusal a Memoir of part of your life. I decline to inspect it. I consider the publication or circulation of such a composition at any time as prejudicial to Ada's future happiness. For my own sake I have no reason to shrink from publicity, but notwithstanding the injuries which I have suffered, I should lament some of the *consequences*.

Byron answered :

RAVENNA, *April 3rd,* 1820.

I received yesterday your answer dated March 10th. My offer was an honest one, and surely could be only construed as such even by the most malignant Casuistry. I *could* answer you—but it is too late, and it is not worth while.

To the mysterious menace of the last sentence—whatever
its import may be, and I really cannot pretend to unriddle it
—I could hardly be very sensible even if I understood it.
Before it could take place, I shall be where " nothing can
touch him further." I advise you however to anticipate the
period of your intention—for be assured no power of yours can
avail beyond the present—and if it could I would answer with
the Florentine, " *La fiera moglie, più ch'altro, mi nuoce.*"

Despite this insulting letter, he wrote to her several times in the
course of 1820, always to request her future kindness for Augusta
—at the same time writing to the Other A. :

The Lady Byron I suppose retains her old starched obstinacy
—with a deeper dash of sternness from the dint of time, and
the effort it has cost her to be " magnanimous," as they call her
mischief-making.

She did not see this ; but one of his letters to herself did anger
her. In it he boasted of his generosity about money—the £200
a year she had as an allowance in addition to her pin-money of
£300 a year ; [1] and " made a modest request—more like a
command " that she would engage to provide for Augusta and
her children. Nevertheless she made that promise, in the last
letter she ever wrote to him. Not until the end of 1820 could
she bring herself to reply ; then she wrote :

KIRKBY,
Decr. 10th, 1820.

When you first expressed the wish respecting Mrs. Leigh
which is repeated in your last letter of Oct. 8th, I determined
to act consistently with it. If the assurance of that intention
would conduce (as you state in a former letter, & as appears
from your reiterated requests) to calm your mind, I will not
withhold it. The past shall not prevent me from befriending
Augusta Leigh & her Children in any future circumstances
which may call for my assistance. I promise to do so. She
knows nothing of this.

He answered in a letter [2] sealed with his pansy seal—motto :
Elle vous suit partout. Her note, he said, was on the whole

---

[1] Byron kept her fortune of £20,000, and was to share her future income
when she succeeded to it.

[2] In full in *Astarte*.

satisfactory, the style a little harsh, "but that was to be expected." As to Augusta : "Her life and mine, and yours and mine, were two things perfectly distinct from each other. When one ceased, the other began—and now both are closed." But in a long postscript he acknowledged her promise much more warmly. He had burned her note, that she might be under no restraint but her feeling. It was a comfort to him *now* beyond all comforts—" but five years ago it would have been something more. Why did you *then keep silence* ? . . . Two words about her or hers would have been to me the *ne plus ultra* of gratification. She and two others were the only things I ever really loved—I may say it now, for we are young no longer."

That was her reward. "Two others. . . . Was one of them myself ? " The question can scarcely not have come to her, recalling his first love-letters. This third, this Augusta to whom she had again promised " to be kind "—she it was who had come between them. . . . Long long afterwards, in 1854, Annabella wrote : " I see what was, what *might* have been, had there been one person less amongst the living when I married. Then I might have had duties, however steeped in sorrow, more congenial with my nature than those I was compelled to adopt. Then my life would not have been the concealment of a Truth, whilst my conduct was in harmony with it."

After the first letter about the Memoirs, for a while there was peace. She left Kirkby again in April 1820, and stayed for a time in London, seeing principally the Miss Baillies and Mrs. Siddons. Round the latter was gathering that sadness of the great actress in her decline. Annabella one night observed in her " a painful irritability. . . . She spoke of herself as a garment out of fashion." Walter Scott was at the same party ; she arrived too late to meet him, and " Joanna seemed distressed, as she knew I had given up another party for this. I said *truly* that Scott was not my principal inducement. She replied that she felt my kind wish to set her at ease, but could not believe the assertion quite sincere (very gravely). If by accident I say a kind truth, such is the consequence ! I was miserably shy and awkward all night."

It was a second phase of reaction—disappointment, disillusion,

the old hypercritical spirit at work. She wrote of Mrs. Villiers :
" She is one of those whose moral standard is derived from the
average practice of mankind. Her deference to the world
amounts, I think, to this—that she would rather not have my
company at, say, Lady Jersey's, if my gown were very shabby ;
but I never looked for more. . . . Timidity is not the cause of
her slight shade of manœuvring, for she is without fear." She
was stopping with Mrs. Villiers when she thus analysed her.
They went to the Opera, and there : " I had the happiness of
receiving a mark of kindness from a friend whom I believed
estranged." This was Lord Auckland, the George Eden who
had been her suitor so few, so many, years ago.

She tried to absorb herself in Ada, noting down her questions,
her wonderings—" Is God a man or a lady ? "—but still there
were traces of the Annabella who had never cared for a doll.
At Hastings, where she had gone to be with M.G. (broken down
by the persecution of her relatives), she heard a woman say that
after a calamity her baby had been nothing but an added pang
for her ; and wrote in her diary : " I know it in myself. Infancy
cannot soothe acute grief, though it may sometimes rouse from
stupor."

Back in London, she went to a meeting where mitigations in
the Prison System were discussed. Of this she wrote a long and
caustic account in her diary, giving a picture of ineptitudes
which might be written by any one of us on any day of the week.
One speaker was well-meaningly insipid, repeating what was not
worth saying once, though his heart was right ; another was
unpleasant, meagre, and ungraceful ; even the great Wilberforce
was perplexed in expression—and there is no one who will not
agree with this :

> I thought the practice of complimenting either the preceding
> or the expected speakers, somewhat ridiculous. Every one
> said that his own exertions were rendered superfluous—yet this
> consideration did not arrest the premeditated discourse.

That kind of clear-sightedness she never lost, in the later years
of public activity. It made her intractable, difficult to work
with ; the blindness to absurdities and pomposities which is so
indispensable to co-operation, she could not acquire—despite her

own transgressions in the sort! Byron had early perceived her
" starchiness "; M.G. had bantered her on it; Captain Boothby
had in 1811 sought to instil the beauty of simplicity in diction.
For herself she never learnt the lesson, though in others she could
instantly perceive " perplexity of expression," insipidity, and the
like. She had been right when she wrote in the MS. book at
Kirkby that her character was unmodified by all she had experienced; to the end she might have written the same words.

And, remembering this, let us read the next entries in her
diary, those for September 16 and 17:

> Saw A.L.'s [Augusta's] children; felt the most tender
> affection for ——. What is the reason?
> *September 17th, Sunday.* Walked early to look at my old
> house in Piccadilly—saw into the room where I have sat with
> him, and felt as if I had lived there with a friend who was
> long since dead *to me.* No sense of past agony—all mournfully
> soft. My thoughts floated peacefully into other channels as
> soon as I had left the spot—where I wished for M.M.
> Spent the evening at Mrs. G. Villiers. I cannot imagine
> why she likes me, for she does not draw out the best parts of
> my character.[1]

Early in 1821 she heard again from Byron. He was tormenting himself about money-matters—wanting her to " get us out
of the Funds," to consent to an Irish loan on mortgage to Lord
Blessington. The latter arrangement fell through, and he
wrote: " As you of course did not do this intentionally, I shall
not upbraid you or yours, though the connection has proved so
unfortunate a one for us all, to the ruin of my fame, my peace,
and the hampering of my fortune." Perhaps it did not seem to
him upbraiding when he continued:

> Yours has been a bitter connection to me in every sense.
> It would have been better for me never to have been born than
> to have ever seen you. This sounds harsh, but is it not true?
> and recollect that I do not mean that you were my *intentional*
> evil Genius but an Instrument for my destruction—and you
> yourself have suffered too (poor thing) in the agency, as the
> lightning perishes in the instant with the Oak which it strikes.

[1] At this time she sat for her portrait to an artist named Newton.

It was a troubled spring for Annabella, apart from this. Her mother was dangerously ill—so ill that Augusta wrote, begging that a good word might be put in for her: " I do not want Lady Noel to die angry with me." Lady Noel partly recovered ; but then came more letters from Augusta about the sale of Rochdale, and more letters from Byron to his sister about the Funds: " That cursed connection crosses at every turn my fortunes, my feelings, and my fame. I had no wish to nourish my detestation of her and her family, but they pursue like an Evil Genius. I send you an Elegy on Lady Noel's *recovery* . . . but the old —— will live forever because she is so amiable and useful."

Lady Noel's daughter did not see this ; its interest for us lies in the fact that Byron had then received her promise to be kind to Augusta.

In September he sent Augusta some locks of his hair. " Select the *best-behaved* curls, and set them in a golden locket for Ada my daughter." There was to be an Italian inscription round the locket: *Il sangue non é mai acqua.* He wished Ada to wear it—" that she may know she has (or had) a father in the world." Of this Annabella wrote to Joanna Baillie that she did not object ; " of course I shall not think myself obliged to interpret." She must have been struck by the aptness of Byron's gift, for in July Ada had one day asked her if Grandpapa and Papa were the same. They were different kinds of relations, she answered ; and Ada went on : " Then mine is not a Papa ? " " I said that I would explain more about that when she was older. Her mind did not appear to dwell on the subject."

The hair sent to Augusta was touched with grey. " Has there been nothing to make it grey ? To be sure the *years* have not," wrote Byron—now irrevocably Teresa Guiccioli's. " I assure you it was not my wish, or fault altogether. . . . You know that all my loves go crazy and make scenes . . . such romantic people, always daggering or divorcing. But this is a finisher. So you see that I have closed as Papa *began* ; and *you* will probably never see me again as long as you live. Indeed, you don't deserve it, for having behaved so *coldly, when I was ready to have sacrificed everything* for you. . . . I am more attached to her than I thought it possible to be to any woman after three years—(*except one, and who was she*. Can YOU guess?).[1]   If Lady B. would but please to die, and the Countess G.'s husband, we should probably have to marry—though I would rather *not*, thinking it the way to hate each other—for all people whatsoever."

And now, on January 28, 1822, Lady Noel, whose health had long been " a source of anxiety and distress," died at Kirkby. Annabella—and consequently Byron—assumed the Noel name, as they were legally bound to do.   "*N.B.*"—these initials gave him great pleasure as being Napoleon's also ; an instance of the child-side that his wife had loved in him.   She was now mistress of Kirkby Mallory and the Wentworth estates ; her £500 was increased by £4000 a year—half the income of her inheritance, the other half going to Byron.   He wrote to Augusta that he bore Lady Noel's memory no malice.[2]

The records for this year, and the following one, are scanty. When in October Annabella did her first " kindness " as mistress of Kirkby by sending Augusta some game (an attention deliberately neglected by Lady Noel !), Byron wrote to his sister that it was a very acceptable thing to him, for hitherto " both sides have proceeded as they did in the feudal times, when people used to shake hands with iron gauntlets through a hole in the door."   He went on :

> You cannot conceive how such things harass me, and provoke me into expressions which I momentarily feel ; it appears to me that persons who are in our peculiar situation, and can never see each other as long as they live again, should at least be courteous in their distance, *because* they never can come in contact.

There was another sign of his joint proprietorship in the Wentworth estates.   He had been asked (through Hobhouse) by the Rev. Thomas Noel—who had married them—to promise him " some living or other " at Kirkby.   " I wish you would ask Lady B. about it, for . . . to *this hour* I do not know whether the

---

[1] The phrases in italics are erased (apparently not by the writer) and hardly legible.

[2] She had sent him a message of forgiveness from her death-bed.

estate is in her, or in me, or in the trustees, or whether the living is in her gift, or mine, or anybody's or nobody's." *He*, if he had a voice, thought that as the " poor fellow," had his father observed the rights of the Church, would have owned the estate himself, some compensation should be made him.   But Lady B. was to decide.[1]

1823 was marked by another approach (already alluded to) from Byron—that through the Blessingtons, from Genoa.   Among the unsent letters to his wife which he sent Lady Blessington to read, there is one alluding to " an old account-book of Miss Milbanke's, which I kept because it contains the word ' Household ' written by her twice inside the cover—being the only two scraps I have in the world of her writing, except her name to the Deed of Separation."   (We have seen that he burnt her promise " to be kind to Augusta " ; he must also have burnt her stern refusal to inspect the Memoir.)   His request was for the miniature which had belonged to Lady Noel—that by Hayter, done in the first flush of triumphal 1812.   It was not sent to him ; nor can we wonder, in view of Hugh Montgomery's gossip about the wearing in a brooch and a bracelet of Augusta's hair.   He also told her of Byron's having spoken of her visit to Newstead, " where she questioned the housekeeper about my conduct before marriage."   (That sheds an unpleasing light on the apparently guileless prattle to which Annabella had listened—unless old Murray was responsible.) . . .   These Montgomerys strike one as prone to inflict wounds which might well have been spared her—for M.M., too, wrote of Byron's wanting the miniature : " I am disposed to believe all this tenderness is directed to the £3500 a year which in case of a reconciliation would return to his possession."   Better left unsaid, one would think ; when Annabella once wrote to Hugh, rejoicing that " the post and my *vindicating* friends have lately left me in peace," to us it seems that these friends may have been silently included.

---

[1] Thomas Noel was Lord Wentworth's natural son.   In 1823 the living fell in ; Annabella presented it to Thomas Noel, and Byron wrote to Augusta that she had done quite right—and he was glad she had done so without hesitation.   He was then just about to sail for Greece.

In their letters came the first news of Byron's Greek plans ; but before that there had been again a thought of return to England. He had written to Augusta in January : " Perhaps we may meet in Spring, either *here* or in England." This letter began on an amusingly, yet pathetically, defiant note : " Do not believe all the lies you hear. Hobhouse can tell you that I have *not* lost *any* of my teeth *hitherto*, since I was twelve years old, and had a back one taken out . . . and so far from being fatter, at present I am much thinner than when I left England, when I was not very stout. I am much reduced since Hobhouse saw me, and more than *you* would like." It was then that Count D'Orsay made the pencil-sketch which is familiar to us all. In it Byron looks very much older than his thirty-five years, " reduced " indeed—a figure touching in its broken vehemence. We feel instinctively that he looked just so, before the adventure which was to kill him.

He embarked for Greece on a Friday, and a Thirteenth—the thirteenth of July, 1823. From Metaxata on October 8 he wrote to Augusta :

> I wish you could obtain from Lady B. some account of Ada's disposition, habits, studies, moral tendencies, and temper, as well as her personal appearance, for except from the miniature drawn five years ago (and she is now double that age nearly) I have no idea of even her aspect. When I am advised on these points, I can form some notion of her character, and what way her dispositions or indispositions ought to be treated, and though I will never interfere with or thwart her mother, yet I may perhaps be permitted to suggest, as she (Lady B.) is not obliged to follow my notions unless she likes—which is not very likely. Is the girl imaginative ? At *her* present age I have an idea that I had many feelings and notions which people would not believe if I stated them *now*, and therefore I may as well keep them to myself. Is she social or solitary, taciturn or talkative, fond of reading or otherwise, and what is her *tic* ? I mean her foible—is she passionate ? I hope the Gods have made her anything save *poetical*—it is enough to have one such fool in the family.

From Hastings on December 1 Augusta received a description of Ada, now eight years old. " Her prevailing characteristic is cheerfulness and good-temper. Observation. Not devoid of imagination, but it is chiefly exercised in connection with her mechanical ingenuity—the manufacture of ships and boats, etc. Prefers prose to verse, because puzzled by poetical diction. Not very persevering. Draws well. Open and ingenuous temper, now under control. Tall and robust."

She enclosed a profile of Ada. It may have been some solace to remember this in the 1824 that was so soon to dawn with its New Year memories, its tidings in her birthday-week of the death on Easter Monday at Missolonghi. An unfinished letter to Augusta lay on his table, asking her to thank his wife for the description —the one " gentle " sign she had made him since the Dearest Duck letter in 1816, the last she could ever make him now. *La fiera moglie* ... who when Fletcher came to her in July with the story of that tormented death-bed, was to walk about the room, sobbing so that her whole frame was shaken, while she implored him to remember the words muttered earnestly, unintelligibly, " for nearly twenty minutes."

He could not remember them, for he had never heard them.

" ' Go to Lady Byron, and say——' Here I told his lordship, in a state of the greatest perplexity, that I had not understood a word of what he had said."

CHAPTER XX

1824-25

AFTER THE END

THE news reached England on May 14; George Byron, now seventh Lord, went down to Beckenham (where Annabella then was) to break it to her. He told Augusta and Hobhouse that her distress had been painful to witness; she had said at last: "I have no right to be considered, but I have my feelings. I should wish to see any accounts that have come." Augusta had already sent her Fletcher's letter, dated April 20—the day after Byron's death; Hobhouse now sent her those received by him.

There is no other immediate record, but long afterwards she wrote for herself alone: "Whoever has once in life seen a *desert* spread before him will recognise the feeling in another mind. It may be lived through, but how much of faith is required to believe this! and we seldom take the right way. It is not, as far as my experience goes, by seeking to turn the whole soul to God and away from earthly things, but by devoting ourselves to help and comfort all (not connections merely) who need what we can give them."

She took that way. To Augusta she now wrote almost daily, advising her on the points which instantly arose—Byron's Will and Byron's Memoirs. Not two days after the news of his death, they were all harassed by Moore's indecent haste about claiming possession in these Memoirs. On Annabella's birthday —the 17th—Wilmot (now Wilmot Horton) wrote to her of their having been burnt that day at Murray's. She had not been consulted; the decision had lain with Augusta, Hobhouse acting as her adviser. . . . We need not dwell upon the story; all Byron biographers do that; but we shall see that

Annabella's part was merely to " concur " in the *fait accompli* of the burning.

Her own first action was characteristic. Within three days it was resolved upon, as this passage from Wilmot Horton's letter on her birthday shows :

> With respect to your proposal of giving up your jointure to George, which you say that I should consider as a matter of course—you pay me too great a compliment in such a supposition. I consider that proposal as one of the most liberal and magnanimous (if the word were not injured by its frequent misapplication) that *ever was made* by Man or Woman—& yet I think it quite that sort of proposal which anyone who knows you, or rather *of you*, as much as I do, might *expect you* to make.
>
> I am *perfectly astonished* to hear from George that an opinion is entertained by those who have the means of knowing that the personalty, or rather the fortune independent of the £60,000, may be calculated *above* £100,000. I can scarcely believe it, & I do trust that if the fact be so, something may have been done for George.

The report was correct. Byron's total property of his own was about £80,000, subject to Annabella's jointure of £2000 a year, secured by the £60,000 in the marriage settlement. She had brought Byron her fortune of £20,000, of which only £16,000 was secured by settlement and went at his death not to her, but their daughter. The remaining £4000 was merged in Byron's personalty, and was bequeathed by him, with all the rest of his disposable property, to Augusta. There were besides " some thousands of pounds of accruing Wentworth rents that were carefully garnered in by Lord Byron's executors for Mrs. Leigh's benefit. They forgave friends of Lord Byron's sums owing to the estate, but they forgave his widow nothing. She did not do likewise. She transferred the whole of her interest in her jointure to the new Lord Byron, who, like herself and her daughter, had been totally disinherited by the poet, and who, unlike her and her daughter, was destitute of all other means of subsistence than this £2000 a year, and even this Lady Byron could only ensure him during her life." [1]

[1] *Lady Noel Byron and the Leighs* : Privately printed. 1887.

Lord Lovelace, in the book cited above, remarks that probably Byron himself did not exactly foresee how his will (dated some six months after marriage) would affect the whole Byron family —that " the Leighs must ultimately engulf all the Byron possessions, and some other possessions too."[1]   He had told his wife of this will ; she had approved, not fully understanding and trusting in Byron's equity.   " She abstained from all interference and cheerfully made the best of what he thought fit to do."   But, as Lord Lovelace points out, " she deserved no credit and had incurred no liability for any single thing in Lord Byron's will. No quotation of words of hers could shift the full responsibility from Lord Byron for making it, or from Mrs. Leigh for accepting benefit by it."

Augusta *had* qualms of conscience about George Byron's disinheritance.   If Annabella died before she did, even the £2000 jointure would come to her !   She wrote a great many letters about her desire to " do something " for George, and might have saved everyone much worry had she begun by addressing him. For he and his wife declined all idea of help from her.   He wrote to Annabella :

> Our feelings cannot allow us to receive anything from Augusta.   We are, thank God, independent, and more than that through your generosity which we have gladly and gratefully accepted—but this, my friend, is quite of a different nature.   The other will not bear thinking of.

The refusal, among other grievances, brought about a complete breach between Augusta and the new Lord Byron.

Such were the pre-occupations immediately thrust upon Annabella.   She had little time to think of nearer things ; there is no diary at this time, no intimate letter.   The first word as from herself is to Mrs. Villiers, on the day after her birthday.   " Ada shed large tears. . . .   It is a great comfort to me that I have never had to give her a painful impression of her father."

One other anxiety, besides those more or less extraneous about Memoirs and money, had been quickly in her mind.   Her

---

[1] *Lady Noel Byron and the Leighs*: Privately printed.   1887.

friend Lady Ravensworth, an intimate from girlhood, wrote on
May 19 :

> I entirely coincide with the sentiments you express respect-
> ing any written documents that may be in the possession of
> *your Friends*, relative to Lord Byron's conduct ; and shall
> certainly destroy some Letters & writings I had directed to be
> delivered to you in case of my death.   The poems you gave me
> I should *very* much wish to keep, both on account of the
> beautiful feeling they display, & because they *must* prove to
> everyone how little justice has been done your real character,
> when the friends of Lord B. accused you of coldness and want
> of sensibility—if however you insist on sacrificing them, I *must*
> acquiesce.

For the rest, her days might be summarised into " Augusta."
Letters about the Memoirs, the Will, George Byron—and Clermont, dragged into the papers again, " shamefully traduced," as she
wrote to Augusta, begging (or rather commanding) her to declare
that there was no truth in the charges against her.   Even about
this Annabella must be told : " You might think it odd in me
not to." ...   And in the midst of it all, Lord Tamworth died
after years of hopeless illness, and the " noblest devotion " from
that Sophy whose happiness had once seemed certain to a passionate child's heart at Seaham.

It was one of those periods that sometimes descend on human
beings, when nothing seems omitted that can try their courage.
In June came the discussion of arrangements for Byron's funeral.
She was asked if she had any wishes ; her answer was that it
might be left to Mr. Hobhouse—he could be trusted.   She must
have read the newspaper accounts of that pageant on July 12,
as it passed from the house in George Street, Westminster (Sir
Edward Knatchbull-Hugessen's) through Nottingham to the
family vault at Hucknall Torkard. ...   She sent—could send—no
message.   The one comment we have is in a letter to Hugh
Montgomery : " I do not like the *unkin*-like action of all the
Lambs, except William, being mourners at Lord Byron's funeral."
For the newspapers were full of lies about her ; even the surrender
of her jointure was unfavourably interpreted.   She took no
public notice ; but the misery of it all broke her down at last,
and she was ill for many weeks.

Her illness did not save her from the Memoirs controversy, nor from controversy about Byron's Will. She had written to Augusta on July 7 :

It has occurred to me that since the contents of the Will are published, *my* authority for opinions concerning it may be falsely alleged by some. I assure you that I have not given any opinion which could possibly be quoted respecting the dispositions of the property. I am, however, very far from wishing to deny now what I have more than once said to my husband—that it was his duty to provide for you and yours. How far *exclusively* is a question which I am relieved to be under no necessity of discussing—& therefore certainly shall say nothing about the matter, whatever may be said *for* me. I am sure you would not consider it as a kindness on my part to *congratulate* you on that accession—but I sincerely hope your cares may be lightened.

Then Caroline Lamb asked if she might come to see her ; " and please ask Mrs. Leigh and Hobhouse for all my letters, pictures, etc., and say it is my wish *you* should have them." She replied that she was too ill to see Caroline ; " Lord Melbourne is the only person I have *sat up* to see for many weeks. I cannot ask for your letters, etc., but they will be all right." Next, in November, came Medwin's *Conversations with Lord Byron*—the collection of half-truths and flagrant lies which did so much to destroy Caroline Lamb's reason. She wrote Medwin a long agonised letter [1]—it caused him to delete in the second edition the whole passage referring to her, together with the verses " Remember thee ! " first published by him. . . . The Byron side was angry, too. There was some thought of Hobhouse's publishing a contradictory pamphlet ; this was abandoned, and Annabella, for one, rejoiced that it was. " Let the excitement subside, and then we shall see," she wrote to Wilmot Horton—telling him also that Moore had written asking if she would send materials for his Life of Byron. She had declined, by her own wish and Dr. Lushington's advice.

The widow of a great public man must always have affliction added to grief ; this widow had contumely and slander besides.

[1] To be read in *Letters and Journals*, iii. 446, and (partly) in my *Byron*.

Byron had become the national idol, after his years of being the national byeword. No one can wish it to have been otherwise ; she did not. Silence was again her chosen attitude, while her generosity was misrepresented, her past and present raked up in every newspaper. These weeks—these months, for the controversy about the Memoirs dragged on until far into 1825—in fact broke her down once for all. She lived to be sixty-eight, and lived a life of more or less public activity ; but she was never again anything but a sick woman striving against the manifold, ever-recurrent sorrows and cruelties that her marriage, and her promise " to be kind to Augusta," had brought and were still to bring upon her. 1824, 1825 ; then 1830 and Moore's Life of Byron, with its long-delayed publication of the *Stanzas to Augusta*, and its slanders on her parents ; then 1831, with the beginning of the Medora Leigh scandal and its long sequel of pain for the saviour of that child of incest, who so belied her father's exultant cry to Lady Melbourne : " Oh, but it *is* ' worth while,' and it is not an ' ape ' "—Elizabeth Medora Leigh, for whom in 1820 Annabella had " felt the most tender affection " and wondered why. And wondering why, had gone next day to look at her old home in Piccadilly, and gaze " into the room where I have sat with him."

1825 began with the question of Moore's compensation for losing the Memoirs. They were not his, but Murray's, when they were burnt, Murray having bought them for two thousand guineas. This money Moore had insisted on returning. He had urgently protested against their destruction, and then and for long afterwards assumed a martyred and magnanimous attitude about it. Though his possession in them had lapsed with Byron's death, it was felt that he ought to be compensated ; there was an idea that Lady Byron should share with Mrs. Leigh in repaying him the two thousand guineas. This distressed Augusta. She told Wilmot Horton that she felt it the greatest humiliation and vexation. " *Mine* was the act of destroying the MS., *mine* and *mine* ALONE ought to have been the consequences. I feel its *not* being so the more as Lady B. says she did NOT ' CONSENT ' to the destruction." Annabella, hearing of this, wrote to say that had she been consulted at the time, the MS. would not have been burnt by her decision, but that *now* she concurred. " It is therefore perhaps as well that I was not."

That was not the end of it ; nor did they spare her even when death intervened—the death on March 19 at her house in Hampstead, aged 78, of the father whom we might think to be the one creature in her life who never caused her any pain. " Bright Daystar." In her fond girlish impertinence she had called him that ; now her sky would hold the steadfast star no more. " Honest red-faced spirit," the Dad whose pot-hooks were always looked-out for, whose home-baked loaves were always the lightest, whose anxiety about the wine for her Romilly-dinner had been so amusingly practical . . . he was gone, now when the shrieking pack of journalists was upon the sick and hunted deer, and the rest—Augusta, Hobhouse, Moore—were worrying at her, frowning on her, " forgiving " her. Now she was indeed alone among them all.

Again there is no diary, no intimate letter. Our knowledge of the love between these two takes their place.

Not a single day was free from Augusta's letters. They were concerned with herself alone—the Moore-Murray turmoil chiefly, but already another book about Byron was brewing. Dallas was printing his *Recollections*, had sent Lady Byron some sheets,[1] which she had acknowledged merely by a formal note, saying she had not yet read them. Augusta was in a fury about the expected publication and George Byron's supposed sanction of the book. She was assured by him and his wife that he had not sanctioned either the offending Preface or the Notes ; but still : " I can never speak to him again." Annabella tried to defend him—vainly. She was again seriously ill ; again it did not save her. From March to June the Memoirs fuss dragged on. She had taken refuge at Ramsgate—thither came a long letter from Augusta " to be read at leisure." Leisure, indeed, was indispensable for wading through the " d——d crinkum-crankum," more exasperatingly itself than ever. Let us see it, as an example of what her sorrow and her illness had to contend with :

---

[1] The printing of this book was stopped by Byron's executors. It was published in Paris in 1825 by Galignani.

To be read at leisure.

. . . .

You really and perfectly *astound* me by saying that W——
throws the responsibility of the *destruction* on *you* ! How can
it be possible after all that passed on the subject between us—
when in consequence of his coming and proposing the direct
reverse of what Mr. Hobhouse had the day before—the most
extraordinary plans, such as locking up the MS. at HIS
(Wilmot's) Banker's ! ! ! publishing the *un*exceptionable parts
& so on—*I* declared *I* would have *nothing* to do with the
thing. He said " You MUST. *Moore will not give them up to
anybody else."* I answered, " IF I DO ACCEPT THEM, THEY SHALL
BE DESTROYED," & that answer closed the whole business !
It is really almost incredible that after *that,* he *can* say *you* did
it—& I feel so strongly that it was *my sole act & deed* that
nothing but absolute inability to pay all should induce me to
hear of your paying one farthing—& I must say it has vexed
me & does vex me more than I can describe to think that
you are to be so taxed for any act of mine. It is certainly true
that after this extraordinary conversation with Wilmot,
between which & the destruction I hoped to be able to have
your opinion, I *did* write & do my best to ascertain it—as you
may remember. . . . Certainly my *first* consideration was my
brother's memory. *Whatever* might be said, *whoever* might be
mentioned in those Memoirs, the disgrace would have been
HIS ! He was not there to prevent or direct—& I feel sure as
of my existence that in his lifetime they wd never have seen
light, & have every reason to hope from the blessed alteration
during the last year that he wd have done his best, had he
been spared, to have prevented it after his death. Mr. Hobhouse knew *from himself,* indeed I believe it is recorded in
writing, that he did not wish them ever to be published. His
words to me, that first wretched day, & after we had been some
time together were : " Well, it can't be helped ! all our regrets
are vain ! But *now,* Mrs. Leigh, we must take care of *his*
fame and *there are* THOSE MEMOIRS." The next [day] he came
and told me Moore had agreed to give them up to *me*—&
" *you must burn them."* I thought *he* knew best—*I* had never
seen them—knew *nothing* of their contents, & it so happened
that my poor Brother *never* mentioned their existence to me !
Some few straggling reports had reached me of such and such
things, this & that person who had read a part of them had
repeated—but that was literally all I had to go by & I repeat,

his fame—his Memory—was my *first* consideration. I could
not but think it was one not indifferent to you, in spite of
circumstances. Wilmot must be *mad*, I do think.

I beg pardon for this long scrawl—but I hope it will tire you
less to read than to write, & I wish that We should understand
each other. It is the more desirable, as it appears from your
account that there exists *somewhere* or *other* the same amiable
anxiety *to set us by the ears* that I have had before to encounter
—perhaps it may be as well *not* to conjecture on the subject
for fear of becoming *as amiable* oneself ! I am very sure from
my indolence & hatred of such *intricacies & want of suspicion*
(*by nature*) I am the very best subject for such malice. I
don't mean to make myself *out* as *amiable* ; all these become
faults if indulged to excess.

At any rate this settles the question of who was responsible.
Interminable—not only the letter but the wretched controversy. The reimbursement to Moore was never made in this
way ; Murray settled the matter with him in 1828 ; but Lady
Byron was ready to pay in part or altogether. We shall see how
she was kept up to that readiness by Augusta, despite the protests
here and elsewhere.

So 1825 fulfilled itself. She was " only well when at the sea " ;
restlessly she fled from Ramsgate to Dover, Cowes, Brighton,
unceasingly pursued. With Moore she would have no communication. She told Joanna Baillie this in November (from
Brighton), adding that as to the newspapers, she had never
attempted to interfere with them, directly or indirectly.

I leave that great instrument to my assailants, at least till
all its offensive powers are exhausted. The time may come,
if my life be prolonged, and my health restored in any degree,
when I shall yet make use of it to counteract some of its own
mischiefs.

I am privately meditating some handsome and ostensible
acknowledgement to Murray, for the sacrifice he made of his
pecuniary interests in surrendering the property of the Memoirs
for the very inadequate compensation of the purchase-money,
at a time when their value was at least quadrupled by the power
of immediate publication. I am thoroughly acquainted with
the documents which prove Murray's honorable and faithful
conduct in this business, and the less it is appreciated in the
world owing to Moore's having gained the popular opinion, the

more do I wish to furnish Murray with some memorial of *my* estimation. What occurs to you for this purpose—a present of plate ? of a marble bust of Lord Byron ? a picture ? I wish it were something that would tell its own story, or at least imply it.

And the year ended—for us who know the future, how ominously ! —with the engagement of Georgiana Leigh, Augusta's eldest child, to Mr. Henry Trevanion, a Cornish connection of the Byron family. Of Georgiana we learn, at this stage, that she was " a very quiet, sensible, retiring girl."

CHAPTER XXI

1826-30 :
AUGUSTA

1826 opened with a begging-letter from Augusta. "When we were contemplating the Moore and Murray business, you offered to lend me my share of the reimbursement which would have amounted to more than £1000, and my security would have been Life Insurance." Could Annabella arrange something of the same sort now ?—the money being wanted for Georgey's settlement. Augusta would not have anything to do with the Byrons, nor with her Leeds and Chichester relations.

Of course she got the money ; and felt " MUCH more gratitude than could be expressed—SUCH a relief ! " This episode produced a sample of Goose's goosishness so exquisite that it must be given here : " We have heard from the *higher powers*, consenting to the immediate conclusion, as *I* (*entre nous* YOU) have provided the needful." That *entre nous*—can it ever have been surpassed in silliness ! But when she added that her heart was " turning with joy," we must grant her one of the vivid phrases that these people so often found.

The wedding came off on February 4, the bride's father refusing to be present. He was violently adverse to the match ; Augusta had " fearlessly opposed " him, as Mrs. Villiers long afterwards told Annabella. It is difficult to associate Colonel Leigh with moral scruples ; here, however, he seems to have had some glimmerings, and with good reason.

Annabella, still helping with money, soon had to advise about something else. Augusta had received a letter from a person named Washington Fleming, telling her that Caroline Lamb had some time ago taken an interest in him " as a literary man," had flattered and encouraged him, deceived him by false promises, treated him " most ungenerously " ; but had also given him the possession of her private journal and confessions relative to Lord Byron " and his Lady." From this he had copied the most interesting passages—quite single-heartedly at the time . . . but now he was perishing, had a mother dependent on him. . . . In short, what would Mrs. Leigh pay ? The alternative was publication ; an immediate reply was demanded.

" His Lady," the first appealed to, could not bring herself to supply the money for this. She saw, as others saw, that they had no real guarantee—who could tell how many copies Fleming possessed ? William Lamb and Murray refused, on this ground, to do anything ; a legal authority told her that at any cost the Byron family must keep out of the transaction. She was alarmed for Augusta, knowing as she did that Byron had confided in Caroline. " I think I cannot go abroad " (as she had arranged to do) " and leave her to such impending danger, if my presence can protect her. A promise of kindness, sealed by death, must ever bind me." So she wrote to Mrs. Villiers. But she was powerless. Finally, against her advice, Augusta sent Hanson to the man. " Half-measures," commented Annabella, " will always be her bane." . . . Except that Caroline Lamb was " very miserable at the consequences of her folly," we know nothing more about this incident ; but Lord Lovelace, in *Lady Noel Byron and the Leighs*, quotes a letter written to him in 1870 by Lady Wilmot Horton : " It has always appeared to *me* to be the most conclusive evidence against poor Mrs. Leigh, the state of abject poverty to which she was reduced—with *no* expensive habits ! And no doubt in consequence of the claims made upon her by those who threatened disclosures."

Against goosishness it seems that " Providence," and Byron, and Annabella had fought in vain.

And now, for the first time in her life, Thursday's Child left England—seeking solace and refuge in the other kind of distance from the Far-to-Go. She spent a year on the Continent ; Ada and Ada's governess, and her friend Louisa Chaloner, were with her. They went from place to place—Rotterdam, Heidelberg, Baden, Milan ; then Genoa, where she was " not observed," and

where Ada had drawing-lessons from a Signor Isola, who had
been " much employed by Lord Byron in this place, and of
course feels a great interest in Ada." The Sole Daughter, now
nearly eleven, would sometimes add a few words in a clear
childish hand to her mother's letters. Of these Annabella
wrote : " I always leave Ada to select her topics and express
herself without restraint. . . . She is full of unarranged
thoughts, which her governess is helping her to arrange." Still
we perceive the slight aloofness—springing perhaps from the
timidity which had made her imagine that her child would
never love her ; that springing in its turn from remembrance
of the bitterness and fear which had inspired the morbid verses
of 1816.

Everywhere she went, Augusta's long screeds pursued her.
Complaints of Colonel Leigh's tyranny and cruelty, his persistent
abhorrence of the Trevanion connection—sinister in its implica-
tions for us who know much of the truth, and something of the
conjectures, about that marriage. So distraught were the letters
that Annabella suggested the family should all go to live abroad.
But no—that would mean a fight with *il marito*, and he would
win. Misery, misery—worries with all the seven children ; the
tyrant husband refusing to let the boys go to school, teaching
them to bet, threatening to leave her. " In all my miseries,
H. T.'s [Henry Trevanion's] conduct and character are a great
source of consolation—he is QUITE what I expected of him."
And money-matters were in their usual state—would Annabella
lend one or two hundred pounds ?

For a wonder, Annabella would not. But not very long afterwards she was again besought—this time for a thousand.
Augusta dared not ask her trustees, because she had already got
money from one of them without telling the others ; her shyness had prevented her. So she had not borrowed enough—
would Annabella help ?

Her appeals disclose, indeed, a most wretched existence.
Written to her who had promised to be kind, they represented a
claim on the disinherited wife which might well have seemed
shameless. Probably it was now that she wrote the verses
entitled *Sent with a Reproof*, and headed " I may not be the
softer friend "—

> The sterner task I dare accept
>   To paint thee as thou art ;
> And when thy better thoughts have slept
>   To rouse—to wound thy heart.
>
> Yet cruel as my words appear
>   It were enough for me,
> Could I believe the silent tear
>   Not shed in vain for thee !

We shall see that she refused the thousand pounds, and her
reason for refusing.

Of the stay abroad—it lasted until December, 1828—she wrote
ten years afterwards to one of the children of her loved M.G.
(then dead), saying that she was much happier now.

> I was fashioning happiness at that time after my own
> imagination, and following with a sigh the path marked out for
> me. I was much more dependent upon my fellow-creatures
> for sunshine than I am now—I do not mean to say that the
> sunshine has yet fallen on me from Heaven, but at least most
> of the darkness is dispersed.

In Switzerland she stayed a while, and wrote with unusual and
touching naïveté that she loved it " because it is like Seaham,
only much bigger."

Back in England, Augusta's troubles were awaiting her at
closer range.   They were *da capo* with the addition of rage against
Moore, now collecting material for his Life of Byron, and much
reviled (poor biographer !) for " ransacking Nottingham and
visiting the Chaworths."   But Augusta had, or thought she had,
a more reasonable grievance ; he was said to be giving it out that
his book had both Mrs. Leigh's and Lady Byron's entire
approbation.

Annabella, then at Bifrons, Canterbury (a house she had
leased, but never could bring herself to like), wrote to George
Byron about this. He answered on March 15 after a long
interview with Murray, who had assured him that there would
not be " one word " in the book to offend anyone, especially
Lady Byron.   Moore had not boasted of her sanction—Murray
believed that story to be " a determined falsehood," and would
be answerable for no such thing being said in the book.   If he

had not joined Moore, an offensive work might have appeared ;
but he had told Moore that if such a work did appear " there were
persons who might reply in a manner he might not be aware of,
and damn Lord Byron's character and those of his friends for
ever." . Murray's last words to George had been : " Lord Byron's
moral character you know I *cannot* defend " ; and Moore had
owned that the Memoirs were of " such a low pot-house description " that he could not have published them.[1]   " I am grieved,"
continued George, " to think how you have been suffering since
we left you."

That suffering culminated in another break-down. From
Tunbridge Wells she wrote to a friend, Dr. King, that she
had been very ill—would he please find her a house in
Brighton, " near the Chain Pier."   Perhaps she had some respite
there ; but in September she was again restlessly on the move.
Clifton, and from Clifton a tour in Devonshire ; then across the
Bristol Channel to Swansea " by steam-packet," up the coast to
Newport, and back to Clifton again. There she saw Mrs.
Clermont—for the first time since 1816.

Her restlessness was, as it always is, symbolic of restlessness
within. It never really left her after she had seen " the desert
spread before her." Though once she wrote that her hope had
been so long crushed that Byron's death could hardly be said to
make a difference to her, something had died with him which
altered her outward—not her inward—life into the very opposite
of what it had been. She had had phases of discontent and
restlessness in girlhood ; now that the word " discontent " was
so inadequate to her sense of desolation as to be an absurdity,
the restlessness became supreme. She could not settle anywhere ; she never had a home again. Once only had she had
one—Seaham, the Seaham which Switzerland could do no more
than recall to her ! It was her sole memory of happiness. . . .   In
after-years some one wrote of her in arresting words :

> Her life was Spring and Winter.   Summer flow'rs
> She ne'er had looked on save in early dreams.

---

[1] On this point there were conflicting voices among those who had read
the MS. Lord John Russell and Lord Holland said there were at most
four or five indelicate pages ; but again, Lord Rancliffe told Hobhouse
that " the flames were the fit place for it," and that no decent person could
regret the destruction.

Her mind, indeed, continually went back to Seaham ; but remember what she might, do what she might, absorb herself in others as she did, " the thought ran through, through—yes, through " ; the thought of her ruined marriage. Kindness to Augusta : that, and his child, were the only legacies Byron had left his wife. Her duties to both were done from first to last, and love was in the doing ; but it was the love of a heart which had learnt to fear that others were " not able " to love her. Intense as she had been from earliest childhood in her own affections, she still was. " But I was fearful of intruding." So she could reminiscently see herself at ten years old ; in that, too, she never changed. An almost painful delicacy ruled her benefactions, even to Augusta—much more than was at all needed with that practised borrower, effusively grateful as could be but always ready to ask for more. To Augusta, borrowing from friends was the most natural of expedients, about which she might feel shy after bamboozling one trustee without telling the rest—but not otherwise ; and least of all with " dearest A," whom B. had disinherited for X.

And before the year was out, she was reproaching dearest A. for a conviction, " equally painful and surprising," to which she had been led—that of A.'s considering B.'s disposition of his property as an injustice to his own child. " It afflicts me to think any act of his could be *so* considered—and by *you* ! It *surprises* me ; for perhaps you will recollect that it was from you —and *you alone*—that I heard of the will . . . and the information was accompanied by the expression of your *decided approval*, founded no doubt upon the feeling that Ada would be adequately provided for. . . . Having reminded you of these facts it is unnecessary to comment upon what your letter has made me feel on *that* point." . . . Augusta had forgotten that when the will was made, Ada was not yet born. Had the child been a son, the settlement would have protected it to a great extent from the despoiling which, as it was, resulted.

Annabella answered, from Dover :

If you will re-peruse my last, you will find that I have not expressed any censure of Lord Byron's will. I merely stated the dispositions of it, and YOU put upon them the *construction*, " an act of injustice to his child ! "

My object was only to show that it would be an act of injustice on my part towards Ada if, *without some strong claim*, I were to alienate her maternal property likewise.   It was, and *is*, satisfactory to my feelings that a provision has been made for you and yours, and however little so regarded, I shall be " a friend to Augusta " *still*.

In the prison of that promise, did she recall her mother's warning : " If I know anything of human nature, she does and must hate you " ?

This 1828 was the year of a death which could not fail to move her.   While she was abroad, Caroline Lamb had passed away at Melbourne House on January 26—six months before, by his father's death, William Lamb became Lord Melbourne.   She had died of dropsy, her husband's hand in hers.   For a while she had been definitely deranged ; the three successive shocks of Byron's death, her meeting with his funeral as it passed Brocket Hall, and Medwin's book, had broken down her always precarious sanity.   She regained it before the last—enough to forget the " beautiful pale face " of her fate for that of the pseudo-Byron, Edward Bulwer Lytton, in the very year of that death and that meeting ! ...   We have no word from Annabella on the end of her rival-cousin in the triumphant, fatal season of 1812.

" Her life was Spring and Winter."   Whoever wrote those words of Annabella was a poet by right of imaginative sympathy.   Yet to herself they would have seemed untrue ; there is, indeed, a sense in which they *are* untrue.   The long winter of her heart disguised itself as fruitful autumn to the nature of the child, girl, woman, whose strongest impulse it was to protect.   We who look more pitifully, if more critically, on her years of active benevolence, can see that the sun never shone for her again—never ripened the fruits of that autumn, nor the richer fruits of her capacity for love.   Something had frozen in her—something always susceptible to frost.   Her affections were too ready for the blight she too readily anticipated.   It did not kill them, but the canker pierced the heart in which they lived.   Though of her girlhood's best-loved friends she kept all until death intervened for them or her, the later intimacies with women knew painful misunderstandings, alienation ; sore hearts on both sides, but hearts too proud—or too sore—for reunion.

And Augusta ? Unique in its complexity, that affection was the phoenix of her heart, for ever rising from its ashes. Not only the promise bound her ; the infatuation, though it indeed could not survive, still held her in its broken chain. Who else had known him, who else remembered him ? The memories were terrible, but Augusta shared them ; the anguish had been supreme, but Augusta had suffered with her. It was the thing apart, the thing that no one else could understand. " I loved her—I love her still—I cannot help it. I shall see her once more in this world before we both die. . . . People have called that in me a want of strength of moral principle, the inability to detach affection from one whom I have found unworthy. It may be, but it is my nature. Can it be wrong ? " So she pleaded to Robertson in 1851. And writing to him the day after, she went on : " Since that one impulse which I acknowledged to you [of the dagger she had almost seized], I have never had any feeling but one of—I can't get a right word. I say this now, because the *utterance* would still try me. . . . Will you not now sympathise more completely ? "

In 1829 the phoenix died its first of deaths. Though from the Return-Scare of ten years before we might date the beginning of the end, it was now that avowed alienation set in, and for a time endured. Even that promise could not prevail against the sense of " wilful misconstruction " which Annabella was justly to feel— and sternly to act upon.

Its origin was the death of Byron's friend, Douglas Kinnaird, who was one of the trustees to the marriage settlement. His place had to be filled ; Augusta claimed a voice in the nomination. (She had a contingent interest in the settlement, but no legal right to nominate a trustee.) Annabella had chosen Dr. Lush-ington. " I have to observe," wrote Augusta, " that he is a perfect stranger to me. . . . It is of the highest importance to my interests that I should be on terms of friendly intercourse or even intimacy with the Party." She added that Lady Byron already had a protector of *her* interests, and requested that her own solicitor might at least be named solicitor to the Trust. She did not think that Dr. Lushington would wish to accept the

Trust in these circumstances, and asked that he should see her letter.

Dr. Lushington saw it, and wrote to his friend :

> Frankly speaking, no one but the most ignorant, or the most selfish, of our species could entertain such feelings—and to this is to be added the base ingratitude to yourself, who have shown every disposition to aid and assist her wishes, to your own great trouble and annoyance.
>
> A trustee of Mrs. Leigh's nomination might injure you and Ada to her advantage. A trustee of your selection could not injure Mrs. Leigh for your interest. You have already extended your forgiveness to Mrs. Leigh to so unparalleled an extent that I must in candour say that all she can feel, write, or say in this transaction is comparatively of no importance. Any personal contact with her is, I think, a degradation to you.

Annabella, too, was strongly indignant. She wrote to Mrs. Wilmot Horton that she could not again have any personal intercourse with Mrs. Leigh after such wilful misconstruction. " I shall not enter into any justification," she added ; but this resolve was frustrated by Augusta, who wrote saying that no future advantage she might ever derive could compensate for the appointment, and the " misery, harassment, and vexation " which all the measures connected with it had caused her. Annabella replied with the utmost sternness. Augusta had no claim to a voice, no reason to doubt that her interests would be promoted, none to suspect Dr. Lushington of " preconcerting with Mr. Kinnaird a plan for obtaining the trusteeship," nor to suppose that his conduct would be unfriendly to her. She could not complain of the communication having been made through Annabella's solicitor, for she had objected to any transaction with Dr. Lushington, and was on good terms with Wharton, the solicitor in question. If Augusta could not assent to these assertions, " I beg you to signify your dissent by silence on the subject."

Augusta did dissent, but would not be silent. She promised " a few words "—and wrote a letter which fills a page of small print.[1] She *had* been unkindly treated—that was the gist ; had been " dreadfully hurt," but could and did forgive freely. Her

---

[1] *Lady Noel Byron and the Leighs*, pp. 94-95.

self-respect would not allow her to say more. She had been
" agonised and almost destroyed."

Insolent was Annabella's term for this letter. " *Forgiveness*
bestowed for all my unkindness "—though measures had now
been carried out for Augusta's benefit under the settlement!
" They could only have been taken at *my* request." So she wrote
to Mrs. Villiers. But though she would not submit to misrepresentation, she declared that she bore no resentment. She had not
yet determined what to do, and here comes a touch of contempt
for which we can hardly blame her : " I cannot give much
time to the subject."

A storm in a teacup—but it had made its splash. With 1830
came Annabella's distress and anger about Moore's Life. Before
this quarrel, she would assuredly have turned to Augusta for
confirmation of her resolve to separate when she left Piccadilly
in 1816 ; Augusta could not have refused to give it ; and this
was the point at issue between Lady Byron and Moore. But as
things were, the Remarks [1] were composed and printed without
any reference to her who had been behind the scenes when
Byron rang up the curtain on his third act.

All readers of Moore's Life of Byron are familiar with these
Remarks. In publishing them, Annabella had to contend
against much opposition from her friends, Colonel Doyle especially. He feared that the whole question would be re-opened,
and did not think Moore's observations were sufficient ground
for the length to which he considered that she would have to go.
Dr. Lushington, too, hesitated ; but did not speak so strongly.
She wrote to him that if he could convince her that she
could be *compelled* to disclose anything injurious to any living
person, she would sacrifice the memory of her parents. " But it
appears to me that if I can endure anything rather than divulge
such facts (tho' this should be known only to yourself), they
cannot transpire in consequence of my statement. I should not
have undertaken to make it without being certain of my own
firmness in regard to accusation and censure—but though I am
prepared to *suffer*, I am not prepared to *inflict* injury." There
was much correspondence ; but, " the more I reflect, the more

---

[1] So she entitled her defence of her parents against Moore's charge
of having coerced her into the separation.

I feel that I should stamp disgrace on myself by remaining silent. . . . I shall have to encounter the charges of retaliation ' after death ' . . . of insinuating what I dare not avow, of cold and malignant proceedings, etc. So be it ! " She thought the most plausible argument against there having been any serious cause for the separation would be that if Byron had been conscious of such, he would not have given so decided a testimony in her favour.

> But the truth is that he always relied on the invalidity of a wife's testimony against her husband, unsupported by any witness—and frequently mentioned that circumstance to me. Mrs. Leigh also endeavoured to impress it on my mind in one of her letters at the time of the separation—as follows : " Without witnesses your depositions will go for nothing . . . the same with regard to those who have only heard circumstances from you." Is not this a curious proof of THE PLOT ? but I did not see through it then.

Finally she wrote that she did not throw on *any* one the responsibility of estimating her duty in the matter, " being determined— whether advised or not advised—to effect to the best of my power the exposure of these calumnies. . . . I *ought* not to be silent."

Of course they had all remembered the Dearest Duck letter, which for so long did make part of the case against her parents. (To this, as the Remarks show, she made a point of referring.) But no fears for herself, no arguments from friends, could shake her resolution.

As we know, Moore offered to bind up the Remarks with his second volume. This was by no means what she desired ; nevertheless she consented, and it was done. Meanwhile the pamphlet itself, of which only a few copies were printed and privately circulated by her, had somehow got into the journalists' hands. Her comment was that though she was annoyed, " it will be the sooner over."

One of the first copies was sent through Mrs. Villiers to Augusta. Soreness about the trusteeship still survived in both women, and Augusta did not in any way acknowledge her copy to Annabella. But she wrote of it to Francis Hodgson, now one of her champions : " God forgive *her* if she has made me what I never was before or believed I could be. Such unfeeling conduct! I agree with every word you say about them." ... Those who remember the Remarks will, on the contrary, agree with Lord Lovelace's comment that " a milder protest could not have been made against untrue accounts." But, as with everything about Byron at this time, they caused a fresh hue-and-cry against his widow, and this in its turn brought about Campbell's (the poet's) disastrous intervention in the *New Monthly*. He had called upon her, for the purpose of making " a frank acknowledgment of impressions which my statement had removed." He offered his services unreservedly, and pressed her very closely " on one point "—as she then thought, from good and generous motives, saying that her silence left a stigma on another's character, and that her motives for such reserve were liable to misconstruction.

> I replied, " I *submit* to that misconstruction." A pause ensued, and Campbell seemed deeply affected. I then added : " It is well known that intercourse has existed between Mrs. Leigh and me since my separation. With respect to reports ... they certainly do not originate with me or mine, and it is for the good of society that they should not be listened to." I trust he did not penetrate the truth ; but after leaving me, he returned to London with a friend of mine, to whom he asserted that he had Hobhouse's authority for *that fact* !

The upshot was that Campbell, in the *New Monthly*, wrote of the matter in such a way as to cast a quite new slur upon Byron's memory.[1] Finally, protesting that such insinuations had never been in his mind, he excused himself for the harm done by saying that he " did not know what he was doing when he published his article." He had printed—but with the confession that there was no authorisation from her—a portion of a letter in which she had refused to give him any private information and had added what Campbell did *not* elect to publish :

> I believe that the most judicious and friendly part towards all concerned is to mark clearly to such persons as may attend to the subject the real object of my statements, though I can scarcely suppose it possible to mistake it.

[1] He was thus responsible for starting the whispers afterwards believed by some to be the subject of that charge which had caused Dr. Lushington to say that a reconciliation was impossible.

My object is *not* to prove myself right and Lord Byron wrong, but to exonerate from all blame those parties who were involved merely *in consequence* of my determination. Having done this act of justice, my mind is at peace. I have other documents, besides *that* letter of Lord Byron's, corroborative of parts of my statement, should such evidence be required by you.

And on a separate half-sheet : " I beseech you, if it be possible, omit that *note of mine.*[1] You *shall* have my reasons, but I claim this as the greatest proof of your friendship. Let no consideration of expense prevent the alteration of the impressions."

Campbell printed only her refusal to give private information —which may be read in most of the biographies of Byron, my own amongst them ; and she wrote of this to William Lamb, now Lord Melbourne :

It is a pity he did not publish my *whole* letter instead of a *part*, if it were to be brought forward at all, for the passage immediately following that published would show how contrary his mode of treating the subject was to my wishes. . . . After this communication you may imagine the [word illegible] I felt at the line of argument he took. I was aware that he intended to say something on the subject, and thought it a good opportunity to have Mrs. Clermont's letter noticed, but this was all I had to do with it. The fact is that his pride revolted at the idea of being guided by any opinion but his own.

She told Mrs. Villiers that the attacks in the papers " comforted her a little for Campbell's puff."

Despite their quarrel, she had made an attempt to see Augusta —had called thrice in one week, only to be told " after long waiting " that Mrs. Leigh was not at home. " You and I," she added to Mrs. Villiers, " have *served her purpose*, and are to be discarded, it seems ! "

Again her mother's warning must have come back to her. Did she perceive, too, what in an earlier letter (referring to the trusteeship) had been so feelingly expressed by Mrs. Villiers— the gradually deteriorating effect upon Augusta of her social immunity ? Almost, in this passage, we might think that

---

[1] Almost certainly, the Dearest Duck letter from Kirkby.

Augusta's oldest friend was reproaching herself and Annabella for that secured immunity ; and now with no trace of the *Schadenfreude* which in the past we have thought to divine.

No one has more reason than myself to know the bad effects that may be produced on the mind by perpetual excitement, by a succession of evils that are to be, or that one fancies MAY be averted—nobody but those who have experienced it can tell how such things absorb and engross all one's attention—how one lays a flattering unction to one's soul by persuading oneself of the necessity of being so engrossed—yet by so doing reflection is stifled, charity diminished, one's sufferings are increased, health injured . . . and one goes from bad to worse in every respect. Ten years ago I was much less aware of this than I am now—and it is looking back on myself that makes me offer now for her this sort of apology—an apology, alas ! for which *she* sees no cause.

This, the one glimpse we have into Mrs. Villiers's personal life as apart from the Two A.'s, explains much of the indulgence she was afterwards to offend Annabella by showing for Augusta's conduct. Here is evidently a woman with some experience from which she had learned tolerance for humiliating shifts and evasions. That lesson-book was one that Annabella never opened. " Faultily faultless," a woman who could not stumble by the way, what Mrs. Villiers could deplore yet understand was to her incomprehensible. Fear—and above all the fear of social ostracism—she knew nothing of ; was unable to imagine how wildly that danger (which nevertheless she sacrificed her peace to averting) could terrify the creature threatened by it. A hunted creature. . . . Thérèse Villiers could follow it in its windings and turnings, subterfuges, baring of its teeth at last ; not so Annabella. She could pity and act on her pity, love and act on her love ; sympathetically imagine—that she could not, because here was no heroic stand, no daring of the issue ; nothing but the purest abjection of terror before an enemy in her eyes so contemptible : " the world."

When Ada's fifteenth birthday came round on December 10, 1830, there arrived a parcel from Aunt Augusta. " I could not resist," wrote Guss in January to her now devoted Francis Hodgson,

" sending her some little token of my remembrance. I selected a Prayer-book (the *Book of Common Prayer*, in two volumes, with the lessons bound up with it). I had them nicely bound, and *Ada*, in Old English characters, engraved on the back, and wrote her name and the date inside, put them up directed ' To the Hon. Miss Byron, with every kind and affectionate wish,' and wrote over this, ' With Lady Byron's permission.' In another outside envelope directed them to Lady B., sent them booked by coach ; and have never heard one word since."

CHAPTER XXII

OUT OF THE BYRONIC ORBIT

AFTER 1830 Annabella passes for a while out of the Byronic orbit. The snub about Ada's birthday-present has temporarily silenced Augusta; Mrs. Villiers, too, drops out of her correspondence; she may be said to " lead her own life," moving chiefly between London and Dover, finally taking a house at Hanger Hill, with a large vacant room in which she proposed to set up a school " on a co-operative plan of education—but I shall not *talk* about it." The children were to be taught, besides the usual things, baking, churning, simple cookery, " which, in rotation, would furnish delightful employments." She was sanguine enough to believe that this would bring together " the class out of which the children would be taken, and the class to which my family belongs. . . . Castes are as much the disgrace of England as of Hindustan." Reading this, we remember the Miss Milbanke who never went to school, and so knew nothing of perhaps the most clannish—not to say snobbish—of lesser communities.

Idealism of that kind marked all her wider outlook—the work she did for the Co-operative Movement, her educational schemes, her attitude towards the Reform Bill riots of 1830. She wrote of these, when her friends were anxious about her : " Few persons possessed of property can contemplate the approaching crisis more calmly than I do. With respect to my personal safety, I trust to the principles on which I have always acted towards my inferiors " (observe the word), " and as to my possessions, if they are merged in any change which is for the public good, I look upon myself as but a cypher ! I have not learned to like riches for their own sake—and I *dare* be poor." Again, to her friend Dr. King :

> For myself, instead of dreading the change of property, I only wish there were a greater probability of it—but I should

not the less disapprove a rapacious or avaricious feeling amongst those who deserve to be benefited. I would rather they should take ¾ of my property in the *right* spirit than ¼ in the *wrong*.

In calling attention to the word " inferior," my purpose was not entirely ironic. Its appearance there adds a piquant interest to its appearance in another letter, referring to the Co-operative Society at Brighton : " A simple and effectual mode of bettering the state of the working-classes directly, and of the *inferior* (commonly called *the upper*) classes indirectly." She did not really mean this—no one of her nature does ; but she really believed she meant it. Hers was the frequent paradox of pride in noble birth and disparagement of the privileges belonging to it. Though in her the sources were deeper than in most Equalitarians, it was as impossible for her as for others to throw off the influence of tradition and environment—the more so because in her parents' lives she had seen that influence at its best. In her *boutade* about the inferior upper-classes she was merely being the Miss Milbanke of the London seasons, sternly contemptuous of " the world."

In a further letter to Dr. King she discussed the question of influence in forming character. " Is it not impossible to distinguish between the outward and inward agency ? "—and, as ever with such reflections, it is clear that her thoughts had gone back to the great experience :

> One happy effect upon my own mind of having early endeavoured to retrace the faults of others to Circumstances, is—that I have *never* felt myself injured, and have therefore never had occasion to forgive. This has seemed very strange & incomprehensible to some persons—is it so to you ?

Dr. King was then Ada's tutor, with a salary of £300 a year. Her mother wrote : " There are no weeds in her mind ; it has to be planted. Her greatest defect is want of order, which mathematics will remedy. She has taught herself part of Paisley's *Geometry*, which she likes particularly." And she had remarked, on hearing that Dr. King was to teach her : " He is just the person to *work out* my ignorance." Among this only daughter's studies was not to be that of shoe-making ; Annabella had been enlightened by Mr. Frend, who calculated that if every one made his own shoes they would cost three times as much as at the dearest shoemaker's. But by then women were permitted by *La Belle Assemblée* to wear something stronger than kid or satin on their feet.

Dr. King's ministrations to Ada were cut short by an illness, requiring absolute rest of mind and body ; for some time she was not allowed to walk. " Everyone laments the interruption of her education, whilst I observe its progress." But we gather that its progress was not wholly what her mother desired when in the summer of 1830 we find a complaint of her " habit of conversational litigation." By that time she was up and about, though on crutches ; and her mind was being formed by a Unitarian Miss Lawrence, who had a school at Liverpool and taught dates " successfully and agreeably " by means of pasteboard rooms without pictures, and with subdivisions which the pupils were allowed to fill up with the events most interesting to *them*. " Children cannot feel the importance of some facts . . . and is it not better to postpone the acquisition of a date till some value can be associated with it ? " Such common-sense was then an innovation ; but Miss Lawrence had found it " curious to observe how the squares were gradually filled up, as the knowledge enlarged."

One piece of knowledge Lady Byron took it on herself to give to the Sole Daughter. Early in 1831 there is the following entry in a diary : " Read to Ada the beautiful lines on Greece in *The Giaour*, the Fare thee well, and the Satire. With the first she was highly pleased, from its *effusion-of-feeling* character ; the 2nd she thought laboured and inferior in pathos ; the 3rd very amusing though very unlike the person." This disproves once for all the legend invented by Teresa Guiccioli that Ada never heard of her father's poetry until a year before she died in 1852 ! Incredible as it was, the ridiculous tale was for some time believed by some people—who in believing it paid a poor compliment to the intelligence of Byron's child. It is true that Lady Noel, on her death-bed, had expressed a wish that Ada should during childhood be kept in ignorance of him, and should not see his portrait until she was twenty-one. When she first saw Byron's portrait we do not know ; she was not yet sixteen when her mother read those poems to her.[1]   The scene has its pathos—and its irony ; that eternally recurrent irony of the younger generation's outlook.   To hear the Satire called amusing must have been at least disconcerting to her who looked back on those months of anguish in 1816.   We know that in the distant future Ada was to ask that her coffin should be placed beside her father's in the vault at Hucknall Torkard ; there is no reason to suppose that her mother felt aggrieved by the request.   In later years than this of 1831 they wrote and spoke much of him ; there was a moment of pain for the mother when the daughter first stayed at Newstead with the Wildmans ; but in a letter of gentle protest she offered her defence, and begged for frank discussion of Ada's view.   We shall see it in its place.

Byron's wife and widow.   Had Annabella Byron done even more, and done it more successfully, for the general good, it is still in that character that she would survive for us.   She had much intercourse and correspondence with the prominent philanthropists, educational reformers, enthusiasts in the Co-operative Movement of her day ; for a time these questions are the sole topics in many of her letters.   Reading them, we are conscious of impatience ; do what we will to share her interest (her very practical interest), we signally fail.   The drama in which she was heroine blots out for posterity the chapters unrelated to it ; we feel them at best as indirect manifestations of character.   But, following her from childhood as we now can, they do help to reveal Byron's wife and widow as a woman who knew no change of impulse through all the disaster of her affections.   Passionate in protective devotion : the child of ten, the woman of sixty-eight, was that.   It was the keynote of her existence.   But—and she was not blind to it—the philanthropic devotion was no more than a *pis-aller* for the personal devotion that the child of ten and the mature woman most longed to lavish.   In 1857—three years before her death—she wrote to the grand-daughter of Sarah Siddons : " It sometimes seems to me as if I were only of some

---

[1] Mrs. Augustus De Morgan tells us in her Reminiscences (1895) that Byron's Poems were all on the book-shelves in the drawing-room at Fordhook, and that Lady Byron had been surprised and disappointed at finding how little Ada appreciated them.

value to those who have no personal connection with me. I accept gratefully the lot of serving *strangers*, and it really comes upon me as a surprise when I myself am the object of deep interest—so many ties have been broken that I say, ' What next ? ' . . . I am not often so communicative." It was the daughter of this Mrs. Mair who wrote to Mary, Countess of Lovelace : " My mother could not admit or acknowledge any sternness in those eyes which (she said) never looked on her but with love."

Yet in the deepest personal devotions of Annabella's life she was frustrated, more utterly than any other woman of whom we know ; and it was not mere indifference, nor even mere ingratitude, from which she suffered. It was contumely, scorn, almost hatred, from Byron, Augusta, Medora—the three phœnixes of her heart. Some fatality was upon her, that she must always give herself most where she could least be loved. Did it originate in the wild strain which she alone could recognise in her nature ? The discontents of her girlhood seem to say so. With her " placid countenance," and the fierce heart that pulsed within, she in-voluntarily deceived the very ones with whom she most wished to be herself. " Inhibited "—so modern psychology has it ; only a word, after all. Having used it, we have got no further ; it does not explain the infatuations. Why was it Byron—why Augusta—why Medora—towards whom she must yearn ? If one name partly answers for the other two, it is but partly. Her love for Byron might just as well have turned her from the sister, and from the child of that incest which ruined her slight chance of happiness in marriage. His reiterated cry upon the wedding-journey, the " now " which echoed lifelong in her heart . . . it was a nature indeed like proof-spirits to which the meaning of that " now " was a claim on love and devotion. Nobility of such a kind is not fit for " common use " ; and common use was made of it by all the three. Byron could have confessed her for what she was, had he allowed himself—had it not been more Byronic to jeer at the paragon. Away from the perfections over which their letters had laughed during the few happy weeks of their engagement, *he* could have seen them truly but for the Legend. She would always have been " no good " while she was with him ; yet even in " the very dregs of all this bitter business," he had paid her tribute : " There never was a better, or even a brighter, a kinder, a more amiable and agreeable being."

It was all thrown back upon her. She must turn elsewhere with her devotion ; these were " not able " to love her. Others could love her—many of them ; she could love others—M.G., M.M., and later M.G.'s daughter, Olivia Acheson, to whom she wrote, as we shall see, some letters which resemble none else of her letters in their unreserve, their brief flashes of gaiety . . . but those three were the chosen three ; those three alienations made each its new winter in her life.

Only so can we regard her generous and frequent public bene-factions, her experiments in education, her work for the Co-operative Societies. She was half self-deceived into enthusiasm —yes ; but only half. The letter to Mrs. Mair almost explicitly confesses them the second choice in which humanity acquiesces with a pang.

Nevertheless, to ignore them would be to leave the picture of her life, and of her character, unfinished. Here, as in the per-sonal devotions, we find the ardour, the wilfulness, the strongly individual point of view ; and no less the impulse to withdrawal when her ideal outlook proved illusory. This was particularly noticeable with the Co-operative Movement, which first inspired her with enthusiasm at the end of 1828. She was one of the pioneers—as indeed she was in each of her philanthropic efforts ; for some years " Co-op " was an absorbing interest. The tentative Hastings experiment was her earliest sphere of action ; she was an original member of the institution in George Street. Hastings was then a primitive fishing-town ; " all round it were open fields, sweet wooded lanes, and breezy downs." She persuaded Mr. Frend, stopping there for the summer, to visit the institution, writing to say that she must study how to employ " all I have " in the service of the poor. When she added that she had been blessed with many poor relations whose claims could not admit a question, there was no irony (if some of her old unconscious humour !) in the use of " blessed."

Mr. Frend threw cold water on this enthusiasm, both in writ-ing to her and in a speech at the institution. The Hastings scheme, as he foresaw, quickly collapsed ; but not before Lady Byron had accepted an invitation to dine with the members.

She went, and described the dinner as one of the pleasantest she had ever been at ; though to Sophia Frend it was confided that " the large proportion of onions in the stewed mutton " had been a little too much for her—a re-entry of the Mutton-theme which we greet with fond amusement.

However, the onions did not daunt her. She persevered in helping with money—and even with land ; in propaganda too she was active, seeking to draw in Dr. King and Dr. Lushington, and writing to Maria Edgeworth in Ireland, only to be told that the Movement could never flourish there : " Parties run too high ! " This proved to be prophetic not only for Ireland. In October 1829 from London our enthusiast wrote to Dr. King that politics had too clearly invaded the movement—she had just come from a meeting at which " goodwill to men was far from being the prevailing spirit. Even *personal* animosity was encouraged."

That was for her the beginning of withdrawal, though still she clung to the idea—or rather, the ideal. " The Societies look too exclusively to objects of *sense* " ; possibly the right tone might be given by Dr. King and other men of " rational piety " . . . but 1830 opens with an account of yet another meeting to which she had sent two friends—one was Mulready, the artist—who reported that " not Co-operation but spoliation of the rich was the subject of the discourses." Robert Owen, pioneer *par excellence* of " Co-op," had fulminated, telling the Society that its members were too ignorant, and that without knowledge the movement was nonsense. But of Owen, with whom she had had an interview in 1829, her opinion was far from high : " Vanity and presumption appeared to me strongly to characterise him."

The note of enthusiasm sounded only once or twice again. A letter at the end of the year seems to say that this, among other things in 1830 (marked by her distress about Moore's Life of Byron), had induced a mood of lassitude in her reforming zeal :

I think I have come to some important conclusions of late respecting human character. I attach more & more weight to original conformation, tho' I see that it can be modified in the first stages of life. With regard to Adults, I expect less than I did from good *influences*. . . . The best we can do for them is to place them in circumstances favorable to the excitement

of whatever right & kind feelings they possess. I am nearly
convinced (and by some painful experience) that we cannot
mould the sentiments of one who is differently *organised* from
ourselves, to any conformity with our own.   Does it not seem
as if each individual had his destined part, which he might
fulfil *faithfully* or not ?   But the part cannot be acted by any
other.

Despairing thus of adults, she turned to an older interest—one
which in 1818, while she was still living with her parents at
Kirkby, had been written of to Mr. Frend.   " I am not surprised,"
he had answered, " at your design of establishing a village school."
(He had himself established the first of all Sunday-schools at
Madingley, near Cambridge.)   There is no record of her having
then carried out the idea ; but when " Co-op " lost its hold upon
her, she turned eagerly to schemes for juvenile communities,
industrial and agricultural schools, the education in general of
the poor.   Here enthusiasm found a better pioneer than in
Robert Owen.   Emanuel de Fellenberg, the Swiss educational
reformer, was in this her pattern ; she sent a man to learn the
system at Hofwyl, his famous school in Switzerland—which she
had herself visited during the sojourn of 1828, then arranging to
place there two young cousins, sons of the Thomas Noel who had
married her to Byron and to whom she had presented the desired
living in 1823.   Her admiration for de Fellenberg was to suffer
no disillusion.   He was everything she believed him to be ; his
influence affected all her larger schemes for the better education
of boys.   Of the school for those of the vagrant class which she
opened at Ealing Grove in 1834, she wrote :

" It will be during the period of *my* management that most of
the difficulties and cavils will be made—and when the transfer
takes place, it will be said that the School has *got into better* hands,
and then I shall be perfectly satisfied."   This venture flourished ;
but the practical experience (as with all of us !) brought at first
its disappointments with it.   The garden-work which was part of
the system proved unsuitable for the younger boys : " No sooner
are they left together, without a superintendent, than they begin
to fight.   They are little better than brutes."   In 1835, however,
things looked less unpromising.   There were more than sixty
boys ; they were happy, and not at all like the brutes ; gardening,

carpentry, and masonry were favourite employments. She felt
that the plan would succeed in every way but economically ; it
would do that only if the scholars could be apprenticed to the age
of twenty-one. In 1839 she wrote exultantly to Sophia Frend (then
Mrs. De Morgan) that the school was becoming so popular that
Lord Lovelace's at Ockham might be stocked from the rejected
boarders. It was not until 1852 that she closed this establishment.

De Fellenberg's method sought to combine the best possible
literary teaching with outdoor life and training in all that per-
tains to agriculture.[1] This departure from the system obtaining in the great public schools of England—in that day far less to
be admired than now—was inevitably alluring to her whose
fanatical abhorrence of them had been inspired by Byron's telling her that Harrow was " the grave of his moral being." (If
she recalled his apostrophe in the youthful Harrow poem— " a
home, a world, a paradise "—this may have been as much of a
shock to her as it is to us !) In 1834 she wrote, continuing the
letter about those boys who were little better than brutes :

> I am led to speak of public schools for the upper classes, by
> the last word.   Parents whose opinions are never in advance of
> the age, are coming to the conclusion that they risk the char-
> acters & happiness of their sons by sending them to these
> nurseries of corruption and crime.   I will give you some facts,
> which have been ascertained, with respect to Harrow, since it
> is said to have been *reformed* by Dr. Longley.   The elder boys
> resort habitually to the Red Lion public house—drink to
> intoxication—have dice and gambling of various kinds, with
> other vicious indulgences.   It is not uncommon for the elder
> boys to insist upon 2 young ones being stripped to fight for the
> amusement of the Spectators, like Cocks !   One poor boy has
> been taken away lately, who says to his parents : " Don't talk
> to me of forgiveness—I have been so cruelly treated by some of
> my Schoolfellows that I never *can* forgive it."   A School for
> exciting revenge in a Christian Country !   It is the law of the
> school that if an elder boy is convicted of getting drunk he shall
> be expelled.   In consequence the Masters never see that he is
> so, unless, as happened not long ago, a boy dropped from the

[1] A full account of Hofwyl may be found in the *Edinburgh Review* for
December 1818 and October 1819.   The articles are said to be by Lord
Brougham.   And see Appendix V.

bench in Church in that state.   But the outcry against these evils is beginning.

Her hatred of Harrow and its fellow-schools was sadly to affect the happiness of the boy with whom she had personally most to do ; but this belongs to a later chapter.

In 1834 she took Ada on a tour through several of the manufacturing towns.   They visited factories—ribbons at Coventry, spar at Ashby de la Zouche, china at Derby, besides many public institutions.   The purpose was educational, for herself as well as for her daughter.   Machinery, then a novelty, had to be studied if she would understand the conditions of the working-classes.   It was an experience how different from the recollections of her own girlhood !

> If in a small village, you cannot go out of the gates without seeing the children of a few Families playing on the Green, till they become " familiar faces," you need not be *taught* to care for their well-being.   A heart must be hard indeed that could be indifferent to little Jenny's having the Scarlet Fever, or to Johnny's having lost his Mother.

But she was resolute to learn the new ways ; hers was the forward-looking vision, as Florence Nightingale [1]—who knew her well—commented, placing her among the women who had encouraged by their example her own great pioneer-work.   Anna-bella Byron's claim to remembrance in this kind rests chiefly, indeed, on her independent and ardent spirit ; as a mark of character it is essential to our knowledge of her.   What she was in the wider sphere, she was in all—practical though idealistic, persevering and long-suffering ; yet, when once disillusioned, stern with herself and others, whatever pain it might be to withdraw the helping hand.

Her allotment-schemes were another instance of her enlightened innovations—she was among the very first to attempt this work, and never to the end of her life lost interest in it.   We have seen, too, that in 1820 she attended a meeting to discuss mitigations in the Prison System ; and though she was caustic about the orations

[1] She said of Florence Nightingale's sister, Mrs. Faunce de Laune, with whom she was more intimate, that she was "more self-forgetting than Florence."

on that occasion (as on many others) this also remained one of her most fervently fought causes. At one meeting, surprisingly to herself, she made two impromptu speeches—suddenly advancing from her seat in the hall. . . . To-day it is ours to read of the plank-bed as still prescribed for hard-labour prisoners ; an instrument of revenge against which, those hundred and twenty-nine years ago, she and Mrs. Fry must assuredly have fulminated.

In these various ways Annabella Byron worked out her protective impulse ; and her endeavours are not forgotten. Fellow-workers still enquire eagerly about her attempts, revering the spirit that informed them all. It was well expressed in the following lines, addressed to her towards the end of her life by a close friend of that period, George MacDonald :

> Men sought, ambitious thirst to slake,
>   The lost elixir old
> Whose magic touch should instant make
>   The meaner metals gold.

> A nobler alchemy is thine
>   Which love from pain doth press :
> Gold in thy hand becomes divine,
>   Grows truth and tenderness.

In his novel, *The Vicar's Daughter*, he drew her as Lady Bernard. " She was like a fountain of living water. . . . I believe no one knew half the munificent things she did " ; and in *David Elginbrod*—dedicated by him to her memory " with a love that is stronger than death "—he wrote of her : " There are a few rich who . . . enter into the Kingdom of Heaven in spite of their riches. She to whom this book is dedicated is—I will not say was—one of the noblest of such."

On her fortieth birthday in 1832—" 40 *years of age*," as she headed the paper, with a solemnity which for modern minds has been postponed by two decades—Annabella Byron wrote an analytic retrospect of herself. Her prevailing impressions were that she had been very much influenced by imagination in her judgments :

My imagination has ascribed to the actions of others motives of a loftier or less worldly nature than really existed. I might have found the springs of action nearer the surface, but I supposed them to be in the mine below. A conduct on my part in conformity with this error, must often have been incomprehensible to others, whilst it seemed to me the straight-forward course. In History & Poetry, the Actors are almost always represented as moved by deep design or intense passions ; and is it not natural that one who has lived a life of comparative seclusion should seek in living characters for the subterranean fire & moral earthquake ? If—besides—such characters had actually been presented to my youthful observation, and had been associated with my strongest affections, would it not become still more difficult for me to conceive the everyday interests by which mankind in general are actuated ?

Not to see things as they are is then my great intellectual defect, and so far from feeling myself wilfully deceived by others in whose characters I have been mistaken, I believe they have often been ignorant of the extent to which they were imposing upon me.

In the same year, two references to Ada gain a deeper interest from this retrospect. The girl was then seventeen ; her mother had been reading Harriet Martineau's *Five Years of Youth*, and wrote to a friend : " It is very good—chiefly directed against Romance, and therefore not necessary for Ada." Was there a drop of disappointment mingled with the perception that Ada would not be led astray by imagination ? A set of verses seems to say so.

ADA'S GUITAR—1832.

Oh ! no—'tis not the stranger's hand
    How skilled soe'er and free,
Could call from Memory's fairy-land
    The dreams reviv'd by thee !

It seems as if the truth of song,
    The soul of Poesy,
Were pour'd those magic chords along
    All, all mysteriously.

Yes !—more than music haunts the air,
    Without the spells of art—
Is it a spirit mingles there,
    And touches thus my heart ?

That inward life was her true life. Those who now met her for the first time were impressed as by one who had undergone great nervous suffering. A Dr. Combe, then famous as a phrenologist (phrenology was a subject in which she was for a time absorbed), told Mrs. Siddons that this interested him so immediately that if there was any coldness of manner at first he did not notice it. He praised her sobriety of judgment, but shrewdly added that it struck him as " that of a mind naturally more excursive and fiery *tamed down* to its present state." Of the " singular conscientiousness and cautiousness," which he also observed in her, she wrote herself to Dr. King that it had produced irresolution and lack of physical courage, for which she had once been remarkable. Her broken health had probably more to answer for in this alteration than she cared to realise ; it is ill confessing to physical reasons for lack of courage, when like her we take for our motto that " what we will, we can." How poignantly she felt the retrogression is shown by a letter to a friend in 1833 : " Your sympathy is as judicious as kind—you seek to call forth the restorative powers of my mind, and you touch the right springs. I have, indeed, never ceased to feel that I should have enough to live for, enough to make me thankful for existence, if every nearer tie were broken, and my kindred were as strangers ! I am absolutely without hope or fear as to any *circumstance*."

Amid such confidences, it is both touching and amusing to come upon a letter to Mrs. King about Ada's presentation at Court in May, 1833 :

You will like to hear something of the young Lioness, beyond what the Newspaper would tell you—that she was drest in White Satin & Tulle &c. She did not suffer from fatigue, as she was not obliged to stand more than $\frac{1}{4}$ of an hour. She was rather nervous about the ceremony of presentation, owing to the injudicious remarks made to her respecting the difficulties and dangers of that moment—but acquitted herself tolerably well. She was amused by seeing for the first time the Duke of Wellington, Talleyrand, and the Duke of Orleans. She liked the straight-forwardness of the first—the second gave her the idea of " an old Monkey "—the third she thought very pleasing. She is going to the Court Ball on the 17th. The expectation of hearing the Band, and of seeing some distinguished persons, makes her look forward to it with pleasure, which will,

I hope, not be damped by any unpleasant consciousness of
notice in a scene where there are so many others to attract
observation. You would have been amused had you seen me
throwing my mind into balldresses ! I find myself obliged to
give more thought to these matters than I had anticipated,
in order to prevent *her* from being called upon to do so—
and I should be sorry were she to become occupied with
frivolities which are not likely to assume more than their
due importance with me. However, I cannot help wishing
the season over. May we have as little " respect of persons "
at the end as at the beginning of it—and be as worthy of your
interest !

No change there, at any rate—how clearly she strikes the note of
Annabella Milbanke in *her* three London seasons ! And when
Ada went (without her mother) to hear Pasta in *Anna Bolena*,
and laughed at " the conventions of opera," did Annabella recall
her own first opera with Lady Melbourne, when she took no
pleasure in squalling and flirting ?   There was yet another trace
of heredity in the débutante's delight at meeting Babbage of the
Calculating Machine—reminiscent of the enjoyment felt by Miss
Milbanke with the professors and the Mr. Walpole of the serious
work on literature. . . . A second London season over, she and Ada
made their factory-tour, the daughter meanwhile studying hard
at astronomy ; she enjoyed seeing the machinery, but she also
showed a great love for dancing.   Forgetting 1812 for a moment,
her mother wrote : " I always before thought that more harm than
good was likely to result from dancing, but I begin to think it
may be a valuable accessory in moulding character " ; later,
growing more indulgent and perhaps recalling the waltzing which
had ceased only when Lord Byron's temporary satisfaction
was spoilt by Cousin Caroline, she reflected : " In avoiding
altogether such amusements, the Evangelicals avoid a snare, but
they also neglect an advantage. . . . They who dance with
temperance will be likely to pray with more pleasure." Yet
she still had qualms : " Perhaps the most unexceptionable of
active exercises is archery.   I mean to have a target at Fordhook
on my return." Nevertheless, she took Ada to the races at
Doncaster, that she might see and judge for herself the amusements of the world.   " But there are few scenes more repugnant
to my feelings. The risk to man and beast—the desperate

gambling among the spectators—the futility of the object—press upon my mind in a painful manner."

There was to be nearer pain for her in the memory of that day at Doncaster—in Ada's judgment for herself of that amusement of the world.

And now, in 1834—ten years after Byron's death—Augusta re-enters. In August she sent Annabella his letters, "although upon reflection I believe it was *intended* they should have been mine—for I now recall words to that effect." However, she professed to be glad to be rid of them.

Annabella replied by refusing to take back her own letters to Byron, and returning those which she had written to Augusta and had then borrowed from her in order, if necessary, to show Byron what their relations had been. Of her refusal to receive her own letters she wrote to Augusta that it was because they properly belonged to the estate and the executors ; but she made a memorandum for herself in which she gave other reasons—firstly, that she wanted to keep other letters which the others might want back ; secondly, that she might be supposed to fear their publication ; thirdly, that she might be suspected of collusion with Augusta. . . . She had learnt her lesson : " Once more take care of X " ; and another lesson, too—that Veracity could not always be entirely adhered to by the heroine of the Byron Separation-Drama.

Two days before this, the tour with Ada had taken her through the grounds of Halnaby, " the very road I have so often ridden on a pony when I was only 8 or 9 years old." . . . No mention of the "dismaying" honeymoon. But earlier, on the way from Bakewell to Buxton, the past had asserted itself. Walking on the road, as she and Ada drove by, she saw Hobhouse—now Sir John. He did not recognise her ; she, who had beheld him last in 1815, knew him at once. Hob had grown stout : " no longer yon spare Cassius ! "

As so often happens, this encounter was a foreshadowing. The Byronic influence was now to come back into her days. There arrived Augusta's letter ; then, back in London, she spent an evening with Crabb Robinson. They talked of Wordsworth,

Goethe, and Byron. She was not among the German Jove's admirers (" the Goethean poison "), but when Robinson told her of what he thought some strangely mistaken notions of Goethe's regarding Byron, she felt that they were true, and proved wonderful insight. . . . And not long afterwards a future already adumbrated in 1829 became the all-engrossing present—it is as if these minor incidents were preparation for the new ordeal.

Meanwhile she continued to lead what I have called her own life, though it was but outwardly her own. Schools, public meetings, hard work—" I doubt if many clerks work harder, but all *under the rose* " ; more intimately, Ada, now showing the extraordinary mathematical talent which was to distinguish her in later life. She was already corresponding with the famous Mrs. Somerville, improving her acquaintance with Babbage and his machine, and bringing these notabilities into close relation with her mother. Of Lady Byron Mrs. Somerville wrote : " The more I know of her the higher she rises in my estimation, and the more do I regret that the world in general are little aware of her superior talents ; her excellence everyone appreciates. I told Mr. Babbage that nothing I had seen could be compared with her critique of his book."

Going back for a moment to 1833, when she was settled for a while at the best-liked of her temporary homes, that at Fordhook, there is an interesting letter to Dr. King about Family Prayers. She granted that it was " our duty to regard the spiritual welfare of our servants " ; but :

I have never had sufficient proofs that the effects were beneficial. I know that in Families where the mode of the performance seemed most unexceptionable, the morals of the servants have been very bad—habits of fraud and profligacy have existed under cover of their devotion. My friend Lady Gosford, who has prayers morning and evening, owns this to be the case, and even says she would never take a servant from what is called " a religious Family," on that account ! . . . I may also mention the testimonies of two very worthy old Domestics of a religious turn of mind, who have lived at different times where the opposite customs prevailed. Both say that Family Prayers gave rise to more vexation and irreverence *downstairs* than was balanced by any practical good. . . . You use another argument, that if not *reminded* of religion we should be worse than we are—but it does not follow that Family Prayer is the best way to remind ourselves and others.

Mr. Trench [1] dwelt on the equality of footing thus established between those whose situations are unequal in a worldly sense—but the servant should take his turn with the master (on this principle). I should like to see *such* equality. It does not exist even with the American Helps.

There speaks her idealism—and, to us who know more than she did of those American Helps, again her unconscious humour !

A little later she wrote : " Facts of a striking nature have lately shown me [that] the religious *sentiment* may ally itself with every error of the imagination—may inflame the ruling passion, and blind its victims more effectually than all the sophistry of infidelity. . . . I tell you my thoughts, though I can't tell you the source from which they spring."

The source was Augusta. That phoenix-love, long failing, was now to die its third of deaths.

[1] He was an Irish landowner, and was interested in the Charitable Loan Societies. She long kept up intercourse with him.

CHAPTER XXIII

MEDORA LEIGH

THE prescience that we thought to see in little Annabella Milbanke's dislike for Halnaby Hall might be again perceived in Annabella Byron's unconquerable distaste for Bifrons, the house at Canterbury which she had leased but never could feel happy in. She had lent it to the Henry Trevanions—Georgiana Leigh and her husband—in 1826 ; they lived there for three years.

At the end of 1829, two people connected with Canterbury—the Baroness Grey and the Hon. and Rev. W. Eden—came one day to call upon the other Lady Byron, George's wife. Their object was to tell her of a scandal about which all their neighbourhood was talking. Mr. Trevanion's young sister-in-law, Elizabeth Medora Leigh, between fifteen and sixteen years old, had been staying for some time at Bifrons and was now with child by him. Mr. Eden had taken depositions which proved not only that, but the sister's connivance.

On learning this from her cousin, Annabella dropped all direct communication with Bifrons ; but she and Lord Byron helped the Trevanions—who were desperately poor—to leave England with the girl, whose child was born at Calais in February, 1830. It died in a few months, having been left in France when she returned, still with the Trevanions, to London in May—going back to her mother's apartments in St. James's Palace. Augusta had not seen her for more than a year, and knew nothing of the intrigue.

In July, 1831, Annabella wrote to Mrs. Villiers : " I thank you for informing me of that crisis, which I had long foreseen." This was the revelation to Medora's mother, and subsequently to her reputed father, of the relation with Trevanion—since productive of a second pregnancy. Soon afterwards she heard that Augusta had " calumniated " Byron as the origin of these abnormal distresses. To Annabella this was inexplicable ; yet surely it should not have been difficult for her to follow the distracted reasoning. A child of incest, the Ape of mediaeval superstition—this was the thought in the wretched mother's mind. Passively B.'s victim, X now turned upon him dead ; the hunted creature, baring its teeth. . . . Poor muddled Guss—we shall see her incredible letters to son-in-law and daughter, and shall not know how to think of the nature to which they were possible.

When Medora came home from France, her looks were greatly altered ; she refused to go out in society, " though hitherto she had much enjoyed the public amusements and children's dances to which she had been taken from a very early age." But Augusta asked no questions. As we know, she was extravagantly fond of Henry Trevanion : " He has been QUITE what I expected of him, and my greatest comfort." He now gave Medora (whom he called Nell) [1] the following letter for her mother, who had apparently noticed a change in *his* demeanour, and of him enquired into its cause.

MY DEAREST MOÉ,

I owe some explanation for the pain I gave you by my wild note—I took laudanum—I promise you not to do so again—would to God that had been all ! Your affectionate kindness distracted me with hopes which are now no more—and Nell had half my consent yesterday to have disclosed the fatal cause of my misery—it shall now and ever be a secret. She cannot speak without the consent I have revoked in my note last night, and you are too dear and good to ask of her a confidence the breach of which involves—my life. Never again allude to the subject if you have love or pity for your unhappy

H. T.[2]

Augusta read this, handed it back to Medora, and still asked no questions. So things went on until February 1831, Augusta going out two or three times a week, leaving her daughter and Trevanion alone in the drawing-room, and often not returning till after midnight. The Trevanions lived in Cadogan Place.

[1] She was called Libby in the family ; but the name Medora so belongs to her, and was by herself so publicly flaunted in later years, that it will be used here.

[2] The original of this, and of Augusta's letters to Trevanion and Medora, are preserved among Lady Noel Byron's papers.

In February Medora gave her a paper written some time before, but withheld by Trevanion's wish. It informed her of the past, and added that a second child was in progress; the blame for this was cast upon Augusta, who then wrote to both. First to Trevanion twice:

Saturday, February 1831.

It would be impossible in the *first* instance to speak to you my dearest—without such emotion as would be painful to us both—and I therefore take up my pen, but only to break the ice! for I feel equal (and in some respects greater) difficulty than I should in speaking.

You know how I have loved and regarded you as my own Child—I can never cease to do so! To the last moment of my existence you will find in me the tenderness, the indulgence of a Mother—can I say more? If I could, tell me so! Show me only how I can comfort and support you—confide in me, dearest—too much suffering has been caused by a want of confidence. What *might not* have been prevented could I have known, guessed, even *most* REMOTELY suspected!—but—I would not breathe a word if I could help it to give *further* pain! Too well do I feel all that has—that is—and that *must* be suffered! my earnest prayer, God knows! is to act for the best for ALL and under the trial *He* has inflicted—no doubt for reasons wise and merciful, though unseen by me! Much do I blame myself! but as He who knows our hearts knows my trials, and the circumstances in which I've been placed, and that I have always acted to the *best of my judgment* for the welfare and happiness of others, I trust I shall find pardon!

I am speaking of myself, the *last* person I wish just now to consider!

I am convinced, dearest, that as I have opened my heart and feelings to you, you will comfort me! I need not point out to you the means! your own heart will dictate them—and as you are dear! MOST dear! *much*, MUCH is in your power!

Heaven bless, comfort and guide you!

(February 1831.)

Your note just received is to me *inexplicable! When* and *how* have you " *witnessed me acting upon a system of distrust* ? " When you answer this, I may be able to meet your accusation —certainly a most unjust one! I will not say *unkind*, for I can make allowances for the effects of your present state of mind upon feelings so sensitive as yours! Dearest—I wish I *could* comfort you!

I was so completely worn out last night from the effort I made to subdue my feelings and to appear cheerful before both the objects of my agonising solicitude, that I *could not* write to you after you left me—if I had, I might have caused you pain from the uncontrollable state of my feelings (the same as on first awaking !). I could not close my eyes till near 4 ! and hurried up, to be able to make sure (while the weather lasted) of seeing dearest G. This is the history of my life since we parted last night—not a word had passed *here*—so that I'm sure the " *distrust* " cannot *truly* be reported from *that* quarter. Now, dearest, to reply to that most heart-breaking letter put into my hands yesterday—and which I dared not look at *again* last night, and you know how I was interrupted in speaking to you on the subject of it. Dearest, do not mistake me by supposing that I have so little consideration for the weakness of human nature as to think of " a TOO *precipitate* execution of my purpose "—a purpose on the accomplishment of which depends my only hope of consolation ! You say, *you do not respect me*—you would *still less* respect me if I did not entertain such a hope, and do my utmost by the most judicious means I can think of to accomplish that on which the *eternal* welfare of that unhappy Being depends ! and the PRESENT welfare—(nay, I may say *existence* and *sanity*) of so many others depends ! Do not suppose anything COULD support me under my present calamity but *this hope* ! but I do not wish to speak of myself, I am as an *atom* in the balance ! Thank God ! I have uttered no word of unkindness or reproach nor anything but what I feel—*that I will be a* COMFORT, if *I am permitted*. I thank you from my heart for your *pledge—I accept it*—and *I trust to you implicitly*. Consult dearest G. on the *most judicious means* of proceeding in such a cruel predicament. I have explained to her my ideas on some *minor* points of *prudence*, which are perhaps more essential than you think for—it is a hateful word where more important interests than mere worldly ones are at stake, but where the ruin of so many may be the alternative of its observance it becomes a serious consideration.

Now Dearest—let me implore of you to be comforted—to do your utmost to make the best of circumstances—to trust in my affection. That you are tried, SEVERELY tried, I feel—and I pray God to support you and comfort you and guide you ! and I feel confident he will never abandon you if you trust in Him !

Do not accuse yourself, dearest, and make yourself out *what you are NOT* !

Remember I *do " depend on your Love "*—and oh ! how I *have* loved you !—how I will always love you and God bless you ! dearest.

To Medora she wrote :

(February 1831.)

As in conversation upon painful subjects one is apt to express oneself strongly, and lest you might misinterpret such expressions, and mistake *that* for unkindness which would be but the effects of agitation, I must write to you, my dearest, what the fullness of my heart and my anxiety would dictate every moment to you !

I cannot describe with what pain I observe much that is passing before me ; and, my beloved and unhappy child, I implore you—*on my knees I implore you* ! to use every *effort of your soul* to cope with those temptations which assault you ! You have the greatest good sense—the best of hearts—you know NOW what is your duty and on what terms alone you can hope for mercy !

Reflect that you are—no, not now—Great God avert it ! that (how shall I write it ?) you have committed *two* of the most deadly crimes ! recollect who you have injured !—and whom you are injuring—not only your own Soul, but that of another, you think *more* dear than yourself.   Think *whom* you have deprived of *his* affection !   Think of others upon whom *shame* and *disgrace* must fall, if even now you are not *outwardly circumspect* in your demeanour !   Think of his Family—of *yours*—of your unmarried and innocent sister—of the broken heart of your Father, for that, THAT would be the result, I am *convinced*—you know not his agonies for the loss of that poor Angel who was from cruel circumstances comparatively an alien to him[1]—think what *this* would be !—and more than that, of the DREADFUL consequences to HIM !—to *another still more*—that no time or place would shield him from their vengeance ! think of what might and *most undoubtedly* WOULD be the consequences even in THIS world ! and think of those more important interests, the *eternal* ones of all those Beings dear to you !   Pardon me if I inflict pain on you—I must in this case " be cruel to be kind ! "—for *could* I forgive myself, did I neglect to rouse you to the consideration of such consequences !   I implore my dearest child therefore, as regards these fears, to be prudent and circumspect to the last degree, and I STILL *more* implore her *on her knees* to pray to God for His assistance to enable her to *forsake* her sins and to repent of

---

[1] One of the daughters was of weak intellect.

them. That He will always do so to those who in sincerity ask, we are assured.

To repeat *my* ardent desire to be of comfort to ALL is needless! Heaven guide me, in its mercy, *aright*—in the labyrinth in which I am involved! I earnestly pray for such guidance —I would not say a reproachful or unkind word to any one! *but*—Dearest, listen to one thing—which is certain and inevitable—a continuance (by which you must not understand that I require *impossibilities*, or *do not* and *will not* allow for the weakness of the human nature and the strength of its temptations)—but an obstinate continuance in this DREADFUL affair —or the least deception, will either *upset my reason or break my heart.* You imagine perhaps that *this* is a way of speaking and feeling—that my disposition is such that no *lasting* impression can be made on my feelings—that I have lived through so much I am like flint or steel at bottom, with only a light surface—but—do not *flatter* yourself that *I* should survive, or that my senses would THAT blow. I have suffered *much*— long (neither you or ANY human Being knows *how* much), but —I never knew sorrow like this!—It was fit perhaps my pride of heart should be humbled—I looked to YOU as the *hope* and *pride* of my life! I felt you might be taken from me by Death! but I was not prepared for this wretchedness—Spare! oh spare me, Dearest! Spare yourself and all you hold most dear! Depend on it your efforts will be rewarded, and in your Mother's heart, surely you might find comfort.

You know that I confidently hoped and intended you to be confirmed this Easter! I suppose it is *now* hopeless—consult your own heart and wishes! There is at any rate one thing I would ask—which would be a comfort to me. I hoped to be able to prepare you sufficiently myself with the help of reading—but I now feel it would be a great satisfaction to me if some Clergyman were to assist in this. Of course his instruction would bear solely upon the preparation and information necessary for such a ceremony—which could be postponed till you felt your mind and heart disposed for it. I pray that the Almighty may so dispose it! Dearest Darling! speak to me, confide in me—and be assured you will meet with all the affection, sympathy, kindness, indulgence that you need and wish from your most affectionate, though wretched Mother.

Can I say more? if I can—tell me *what*—and let me comfort you if I could do so! God bless you!

The pitiful absurdity of these letters paralyses the judgment. They are the authentic voice of Goose's bewildered spirit—from every word reflecting the chaos within. Just as she had offered the nature of her feelings for B. to his wife's approval, so did she now cling to the thought of Medora's mind and heart being " prepared by some clergyman " for confirmation at Easter.

But on the girl's refusal to go through such a mockery, she allowed her to accompany the Trevanions when they went in March to Bath. There Medora remained until the first week in June ; then Georgiana (who had urgently begged for Medora's protection at Bath, because otherwise she dreaded personal violence from her husband) wrote to Augusta that she could no longer bear his treatment of herself. On this, Augusta—through her friend, Colonel Wyndham—informed Colonel Leigh of the state of affairs.[1] We remember his marked disapproval of the marriage, and that he had been " fearlessly opposed " by Augusta. Now it was his turn to be fearless. He arrived at the lodgings in Bath with a solicitor and a Bow Street officer, to carry away his—reputed—daughter Medora. She was placed under the care of a Mrs. Pollen, in Lisson Grove ; her windows looked out upon the drive through Regent's Park—there Henry Trevanion soon appeared.

Georgiana had written, imploring her to join him at the first opportunity ; Mrs. Pollen connived at her escape. In the first week of July she fled with him to France, and they lived for two years in a town of Normandy.[2] Then Medora wrote to her mother, begging to be enabled to go as boarder to a convent in Lower Brittany. Augusta promised to allow £60 a year, and Medora entered a convent at Carhaix. In a month she found herself for the third time pregnant ; she then left the convent without her mother's knowledge but with the consent of the Abbess, who helped her to deceive by allowing her to have letters addressed there. In 1834 a daughter—Marie—was born ; where

[1] In *Lady Noel Byron and the Leighs*, privately printed by Lord Wentworth (later 2nd Earl of Lovelace) in 1887, at p. 111 there is this : " If Lord Lovelace's [his father's] recollection may be trusted, in 1840-1-2, Libby accused her mother of various acts of profligacy. One charge was (perhaps originally made by Henry Trevanion) that Henry Trevanion had first been Mrs. Leigh's lover. . . . " It is added that on Libby's unsupported word, " and still less on that of Trevanion," these charges are not credible, but " it is impossible to be absolutely certain of [their] falsehood."

[2] " The child appears to have been still-born." *Lady Noel Byron and the Leighs*.

we do not know, but Medora's narrative declares that she and
Trevanion were not then together. They afterwards rejoined
one another, living (she says) " in an old château in a secret and
unfrequented spot, in great poverty, but as brother and sister."
(It was in the neighbourhood of Morlaix.) Trevanion had a
mistress, to whom Medora was made to act as a sort of servant ;
after some years the hardships and his cruelties made her fall
dangerously ill, and in 1838 she wrote to Lady Chichester
(Augusta's half-sister), imploring to be enabled to escape. The
means were given, and she went to the neighbouring town of
Pontivy.

Augusta wrote to her affectionately for two years, and promised to allow £120 a year, but this allowance was irregularly
paid. Medora, in great want, was advised to sell her reversionary
interest in a deed executed by Augusta in 1839, whereby £3000
was to be payable to Medora on the deaths of Mrs. Leigh and
Lady Byron. But she found that the sale could not be effected
unless the original deed was in her possession. Augusta had
retained it, giving her a legally attested copy, to prevent that
very step, the £3000 being intended to enable her to provide
by will for her child. In this, as we shall see, Mrs. Villiers
upheld Augusta's action, and Lady Byron (" on high legal
authority ") condemned it. Medora in 1841 instituted a suit
against her mother for the possession of the Deed.

Before that, however, she had appealed through her solicitor,
Sir George Stephen, for help. He sent her application to Lady
Byron, who then wrote to Medora " a most kind letter, with
money and offers of protection for me and Marie." This was
in July 1840.

We must now go back to 1835 when, with knowledge of the
scandal, Lady Byron received from Mrs. Leigh a letter asking
what it was wished that she should do about Ada, when they met
in Society. Augusta had hitherto refrained from speaking to her,
" doubting whether (from the line of conduct you have pursued towards me during the last five years) it would be agreeable to you
that I should do so." This had been such pain to her, and looked
so strange, that she now asked her question. If no answer

came, she would understand that she *might* speak to Ada when they met again. And there was something more. It was said that Annabella was going abroad. If so, Augusta wished to see her before she went.

Thus coerced into replying, Annabella answered—acknowledging the " obliging " reference to her wishes about Ada, but adding that she should not consider herself justified in sanctioning *any* intercourse, now that she had additional reasons to feel mistrust. " You have placed me," she went on, " under the necessity of saying what is exquisitely painful to me, but of this probably no words could convince you." A postscript added that she was not going abroad.

The phoenix was dead indeed.

But Augusta then more imperatively requested an interview ; her duty to herself, " and MORE than herself," obliged her ; in common justice it could not be refused. Seven letters, covering two months, passed between them—the one refusing, the other persisting. Dr. Lushington strongly advised against consent ; Annabella then suggested Mrs. Villiers as an intermediary, but Augusta declined to say what she had to say through any third party. Finally Annabella wrote : " If the object of your intended conversation regards *my* interests, I take the consequences. If it regards *yours*, I can only regret that [my proposal] should appear to you inadmissible."

So matters stood between the Two A.'s when Annabella (convinced by Medora's letters that her one desire was to be placed anywhere out of Trevanion's reach) invited mother and child to join her in France—at Tours, where she had gone in the July of 1840. They met on August 21. " I found her altered beyond the possibility of recognition, and in a confused and stupified state of mind, attended at times with great excitement." At first she had intended to place Medora at Tours with some friends ; but her desolate situation and her illness—believed to be consumption—so worked upon compassion that she took her entirely under her own care. " By my desire she assumed another name, and under that name she travelled with me." [1] The name was Mme. Aubin—already assumed by Medora during her cohabitation with Trevanion, who had passed as M. Aubin. (Lady Byron

[1] From a narrative by Lady Noel Byron written in 1841.

was afterwards accused by blackmailing servants of having represented Medora as a widow. She had never done so, and in one instance—as she wrote to Dr. Lushington in 1843—had acknowledged the truth rather than equivocate.)

From Tours they went to Paris. One day at Fontainebleau Medora was told " the cause of the deep interest Lady Byron felt, and must ever feel, for me. Her husband had been my father." So it is stated in Medora's narrative ; in a letter from Annabella to her friend Selina Doyle in 1843 we read :

> She was unfortunately in possession of that fact before she was connected with me, and after much embarrassment from her allusions to it, I determined on admitting it, as it materially influenced the course to be pursued in the suit ; [1] and by communicating the danger of disclosure, I hoped to prevent the necessity of it in Court—and have succeeded ; but had I known her better, the contrary course might have been more expedient. Of *late* she has appeared, as you imagine, desirous of being pointed at as a monument of infamy ; but, besides this, she thinks it a *power*. I can never be acted on in that way, whatever may be the consequences. [2]

Much water had run under the bridge before that letter was written. On the day at Fontainebleau Annabella's *protégée* was to her Medora—not Elizabeth, as she later became ; and it moves us to a strange mixture of sympathy and something not far from scorn for infatuation, to find in a letter from the girl that she was permitted to use Byron's old nickname of " Pip " to her protectress.

Augusta had not been told by Annabella of the rescue ; but the Pontivy doctor had some months before informed her that her daughter was under Lady Byron's protection. She now wrote to Annabella, " however reluctantly," begging for news. She herself placed " unshaken confidence " in Medora's (and the doctor's) earlier assurances of the girl's having freed herself from Trevanion's influence ; but : " I cannot conceal from *you* ... that there are those who view them differently, and consider ME their *dupe*. God knows, I have been too often and too

[1] Brought by Medora against her mother to obtain possession of the deed of 1839.

[2] The Trevanions had told Medora the secret of her birth ; in her narrative she represents herself as having refused to believe them.

cruelly deceived to be in a position to give a very satisfactory answer to such suspicions!" Very humbly she apologised for appealing to Annabella in her suspense and anxiety.

... Byron's daughter, over her deep tenderness for whom at six years old Annabella had wondered in the September of 1820! The protective devotion had indeed found an outlet now. All was combined in it—rescue, protection, sacrifice of pride, proof of magnanimity ... all but the phoenix love which so recently had died its third of deaths. That love was doubly slain, for jealousy had entered in a new guise, strangely more potent than the earlier one. She who had cried from her inmost heart to Guss when her own existence was being devastated, had now no shred of fellow-feeling for her. This broken life had been given her to mend—and everything that was fierce in Annabella, as well as everything that was tender, responded to the claim. But also, everything that was rigorous. Had she not found this daughter—Byron's, but Augusta's too—on the brink of starvation, threatened with mortal illness, deserted with her child in a foreign country? Promises, fine words, appeals to Providence— how well she knew it all! And she wrote to the mother: Yes, it was true; *she* was henceforth responsible for Elizabeth's safety and comfort (Elizabeth, not Medora, to this correspondent), and Augusta might reveal it or not as she pleased. "If it should become known, I am prepared, in justice to Elizabeth and myself, to explain fully the reasons for my thus interesting myself in her welfare."

Could I have believed that you had a Mother's affection for her, you would not have had to ask for information concerning your child. But facts are glaringly opposed to your professions on that point. ... Your affectionate letters to her must appear a cruel mockery to those who know that you left her, for so long a time, only the alternatives of vice or starvation. Her malady, the effect of physical and mental suffering combined, can be retarded ... only by extreme care and by her avoiding all distressing excitement. The former I can secure, but not the latter—I would save you, if it be not too late, from adding the guilt of her death to that of her birth. Leave her in peace! This advice is given in no hostile spirit, but with the firm determination to protect her to the utmost of my power.

This letter drove Augusta to implore Mrs. Villiers's mediation. There followed a long and painful correspondence with Lady Byron, wherein Mrs. Villiers sought to defend the mother both on her failure to maintain the allowance and her retention of the original Deed. She represented the extreme difficulty of Augusta's position, tugged at as she was for money by a worthless son and (on this Mrs. Villiers naturally laid much stress) with her deserted daughter Georgiana and *her* three children, now left penniless, to provide for entirely. Lady Chichester had testified to Mrs. Leigh's having deprived herself of all luxuries and many necessities to maintain them. A detailed statement of Augusta's difficulties followed :

> Her income is £800 per annum. Out of this she has to board her husband when at home, and her son Henry always, to maintain herself, Emily, and her servants entirely. She gives her eldest son George £100 per annum—her son Frederick has never cost her less (if so little) as £200 per ann: and she has *entirely* to provide (as far as she can) for the wants and really necessaries of Georgiana Trevanion and her three growing-up daughters ! As may be supposed, however, the supply has been quite unequal to the demand, and Georgiana is deeply in debt for the bare means of subsistence.

Mrs. Villiers further commented : " The Parable of the Prodigal Son " (alluded to by Annabella) " can only be applicable to cases where there is a fatted calf to kill. In this case there was no Calf at all." She had not seen Augusta for ten years, their estrangement having been caused by disapproval of her conduct towards Lady Byron. Now she had found her in agony over the letter, " and *that* was not the moment when I could refuse any aid which it might be in my power to afford." She had advised Augusta to make a " perfectly correct " statement of what had passed between her and Medora since the flight to France with Trevanion, ask the Chichesters to attest it, and send the whole to Lady Byron.

Augusta had done this. On February 12, 1841, the packet had reached Paris. Lady Byron had not opened it, had returned it next day to Augusta's solicitors. " I wrote in the envelope to Mrs. Leigh that I considered the correspondence terminated by my answer to her inquiry." It was upon this that Mrs.

Villiers intervened, begging permission to reforward the unopened packet.

Her intervention was warmly accepted; her request was refused. Any " *facts* " which might have favourably impressed her mind would be listened to. They were stated; but though listened to and argued on, were wholly unavailing. There was much, indeed, to urge against Augusta—not only in the matter of money; in letter after letter her opponent urged it all. Mrs. Villiers acknowledged its force; but though her warmth of heart, her long affection, did not blind her to the many obliquities of the recent past (the remote past was barely alluded to by either), she strove to palliate, once more repeating that the effects of " *intense fear* " could not be estimated by anyone who had not experienced them. Her vindication was eloquent; on money-matters, convincing. To clear Augusta of the charge of complicity in the Trevanion affair, she copied part of a letter from Medora to her mother in December, 1838.

Heredity has seldom been more strikingly shown than in this composition; it might have been written by her to whom it is addressed.

My own dearest kindest Mamma, Your dear kind letter has made me *so* happy—but has given me the certainty of how far too good you are. My own dearest dear Mamma, never think that you have ever pained me by even a harsh word or thought. If, when under the influence of other feelings, my conduct towards you may have led you to suppose you seemed harsh, or anything but what you are, and always were—the best, the kindest and most devoted of mothers, forgive me this amongst my other faults—believe the fault was not on your side—no—no—indeed—I well feel and know *that*. God Almighty be merciful to those who betrayed my confidence in you, my own dear Moé—*that* confidence existing, my ruin could not have been effected—but no—you are right—we must not look on what can only pain us. Only remember, My own DEAREST Mamma, you have never erred but by too great kindness. You did *for* the best, *and* the best, believe me. I have no interest in this world—no good can come to me of deceit—I cannot even hope for the respite of a long life before I answer to God Almighty for all I have done and do. I, who know more in this sad misery than any one, know *only how* innocent you are —how good and kind you have been and are to all concerned therein, and God Almighty will recompense you—we shall be happy hereafter *together*, my *own* dear mamma—pray for me —do—do—pray for me as you alone can do.   Keep my letter —and if ever at a future period your kind heart fears having occasioned a pang to your own unfortunate Libby, read this over and believe we *have* been CRUELLY deceived towards each other ! ! ! !

" Did I not see," added Mrs. Villiers, " and know this to be her own handwriting, I could scarcely believe that this is the same daughter who is now engaged in a law-suit against the same mother . . . and all because she *could not* do what she only promised to do IF SHE COULD."

The answer was : " Let Mrs. Leigh have the benefit of her daughter's affection. . . .   [The letter] was very natural from one who believed herself dying, and was worked upon by such a letter as that to which this is obviously a reply. . . .   Undoubtedly you are an able advocate."

Able, but entirely unsuccessful.   Mrs. Villiers had pleaded, and continued to plead, in vain ; the conclusions to which Lady Byron had " *most reluctantly* " come were unaltered ; and the correspondence ended in an estrangement between her and Augusta's friend.

Infatuation was once more possessing that strong and wilful nature.   From Fontainebleau she had written to Lady Olivia Acheson, daughter of her loved M.G. :

> I am particularly happy just now.   Feelings that have long lain, like buried forests, beneath the moss of years, are called forth, and seem to give happiness to one for whom I have something like a Mother's affection.   This is a little gleam in my life—it will not last, but its memory will be sweet.   The object of my affection is marked for an early grave.   Show this to your Mother, who will understand it better than you.

But at the end of the same year, to the same correspondent, there is a letter which seems to say for all its playfulness that disillusion was casting its shadows on that happiness :

> This is to give you warning that for the year 1841, I shall not want or wish for you, because I have got a Lanky Doodle who instead of taking the sugar-bason away from me, makes me what she calls " *conscientious* lumps of sugar."   She knows

that the throat of my conscience is small, and she adapts the sweet sin to the size of it, with wonderful precision. Let me recommend this morality to your particular consideration ; and as it comes from a Roman Catholic you will be the more disposed to adopt it. If a Sin would choke you, break it in two—for instance if a Man should ask you to run away with him, & you can't make up your mind to so decided a step, refuse, and go somewhere from whence he may run away with you.

Again, if you want the contents of your neighbour's pocket, don't steal, but borrow them ; and add to the first little *lump* a second—the failure of payment.

One more edifying instance—if you can't tell a downright falsehood, tell that half of it which will convey the other half inaudibly to the mind of the receiver.

Love & all friendly wishes to my *three* young friends from
Your personified Bon-bon
A. I. N. B.

My address—24 Rue de Rivoli
Paris

Grave P.S.
I think that illness has much to do with the painful circumstances in which you so kindly sympathise. There are some kinds of illness which are manifested only by their effects on the mind, at least in a certain stage of their progress. We are always expecting our fellow-creatures to be endowed with the discernment of disembodied spirits. I will not say however that I can reason myself quite out of painful feelings, on such subjects.

Much was adumbrated there which later filled the entire picture. The correspondence with Mrs. Villiers ceased in July 1841 : in the April of that year Ada, now Countess of Lovelace,[1] had come to Paris with her husband, and the two daughters of Byron had been introduced to one another. From Ada her mother had in March received this letter :

St. James's Square, *Saturday, February 27th,* 1841.
Dearest Mama, . . . I am not in the least *astonished.* In fact you merely *confirm* what I have for *years and years* felt scarcely a doubt about, but should have considered it most improper in me to hint to you that I in any way suspected. I told

[1] Ada Byron had been married to William, eighth Lord King, in July 1835. In 1838 Lord King was created first Earl of Lovelace.

William last summer or autumn the *whole* of my ideas respecting the wickedness of Mrs. L., otherwise I scarcely think he would have seized the import of your present letter to him.   In fact the very idea is so *monstrous* and *hideous* that I remember when I communicated my own *more* than suspicions to William, I felt ashamed at having done so when I found how little definite and tangible *grounds* I could bring forward when he questioned me on what *could* have suggested so extraordinary a conviction to me. . . .   I only feel now upon it as I have long done, that the state of mind in both parties in which such a monstrosity could have originated, is indeed appalling.

I will not now add more.   But believe me, Dearest Mama, your *Hopeful Bird*.[1]   Yes—I must hope well *even* for Mrs. L. ; and I fear *she* is more *inherently wicked* than *he* ever was.   I question if there is as much in *her* of the *defying principle* as of the *Love of Crime*. . . .

In reply Lady Byron wrote :

I must write a line in answer to my dearest Children's joint letter to-day, though I have not yet become composed after reading so much that affects me deeply.   I know not, dearest Ada, what I ever said to you that could even suggest the idea of *vice* on her part.   Of her want of veracity and artfulness I have spoken.   When you alluded to the poems in which there was a remote reference to the fact, I have always avoided discussing them.   It is, however, another proof added to many in my experience that the truth always makes itself felt, at least to persons of a certain kind of intellect, by means which are neither tangible nor imaginable.

I have been told by some that it was a weakness—almost a want of truth on my part—to wish, as I have done, to leave your Father's aberrations sufficiently indistinct to enable you still to contemplate his memory with a sort of gratification. I will hope that the true charity which replaces the imaginary feeling is better for *you* &, if he knows it, more acceptable to *him* in his purified state.   It is indeed consolatory to me that I can make you the friend of my past as well as of my present life, *without reserve*.   All you say appears to me true to the character of the Parties.   Strange to say I have been led to acquit *him* of some portion of the guilt by recent disclosures respecting her conduct to her child—for one who could, *as she clearly did*, connive at the ruin of a daughter, must have been capable of injuring a brother in the same way.   I had believed

---

[1] This was Ada's pet-name, with mother and husband.

her to have been wholly a victim.   But more of this—I scarcely know what to state on the subject—ask what you please—I thank you for all your delicacy & consideration, but it need no longer exist.

To my dear Son only say that whilst I should trust him with my nearest interests, I hope to have no occasion to give him the painful task of acting in this business.   It is enough that if misrepresented after my death, he will know how much to believe of the statements made on her part.

Ada replied :

March 3, 1841.

I cannot recall the precise moment or circumstance which *first* suggested to me the idea of the miserable events we have been writing about, although I can remember *several* which have confirmed and strengthened the impression already in my mind.   I think however that it is some years at least— perhaps six, seven, or eight, if not more, since that impression has been very distinctly traced out. . . .

I should tell you that I did not suspect the daughter as being the *result* of it.   In fact the notion would not naturally occur, because Mrs. L., being married at the time, it might not have been easy to prove this, or even to feel any degree of certainty about it.

I should like some time to know how you came ever to suspect anything so monstrous.   The natural intimacy and familiarity of a Brother and Sister certainly could not suggest it to any but a very depraved and vicious mind, which *yours* assuredly was not.   I cannot help fancying that *he* himself must have given you some very clear hints of it.   He too well liked to taunt you with his crimes.   Alas !

A definite affection sprang up between the two younger women during Ada's stay in Paris.   Medora was described by Mrs. De Morgan, who often saw her in 1841-2, as very like Ada but much taller.   " She was excessively slim ; her face—like Lady Lovelace's—had a strong family likeness to Lord Byron, and her gestures recalled his.   One was particularly noticeable—her quick way of turning round to look, if anyone suddenly entered the room, when she would hold her head in Lord Byron's characteristic position."   Later, in the days of Medora's rebellion, there is an amusing comment on her slimness in a letter from Ada : " She is such a fool to stand in her own light—with that great tall childish figure of hers, too ! "

But in Paris they were as sisters ; and thus encouraged, Lady Byron brought Medora and the child to England in June, 1841. The law-suit about the Deed had ended in May. Augusta's counsel had agreed to surrender it on the day when the cause was to have been heard ; the original was now in Medora's hands.[1] Of this her protectress wrote to Lady Wilmot Horton : " Much and perhaps irreparable mischief has been done by the anxious suspense of two years to Elizabeth—and the best hopes of her restoration to health or peace destroyed."

That was written on the 6th of June. On the 9th is dated a document in Annabella's handwriting, sealed and with the inscription : " Not to be opened without my leave." Headed " Remarks on E.," it states that for some time it had been impossible for her not to suspect that " the wild and wayward temper is in this case, as in many others, only an instrument for selfish purposes—assumed and cast aside, not according to natural impulse, but for effect." There had also been, " in un- guarded moments," slight allusions to working upon Augusta for future advantages—" which betrayed, to my apprehension, an intended object. In consequence I must, without disclosing my reasons, protect the mother by my future arrangements."

Thrust back into the prison of that promise, by the child of that incest—could irony go deeper ? All the cold anger against the mother, all the fierce championship of Byron's daughter, had ended in the old refrain : " Be kind to Augusta ! " And the sealed paper goes on :

There are in my opinion but two holds on this character. Love of approbation and of money.

The first is comparatively feeble, because it can never be fully gratified, but it ought to be cultivated as the best of the two, and as affording a certain check.

The latter must be used indirectly, and not in a way to lower her in the estimation of others.

In attempting to hurt those who oppose her, she will hurt herself ; but this will be, not from recklessness, but miscalcu- lation. She expects to make people serve her better by bullying.

[1] It was afterwards transferred for some time to the care of Lord Love- lace, and Lady Byron's allowance to Medora of £150 a year represented the equivalent of its sale.

Let us read here some letters to Medora, written little more than
a month later ; and compare them with that dispassionate
judgment, and the gay " lumps of sugar " letter to Olivia
Acheson.

> Do you remember, dear E., that I asked you early in our
> acquaintance not to use affectionate expressions towards me ?
> I then felt the possibility of a change in your feelings. You
> did not regard my request, and I suffered myself to believe that
> you had conquered the early impressions to my disadvantage
> which were made upon your mind, and were able to love me.
> But I ought not to have let you deceive yourself and me (much
> pain would then have been spared), and should not have
> accepted your expressions of entire confidence and affection.
> I will endeavour to forget them. It is enough for me to be
> your friend. I have never expected anything in return.

And again :

> You mistake me very strangely, dear E.—and I lament it
> more for your sake than my own, as it must render your
> relative position, which might be a very easy one, far other-
> wise. I see how hopeless it would be to attempt to convince
> you at present, but you will not always do me such injustice.
> From some of your recent letters you have appeared to suppose,
> contrary to my repeated assertions, that I wished for *expres-
> sions* of affection. Far from it. My bitter experience of them
> in your family has made me almost shrink from them. . . . I
> shall now dwell only on the many many kindnesses I have
> received from you—on your patient and tender care in illness.
> Do not think *these* remembrances can ever be effaced.
>
> I am perhaps better. Can you expect I should be well ?
> Pray mention your health always. . . . As for expense in any
> matter concerning [it], pray do not pain me by speaking of it.
> . . . On all other [points] believe me as fallible as you please—
> but *trust my affection*. It has never varied. You will always
> be my very dear child, but let us profit by experience, and
> do not try to fancy that you have corresponding feelings
> towards me. It is an illusion which, having been once broken
> through, ought in future to be equally resisted by yourself
> and me.

As resolutely dispassionate as the sealed verdict, yet what pain
throbs through those words ! For a while to have believed that
one of these three " was able " to love her—illusion most cherished,

ADA, COUNTESS OF LOVELACE

After the portrait by Margaret Carpenter at Ockham Park

most infatuate. . . . The gamut was run through—himself, Augusta, and their child. Now there was nothing left but to profit by experience.

What had been happening was what might have been anticipated. With possession of the Deed had come a change in Medora. The " wild and wayward temper " had expressed itself in a kind of blackmail on her protectress. She complained that the Chancery suit had been settled without consulting her, that she had been sacrificed to her mother's interests ; and now it was plain that the knowledge of her parentage was to be used as a weapon against both. She refused to stay in England, to be under guardianship of any kind, there or elsewhere. " I would not submit to any such restraint."

She was at this time living apart from Lady Byron. " She obliged me," wrote Annabella to Selina Doyle in 1843, " to quit my house some weeks before she left England, by rendering it intolerable to me—but I loved her still. One chapter more in the self-incurred sorrows of your friend." . . . It was Moore Place, Esher, which had thus been made intolerable. Unable to endure the scenes of fury, she had left Medora there under the care (for some little time) of Mrs. Anna Jameson—the well-known writer on art, and author of the *Diary of an Ennuyée* and Shakespeare's Women-Characters. She and Lady Byron had met early in 1834, and were now closely intimate. In Paris Mrs. Jameson had seen much of Medora ; she too was at first attracted —it is evident, indeed, that this girl had the Byronic fascination, for her adherents in the future were all in the beginning infatuated, though they, like these others, were each to be disillusioned. Mrs. Jameson's eyes were already opening in the April of 1842 ; for she then wrote : " There is the wish to be and do right, with an utter blindness to the right."

And now, in the July of the same year, when Medora's resolve to leave England had become immutable, Mrs. Jameson—not then in charge of her—went down to Esher to make final arrangements for the journey to, and sojourn at, Hyères, which was the retreat agreed upon. Medora was absent in London when she arrived ; she found the French maid, Nathalie Beaurepaire (engaged during the Paris period), worn-out by her mistress's tempers. " Je ne puis plus la contenter ; Madame est d'une humeur inconcevable. Elle me reproche de ce que je suis plus dévouée à Lady Byron qu'à elle.''

Medora, on her return, received Mrs. Jameson amiably but seemed agitated, which she accounted for by having accidentally seen her mother. When the arrangements were explained to her there was one of the scenes of fury ; '' she lavished on her protectress and me every term of unmeasured abuse,'' and at first refused the £40 assigned her for travelling expenses. When finally she consented to accept it, Mrs. Jameson gave it her in bank-notes,

> which she clutched with a sort of contemptuous eagerness & impatient haughtiness—saying it was not half enough, & there were things she *would* have, in spite of everybody, cost what they would, & Lady B. should pay for them—she would *make* her do so. . . . There was from beginning to end a purpose of which I had the clear conception—the purpose to get as much money out of her protectress as possible.

Of the accidental seeing of her mother Medora had written during the day from St. James's Square, the Lovelace house in London, to Lady Byron.

> If dearest Pip I began my letter with anything else than what occupies me at this moment you might attribute the natural constraint of my letter to other causes, & I *know* you will sympathize at what I feel. I have this instant met my Mother. She was crossing the Square coming from York Street as the Carriage drove up to the door. I instantly recognised her—she is unchanged in face—& turned my head as if waiting for William who was ringing at the door. She could not have seen my face—my veil being down—& I saw her before she saw me—her sight and perceptions are not quick —& between the door being opened & my speaking to William, she had reached the Duke of Cleveland's before I got out— which I did quickly. She turned round & looked at the carriage—for I observed her from the little back window— probably from curiosity or thinking it might be you. She was followed by a dirty-looking rascally kind of servant out of livery who was playing with his glove, & was dressed in a dark brown kind of muslin gown with white pattern, a black silk shawl with long fringe and gathered round her as if she was afraid of losing it & a straw leghorn bonnet trimmed with white satin ribbons. Her large eyes are ever & indeed *unchanged*, her

walk is most altered—she shuffles along as if she tried to carry the ground she walks on with her & looks WICKED. Oh, were there a thing I had hoped to be spared it was this. If her curiosity were awakened it is lucky this took place at Lord L.'s door—be sure she fears him. . . . I was very quietly dressed in my old dark silk gown black scarf & white bonnet—& she did *not* see my *face*, & I well remember how she never saw or knew any one & always used to say no one ever knew people or observed as quickly as me save " poor B."—& she used to rely on me for observation.

This has shocked me—pained me, but it is over. I have drunk quantities of wine since, & now there is nothing left for me to suffer that I dread. Oh how dearly fondly I loved her, & had she only stifled the existence her sin gave me—but God *is* there—& I will do my best to bear as I have ever done but it is so long, so constant—God forgive her. Oh how horrible she looked—so wicked—so hyena-like—That I could have loved her so ! Bear in mind one feeling the sight of her has given me yet more strongly—if for my good or that of Marie— intimidate her—she will grovel on the ground, fawn, lick the dust—all—all that is despicable & bad. You she will not fear, you personally—but Lord L——, Dr. L——, or Wharton. Now we will try & never mention her name—she will live for *years*. Oh could I only have loved the memory of my mother, but had death passed over me the chill—the horror—could not have been so great. Pity & forgive me if I involuntarily pain, I do not mean—but I *do* suffer. . . .

Ada's visit gave me GREAT pleasure yesterday ; to-morrow the children come to me & Thursday she and Ld. L——. My will is signed & most satisfactorily to me & I hope to every one hereafter. If climate does not do me good & I never come back you will find all my letters & papers in order & I feel that all I have done will satisfy you & not make me a less dear child to you.

Dearest Pip, I have come up to-day early on purpose to get you a Daguerotype done of me—I have heard you say it would please you to have one—but the Sun is clouded over but you shall have one & as little ugly as possible. I do not contradict what you say about affection—time will best show you. I no more wish for a " farewell " than you—we have parted—if we meet not again here we shall only meet in happiness hereafter & if we *do* meet again as we *shall* & when I am happy and well —we shall not be the sadder for having had an agony less. My health is as ever bad and tiresome. I have had the little yellow smelling-bottle you gave me filled with salts that are

now become necessary to me & it never quits me. Oh only
think I have a way you can constantly & when you like get
parcels to me at Hyères—this will please you—Ada is delighted.
I suppose I shall quit London Saturday for I cannot begin a
journey Friday. . . . Ada & me will consult about road.   God
bless you.   I will be strong & get over all I cannot help feeling.

> ever yr affecte Child

When she wrote : " I no more wish for a farewell than you," she
was answering these words : " We *have* parted.   For my life's
sake I dare not encounter the agitation of saying farewell—but
you are nearer to my heart than ever."

Of Medora's vision of her mother, Lady Byron wrote : " I could
not read of that meeting without great pain, and yet I believe it
best that you should see what *is*."

Was it indeed what was ?   Shuffling along, behind her an ill-
trained man-servant (presented to us, through Medora's syntax, as
dressed in a muslin gown), " so wicked, so hyena-like " ?   As
little as we believe in the muslin footman do we believe in the
hyena Augusta.   Her large dark eyes unchanged, herself unchanged—no hyena, only the bewildered muddled Goose, who
clutched her slipping shawl around her as she had clutched her
slipping reputation. . . .   The picture is Balzacian, and (for all
the erring English) drawn with such swift spontaneous force as
yet again we must grant to yet another of these people ; con-
straining our hearts to pity, though to neither of these hearts did
it appeal—not to the daughter's, not to her second mother's,
who yet had learnt, was learning, was still to learn, what that
daughter could be.

Like the third episode in a fairy-tale—the episode which breaks
the spell at last—was the third Byronic infatuation for Annabella.
Not again would she believe that any of these three " were able "
to love her.   Soon she was to hear from Ada that herself was the
Gaoler, Mrs. Jameson the Turnkey.   " I can't help laughing
after all," the other daughter added, cured of *her* infatuation.
And to " Mme. Aubin " in France the Gaoler wrote, after reading
Ada's letter : " Guard against imagining injury, or you will at
last estrange the suspected (if estrangeable). . . .   You are happy

in the fancied emancipation from fancied chains. Go, and buy experience."

It was rather she herself who was to buy experience, though by this time she had learnt some practical lessons as to the wise treatment of her *protégée*. For on two points she was adamant. She was to retain some control over Medora's expenditure ; she was to have sole charge of Medora's maintenance. If money was asked or received from any other person, their agreement was annulled. " And," she added, " you will deprive me of one of my greatest gratifications, which you have led me to believe would never be oppressive to you." But before the departure Ada had had an interview with Medora at Esher. " The last half-hour I was there," reported Lady Lovelace, " I was compelled to hear a discourse on the bitterness of dependence and threats of throwing herself down the throat of the first man she could get hold of to marry. . . . ' At least I should not depend on *charity* '—and then came all sorts of vituperations." . . . Next day she was gone.

In April 1843 Annabella wrote to Selina Doyle : " The Serpent-race will finish my life, as they have certainly shortened it." For with this year, Medora's infrequent letters had become haughty and insolent. Her birthday (April 15) was approaching ; Lady Byron had intended to mark it by an increase in the allowance. " But," she wrote, " you put the veto on that intention (to which others can bear witness) by your conduct. When I recollect your birthday last year, am I to believe that your tears and your tenderness were feigned ? I *cannot* do so—I must first hear from yourself that you were playing upon my affection. Tell me then at once what I am to think—that I may know whether I am still to be as I have been."

Medora was then in Paris, where she had gone in direct violation of the agreement. " I am not surprised," wrote Annabella to Miss Doyle (also in Paris). " And as to my pounds, they will only follow many others into the vortex of that family. . . . I suppose I was Cat's Paw to pull the Deed out of the fire, and when I had served that purpose, I was to be turned adrift." But still she clung to one shred of infatuation—Medora *had* been better when they first met. " Adversity is her best friend, and she cannot bear kindness. The Slave is not fit for perfect freedom.

You cannot imagine," she went on, " the scenes of fury before her leaving England. I had *never* seen anything like them. She has told me that I was her bitterest enemy, and threatened revenge."

Medora represented her in that light to the Miss Doyles, who (despite a caution from Lady Byron) did see something of her in Paris, when the elder—Adelaide, not Annabella's intimate, Selina —was prevailed upon to pay an hotel bill for her, on the ground of her destitution. She was now resolute to defy her protectress in every way. By leaving Hyères for Paris she had sounded the challenge, her pretext being that the allowance was paid through Nathalie, and that *she* was expected to give a receipt. Of this she made a vast grievance.[1] Some time before, she had put herself in the power of Nathalie and Nathalie's husband (permitted by Lady Byron to attend her on the journey as courier) by confiding to them the secret of her birth. The man was of course blackmailing her—so much excuse there was for her flight to Paris, where she consulted the famous lawyer, Berryer. He too was at first fascinated ; she told him all—her birth and Marie's birth ; and not only him, but a Mr. Bulwer of the British Embassy, and a Captain de Bathe, R.N., whom she had known during the Trevanion period. . . . Like her father, as like his sister—the loquacity, and the appeals to Providence !

Meanwhile, Lady Byron had despatched her friend Dr. King to Paris with the offer of £300 a year on condition that Medora should resign all control over herself and child to her protectress —who wrote to Dr. King on April 27 :

" The suffering has been great to me of expressing myself harshly towards one who has been the object of such tender interest—one whose cradle I had watched with peculiar feelings (she is a year older than Ada), and whom I had given a promise that I would befriend. But the ' law of love ' is not for characters in such a state." She added later : " I have felt that there is a process going on for the disclosure of some truths long hidden, which it may not be in the power of any of us to prevent or retard."

---

[1] There was no other way, for to use a false name in transactions with bankers is liable to a penalty—as Lady Byron had told Medora before she left England.

On the same day Berryer was writing to her. Almost his first words proved her prescience. " Mlle. Leigh "—not Mme. Aubin —had revealed to him all the sad circumstances of her and her daughter's birth ; she had also told him of the extreme kindness, the tender protection, she had found in Lady Byron ; and now it was his mission to point out that the allowance of £150 was " *tout à fait insuffisant.*" He had listened " *avec prudence* " to her story ; he now answered to Lady Byron for the purity and nobility of Mlle. Leigh's sentiments, and pleaded for an increased allowance, her entire authority over her child, and free choice of her mode of life. " He has forgotten the lawyer in his senti-mental advocacy," wrote Annabella of this to Selina Doyle ; but her answer to him was studiously courteous. It refused to discuss such delicate family affairs with a stranger—there was no need to do so, her friend Dr. King being in Paris and the interpreter of her sentiments towards " Mlle. Leigh."

To Olivia Acheson, on first hearing of the confidences to Berryer, she had written bitterly : " She has gone so far that I can never hold intercourse with her again. I think of having a seal with a large *Gull* engraved on it—can you give me a motto ? "

Dr. King, as we know, was to offer a doubly increased allowance, but on conditions. His mediation failed. He declared Medora to be of sound mind—a point which had been debated ; her protectress then relinquished all direct communication with her, and no longer paid to *her* the annuity of £150, but reserved it to be placed in the hands of trustees and administered for her benefit, provided that the Deed was not sold and that she did not " return to a life of vice." In the letter communicating this to Lady Wilmot Horton (who was Medora's godmother) Annabella added : " When I first entered into correspondence with Mrs. Villiers on this subject, I wrote to her : ' It remains to be seen, as regards E.'s character, whether I have interfered too late or not.' It *was* too late."

Too late, indeed—if it could ever have been in time. Medora now came to London under Captain de Bathe's protection, and a system combined of persecution and blackmail of Lady Byron and Lord and Lady Lovelace was instituted by her and the two servants—whether acting in collusion or not was never fully ascertained. A letter from Annabella in July 1843 speaks of an hour in which she had given herself up to despair, but then roused herself to take measures " to arrest the further circulation. I feel resolute and courageous, since it is for *others* I am fighting." . . . Those others were Augusta, and the memory of Byron.

The disclosure had been made in three quarters—the Palace, the French Embassy, and to " a lady of high rank in London." Everywhere the Beaurepaires were countered by Lady Byron's action, and met with indignant repudiation ; they then threatened an action for defamation of character, on the ground that they had been induced to enter Mme. Aubin's service by a false description of her as a " respectable " widow.   They sent letters, both signed and anonymous, full of the grossest abuse ; the envelope of one was addressed : " The Lady Noel Byron, *femme de mauvaise foi*, Esher, Surrey."   The man announced his intention of assaulting Lord Lovelace in the street, so as to be taken to Bow Street and there make a statement. . . .   Meanwhile Medora was bombarding her Leeds and Chichester connections (half-brother and -sister to her mother), with appeals for money, at the same time demanding interviews with Lady Byron and Mrs. Leigh.   Both refused to see her—the letter to her mother was so insolently cruel that a new champion, a Mr. Smith of a firm of London solicitors, was revolted to such a degree that he refused to insert it in the narrative of her life (and her " wrongs ") which he then compiled for her, but which was not published until 1869.[1]   Lady Byron, too, declined to see her, giving Dr. Lushington her reason.   " A person guilty of such *parricidal* conduct " ; nor would any measure Medora could take ever induce her to resume the character of protectress, or give her the slightest reason for saying that she was restored to favour.

The servants' action-at-law was never taken.   Much against the grain, but on Dr. Lushington's advice (he feared the action would go against Lady Byron, the engagement having been made for " Mme. Aubin," and foresaw that anyhow exposure of the long-kept secret would be inevitable), Beaurepaire and his wife were bought off, and no more was heard of them.

[1] This Mr. Smith seems to have been highly susceptible to the Byronic spell.   He had met Byron in Greece, and (by his own confession) had been so overwhelmed that " my faculties were visibly affected."

Through Sir George Stephen—acting for Lady Byron, but not avowedly so—an offer of assistance was made to Medora. There were three conditions :

1. She must surrender the Deed of Appointment to trustees, " as a sacred provision for her child."
2. She must sign a statement of the sums received by her during the period when she represented that she was " abandoned " to the charity of servants, and deprived of Lady Byron's protection.
3. She must return to seclusion in France.

Medora consented to 2 and 3, but refused to surrender the Deed. While matters stood thus, she suddenly disappeared from England (and from the knowledge of all concerned) with her child and the Deed of Appointment.[1] The final arrangement was that the funds for her and Marie should accumulate till they could be applied, and the annuity of £150 a year be placed in the hands of trustworthy persons for that purpose, " taking care that it is *unknown to her.*"

Nothing more was heard of her until in the September of 1849 she died at Saint Afrique in the South of France, where she was stated to have been married for some years to " *un soldat retiré du service,*" and to have left a legitimate son named Elie, who in 1857 was eleven and a half years old. Her daughter Marie lived for many years in Paris, and was much respected there for her devotion to good works amongst women. She was known as Miss Ada Leigh ; the Ada Leigh homes in Paris were named after her. In 1899 she had been married for some years to the Bishop of Ontario (afterwards Archbishop of Ontario), John T. Lewis, D.D., LL.D.[2]

---

[1] It may be said here that she never did sell the reversion, though in 1844 she borrowed £500 on the security—the lender " becoming by indenture first encumbrancer " of her reversionary interest. She must have married (see above) between 1845-6. She died before both Augusta and Lady Byron, so that she never profited by the Deed except through the allowance which represented the equivalent of its sale, and the above-mentioned loan.

[2] The above statements referring to Medora are from an undated paper " once " in Lady Noel Byron's possession, but of unknown authorship ; and from a letter to her of February 10, 1857, from " G. de Waroquier, ancien officier d'état major " (*Lady Noel Byron and the Leighs*, p. 206). Those referring to Marie (" Ada ") Leigh are from Ralph, Earl of Lovelace's Papers.

When in 1869 the Autobiography of Medora Leigh was published
—as an indirect result of Mrs. Beecher-Stowe's disclosures—the
Quarterly Review made the following charges against her protectress : First, that she neglected Medora ; second, that she
reported, as coming from Medora, the statement that Mrs. Leigh
had co-operated in her daughter's ruin by her son-in-law ;
third, that she told Medora of her paternity without any justifiable
motive ; fourth, that she submitted to Medora's overbearing
conduct because she feared the revelation that she was Medora's
informant.[1] We have seen how little truth there was in any of
these charges. What fear she ever felt regarding publicity
was not for herself ; it was for Augusta and Byron's memory.
But the story was a stick with which to beat her in her grave,
and it was vigorously used. Dead, she was reviled more grossly
even than alive. Her mother's phrase comes back to us once
more : "Like proof-spirits, not fit for common use." The Christopher North who knew so thoroughly the common use of spirits
that are not proof excelled himself in coarse abuse ; the barrister
Paget launched his moral anathema : "The most degraded of
street-walkers in the Haymarket, etc." ... They judged
according to their darkness ; such things were not for them.
One writer saw clearly, wrote with insight and sympathy—the
author of the articles in *Temple Bar* which were afterwards
published anonymously as *A Vindication of Lady Byron*. He is
now known to have been Mr. John Fox, father of Sir John Fox,
late Senior Master of the Supreme Court, Chancery Division—
who in his turn has written (and he with knowledge where his
father could only guess) a book which all interested in the story
of the Byron marriage and separation should read, and which all
who write of it must find indispensable.[1] His father could
only guess, but, guessing, displayed an insight—and a shrewdness
—remarkable indeed.

Well—when in 1869 they found their brand-new stick, the
Christopher Norths and Pagets were no longer able to hurt
her. She had been dead for nine years.

... The three winters of her heart were over when in 1843 the
third phoenix died once for all. Perhaps that winter was the

[1] *The Byron Mystery*, by Sir John Fox, p. 49 (1924).

worst, because it was the last. The promise had been kept—to befriend Augusta and her children ; kept with love as well as with money. Once more the love had been flung back to her, though not the money. " *I* could be no good " : the lesson was learnt to its end.

She had her own daughter—Byron's daughter ; but the fairy-tale was finished.

CHAPTER XXIV

1838–50
FRIENDSHIPS WITH WOMEN

BEFORE the Trevanion scandal touched her personally there had been another brief respite from the sordid aspects of Byronism ; and this gives us a fresh angle from which to view the heroine of the Separation Drama. In 1838 she was living at Windsor ; the new little Queen Victoria, in residence at the Castle, was told of her interesting neighbour. Even to Royal maiden ears that story—twenty-two years old though it was—must surely have been imparted (if in an expurgated version) ; and besides, Lady Byron's first cousin was Her Majesty's adored Prime Minister. To the imagination opening under the mellow sunlight of William Lamb's influence, his relative offered more than one reason for curiosity—the Queen expressed a wish to see Lady Byron at the Castle dinner-parties. But Lord Melbourne was obliged to tell her that his cousin did not go out in the evenings. Then would she visit the Queen in the mornings ? It was January, the weather was severe ; this, too, proved to be impracticable— though doubtless the refusal was conveyed in words other than those of the much-desired guest to a friend : " I have no notion of slaying myself for what is after all of so little importance."

Of little importance, perhaps ; yet, one might have supposed, of some interest. That the girl-Queen awakened no reciprocal curiosity not only impoverishes our chronicle, but betrays the lack of imaginative sympathy which more than once explains the lapses in Lady Byron's conduct to others. For Queen Victoria left Windsor without having been allowed to gratify her desire.

The Prime Minister, however, paid his uncourtly cousin a long visit of which she wrote an account to her son-in-law (soon to experience the graces of that connection, for later in the year he was created first Earl of Lovelace) ; and here we find a moving touch of—how many memories of pleasure and pain ! They were

370

both agitated ; William Lamb so much that he never fully recovered his self-possession ; she was outwardly calmer, but inwardly even more overwhelmed, for " his resemblance to my father made it almost like a resurrection."

She was now forty-six, and already a grandmother ; her father had been dead for thirteen years ; but in her Windsor abode she had gathered round her many who belonged in one way or another to her youth. There was Lady Olivia Acheson, daughter of M.G. ; there was Fanny Smith, a young relative of her Doyle friends, rather lonely, very sentimental, much loved and at this time devoted ; there was Mrs. De Morgan, known since 1816, and daughter of the William Frend whom Annabella Milbanke remembered as far back as she could remember anything. He, unorthodox, hot-headed, had in youth been the quarry of a partially successful heresy-hunt, had then abandoned his Orders, and to mark the withdrawal had worn always afterwards (long after the fashion had become obsolete) a blue tail-coat with brass buttons. This odd, imperious, warm-hearted man had instilled his freedom of thought into the daughter of the house at Seaham ; from Frend, with Sir Ralph as abettor, she had imbibed her pronounced distaste for dogma, her horror of " priest-craft "—the latter so deeply that it might have become a King Charles's Head if from her father she had not also inherited a tolerant spirit. But priestcraft was, in the coming years, to draw from her one of the few bitternesses found in her many letters on religious subjects.

So, in this 1838, it was a sort of renewal of Seaham days that William Lamb came in upon, with his family-likeness and his largely-opened brilliant eyes that so belied the pose he still pre-served—because it truly represented one side of him—of being indolent, used-up, little-caring. In 1812 Miss Milbanke had pro-nounced him " self-sufficient " ; Lady Byron was more perceptive, though still disparaging. Mrs. De Morgan (present during the visit) remarked upon Lord Melbourne's " very small self-esteem"; the hostess agreed, commenting to her son-in-law : " He would have kept better company had he respected himself more." Gossip had long been busy about the widower Prime Minister, either with Mrs. Norton or a far more exalted lady ; his cousin now wrote to Fanny Smith that " the report " was plainly unfounded—those who " observed his proceedings " could testify that the chief interest did not lie in *that* quarter. " Time will show." Initiated as she probably was, we could wish that she had been less maddeningly discreet.

The Windsor sojourn, like most of her sojourns, was brief. From there she went to Fordhook near Acton (" then a pleasant country-place "), which was the best-loved of all her makeshift homes—" Ford-happy-hook," as Fanny Smith vapidly called it. Here Ada and the first-born son—Byron Noel King, soon to be Lord Ockham—stopped with her : " A very good bird it has been," she wrote to Lord King of Ada, who was hung about between them with bird-names, Brown Thrush, Avis, and so on ; her husband being the Crow and her mother the Hen—a designation almost exclusively used for Lady Byron in her son-in-law's letters to his wife. Sometimes this has a comical effect, as once when he wrote, rather annoyed with her, that the Hen showed little consideration for Horses, taking them out far too often in the day. She seems, indeed, to have been entirely indifferent to animals ; there is never any mention of a pet—Byron's parrot in the Piccadilly days is the sole instance. To him who kept a menagerie wherever he lived, and had possessed two dogs which are (as Henley has said) " among the world's dogs," that must have been a distressing incompatibility.

This letter of April 21 from Fordhook reveals that the Byronic respite was over :

I send you two letters about Fletcher. The poor man has been defrauded of the Annuity positively promised him by the inheritor of the unsettled property—which property was calculated to be, including the reversion of my Jointure, copyrights, etc. near £100,000. The blame of his being destitute ought not to fall on other Members of the Family—the difficulty is to exonerate them from having failed to fulfil a claim, without bringing forward personally one whose interests I must always wish to consider, as far as justice to others will allow.

Any sum raised for Fletcher must be placed in the hands of Trustees to be given him *at pleasure*—else he would pledge his Annuity from folly and extravagance. I would give (anonymously) £100, and as much more as might appear desirable after application had been made to certain persons—Sir John Hobhouse, Mr. Harness, Mr. Hodgson of Cambridge and other

surviving friends, could scarcely decline to contribute, and it
might be proposed to two of them to act as Trustees ; or
perhaps two of the Family would be preferable—in which case
perhaps Lord Byron & Sir Robt. Horton. . . . At Fletcher's
age money sunk would give 8 per cent.—so that an annuity of
£50 per ann. might be purchased for about £600.

As to the form perhaps something of this kind would be the
least invidious :

" Lord B.'s faithful & most attached Servant Fletcher—the
companion of his Travels & the attendant upon his death-bed—
having been deprived by circumstances (for the truth of which
the promoters of this appeal can vouch) of the means to which
he had looked for support, is now left dependent on the generous sympathy of the Public (or of the friends of his deceased
Master)." . . .

Augusta's name, so carefully avoided, was not then the name of
stern reprobation it was in 1840 to become. Indulgence still ruled,
despite the long estrangement and the knowledge of her obliquities
in the Trevanion affair. It was not until Byron's daughter was
found deserted that pity ceased to plead for " dearest A."

Fanny Smith (for whom a perhaps irrationally imperfect
sympathy rules the present writer from first to last) was much
with her in those days. They were Knight and Ladye of Fordhook to one another—the Knight apparently a fire-eater : " And
when you have had a lance through your foolish heart, do you
think the Ladye will thank you for dying in her cause ? I know
her better. She will say, ' If the fellow had had any common-
sense I might have regretted him, but there will be some peace
now Orlando Furioso is disposed of '." Orlando Furioso was,
however, to be otherwise disposed of—he turned into another
Ladye when Edward Noel arrived on the scene from Greece.
This was one of the sons of that Thomas Noel whom we met at
the Seaham wedding ; he fell in love with Fanny, she with him,
and in that August (1838) they were married. The Ladye of
Fordhook was then transmuted into the Troubadour, and wrote
a copy of verses—not very good—for the occasion. The second
stanza is interesting :

O better far than all I once surrendered—
    Could I desire for *self* again to live ?
Heaven hath o'erpaid the Sacrifice I tendered
    With more than even my dreams fulfilled could give.

She must have looked back upon those words with feelings all too familiar when in time to come this pair estranged themselves for some obscure but violently resented reason, and left her appeals for reconciliation unanswered.

Just then, however, the relation was close indeed, for she joined them at Wiesbaden during their honeymoon. From there to Ada she wrote one of the most amusing of all her letters—giving yet another angle from which we (like herself) may view the heroine of the Byron story.

A droll incident has occurred at the Table d'Hôte, where I was with the rest of the Party. Next to me sat an English Miss, and opposite to her a young man, of the demi-gentleman cast. He observed that Lady Byron had arrived here yesterday. She replied, " Oh, what I would give to see her ! " " You would be very much disappointed if you did," said he ; " she is very short, of a swarthy complexion, and looks as if she could never smile." He went on to say that he had seen me five years ago with you, and then you came in for your share—as being " very fond of accounts. What a thing for a Poet's daughter ! " Still my fair neighbour persisted in wishing to see me & asked where she could meet with me. " Oh, you will be sure to see her at Church, she is very *pious* ! " I thought it honourable to hear as little of the conversation as possible, but it was loud enough to compel me to do so. My only anxiety was that the unfortunate man should not find out his blunder, but the Noels looked so angry that I feared he would ; and I am told that he appeared conscious the latter part of the time. Had anything really unkind been said of *you*, I should have made some observation—but otherwise I wished to remain incog. He was a tall young man with rather light hair, and certainly not classically educated, by his language. Do you remember that Forester, in Miss Edgeworth's story, *made believe* to die, in order to hear what would be said of him ? He had better have gone to the Table d'Hôte ! Dr. Wilson had told R. Noel [1] before that he heard great curiosity expressed on the day of my arrival, to see me. I thought this gone by ; but as it is not, I shall get some rouge and a brown wig & make myself captivating. I ought to get stilts, too, it seems.

A postscript finishes the story ; " Ealing " evidently refers to her innovating Industrial School there.

[1] This was Robert Noel, Edward's brother, also of the party.

P.S.—I have just ascertained that the Gentleman who abused me is the Clergyman of the place ! This will not add to William's respect for the Church. I had subscribed to the English Minister that very morning. It was certainly unbecoming in the Minister to hold such discourse at the public table. He had been a curate at *Ealing*, which explains all.

These Noel cousins were among her beneficiaries. Their father, Lord Wentworth's illegitimate son, would have succeeded to the estates had his parents been married ; hence she regarded it as a duty to provide for the sons, two of whom, as we have seen, she had placed at de Fellenberg's school. There were four of them— Thomas, Robert, Charles, and Edward ; for each she interested herself. The most interesting to posterity are Robert and Tom —the former cultivated, much-travelled, a noted phrenologist in that golden age of phrenology, and the friend of many well-known men and women, among them the Count Francis Thun who was George Sand's model for the hero of *Consuelo*. He married a German girl of aristocratic parentage ; Goethe's daughter-in-law Ottilie was an intimate of him and his wife, for they lived much in Austria and Bavaria.

Tom was in his youth a black sheep ; there are anxious letters about his " tendencies " and the bad company he kept. But his name is more familiar to us than that of any brother Noel—or rather, the poem he wrote ; for perhaps to others it will be the surprise it was to me that Tom Noel, and not Tom Hood, was the author of *The Pauper's Funeral*. " Rattle his bones over the stones "—we seem to have been born acquainted with these words, though not, I imagine, most of us with the rest of the poem. Tom finally settled down, married and had children, occupied himself with gardening, and his poetry—of which there also survives (as another surprise) " Rocked in the cradle of the deep."

Edward lived for some years in Greece, on an estate in Euboea bought for him by Lady Byron. He made a success of it, was " loved and revered by everyone who knew him "—a de Fellenberg fervent, but more judicious than his model. When Fanny died, her one-time Troubadour wrote of Edward's outbursts of tempestuous grief : " No one can soothe him but the rough Charles, who is called upon by them all in times of trouble ! " Charles was her agent for the Kirkby estates (she never lived at Kirkby Mallory after her parents died, finding the expense of upkeep too heavy).

These " children of mine," as she called them, were all established in life by her. As usual, each—except the rough Charles —was associated with some pain ; Edward most of all, for after Fanny's death he kept up the mysterious quarrel. Certainly no woman was ever more scurvily treated by many of those on whom she lavished benefits. We speculate on the reason ; it cannot have been lack of delicacy in the conferring, for in delicacy she was even excessive. There was perhaps a touch of the autocrat —which had nothing really to do with her state as benefactress and would in any event have shown itself ; but gratitude, on which Miss Milbanke had so solemnly reflected, is an emotion whose victims are kittle cattle. She who had all her life so few material benefits to receive from others may not have allowed sufficiently for her restive team's susceptibilities. She did complain that to Edward Noel her friends had not spoken up for her. " The poet, the painter, in him would have answered to the touch. . . . It never seems to strike M. M., when he goes to her for aid and comfort, that heartily as I rejoice in his receiving that comfort, I am not quite so sublimated as to rejoice also in being cast aside." That was written to Lady Olivia Acheson in 1846 —in the same letter she said that the loss of Olivia was the only severe personal grief that now remained for her.

The sense of obligation was for Robert Noel the cause of a deep personal sorrow—temporary, but for its hour most painful, and by him unwillingly acquiesced in. During the Medora period we saw that Mrs. Anna Jameson was closely intimate with Lady Byron. Introduced to one another by him, who was one of Mrs. Jameson's most devoted allies, they had met in 1834. When he soon afterwards asked his friend what her first impression of his cousin had been, her answer was : " Implacability." . . . There can seldom have been a more striking instance of personal premonition ; and though the two were to become (in the words of Mrs. Jameson's niece, Gerardine Macpherson) " almost one being," for us the foreboding seems to have haunted their relation from first to last.

One thing they had in common—both had had impossible

KIRKBY MALLORY HALL

husbands, from whom both had separated. Mrs. Jameson's vicissitudes were greater, but her sorrow was far less crushing—it was scarcely sorrow at all. She had got rid of a pestilent man whom she was evidently relieved to get rid of.[1] Impoverished, but with talents that were widely recognised, she was never without congenial if laborious work by which she could live ; she had an adoring home-circle—an interesting father and mother, sisters and nieces who filled her days with love ; she had many friends both at home and on the Continent, in Germany especially, where her intimacy with Ottilie von Goethe was one of the enthusiasms of her enthusiastic heart. . . . The " Sphinx-Woman," as Gerardine Macpherson calls Lady Byron, had fewer compensations for the loss of a husband infinitely dearer than Mr. Jameson had ever been to his wife ; and, moreover, it is clear that Mrs. Jameson was—in a very much more significant sense than Lady Byron, of whom I have used the same words—a woman's woman. Her emotional life lay wholly there, beyond a doubt. Hence the joys and pains of feminine friendship had for her a morbid intensity ; she could be virtually broken by the alienation from this intimate of twenty years.

But indeed we never at any time feel that Lady Byron fully responded to her friend's extravagance—of language, at all events. Mrs. Jameson (she had been Miss Murphy) was Irish by birth—a fact which, to Irish people, does not at all account for effusiveness ; but for English people the legend of the Stone still turns to farce the tragic beauty of Blarney Castle, and here no doubt it found a believer more critical, more embarrassed, than most. It is amusing to picture the Annabella we have known, as she read the countless pages of adulation—but adulation borne out by a warmly sympathetic love. Mrs. Jameson was tireless in service spiritual, mental, and physical ; and despite the flatteries, very far from sycophantic. She would criticise with just acumen the verses frequently sent her—though not, we may conjecture, the sonnet addressed to her own portrait ! It was painted by her father, a professional miniaturist ; and

---

[1] He was a brilliant lawyer, and became head of his profession in Toronto. Thenceforth he made her an allowance of £300 a year ; but on his death left everything he had to a married woman whose name she then heard for the first time.

represents her as a very young girl, with the bright red hair of which she was proud and an ardent eagerness of look and attitude that answers to everything we know of her. To its reproduction in Mrs. Steuart Erskine's interesting memoir, a facsimile of Lady Byron's sonnet forms the transparent covering-leaf—not a successful sonnet, but here at least there is a note of fervour. Nevertheless Mrs. Jameson's words about other efforts apply to this one also :

> " The thought in your verses is very beautiful and poetical, but as usual you almost strangle it in the expression. I think it is part of your character ... that you shrink from making *words* the vehicle of feeling."

That might be taken as the note of their intercourse. Words were to Mrs. Jameson the most facile, to Annabella Milbanke the most intractable, of instruments ; the one could glissade from end to end of the gamut, the other with difficulty get through five-finger exercises. It was only when Annabella forgot to try that she ever really expressed herself on paper ; once let her try, and the dictionary fell with all its weight upon her fingers.

Whether she tried in her letters to Mrs. Jameson will never be known. All those (and they were very numerous) belonging to the happier years were destroyed by the Irishwoman—in that, at any rate, typically of her nation ! She could not bear to see them, the pang had been too rending ; she kept only the two which had—in sober truth—destroyed herself. For from the time of the rupture she never knew health or happiness again.

There is tragedy here, and on one side something not far from cruelty. Those two letters betray the harsh, unyielding temper which did underlie Annabella's tenderness, devotion, yearning for the love of chosen fellow-beings. Once more it is the lack of imaginative sympathy ; she could not bring that to her friend's dilemma. Mrs. Jameson had unerringly divined the deficiency ; maybe because she had a streak of the genius in her day so lavishly assigned her ; maybe because for her it was to show itself so ruthlessly.

The breach came with Ada's death at the end of 1852. Mrs. Jameson had been deep in the daughter's confidence ; when that secretly tormented life (which was, besides, so physically

tormented at the last) passed away, it was found that the friend
had known much that was unknown to the mother.

At once jealousy flamed.   Byron's daughter and her own . . .
another knew that daughter's secret, hidden from that mother,
his wife and widow !   As always when the note of him was struck,
everything that was fierce, everything that was rigorous,
responded.   And now it was not between themselves, between
the Byrons ; now there was an alien usurping the mother's place.

It was the end.   Fierceness froze into rigour.   But rigour took
the semblance of dispassionate philosophy.   In 1853, the year
after Ada's death :

> Yes, we " get over " all things, but as the earth gets over a
> deluge—showing desolation where there was fertility, a Dead
> Sea where there had been a volcano. . . .   Transmuted our-
> selves every moment whilst we contemplate transmutation—
> the very affections which mourn it are being altered.

The Irish volcano could not take that Dead Sea of words for
an answer.   On May 16, the day before her friend's birthday,
Anna Jameson wrote :

> You will know without my saying how I shall think of you
> to-morrow, *the 17th*.   If the past, my once so dear and kind
> friend, cannot be restored, at least it cannot be obliterated.
> Many things may pass away, but not the least particle of
> Memory as far as you are concerned.
>
> It grieves me that pain has come between us—that you are
> alienated from me and that I can comfort you no more.   But
> let me only know that you are happy . . . no matter through
> whom—whatever the healing influence—I shall bless it and
> love it for your sake.

The next letters we have are those kept by Mrs. Jameson.
They were written in 1854.

> Though I declined to make use of your kind offers in regard
> to my Daughter's Monument, & to the Robertson concerns, I
> do not see what *that* has to do with mutual good-offices in
> matters which are wholly unconnected with either, and the
> fact that I had accepted other proofs of your good-will since
> the time when we differed on certain points, gave me a right
> to expect that you would permit me to render any trifling
> services in return.

Your habit of fixing your attention exclusively on some particular passage in my letters, apart from the context or from previous communications, is the cause of your doing grievous wrong both to yourself and me. By thus *selecting* certain words, you deceive yourself as much as any one else would be deceived by such a representation.

You say " *Be* just," as if I had been unjust! My justice towards you has been *Gratitude*. How could it be otherwise when you, who could so often command the first place in the regard of others, were generously content, as you have told me, with the second in *mine*? But our differences are not, I believe, personal. They depend at least *more* upon my being unable to acquiesce in some of your views on general questions. Would you have me say I think these right when I do not? would you have me concur in them when put into practice by you? Would such a course be more faithful to friendship than to truth? Of this be assured, that I should live to see my error. It will be a far less effort to me to acknowledge it than to maintain an opinion contrary to yours, especially when I think of you as watching by a death-bed.[1]—In that sorrow I offer my deep sympathy, dear Mrs. Jameson.

Yours faithfully,

A. I. NOEL BYRON.

February 13, 1854.

I must trouble you with the correction of a date, of some importance to Truth.

You say, " I never believed your feelings alienated from me, TILL you told me they were."

Now, on the contrary, in the close of the year 1852, when my whole being was so absorbed that I could not have borne any added excitement or agitation, & whilst you were accusing me of being false to friendship, I maintained that I was " as ever your friend." This passed in writing, for we did not then meet, owing, as I told you, to the peculiar circumstances of my position.

The year following, in Dover St., you drove me, by your persevering attacks, to say something about " alienation "— but if you would look to *facts*, my subsequent intercourse with you, my visits in your society, would shew how far that *word* was from being verified.

You tell me you have " shielded the memory of Lady Lovelace from the cruel world." If the world is cruel, let it alone.

[1] Mrs. Murphy died in January, 1854. Anna Jameson's father had died in 1842.

If the " Repentance " which is now by her own direction & in her own words, inscribed on the monument to her at Kirkby Mallory, cannot disarm the Pharisees, they must be left to convince themselves. Your reiterated expressions of *Forgiveness*—in fact so many accusations, might need Forgiving, if I were not in many respects still your Debtor, & in spite of yourself, always so truly

Your friend
A.I.N.B.[1]

The sternness might have been meekly accepted ; the reiterated, self-approving assurances of " friendship " were the intolerable. If it afflicts us to read them, what must have been the revolt in Mrs. Jameson's feeling ! Open alienation could have left no such bitterness behind it. . . . Lady Byron had felt herself betrayed by daughter and friend ; not only so, but bound up with Ada's secret was a second rending estrangement (to be read of in a subsequent narrative by another hand than mine). Her life for the time lay in ruins around her. Strange that these sorrows could so act upon the woman who had known Anna Jameson's devotion—that she could not or would not perceive the dilemma of a confidante sworn to secrecy.

For epilogue, the letter which follows. Here the tragedy lies bare ; comment is needless. It was written in the October of 1854, to Robert Noel.

Dearest Noel—It is a hard struggle but I cannot see you nor speak to you nor write to you about the relative things—you are every way bound to Lady Byron ; be to her all you can and ought to be—leave me alone—I will not see again any friend who reminds me of her. These long years—ten years now—in which I have suffered—first for her, then thro' her— the idea of having been sacrificed when I so entirely loved and trusted—the expression of that face as I last saw it—these

---

[1] The monument alluded to by Lady Byron is a cenotaph bearing this inscription :

Inscribed by the express direction of
Ada Augusta Lovelace,

Born December 10th, 1815, died November 27th, 1852.
To recall her memory.

And the prayer of faith shall save the sick,
And the Lord shall raise him up ;
And if he have committed sins,
They shall be forgiven him.

have pressed into my life deeper and deeper with time. You
do not understand how it is—but be assured that I will do my
best and work on bravely. That I may do so—let me not see
you—dear Noel—not yet—at least. I am kindly and faithfully
yours   A.J.[1]

In every way it is a relief to turn from this. Far more spontaneous (as were all, I feel, of the friendships with women younger
than herself, and of her own social standing) was her love for
Lady Olivia Acheson, daughter of Lady Gosford, the M.G. of
girlhood. Lady Gosford had died in 1841, during the Medora
infatuation. The fires of that lurid domesticity finally put out,
it was (as if in a symbolism of the seasons) a renewal of older
affections when Lady Byron turned to this girl—one of four
daughters who were all as her own, though Olivia was the
favourite. There was a namesake, Annabella; the third of
whom the letters speak was Millicent, namesake of M.M., also
one in the trio of early days. Since their mother's death, these
daughters had become subject to the tyranny of their formidable
aunt, that Lady Olivia Sparrow of whom Miss Milbanke had
written in her diary : " She has more humility than I have."
If that had ever been true, it was true no longer. Lord Gosford
was now his sister's thrall more abjectly even than in the
Lowestoft period when the Sparrow household was characterised
as " the devil " ; and there was, besides, a development which
we may grant to have been inevitably painful to the elders.
Olivia Acheson had 'verted, as one says, to the Roman Catholic
creed—most anathematised of all creeds by that savage sect of
Evangelicals. These hot-gospellers looked on the girl as a
criminal. Before her mother's death, there had been trouble ;
not only Lady Olivia but Lady Annabella had betrayed a fancy
for the Scarlet Woman. In Annabella it had been quenched ;
Millicent was apparently immune from the infection—she too however, learnt how bigotry could avenge itself. A system of persecution was set up, which grew more pronounced as the battle

---

[1] In 1858 Mrs. Robert Noel wrote to Mrs. Jameson. No answer came ;
when Mrs. Noel's letters were returned to her after Mrs. Jameson's death
in 1860, the seal of this one was unbroken. These friends had, however,
seen her before the end ; Mrs. Jameson was still unable to speak of Lady
Byron.

with Olivia grew bitterer ; soon the daughters were forbidden intercourse with any of their mother's friends, and Lady Byron —" halting between two opinions " as she was held to be—was of all the most fiercely ostracised.

We have seen how in 1840, during the rosy dawn of hopes for Medora, Olivia was told that a " Lanky-doodle " had supplanted her for the coming year. From the letters of both we gather that she was herself the original Lanky-doodle—a tall, attenuated young woman with a long nose (who in many ways recalls, to us of the Victorian era, Ethel May in *The Daisy Chain*). The nickname is typical of the gayer mood which she frequently inspired in those days ; but there was anxiety besides, for here again was a life threatened by consumption.

Mütterchen, Mother the Second—so Olivia called her mother's dearest friend ; and with the aunt's ostracism instantly awoke the girl's defiance. It was not encouraged ; for here (and this before the bitter experience of 1842 had taught a bitter wisdom) the protective impulse in Lady Byron took a wiser way. Fierceness, jealousy, infatuation—those were for others ; the Byronic spell alone could call them forth. . . . The duality which lies in all of us lay there in her. Hot-hearted, blinded, wilful there, elsewhere she was serene, far-sighted, even cautious. Olivia's revolt was quelled, a degree of withdrawal was at once acquiesced in, though the girl was shown that only the sense of a daughter's duty and (more surprisingly) a dependent niece's prudence, had dictated the acquiescence.

By 1843 a tenser strain had come into Olivia's fervour. A few years before she had been counselled by her friend : " Don't try to be too spiritual at your age. That mercifully comes later." But for her such words had no meaning. Her longing for the cloister did not take effect for many years, as we learn from a letter of hers to Millicent, who in 1842 had married Dr. Henry Bence-Jones. There is no date, but it clearly belongs to a much later period. From this we can estimate what the nieces had suffered during their aunt's domination—for Millicent's marriage seems to have been a happy one.

Oh dearest, don't *you* say " the laugh is gone out of you," with your five little ones that so hang upon your laugh. It is out of *me* for ever—but my heart often smiles yet. When you said that in your letter it made me cry so bitterly, for it is so the abiding state of my dried-up heart. Oh, don't say so—if I thought it was so with you I w$^{d.}$ try what my old bony arms round your neck w$^{d.}$ do to win back a merry thought, if not a laugh, my own precious Milly. Though I am seeking *occupation* for my mind's health here, dearest—a call from you will always bring me to your side, there to find all that this world contains of the only love I care for now. When I leave you it is not to seek what I can only find near you—but work I must do if I am to live, & that I can best do when my affections are away, but I am not going into a C. while my Milly wants me ; don't fear that.

But the call prevailed. Before Olivia died, she was already lost to Millicent.

There seems to have been no direct dissuasion from her second mother. Once, from Paris in the first Medora period, she did say : " I shall not try to convert *her* " (Medora had also become a Roman Catholic), " but I might try to convert *you*." They often discussed the question—no more ; Lady Byron was firm in her own unorthodox faith, averse from proselytism in any sort ; and moreover (we may hazard), sympathetic for the inevitable revolt of these girls against the fanaticism of their father and aunt.

There may have been, besides, the fear of alienating Olivia. Such love as fills the letters to her has its apprehensions.

I think I might retaliate about the want of Self-esteem, when you talk of my having *some* affection for you. You may have forgotten, but I have not, a certain evening at Windsor when I told you what I should be to you *for life*. It is a wonder that I have ever uttered a word from my heart since, for having sealed my bond, I thought it quite superfluous to say any more. But as it is not usual, I believe, to put so much meaning into expressions of that kind—I ought perhaps to refresh *your* memory at times, tho' *my own* needs it not.

How can I send you a scarf wherewith I wish you to conceal your ugly bones ? I have worn it once myself.

And then (signing herself Eve) : " Heaven upon earth be yours—apples of Paradise ! " But the next letter says :

Every evil is an egg of good—but we do not understand the art of hatching. Still we are often benefited against ourselves. Take away from the best character in the world the graces which have been born of pain, and it would be but a poor specimen of humanity. Therefore do I endeavour to thank God not only for more dignified trials, but for little *rubs* and *scrubs—kicks* and *pricks*. I can conceive no greater ruin to the character that to have *all* go smooth !

That philosophy was put to the proof when Olivia finally resolved to become a postulant at Birmingham under Newman's teaching. Her friends, apart from the grief of separation, despaired of her health under convent-rigours. But if there was bitterness for the second mother, it was not towards the girl. In 1850 the step was taken ; the following letters tell the story to its end :

LADY NOEL BYRON *to* CAROLINE BATHURST.[1]
LEAMINGTON,
June 12, 1851.

I don't know whether I ought to write to you this morning —certainly not to talk about myself. All went off better than well yesterday—that is enough. On Saturday I shall have a much larger audience of poor Stockingers at Kirkby, and on Sunday I meet *all the World*, some hundreds I suppose, in the People's Park—not to talk, but to see and be seen.

But I ought to tell you that when I was at Birm^m. on Monday & Tuesday. . . . O— said to me : " I could not help thinking this morning how happy it would make me to see you a Catholic *before I die*! " You will conceive that this was to be met by sympathy, not Opposition, & with tenderness & gratitude. She cannot conceive Faith to exist *out of a collective body*, & because she sees me *alone*, she believes me without Faith. I reminded her how many of *her* Catholics had in their day stood alone—what self-denial it required, what fidelity to God, not to join in outward as well as inward communion with the beloved, and I felt it at that moment. I was introduced to Newman. My mind was made up at once about his character. He is no Hypocrite—but a man in whom the elements are discordantly combined, and chiefly from great deficiencies. The talents are wholly perceptive & executive—these very great. Logic and Benevolence, phrenologically, are absolutely wanting ; Veneration excessive—the rest of the head strangely irregular. I did not feel power in him—and he was evidently not at ease with me. Dialogue :

N.—You think Lady O. better, I hope ?
I —I do not—I suppose I must answer sincerely.

[1] She was an intimate friend, the daughter of Lady Caroline Bathurst.

N.—But since—I assure you she is much better.

I —Of that I can be no judge. I wish I could think her better.

I was in my own mind displeased with him for having encouraged her to violate Dr. [Bence-] Jones' injunctions about going out, so we had a secret Antagonism, & he felt it.

Next comes a letter from Newman to Dr. Bence-Jones :

I thank you for your kindness in telling me your and Dr. Watson's judgment about Lady Olivia. It concerns me to find you still think so seriously of her case. As to the particular object of your writing, of course I am obliged to speak as her spiritual adviser, just as you speak as her medical ; and certainly I have as strong an opinion, which is not my own only, of what is necessary for her tranquillity and comfort as a physician can have of what will conduce to her health. I have a deep conviction, which I hardly think any one who knows her but will share, that, till she is here, she will not be happy ; I do not believe that she will have a day of peace till she returns. Indeed, except it were going out of my province, I would say further that it seems to me as if her want of peace would prey on her health, which would suffer more in one way by her absence than it would gain in another. Would not Dr. Evans, in whom you have so great a confidence, be equal to *watching* over her here ?

Olivia died at Birmingham on March 28, 1852. Lady Byron wrote to her sister :

BRIGHTON,
Apr. 5th.

There is another point of view, dearest Millicent, in which I look at her death ; & perhaps *you* will take the same view of it. It has emancipated her from that tyrannical Church under which she suffered such thraldom. It was clear that in life she could only have been a slave, and that every better feeling & every natural affection was secretly at war with the Priestly rule. *They* may say what they will of her happiness—*we* know better. I saw even as regarded myself that every affectionate feeling called forth caused a painful conflict, & I thought it better not to awaken it latterly. Do not then be shocked, if I rejoice that she is out of their power—that no Masses can any longer reach her—that she is *ours* more than before.

Mother never loved Daughter better than I did her. Some of my friends know that I could hardly refrain from giving her my life by going to Birm^m. this Spring, where I should most likely have died—but it would have been selfish indeed.

There is one fact only on which you can dwell with unmixed gratification—your husband's generous devotedness—the more generous because, as I can testify, it was throughout unaccompanied by any *illusion*. He well knew she was absolutely in the hands of the Priests.

Lone as you are, Millicent, in every *other* respect,[1] you must almost feel as if a Stranger upon Earth. Believe there is one who feels for that loneliness.

Before Olivia's death she had written to her :

Even in illness the thought of you is more happiness than pain to me—the thought of a spirit which always seems to me to shed its light through an alabaster vase—so softly, so tenderly, that the weak may look upon it without pain, and the hardened find it has power to melt. . . . Only one severe *personal* grief remains to me—the loss of *you*.

That was in 1846. The letter to Millicent in 1852 reveals that, like the sister, she had lost Olivia before the end.

But the bitterness in that letter did not endure. To priest-craft she could never bend the head ; yet her grandson Ralph wrote in after-years that now he was older he felt confident she would have sympathised with him, though not encouraged him, in his own youthful leaning towards Roman Catholicism.

" Halnaby, Raby—how names fade away ! The Milbankes having disappeared from there and Seaham."

So in 1850 Lord Lovelace wrote to Annabella. He and Ada had been paying a visit to Newstead, as the guests of Colonel Wildman ; Ada had written of the Abbey and its associations. We can divine the tone of her letters from her mother's answers :

I have had your letters from Newstead. . . . I had been most anxious that the family mansion should not be sold . . . and it might have been saved—but he had (to me *then*) an unaccountable horror of the place, and was resolved to get rid of it for ever. How strangely the mysteries of the past are solved ! There was more than one reason for that feeling.

---

[1] All Lady Millicent's sisters were now dead.

And then :

Your letter from Newstead Abbey. If the Mythic idea generally entertained of your father affords you satisfaction, do not forget, dearest Ada, how much of it is owing to my own line of conduct. The partizans of Byron amongst whom you have lately been living, consider me as having taken a hostile position towards him. *You* must not be infected with an error resulting from *their* ignorance & his mystifications. I was his best friend, not only in feeling but in fact, after the Separation, & saved him from involving himself in what would have injured his private character & reputation still further. The proofs & witnesses are in existence. To his Memory I have also been a friend to the utmost that truth permitted, *if not beyond it*. Of this Lovelace is fully aware.

The very serious social disadvantages under which I have been placed, if of less importance to me than the objects accomplished by my silence, ought not to be forgotten. But setting these aside, there is a consideration nearer to my heart of which I will now speak, for the sake of our being all united in feeling as long as I may live.

It often occurs to me that my attempts to influence your Children favorably in their early years will be frustrated & turned to mischief—so that it would be better for them not to have known me—if they are allowed to adopt the unfounded popular notion of my having abandoned my husband from want of devotedness & entire sympathy ; or if they suppose me to have been under the influence, at any time, of cold, calculating, & unforgiving feelings—such having been his published description of me, whilst he wrote to me privately (as will hereafter appear), " I did—do—and ever shall—love you." But from the whole tenor of my conduct, & more particularly from the circum[s.] a few years ago which necessitated a disclosure till then withheld from you & Lovelace, you must be convinced of my repugnance to anything like self-justification. Only the strongest conviction of its being a duty towards others would force me to enter into it.

I do not judge for you & him as Parents—but surely you could not *as such*, come to the conclusion that your Children had better—for the sake of Lord Byron's fame—believe me *what I am not*. Write to me what you think & feel openly.

For a while after this mother and daughter were estranged. Lord Lovelace, at any rate, felt that Lady Byron had been justly wounded. He wrote twice, after the Newstead visit, to assure her of Ada's affection and his own. We have seen to what the daughter's feeling prompted her at the last ; in that sickroom, two years later, assuredly no resentment listened to her dying wish.

Not only from Halnaby, Raby—from Seaham, too, the Milbankes had disappeared. In 1841 she heard of the house dilapidated, " not even a servant kept there, grass growing green at the door." But in 1842 Mrs. Jameson (expressly for her sake) made a pilgrimage to the one home her friend had ever known. The house was then inhabited ; the visitor made friends with the gardener and housekeeper, went into the pretty little flower-garden.

> From the great hawthorn, which they have christened Lord Byron's Hawthorn, and from the beautiful large myrtle. . . . I gathered a branch from each to bring you ; then went over the house, where they pointed out the room in which Lady Byron was married. Then down to the beach : tide coming in, a grey veil over the sky. . . . It would please you to know, but I daresay you *do* know, with what respect " the old family " is remembered.

The sole daughter of the Milbankes reads of their hawthorn named for him who had so little loved or known her home and her ; of the room in which Lady Byron—not Miss Milbanke—was married. Throughout the coming generations strangers will think of only Byron in the place where the " old family " is still remembered. Not long afterwards she heard Sontag singing Home, Sweet Home ; it made her " rain tears." Sontag's voice, her parents' voices, that other voice, the sound of the sea. . . . " I stand on the craggy brow "—and the tide going out, a grey veil over the sky.

CHAPTER XXV

FRIENDSHIPS WITH MEN

BRIGHTON, Fordhook, Esher and Brighton in combination (Moore Place and Junction House, the latter now pulled down, near the Pavilion) Hastings on the Tackleway,[1] Ham Common, Richmond —in all these places she pitched her moving tent, with many a flight for still briefer sojourns at Clifton, Canterbury (not in the detested Bifrons), Southampton. . . . Was her wandering life no more than the search for health—did it not symbolise the search for rest in some affection ? Too many had proved illusive— other women's chiefly, leaving the first supreme illusion aside as too great for comparison with any second.

Now (we might think to see) after the alienation from Augusta, Fanny Noel, Mrs. Jameson, and the loss of Olivia Acheson to " the Priests," she turned to men for friendship. There were alliances with women still—Mary Carpenter, Caroline Bathurst —to whom she wrote many interesting letters, and many prosy ones too ; there was the unfortunate confidence to Mrs. Harriet Beecher-Stowe in 1856, at their second meeting [2] ; but not again are we conscious of more than what Mary Carpenter calls " soul-communion "—a separate thing, especially with Annabella Byron, from heart-communion. She could talk about religion with almost anyone, despite a comment on " the worst kind of gossips —religious ones." There we find again the Miss Milbanke of the London seasons, too ready with detraction of what she could herself enjoy.

[1] Among her several abodes there was East Hill House, a small low-gabled, bow-windowed house, which has a plaque above the door to say that the Duke of Sussex, Lady Augusta Murray, and the Comte d'Este stayed there. George MacDonald visited Lady Byron at Hastings in August 1857.

[2] So much has been written of this by myself and others that it will not be dwelt on here.

But with two men she formed, towards the end of her life, friendships which in strongly contrasted ways awakened deep affection on both sides. Each was much younger than herself ; each unusually gifted—and unusually good-looking. Her girlish List of Qualities for a Husband had speculated on beauty and genius as possible essentials ; however essential for " interest," they had not proved efficacious for happiness—yet once more we see that she knew something about herself when she considered them.

Of these friendships the later in time shall be the earlier chronicled, because it is as water to wine compared with that which was closed by death before it began. Frederick Robertson " of Brighton " she met in 1848 ; George MacDonald she did not meet until 1855, when Robertson had been dead for two years. Of Robertson's intercourse with her another chapter will tell, for there alone it finds the fitting place. She lived her sorrow through again with him, in a kind of renascence of the heart—touched to life by the reciprocal attraction he felt for her, though in years she might have been his mother.

With George MacDonald her relation was not at all like this. The difference in age was marked all through, as we never feel it to have been with Robertson ; Lady Byron was to MacDonald the protectress, the adviser, and once at least the extremely rigorous critic.

It was through the reading of his narrative poem, *Within and Without* (published in 1855, but written a few years earlier), that their acquaintance began. She wrote to him of her admiration, and soon afterwards they met. He was as yet quite unknown either as poet or novelist, married, struggling for a livelihood. Thirty-one, a handsome Highlander, raven-haired, aquiline, keen-eyed, of unorthodox faith, no ascetic (for, in the one vivid phrase—and that a quotation—found in his friend Johnson's Memoir, " he came eating and drinking "), George MacDonald at once awakened the protective impulse, and the critical impulse too. A pronounced idealist, he stirred to protest the realist in her on whom realism had so pitilessly been forced. She recommended " a course of the Newgate Calendar " ; and whatever his surprise at this from the impressive, ermine-cloaked lady, he had humour enough to see the fun of it. But when she wrote in far more

destructive criticism of his public readings of poetry, the Highlander in him rebelled. He used the sanctioned phrase, " a true
sign of friendship "—true sign of a wry face in the user ; but
added that hers was not the universal opinion. Something
painful he granted there must be—it was for *him* to find out
what it was. Had he but known, she went a good deal further
than painful—had pronounced the excess of emotion to be
" intolerable," and feared he could never succeed as a lecturer.
(We know that he did succeed, whether or not by obedience to
her strictures.)

But by that time their friendship was too secure to be shaken
by home-truths. In a packet of letters to him, written during
these five years before her death—in the clear, regular hand
which had always been hers, more flowing than graphology would
lead us to expect—we find many a proof of her active interest.
" I hope my play will be wicked enough to please you," wrote he,
sending the MS. ; and she of an expected visit from him :

> You shall be treated most inhospitably—put into a room
> apart with a private entrance. . . . No note will be taken of
> your goings out and comings in. When socially disposed,
> you will *invite yourself*. My house has often been called
> Liberty Hall.

(That is unexpected, and the *sans gêne* was sometimes carried
too far ; in a letter to Caroline Bathurst there are apologies
for having forgotten to give her any luncheon !)

The already quoted dedication of *David Elginbrod* to her
memory (it was published in 1872, twelve years after her death)
is sufficient proof of what the friendship had meant to George
MacDonald and his wife ; their children, as a letter in 1922 from
one of the daughters testifies, " grew up in the knowledge of our
parents' love and reverence for her." She confided part of her
story to him ; in verse he recorded the memory and the effect it
had upon his own anger in 1869, when *Blackwood's* and the
Quarterly were reviling her who had been nine years in her grave.

> Dead, why defend thee who in life
> 　For thy worst foe hadst died ;
> Thou who, thy name a word of strife,
> 　Didst silent stand aside ?

Grand in forgiveness, what to thee
        The big world's puny prate !
Or thy great heart has ceased to be,
        Or loveth still its mate !

In a private letter he wrote : " I would as soon discuss my
father and mother as her. This much only would I say, that
knowing her for years, I counted her one of the noblest as well
as one of the ablest of women ; and that so far from being cold-
hearted, I believe she loved her husband to the last, whatever
the *last* may be interpreted as being."

Mrs. Mair, a daughter of Mrs. Henry Siddons and grand-
daughter of the great Sarah, writing of the friendship with
MacDonald, added some words on her own account. She, then
a child, and her mother had stopped with Lady Byron during
the sojourn at Seaham which followed on the impetuous flight
to Newstead in 1818.

> She was in great grief and suffering, and she has often told
> me that the interest she felt for me—the occupation of teach-
> ing, playing with, and loving me—brought her more cheerful-
> ness and comfort than anything could have done. If I was a
> comfort to her, what has she not been to me since ? a true,
> tender, and maternal friend. She has been thought cold by
> those who did not know her, but I often think of those soft,
> almond-shaped blue eyes, which never looked on me but
> tenderly, and wish that she could have been known more
> truly as she was, and less as a somewhat reserved, shy manner
> caused her to appear.

Frederick Arnold, in his Life of Robertson, writes of the
" beautifully blue eyes, with an expression wild and keen " ;
Mrs. De Morgan described her as one whose face (" as Mr. Carlyle
said to me many years after ") could never be forgotten. " Her
complexion was fair and clear, and her features delicately formed,
though not regularly beautiful, with the exception of her eyes.
These were large and tender, and of a deep blue which seemed to
kindle as one looked into them. She had fine eyebrows, and a
quantity of soft brown hair ; [1] but the great charm of her face

---

[1] The present Baroness Wentworth, daughter of Lady Anne Blunt, tells
us that her mother and her uncle Ralph " used to consider it their greatest
delight to be allowed to brush Lady Byron's hair, which was so long that
it touched the floor when she was sitting on a chair."

was its sweet and intellectual, though rather mournful expression." There is an interesting anecdote here. One evening Mrs. De Morgan was at Fordhook with Lady Gosford and Miss Montgomery—M.G. and M.M. They were talking about wishes: what would each desire if she could have her wish? When it came to Lady Byron's turn, she said: "If I had been asked when I was beginning life, I should have answered, 'To love and be loved.'"

In Frederick Arnold's book there is a vivid description of her. Arnold was reminded of Mère Angélique of Port Royal; but this observer seems to have seen with a prepossession of her sternness and formality. He goes on:

> To the last she was rather striking. The forehead was abnormally high—the head seemed half face, half forehead. The face was noticeable for its extreme pallor. . . . Her favourite attitude was to stand on the drawing-room hearth, the little fist clenched somewhat imperiously; the tones of her voice somewhat dogmatic.[1] The attitude was always graceful. Her singular appearance was partly due to the state of her health. She suffered greatly from heart-complaint, which caused her intense pain. . . . As she stood on her hearth, it was a great delight to her to lecture young people on phrenology.

Phrenology was for a long time one of her crazes. Every one was considered in the light of his bumps; and the lack of humour apparently inseparable from this pseudo-science comes out very ludicrously in her description of a much-revered American divine: "The countenance is of a hallowed caste, meek and tender, the speech milk and honey"—a picture from which we turn with blushes of vicarious shame for both. And again in Mrs. De Morgan's ingenuous comment on Lady Byron's specifically philanthropic friends: "We remarked—those of us who took note of heads—that in all the real earnest friends of their species the head was high in front and at the top." To imagine a dinner-party—and there were many—consisting of these first of all High-brows is a dangerous exercise for the biographer, solicitous to be respectful. I gladly fall back on a further reminiscence of Lady Wentworth's: "My mother said Lady Byron was the sweetest and gentlest person she ever knew, and *very amusing*."

[1] Robert Noel wrote of " her beautiful diction."

Sooner or later the story of any life at all prolonged must give a list of deaths. The closest of all ties had been broken in the eighteen-twenties; now begins the catalogue of friends. In 1840 Hugh Montgomery, fictive possessor of her girlish heart; in 1841 M. G.; next year William Frend; Sophy Tamworth in 1849 (" the last for whom I should truly mourn—I mean of my own family"); in 1850 Mrs. Clermont and (scarcely to be reckoned among friends, it is true) Colonel Leigh. Then came the crushing 1852 which saw Olivia Acheson first, then Ada Lovelace, pass away.

Lord Melbourne died at the end of 1848. To Mrs. Jameson— not yet driven out from affection—his cousin wrote :

> His death is a consolation—better than the living death of his last days. The epileptic fits were fearful ; he was rarely conscious. All the papers are full of falsehoods. . . . Sydney Smith's is the only [character] at all like that I know. The biographer should know the world in which Lord Melbourne moved—should understand how its malaria could poison or neutralise Nature's best gifts—how the nature thus poisoned would mock itself in bitter remembrance of its own higher type. . . . His memory must rest with the Queen. She only can render to Caesar at some future day.

And six years later, when there was some idea of publishing his private letters : " They are the only proofs of his extreme tenderness and generosity, and they reflect great credit on poor Lady Caroline also—are calculated to *protect* her memory from the Pharisees." The former judgments of self-sufficiency, lack of self-esteem, were thus atoned for ; that youthful hostility for the " little sheep " was forgotten in the sense of Melbourne's charm. A long story it had been, dating from earliest memory —Mam's suspicions of " the Viscountess," Dad's much-combatted affection for his sister ; Caroline and the waltzing at Melbourne House, the painful interview and the spoilt season that resulted ; the scandal at Lady Heathcote's ball ; William Lamb's argument with Byron about *Evelina*, his silent championship of herself, when at Byron's funeral he of all the Lamb-connection was the only one not represented—and then the likeness to Sir Ralph which had made the seeing of him " almost a resurrection." . . . Annabella Milbanke ; Lady Byron—which was she as she wrote of him to Mrs. Jameson ?

That 1848 was the Esher-Brighton period. Moore Place, the Esher house, she had lent to the Duchess of Orleans, exiled with the other French Royalties. Little Annabella King (the Lady Anne Blunt of our time) had seen them all at some railway-station ; her grandmother—more sympathetic than for her own Queen ten years before—had soon afterwards offered Moore Place, so near to Claremont as it was. The tenancy was in every way successful ; Lady Byron granted an interview to *this* Royalty before the Duchess of Orleans left England, and many little graces passed between them.

But 1848 saw, too, the re-entry of a theme incongruous with Royal amenities. It saw the re-entry of that development of the Medora-subject introduced by one Washington Fleming two years after Byron's death—blackmail.

CHAPTER XXVI

1848-51

ROBERTSON: THE LAST MEETING WITH AUGUSTA

Not upon Lady Byron ; upon Mrs. Leigh.

Since the rescue of Medora in 1840 Augusta had been shut out from all intercourse. " God knows whether my poor child is alive or not ! "—so it was reported that she had written to a friend ; but this was scornfully shown to be an instance of her duplicity. " Mrs. Leigh must be well aware that she would have to be legally informed of her daughter's death." She might be told (" but not as a message from me ") that Elizabeth was alive and well, in comfortable circumstances ; no more could be imparted to her ; the daughter's conviction that she would be molested forbade that.

In 1846 Sir John Hobhouse, as the surviving executor of Byron's will, filed a Bill in Chancery empowering the Court to administer the funds ; " for the numerous deeds executed by Mrs. Leigh had created so many claimants that he wished to be relieved from responsibility." The costs of this Bill would (wrote Lady Byron's legal adviser) seriously reduce the Trust Fund. Resigned though she was to that, she would not surrender to indirect blackmail when two years later there came an urgent but humble appeal through Dr. Lushington—would he obtain for Mrs. Leigh an interview with Lady Byron ? Both guessed what the urgency was ; the interview was refused ; Mrs. Leigh was asked to give her reason for desiring it. She declined to do that, and added : " The time may come when Lady Byron will regret her answer—it may easily be believed that no common causes would have induced me AGAIN to address her." But next year she still more urgently and humbly implored an interview, this time giving her reason. She was in desperate need of an " IM-MEDIATE " sum of money ; refusal would and must end " in the ruin *of us all*."

Now there could be no doubt ; and, feeling the wretched futility of giving for such a purpose, Lady Byron " with very great pain " refused. But might she not have consented to see Augusta ? Herself betrayed, cast off by the daughter, was it that she could not face the victim of her unmeasured condemnation eight years ago ? Whatever the other delinquencies, had Mrs. Villiers been justified in her defence—had Medora been to her mother what she had been to her protectress ? Before this Lady Horton had written that Augusta's champion now believed she had been misled on some points, but also believed that Medora had deceived Lady Byron on others.... The old story— subterfuge, evasion, half-truths ; the " lumps of sugar " that had been ironically commended to Olivia Acheson ! It would not be so bitter to confess to Mrs. Villiers, who had just (on what pretext we do not know) reopened correspondence. To admit the blindness of that infatuation might even be relief ; and (still firmly repulsing the humble, desperate suppliant) Lady Byron wrote to Augusta's one-time " able advocate "—herself in a tone of humility. She had not expected, she said, ever again to read such kind expressions from Mrs. Villiers ; she was most willing to join the end to the beginning and become again hers most affectionately.

> Since you have alluded to *that* unhappy business, I will just say that I regret having yielded to legal advice in avoiding to discuss it *vivâ voce.* Had we conversed upon it, I am persuaded that some mutual misapprehension would have been prevented. I am still ignorant in what respect I was *really* deceived.

When the September of this 1849 brought the news of Medora's death, no word passed between mother and one-time protectress ; the alienation was complete.

Yet within a year and a half the Two A.'s met again, this time at Annabella's suggestion.

It came about through her friendship with the Rev. Frederick Robertson " of Brighton," as one still says in recalling him. She had been introduced to him in 1848 by Robert Noel, to whom she wrote soon afterwards : " I must thank you for the greatest gift that human being can make to his fellow—the means of intercourse with a great soul—Robertson's." To another correspondent she wrote more simply, and (as usual) more expressively : " I love him."

" Great mutual attraction " had been Mrs. Jameson's comment when she first saw them together ; to her Lady Byron called him the Genius of the Soul's world. " His images will be fixed for ever like stars in my mind's Heaven." She could disagree with him, however—in the early days at any rate. " Robertson thinks too much of Heaven and too little of this world. . . . We are made largely to enjoy, and does it become us to undervalue the present gift for the sake of the future ? " Unexpected in her, who does not strike us as having had much of the *joie de vivre* ; and a semi-contradiction of her words to Olivia Acheson : " Spirituality mercifully comes with later life "—for she was fifty-six when she met Robertson, and he was in the early thirties.

Almost a quarter-century between them ; yet each, it is clear, felt the other's personal no less than spiritual attraction. When Lady Byron first met Mrs. Robertson, she pronounced her to be " simple, not silly." The negative clause does its work ; it is with amusement that later we find confidences from Robertson about vague distresses, soon to develop into revelation of " that old unhappy sense of loss, or want of something," made by a more famous man about his own married life. Most time-honoured, most irresistible of appeals from a husband to a " soul-mate "— and this husband, in a long series of gradually more explicit letters, made it with all his powers of graceful eloquence.

Nevertheless, the protective impulse did not here come into play. *She* was the protected, if either was. A new relation, that, for Annabella Byron, everyone's benefactress ! Easy to imagine the delight, the repose, it must have given her ; and when to this were added Robertson's unorthodox saintliness, vivid radiant personality,[1] and remarkable good-looks, the Brighton period may be regarded as one that brought her more happiness than any other since her girlhood. Though she was now a confirmed invalid—the heart-disease was far advanced—

---

[1] After one or two meetings an acquaintance wrote of him : " I need hardly say that a more *taking* man never lived."

his visits, her church-goings, were supreme enjoyments ; she leant upon him with a charmed trustfulness which neither Mr. Frend nor Dr. King had inspired. It was a real renascence ; almost the girl in her came out again, and the more because of Byron they soon wrote and spoke.

Holy Trinity Church—originally a Nonconformist Chapel, the centenary of which was celebrated in 1926—was Robertson's field of action at Brighton ; it was crowded whenever he preached. From a woman who heard his first sermon there, the *Daily News* printed in 1926 some interesting reminiscences. She could vividly recall his beautifully clear voice, dark-blue eyes, rich brown curly hair, clean-shaven mouth and chin—and (sad anti-climax) mutton-chop whiskers. " He had a remarkable way of looking straight at you " ; and once when an Electro-Biologist (as Spiritists then called themselves) was lecturing at Brighton, Robertson went to hear him. It was not long before the lecturer exclaimed : " I cannot do anything while that gentleman is here ! "

Confidence begets confidence ; soon Robertson's was reciprocated. She knew him to have an intense sympathy with Byron as revealed in the poems ; could give him intimate revelations " which would certainly not lessen that sympathy." But (she told him) it must be by letter ; she was uncertain of her self-command, and besides she wished to leave a written record of such recollections. So with her old habit of classifying by 1, 2, 3, she proceeded to " lay open " Byron's mind on religious matters.

To us the analysis brings few surprises. " He was no sceptic "; " conscience was always alive " ; " the Bible was viewed through the fearful medium of Calvinism ; God was a God of Vengeance " —we have long known these things. By Robertson too Byron's cry : " The worst of it is, I *do* believe ! " had always been heard through the tumult of Byron's verse ; but when she told him of another : " ' Too late—too late ' ; words ever in his mouth," he wrote that it opened a fresh vista, and added (unexpectedly even from the unorthodox clergyman he was) : " Religious people, as usual, never penetrate below the surface."

There spoke two traits of Robertson—the ingenuousness which made him feel a deep significance in those emptily melodramatic words, and the somewhat censorious strain which had always

had its counterpart in her. Like her, he could be violently prejudiced ; was prone to gaze upon a narcissistic vision of himself,
as she on that of herself—he more conscious than she of the lapse
from wider vision. It was a weakness which influenced both at
an hour in which vision was tested.

For a while her revelations were impersonal ; soon the more
intimate note crept in, and prevailed. So long ago as 1836 she
had set down—then too calling the reminiscences religious—
some details of her life with Byron. These pages were now handed
to Robertson ; in them were disclosures far more interesting.
Relating the suffocation-scene at Seaham, with Byron's : " Perhaps I shall go to Heaven holding to the hem of your garment,"
she had written of that and kindred sayings :

> Could there be anything more mortifying, as well as afflict-
> ing, than to be the object of such sterile approbation ? It did
> not enable me to render him better or happier ! From first to
> last this was the case. . . . The fancied contrast between him-
> self and me rendered me habitually an object of the greatest
> irritation. As if in order to aggravate that morbid and per-
> verse feeling, he would not see my faults ; he more than once
> said : " Had I known *what* you were, I would never have
> married you." It may be supposed that such expressions were
> ironical, but it is improbable that my vanity should so far have
> deceived me. . . . Some of his published sentiments may be
> alleged in opposition to this view, but they were obviously *for
> effect*. Byron knew himself—he was no self-righteous Pharisee.
> How often did he exclaim, with mingled bitterness and despair :
> ' B. *is* a fool ! ' (Of course he did not mean intellectually, tho'
> in that respect he did not rate himself as highly as he was
> rated.) I have ever believed that his Conscience was not thus
> kept alive *in vain*. How he communed with his own heart
> before he died, none can tell—he *would* have told, but could
> not !

And sending the picture we have seen of Byron's " child-side,"
she added :

> There were moods in which he would have gladly exchanged
> all his fame—I am sure he spoke sincerely—for the obscurity of
> some *harmless* writer. . . . Conscious as he was of the weakness
> of his own character, of its extreme mobility and impressibility,
> the aspiration after its opposite (or what appeared to him such)
> was the more natural. . . . He disclaimed with sincerity that

he had drawn his own portrait, though he told me, I believe as truly, that all his then published poetry was *fact*.

(Incidentally, this paper of 1836 affords another proof that there were moments of real confidence between them during their married life.)

When letters were exchanged for talks with Robertson, the more painful revelations began. They repeat what we know in notes taken down at her request, for she intended to entrust the posthumous defence of herself—and Byron—to him. Elaborate preparations were made by both for this ; Robertson's death frustrated the purpose. One curious anecdote is new :

> In November 1815 (residing in Piccadilly) I was informed that bailiffs were coming into the house to take possession of everything, even the bed on which I lay. Resources were suggested by me in vain ; I was told it could not be avoided, and the dreadful consequences to myself particularly were dwelt upon and exaggerated. In my then state of mind, outward matters were of little significance ; and I took it very quietly when a man *said* to be the bailiff walked in, went over some of the rooms, but took nothing away—and there it ended. I could not understand it then ; I think I can now. . . . Almost every fragment of that period seems, since I have viewed it at a distance, to take its place and become intelligible in connection with the whole. There were some spots long mysterious —one or two still.

She meant the system avowedly designed to " make you run back to your father, like the spoilt child you are " ; but there was also in her mind the plot alluded to in a letter of 1830.[1] This latter idea came to be called hallucination by the champions of Byron—too strong a word for what was simply a confused attempt to understand the persistent enmity he showed her after their marriage. In the first hour he had told her that " it *must* come to a separation " ; those who put all the odium on her forget that strangely. During her lifetime, it is true, not many knew of Byron's instant cruelties ; but after her death Lady Anne Barnard's narrative (to say nothing of Mrs. Beecher-Stowe's) appeared in print, and left no doubt that from the first moment he had shown his resolve to drive her from him. When—still in

[1] See Chapter xxi, p. 318.

the earliest days of their life together—she learnt from his lips of the liaison with Augusta and of the (invented) scheme with Lady Melbourne to revenge himself for the refusal of his first offer, how could she escape from the conviction, so borne out by events, that she *had* been the victim of a plot ? As time went on, this was over-emphasised—a different thing, however, from hallucination. Certainly the plot would not have produced this brief note from Byron during the first weeks of separation :

> DEAREST PIP.
>   I wish you would make it up. I am dreadfully sick of all this.

Affronting enough in its slightness for her who had had a good deal worse to be sick of ; yet with a touch of the " child-side " which partly redeems it. Robertson, under the spell of her confidence—known to be then so rarely given—and as a result losing much of his sympathy for Byron, could feel only the affront ; in all these discussions he was the listener indignant and appalled, though as yet he had not been fully enlightened. The time of course came when all was told him ; but this again by letter. On the New Year's Day of 1851 they met and talked as usual of her past. It was then that she said : " I thought Mrs. Leigh my friend—I loved her—I love her still ! I cannot help it. I shall see her once more in this world before we both die."

No more was then said of Augusta. Lady Byron soon afterwards went to Ockham for a while ; on January 8 she wrote to Robertson :

> A hope has risen in my mind that through your ministry good might be done to that survivor for whom I am so deeply interested. . . . You shall know then. If you recollect, in our last conversation I said there was one whom I had not seen for years, but hoped before death to see again. That was the person whose *guilt* made a great part (*not* the whole) of my wretchedness. . . . Will you not now sympathize more completely ?

And before she could hear from him she wrote again :

> It was not Passion nor Circumstance that occasioned the worst aberrations. There was a deliberate purpose to set God's will and human law at defiance. Transgression was desired *as*

such. Vice in itself was spoken of as insipid, as deriving its zest from its unlawfulness. . . . " How I should have loved you if you had been another man's wife ! "

With respect to my testimony, I desire to be subjected to rigorous and unsparing enquiries. On *that* subject I cannot be hurt by any view or opinion concerning myself. If I could, I must have died long ago, or been driven mad—not that I am naturally without a strong desire to be approved.

As commonly happens with such confidences, the dramatic element was encroaching. To increase sympathy for Byron was no longer her single aim ; as he himself had been, she was unconsciously impelled by the vanity of suffering, of all vanities most specious.

Robertson's reply to the unmistakable indication overdid amazement and horror ; to a student of Byron it could not have come as so startling a shock. " Surely I have—I must have mistaken the implied meaning ! I shrink from suggesting," and so on ; finally : " Did *Manfred* shadow a truth ? " But we must remember that he was a young man writing to a much older woman ; he might know very well that he had not mistaken her, yet how to convey his comprehension ! He found the way ; she too found the way to let him know he was right : " My silence has of course confirmed your supposition." So she wrote after her return to Brighton on January 15, asking him to come to her that evening.

But in the interval at Ockham, away from his exciting presence, she could remember her original motive. In a letter unsent (but afterwards dated by Robertson's hand) she had exclaimed :

Shall I survive to bear witness to the evil, and not to the good ? Can I not be believed when after all I have disclosed I say that there was a higher better being in that breast throughout . . . one which he was always defying, but never could destroy. . . . Let it be supposed to have been the illusion of love on my part *then*—but the conviction remains unaltered now.

So, tossed between her human and what Robertson had called her superhuman nature, she wrote—and was. Here, as in a score of other instances, we find the real woman under the reviled, and the apotheosised, heroine. When Robertson called her superhuman, he was mistaken as so many have been mistaken ; her mother, long ago, had found a truer word. But it was not for either to feel as we can feel the drama in these confidences. When self-consciousness did enter in, its influence was disastrous.

Soon—her emotional life renewed under the dual influence of spoken memories and Robertson's ardent sympathy—the defence of Byron induced anger against those who had been, as she said, " unfriendly " to her after they had parted.

> It is not possible, if I have read human nature rightly, for any one to keep up such bitter resentment without believing in some cause for it. . . . Towards the close of his life his feelings towards me were softening—but evil influence had not yet lost its hold entirely. He *must* have come, had he lived, to the belief that *from first to last* I had been his only truly devoted friend—it was not permitted !

Such thoughts, written to Robertson, brooded over in solitude, gradually led her to reckon Augusta among those who had kept resentment alive. She recalled that interview during the separation-proceedings which had resulted in Byron's sending her letters from his friends ; recalled other duplicities (as she held them to be) in the Medora episode. Could she not now wrest a confession—a further confession—from Augusta ? Would not that inspire a more perfect " forgiveness " ?—which nevertheless she constantly denied having felt to be required of her, saying that she had never regarded herself as injured. This delusion Robertson might have dissipated ; with the insight so remarkable in him for others, he could have shown her that, on the contrary, she was pluming herself complacently on forgiveness in her talks with him. Instead, he encouraged both delusion and doubts ; they decided that an interview should be offered, in which the suspicions were to be laid before Augusta for refutation —or the reverse.

In 1850 Augusta had been widowed. Early in this 1851 of the talks with Robertson there came (through Dr. Lushington once more) an appeal from her daughter Emily, the only one who had been as a daughter to her. Emily was Lady Byron's godchild ;

this was not her first letter since her father's death. There had been two ; they had not been answered. In this one the appeal was for money. Her mother, she wrote, was in a wretched state, no longer equal to the continued anxiety of so many years ; ruin was staring them in the face ; Lady Byron was their last and only hope. The tone was very humble ; blackmail was clearly not now the terror—creditors of the worthless son Frederick were known by Lady Byron to be clamant on his mother.

She sent Emily's letter to Robertson, asking for its return, as she wanted to show it to Lord Byron. " He and Lady B. gave me a frightful description of the hatred now raging between the mother and her eldest daughter [Georgiana Trevanion]. *This*," she added, referring to the discussed interview, " is not the moment, I think ? ... I would write, however, to this effect— that I had determined on offering it, but felt that in consequence of the application from Emily it must now be given up.... It will then rest with her to urge it, and to promise the necessary conditions."

Not the time to be *chosen*, Robertson agreed, but he thought the interview indispensable to her peace of mind. Accordingly she wrote on February 11, as from the Post Office, Brighton—a precaution which forgiveness would, one thinks, have forgotten.

> Since the cessation of our personal intercourse you have more than once asked me to see you. If you still feel that wish, I will comply with it. We may not long have it in our power, Augusta, to meet again in this life, and to do so might be the means of leaving to both of us a remembrance of deep though sad thankfulness. But this could not be the effect unless every worldly interest were absolutely excluded from our conversation, and there were the most entire and mutual truthfulness. *No other expectations* must be entertained by you for a moment. On any other terms I cannot see you again, unless summoned to your death-bed.
>
> If you decline, these will be the last words of mine ever addressed to you, and as such I wish they could convey to your heart the feelings with which I write them, and am
>
> Yours
>
> A. I. Noel Byron.

No answer came for some days. " I shall now cease to expect," she wrote to Robertson ; but Augusta's letter was in the post.

She was almost too ill to write, but " unhesitatingly and thankfully " accepted. At the moment a meeting was impossible ; she would write again as soon as she had any strength—" and I suppose to the same address." That was all her reproach ; she added that she was prepared to give and receive any explanations that concerned herself.

" It reads well," wrote Lady Byron, sending the letter to Robertson ; " but to me who know it not to be her own language very painfully. It is for *third parties*, not for *me*—heartless."

Assuredly it is not the poor muddled language we know—strange if it were. There had been enough to congeal that torrent. Heartlessness for heartlessness, if indeed Augusta's answer was heartless at all. The withheld address—in that the other two perceived no heartlessness ; and Robertson replied : " A *most* unsatisfactory letter. I certainly was not prepared for anything so deep as this."

What nonsense ! Laughable, were we not so repelled, did we not recall the confessional interviews of 1816, did we not see that this one was foredoomed, that Augusta would walk into an armed camp when after some time it was arranged that she should meet —not Annabella alone, but Robertson too, at Reigate. Lady Byron must have with her a friend to attest what *she* might say. She would hear Augusta in private ; then her witness should be introduced.

The other tried to dissuade her—in vain. " It would not be right." Under protest Augusta consented ; Robertson was then for the first time named. Not until the end of March had they got so far ; a Thursday or Friday in that week was suggested. Lady Byron wrote to Robertson : " I will say nothing of my feelings, and would ask you not to refer to them until the meeting is over." But then came a fresh delay. Augusta could not manage Thursday or Friday ; any day after Monday was offered. . . . Strung up for the earlier date, Annabella felt " for a moment as if trifled with. ' What is play to you is death to me '—but perhaps I am mistaken. Still I don't like the postponement."

Too plainly now we perceive the self-dramatisation ; and it was assiduously fostered by Robertson, whose influence just then strikes us as the worst she could have had. Instead of toning down, he keyed-up the situation to concert-pitch. . . . Tuesday was offered and accepted, with an apology from Augusta for her helplessness about trains. She had taken only one journey and back in her life—" and that in 1847." [1]

Strange to read that to-day—strange even then to read it, for the never-resting wanderer from place to place ! She gave the necessary details, adding : " My servant in Drab Livery, holding up a visiting-card, will look into all the 1st Class Carriages," and would then convey Augusta to the White Hart Hotel in Reigate.

Alone, ill, scared of the " railroad " ; watching nervously for Reigate, peering out (with the large dark eyes that saw, as her daughter had said, so little) for the servant in Drab Livery with his visiting-card, Augusta came, alighted, drove to the White Hart. It was no less fragile a woman who awaited her ; but not alone, not suspected. In Annabella's bag there lay a memorandum ; among the headings this : " Questions—*you* kept up hatred ; *you* put things in a false light ; *you* suppressed what was kindest, most calculated to soften "—accusations that Augusta never dreamed of having to answer.

The White Hart had set aside two private sitting-rooms for a few hours. A clergyman with an elderly lady arrived ; then an elderly lady alone ; figures that we may guess to have been baffling for the inn's curiosity ! So the Two A.'s met after many and many a year. " I saw Death in her face at once," wrote Annabella, months later.

In Robertson's presence the interview opened with Annabella's promise not to divulge anything Augusta might desire to say, and an assurance of her unaltered affection ; then (as we surmise) the women were left alone for the " communication " which remains their secret.

Lady Byron's account—the only one we have—was written for purposes of record, and attested as " most accurate " by Robertson, though he was present at only part of the interview. The most unsatisfactory of documents, it leaves us so much in the dark that we can scarcely follow the emotional fluctuations.

---

[1] An amusing side-light is shed on this by a remark quoted from Lord Meath—who is 88 years old—in the *Daily News* of April 16 or 17, 1929. "In my young days, anyone travelling by train definitely lost caste." Mrs. Leigh, Court-lady, lodged in St. James's Palace, had probably shunned "the railroad" for this reason ; while Lady Byron cared for none of these things.

Annabella was in a state of strong excitement—the work of weeks, of months ; Augusta, at all times far less intense, was besides unaware that Robertson knew the whole story. She accepted him not as her judge but as Annabella's witness—painful enough (as she had pleaded) but not overwhelming. There was everything to make this 8th of April the supreme climax of their drama for the one ; an occasion of almost happy reconciliation for the other, sanguine as even still she could be of things coming right by some intervention of that obliging Providence of hers. . . . The narrative states :

> Her communication was very short. I made no comment on it whatsoever, except, when she ceased to speak : " Is that all ? " Had I spoken, I must have said : " False—false." There appeared to be no motive on her part but *self*—no feeling for the nearest of kin to her who were gone. The language (now that I reflect upon it) was studiously *equivocal*—no faltering— —I think it had been learned by heart.

Augusta went on to express gratitude for kindnesses to herself and her family ; the narrative continues :

> My feelings broke loose from all control, and I said something about its having been all in vain—I felt utterly hopeless, and asked to be left alone to compose myself.

Was not the interview foredoomed ! Byron's enmity and the supposed fostering of it were evidently not touched on during their tête-à-tête, for when after a few minutes Annabella went in to the others, she " determined to make one appeal to her [Augusta's] sense of justice towards the dead " ; and then spoke of the suspicions, saying that they referred only to correspondence after Byron had left England in 1816 (" for I felt that she was apprehensive "). Probably in that moment it dawned on Augusta that Robertson knew the whole. She defended herself, said that Byron's letters to her would show that she had never done Annabella any injustice in her correspondence with him (we have seen that this was the truth), that he, " poor soul," was very unjust, but not through any irritating words of hers. Annabella remarked that there was a difference between exasperating and not softening (" I thought of her smooth way of making mischief ") ; but added that she did not speak as Augusta's judge.

The subject was dropped ; after some time Augusta resumed it. " I then declared, and in the strongest manner, that I had not had any feeling about *myself* in making this appeal."

Now—but in all her goosishness ; no worse, as her letters afterwards will convince the reader—Augusta took the false step which seemed to her accuser unforgivable.

> She said that she had recollected a proof that she had acted justly towards me, for Sir J. Hobhouse had said to her, in speaking of what she had said of me to Lord Byron : " You risked his affection by doing so." [1]

> At *such* a testimony I started up, and all but uttered an ironical answer—but she had *trusted me unconditionally*, and I replied : " I don't understand it." From that moment there was a mingling of indignation with the intense pity I had before felt—and I was afraid of myself. I said, I believe, that I should always wish her the blessing I could not give her, or something kind if my tears did not prevent my uttering it— but the strongest desire to be out of her presence took possession of me, lest I should be tempted beyond my strength.

And the narrative ends :

> My calm conclusion is that the state of her mind was absolutely unimpressible by any representations of mine, which is some consolation for my own deficiencies or want of judgment in any respect, overcome as I was by feelings that have not yet been brought under perfect subjection.

Did she know what one of those feelings was ? Like a long tongue of flame it had crept—had always crept—among the ashes of her ever-dying, ever-reviving love for Augusta. Jealousy that was latent hatred, flickering up, repressed ; breaking out again, repressed again. . . . Did Annabella know anything of this ? Nothing, adept at self-deception as she was. Words had been her snare from childhood—words in which she believed, to which she trusted. . . . For an instant, now, they failed her ; helplessly she cried out, not knowing what she said : " I don't understand it ! " There was no meaning in that cry. What was it that she did not understand ? The thing that had happened

---

[1] In Robertson's " postscript," attesting this memorandum, Hobhouse's words are given thus : " You not only risked the loss of property, but what was much dearer to you, his affection " (*Lady Noel Byron and the Leighs*, p. 222).

was plain enough—in this hour of stern accusation, it was to Hobhouse that Augusta had appealed. That was the insufferable ; but why ? Was it because for Hobhouse too a jealousy as fierce, and still more ambiguous, had smouldered in the past ? Distrust and resentment had soon ruled her feeling for Byron's bosom-friend ; had these grown into suspicions unavowed, inex-pressible ? Hobhouse and Kinnaird—" the Piccadilly crew "—had stood openly for drink, dissipation, low company ; what besides had they come to stand for in the young wife's roughly-awakened perceptions ? . . . But only for a moment was she now inarticulate. Clutching at set phrases of forgiveness, of " blessing," she regained her poise ; and never knew that for an instant she had hated Augusta with all the force of her being.

They parted. She who had already resolved never to see again the face in which she had now seen death, went out with her friend ; the servant took Mrs. Leigh to the train for London ; and the White Hart's private sitting-rooms were free for the more usual kind of rendezvous.

Each woman took away her clear impression of the interview, different as could be from one another. Letters were at once exchanged. Augusta was (even in her it is surprising !) " unable to resist signing herself yours affectionately " in answer to a note —not in Annabella's hand—announcing safe return. " The tone," wrote Lady Byron to Robertson, sending him the letter, " is very unpleasant to me—its *glissant* character, as if everything were smoothed over. To give that impression to others was perhaps her object. I have sought to give a mild rebuke."

Here is the mild rebuke :

> Your letter . . . affords the last proof that during our inter-view, trying and painful as it was to me, I did not for a moment forget the consideration I was bound to observe by your having trusted me *unconditionally*.
> As I have received the communication which you have so long and anxiously desired to make—and upon which I offered no comment except " Is that All ? "—I have done all in my power to contribute to your peace of mind. But I remain

under the afflicting persuasion that it is not attained by such means as you have taken.   Farewell.

A. I. NOEL BYRON.

A copy was sent to Robertson ; he was to add his initials— again for purposes of record.   If any answer came, she would send it unopened to him to be returned to the writer, if he approved that course.   But (she went on) his moral view of the circumstances would be incomplete if she did not tell him the retribution which her failure had brought to herself.

I am made to feel still more strongly than in other cases where I have been powerless to do good, *why* it is.   I am made to recall even what is so far back as my defective filial duty— my self-pleasing in the *choice* of duties—my indulgence in wrong trains of thought—my acting under the influence of secondary motives instead of doing right for right's sake.   .
By all these I have lost, or failed to gain, the moral power which might have been instrumental to another's salvation.

Humble enough in spirit ; but like so much self-analysis, too elaborate !   One word, in this instance, would have summed-up her failure—Mrs. Jameson's word, Implacability.   Easier for human nature to confess any fault than that fault.

After some little time an answer did come.   It was returned by Robertson : " Lady Byron considers the correspondence to have been entirely closed by the last letter which she sent."   Augusta had written :

I feel sure that you would not willingly be unjust. . . .   I have therefore determined again to address you.   My great wish for an interview arose partly from a secret desire to see you once more in this world, and still more to have the means of convincing you that accusations . . . brought against me were unfounded ; and at this, if only from the recollection of the affection that once subsisted between us, you cannot be surprised.   I had not, and never implied that I had, anything to reveal to you with which *you* were not previously acquainted on any other subject.   Nor can I at all express to you the regret I have felt ever since those words escaped you, showing that you imagined I had " encouraged a bitterness of feeling in Lord Byron towards you."   I can as solemnly declare as if I were on my oath or on my death-bed that I never did so in any one instance, but that I invariably did the contrary.

She added that it would be a comfort to her to see Mr. Robertson, and afford him every proof in her power of her veracity. " It was clear that he thought I was keeping back some communications which ought to be made to you." And when her letter came back to her, she sent it to him (re-writing the second sheet) and begged that he would read it. " There was a kindness in your manner which makes me very desirous that *you* at least should know the truth."

Robertson evidently wished to see her, though to Annabella he wrapped up his willingness in phrases about injured innocence and sins, and this further interview being no more than a forlorn hope. He would do exactly as his friend thought best. His friend " confidently " took upon herself the responsibility of " precluding Mrs. Leigh's intended justification. . . . The opportunity for garbled representations could not be resisted." Accordingly he declined in a long letter, very little expressive of the kindness Augusta had thought to perceive. " The proofs you desire to give could only be given in Lady Byron's presence, and she will never consent to another meeting."

It is clear, from Augusta's vehement words, that the explanations to be given had by her been expected to refer to the Medora episode—her own ambiguous conduct, the failure to maintain her daughter ; and, for herself to receive, some expression of regret for the persistent harshness shown to her. Among the headings in Annabella's memorandum there had stood : " Elizabeth—how, where—my line of conduct." . . . What was said of this is hidden from us ; our one clue is : " The things I had meant to say, had the character of her communication been different, would have been out of place altogether." These may have been what another heading points to : " I have wronged, by assisting self-deception—will repair it." Incomprehensible, as it stands ; the whole incident is indeed so baffling that it is vain to dwell upon it further. What Annabella and her witness had hoped from it, they alone could tell ; to us it seems that—even without her fatal blunder—Augusta was condemned beforehand, that nothing she could have said would have saved her from that " afflicting persuasion."

A few months later she was dying. Annabella wrote, went to enquire, offered assistance. Her offer was at first declined ; a fortnight afterwards Emily wrote that there " *was* a pecuniary difficulty." . . . The old tragi-comedy—and it was felt. Though it was " gratifying to be able to render this poor service," the service seemed poor indeed ; memories came, and remorse came with them. She wrote to Emily, alone by the death-bed, bidding her whisper " two words of affection long disused." *Dearest Augusta*. . . . " I was told in answer that tears long dry had flowed again, and that those words were ' joy—her greatest consolation,' with a message unintelligible to the hearer. . . . A *second* message lost ! "

Three or four days later, on the morning of October 12, 1851, Augusta was dead. " A second message lost "—it need not have been lost, she would gladly have spoken it on the day at Reigate ; and still for many months the Other A. brooded on her failure. In 1853 she wrote of it again to Robertson with a like humility, a like blindness to the real failure—human in that as in so much else.

Even for herself she had the lack of imaginative sympathy which accounts for so many of her severities. She could not follow her own windings and turnings, her own flight from self-recognition ; she never saw the flickering tongue of flame among the ashes—the latent hatred, seen by her mother in Augusta though not in her. More truly, perhaps, to be seen in her— deluded as she was by her words and deeds of kindness, fettered by her promise ; and loving too, although unconsciously hating, the one who had frustrated what " might have been."

But there was endeavour after endeavour to understand, to explain herself. Letters to Mrs. Villiers, to Robertson, to Emily Leigh. To Emily she showed every kindness—advised her, helped with other relatives and friends to maintain her, left penniless as she was ; but was met with a certain aloofness and mistrust. She sought to dispel this by a long sad letter. " I only wish my poor mother had been aware of your strong affection," wrote Emily in answer ; " she grieved so very much over her interview with you."

It was the irrevocable. Her sense of failure grew ; but with it her sense of injury. " I have never," she wrote to Robertson,

" been ill-used to any great extent except by those for whom I had gone beyond the common limits of kindness." And the last touch of irony was given when in 1854 the Byron affairs were brought forward in the Court of Chancery ; " where 26 Money-Lenders appeared as the present Claimants of all property over and above the Capital necessary to secure my Jointure, and of that after my death. How little was such a result anticipated by the Testator ! "

" Be kind to Augusta." She had kept her promise so nearly to the end that to have failed at the end was bitter. It haunted her ; only that last message could lay the ghost. " There was enough to make me thank God that I had done it."

CHAPTER XXVII

1851-1860
DEATH OF ROBERTSON: THE END

THERE was still a Leigh to be kind to—Emily ; " poor child !
left penniless alone at the Palace with Birds and a Dog," wrote
Mrs. Villiers, whose capitals somehow suggest that Birds and a
Dog would have been an aggravation of solitude for her.   It was
not a period for household pets ; Augusta had perhaps copied her
dearest B.'s fancy for having animals about him.

One of the many anxieties was for the safety of Augusta's
letters from Byron.   She had sold some of them to Murray, but had
enjoined on Emily to buy them back " whenever she had money
enough."   It was soon evident that Emily never would have
money enough, for though everything was left to her, the little
that everything represented would be swallowed up by earlier
appointments to the rest of the children.   Relatives and friends
combined to provide a " pittance " ; Lady Horton promised to
contribute, but added : " All I protest against is having anything
to do with any other members of her Family.   They have long
enough been " Beggars " to be quite inured to it, and I fear
worse.   The Furniture had far better be sold for what it would
fetch . . . most certainly I would give *nothing* to save Furniture
or things in which others of course have interest."

Poor Emily, with Furniture, Birds, and Dog reft from her by
these kindly hands, and these kindly voices assuring her that all
was for her good—it is no new situation, but always newly
piteous.   Among them they raised £120 a year—" not to be considered permanent at present."   Distrust of the brothers inspired
this condition, as also that by which Emily had no control over
her annuity.   She was asked where she wished to live, and chose
London, for there alone she had friends and felt that she would
very soon be forgotten by all if she did not see them.   So, " truly

and humbly enough," she was reported to have said.   They all assured one another that she was much improved, wished to do right, was grateful and submissive. . . .   Perhaps the inner workings of benevolence should never be laid bare.

Mrs. Villiers, the moving spirit, had named several relatives as possible contributors ;   " but the poor girl says her mother has been so helped by Lord C. [Carlisle] and the Duke of Sutherland, the Duchess of Norfolk, etc., that she can't bear to have her name mentioned to any one of them . . . indeed Emily says that every friend they had has helped her mother—the money-lenders must have been the robbers, or how could it all go ! "

" Blackmail," Lady Byron might have answered from her knowledge of Augusta's terrors ; instead, she wrote :

> In every life that I have looked into with close intimacy, the mystery of its course appeared to me explained by the results of that course, except in cases where there had been a kind of Moral Idiotcy from birth, as in that of my poor sister.

Yet could there have been a stronger confirmation of her theory than that very Moral Idiotcy and those results !

Lady Chichester, Augusta's half-sister, was stopping at Brighton in the month after Augusta's death.   " Shall I be *cruel* enough to visit her ? " wrote Annabella to Mrs. Villiers.   " Of course I should avoid, as I always have done, Family matters—and this reminds me of the reason for not opening that packet sent to me . . . about poor Elizabeth's concerns, several years ago."   She went on to explain this as having been regard for Lady Chichester's feelings, for she had felt morally certain then, " and *am still more so now*," that she would have to expose misrepresentations and enter into the whole story of her relation with Augusta.   " I preferred being misunderstood to . . . giving so much pain to so good and kind a heart as the sister's."

She was then under the influence of that ploughing-up of the past with Robertson.   Eleven years do much either to open or close our eyes to motives long-ago ; if hers seem to us rather to have closed than opened, we must not forget the excitement of such daily confidences.   It was now that she drew up the synopsis for a memoir of herself in which—with a transparent veil thrown

over minor circumstances—she proposed to recount her experience
with Byron from their first meeting to the end. Here, however,
we find little self-deception ; writing alone, without Robertson's
extreme of sympathetic horror to shed limelight on the past, she
could read it with clearer vision. Of her final resolve to separate
she wrote, in this mere jotting-down of notes to be worked from
later :

> The responsibility of her future course was thrown upon her,
> beyond the possibility of escape. Her belief in the reality of
> Good and Evil, often as he had tried to confound them, had
> not been destroyed ... but the Will recoiled. ... She was
> helped by his conduct—and above all by the consideration of
> what might be saved to *him*, what mercy it was to *take away
> power* from one who was bent, whether sane or insane, to abuse
> it. She said to herself : " It is *for his sake.*" Those words
> returned to her memory when he died.

> And it was *done*. She parted in tender peace from him, he
> from her with icy coldness. ... It was before midnight—
> another night to be passed under that roof—and where his
> steps were still heard. Might there not be an alternative ?
> This thought came with the morning light, and her resolution
> seemed unnerved. She *could not* have passed his door, she
> must have cast herself on the ground (such was her violent
> impulse) but for the hope that he was insane, and she should
> be recalled.

> From the moment that he had accomplished the end which
> he repeatedly confest that he entertained from the first, of
> estranging her and throwing the blame of the desertion on her,
> he began to regret it ; next, he defied those regrets ; but
> whether he ever conquered them, none can know. She, on the
> contrary, who had resisted his designs to the utmost, and had
> felt it would be the greatest of calamities, never afterwards
> wished to be re-united. The future state of each mind was
> unknown to itself.

> The World's voice was heard. ... It was nearly the echo of
> his Will. She was passive. ... Had she desired to " justify
> herself," who was her witness ? He only, who had accused
> her under the mask of tenderness. ... Often, when kindly
> sympathies were denied, she has made the reflection that had
> the positions of her censors and herself been reversed, she
> would in all probability have spoken and felt as they did—
> from her natural feeling for the class of characters to which he
> belonged. She has no impression, therefore, of having been

judged unkindly, in any single instance, by individuals.   As to the Press, its condemnation was obviously the result of prejudices and illusions.

And now with the lapse of 35 years, she looks back on the Past as a calm Spectator, and *at last* can speak of it.   She sees what was—what *might* have been, had there been one person less amongst the living when she married.   Then she might have had duties, however steeped in sorrow, more congenial with her nature than those she was compelled to adopt.   Then her life would not have been the concealment of a Truth, whilst her conduct was in harmony with it (no wonder if she was misunderstood).   But such visions may even now be dangerous. . . .   Let the Fact work out its end.

The one exaggeration there is of her own unshaken resolution ; we have heard the cry from Kirkby to Augusta : " Oh, that I were in London, if in the coal-hold ! "   But the rest has all her sincere, and justified, conviction that *she* " could be no good," that only because Byron had lost her did he wish for her return.

Her absorption in these memories coloured another interest of 1851—the attempt to instil her own unorthodox religious creed into her young friend, Caroline Bathurst.   There were many letters—for the most part negligible, but in one we find a revealing passage.   They had been talking " in Regent's Park " of the love of God ; from Brighton she afterwards wrote of this :

In how many external ways can we love a person ?   With our voice—in its tones and utterances ; with our eyes in their expression ; with our touch in its heart-pressure.

These are the symbols—but after all *only* the symbols.   What the temple is to the worshipper—but he has a shrine within independent of them. . . .   Is it not better to recollect that the outward is but the passing sign of the inward, & to keep it in such subjection that it shall never become in itself of importance ?   Then it will never be worth a question.   If we were suddenly transformed to spirits there would be no change.

These are not the doctrines of age.   The only difference with me between the prime of life & the decline is that I dare

now own what was concealed in earlier years. Every temptation to indulge in the sign has been known to me—*is* known,
strange to say ! But instead of sternly repressing my impulses,
I infuse into them such reverence for their object that they
form a halo, " a charmed circle," round it.

There ! Make what you can of it !

We picture Byron thus haloed ; and if we smile for him, must
sigh for her. Imaginative passion, without the imaginative
sympathy which would have yielded to " the temptation to
indulge in the sign "—what was this but the sublimated self-
sufficingness, the narcissism (as we call it now) which more and
more reveals itself as the essential of her nature ? She dwelt in
an Atlantis of her own creation, gazing on the image of a woman's
love, *her* love, and reckoning with no other's image of what
woman's love might be. With her unconscious arrogance of
spirituality, her " reverence for the object," to Byron she seemed
—inevitably—*la fiera moglie*, the cold concentrated paragon
against whom he raved when he finally repulsed him. Himself
(despite his cynicism in love-affairs) a creature of the affections,
with heart that " always alighted on the nearest perch," the last
thing he wanted was to have a charmed circle drawn around him.
Guss, with her " finger in eye," her lavish phrases of endearment,
locks of hair and secret signs and trinkets worn because B. wore
their counterparts—the fool delighted in because she could be
such a fool, could be made to laugh at anything . . . that was the
love which suited him, torn as he was between two extremes of
consciousness—what we now term the " inferiority complex "
and its opposite. He too had his narcissism, heaven knows ; but
had as well his sense of predestined disaster, of " ruining all I
come near " ; and, besides, his memories ineffaceable and mortifying of life with his mother, of the long social obscurity, the
scorns of his frigid guardian. He needed above all the very
things which Augusta alone could give him—knowledge of his
blighted adolescence, without overweighted compassion, without
insistence on his darker moods. Guss did not need to be told he
was " facetious " ; Guss drew no charmed circle, fitted on no halo,
worship him as she might. . . . " There—make what you can of
it," said Annabella of her transcendental love ; and perhaps
Caroline Bathurst was like Byron, and could make nothing of it.

This remoteness was increasing as she grew older. Of Robertson she wrote at the same period to Caroline : " I heard him preach yesterday . . . and felt that he was calmer, more at rest within. It made me happier—yet I did not care to see him ! I hope it is a preparation for invisibility that I so delight in being unseen and near my friends." That—despite her constant kindnesses, her house that was Liberty Hall, her many and often-welcomed friends—is the keynote of her narcissism, which was by no means egotism, which indeed lies oftenest in natures that know not egotism, that are ardent in the service of others precisely because they suffice unto themselves. . . . It was in this 1851 that she wrote in her note-book—not long before the last meeting with Augusta : " Pure passion never dies. Impure passion has death in itself. The line ' Alas ! they love not long who love so *well* ' (B.) should be corrected ' who love so *ill* '." But we feel decidedly less sympathetic when with all her pedantry she adds : " Stages of declension : romantic—sensual—vicious—cold— callous (*with men*, malignant)." Something too much of detachment there ! And later in the year she spent an hour with Rogers ; of this she wrote afterwards to Mrs. Jameson (then as yet uncondemned) :

Mr. Rogers alluded to Lord Byron touchingly—& in that affectionate feeling we were one. He went on to say, " And with all his faults he was so generous." Could I, ought I, to have been anything but *silent* ? I might have replied, for these thoughts rose in my mind : " What—he who betrayed the women he seduced, & turned the whole power of the Press against the defenceless ? "

On what grounds can Rogers like or esteem *me* ? If Lord Byron were " generous," whatever might have been his faults towards me, my line of conduct was ungenerous. To one capable of generosity of *conduct* I should have been indulgent and relenting, instead of inflexible, when I was asked for re-union.

With Mr. Rogers, when I did speak, I turned the conversation to Lord Byron's freedom from all literary jealousy, & told the anecdote of his calling the Reviewers " fools " for preferring *Lara* to *Jacqueline,* in private with me. I added, " I must confess, Mr. Rogers, that *I* did not agree with him." It was not, I feel certain, without a deep conviction that Rogers replied, " *You* were right."

What Mrs. Jameson said in reply we do not know; she was answered thus:

"Generous" was used unequivocally in its moral sense, as opposed to selfishness and meanness. There were *acts* of pecuniary generosity to which I willingly bear witness. I will mention two gifts made by Lord Byron some years before my marriage :—£1000 to the Falklands, & a sum not less, perhaps larger (for I forget), to Hodgson first as a Loan. With his (Lord B.'s) embarrassed circum^s: & desire of those indulgences which money would have procured, those donations must have been greater sacrifices than they would have been to one content with the common pleasures of life. My opinion was, from the contrast which I observed in his pecuniary dealings after I knew him with those previous facts, that the former phase of character had passed away, or was clouded over by the pressure of existing interests. Indeed he told me as much, & before he wrote it in *Don Juan*, expressed his consciousness of the "old-gentlemanly vice."

That was written on the Christmas Day of 1851; "the only Christmas I ever spent alone," she wrote to Caroline Bathurst, "and but for one feeling none would have been happier." She was alluding to Robertson's having been taken ill in church. "The hollies seemed to change to cypresses." ... It was the warning before the end; the invisibility welcomed in anticipation for herself was drawing near for Robertson. Ever since his coming to Brighton he had been overworked beyond all measure: "he never seems to have had the art of managing himself wisely," writes his best biographer, Frederick Arnold.[1] The two sermons on Sundays came to seem an impossibility: "Would to God," he exclaimed, "that I were not a mere pepper-cruet to give a relish to Brightonian palates!" From this time he failed visibly. Though when Ada Lovelace died in 1852 he was able to be with her to the last, it was plain that he would not long survive her; his last letter, written in the first week of July 1853, gives a piteously humorous account of his incessant fainting-fits: "F.W.R. looking like a ghostly turnip ... blisters behind the ears to allay suffering in the brain, morphia to give some chance of rest. ... I am tired. I can write no more."

---

[1] *Robertson of Brighton*, by Frederick Arnold, 1886.

On August 15 he died. His funeral was such as Brighton had never seen before or since—so Arnold wrote in 1886 ; and he continues : " There was in the immense *cortège* one illustrious lady, sincerest of mourners. With a singularity that was in full unison with an eccentric but noble life, Lady Byron ... refused to use her carriage. She was not worthy, she said, even to walk behind the hearse." ... Soon afterwards she heard (from a distance) of his grave being covered with flowers ; this inspired some lines which were printed and privately circulated.

> I may not strew with earth-born flowers the turf
>> where thou art laid,
> But flowers there are which Love may rear, and
>> such as cannot fade. ...
> If parted clouds a moment showed the blue
>> depths of thy soul,
> 'Twas but to prove them far beyond the
>> skies where thunders roll.

Had Robertson been free, had their ages been less disparate, this was the one other man she could have loved ; and he could have loved her. But the gods saw it otherwise ; she was to be Byron's to the last.

For a while she thought of writing Robertson's biography, as she had been asked to do. " If I did not feel sure I could prevent mischief I should decline." But this was not to be ; his brother ultimately edited the sermons, with a short notice of the life. ... Much is said in Arnold's book of Lady Byron's literary powers ; he tells us that " in early life she had begun to form literary plans of some extent." We cannot agree with his ingenuous admiration for her writings ; nor do we find anything in the Lovelace Papers which points to such ambitions—unless the girlish dream of Translations from Horace (indubitably an extensive plan) are to be so regarded. But Arnold is often grossly inaccurate in his chapter on her—nowhere more so than in the statement that she placed a quantity of *printed* matter in the hands of a well-known resident of Brighton, " supposed to constitute a case completely exculpatory of herself and condemnatory of Byron." No papers were ever printed during her lifetime. Arnold goes on to declare that this gentleman, finding nothing against Byron in the documents, returned them to her as " a brief which he was unable to hold " ; and that after Robertson's death they were handed to another clergyman, then a Presbyterian but later " beneficed in the Church of England." This was the Rev. Alexander Ross, of whom there is mention in *Ralph, Earl of Lovelace* [1] as having been desirous of editing a collection of Lady Byron's letters. Mr. Ross was acquainted with the whole story, and had long been among her correspondents. In 1869 Lord Wentworth (as the second Earl of Lovelace then was) had intended to collaborate with Mr. Ross in this publication of his grandmother's letters ; but other things intervened, and the plan was never carried out.

In 1853—before Robertson's death, but not before his health was evidently shattered—there is the following letter to Lady Byron from her friend, Francis Trench, brother of the renowned Archbishop of Dublin :

It appears to me that to seek confidence or communications on subjects of the kind, at once so important and delicate, to which your note refers, is the part of a busybody ; but to *reject, or feel indifferent* to them, when offered by a valued friend like yourself, would be most unsympathizing, and wrong in many respects. I therefore accept with sincere thanks the permission you give me, seeing and feeling strongly how much and on how many points the death of Lady Lovelace may bring altered claims and duties into requirement, and how entirely you and you only are now to be the *one*, by whose judgment and decision the matter in question is to be settled.

And at the same time she wrote to Miss Montgomery (" M.M.") : " To the explanation I propose to give, it should be added that there were *pre-existing* causes of separation."

We know no more. One thing does seem certain—that towards the end of her life the impulse to confide in others, and those others men, not women (as had hitherto been the case) became frequent. But in contradiction of Arnold's statements there is the fact that all her papers were left to three trustees—Miss Mary Carpenter, Miss Frances Carr, and Mr. Henry Allen Bathurst—with instructions that they should not be published before 1880, and then only in these trustees' discretion. In 1856 there were the disclosures to Mrs. Beecher-Stowe—made, however, under a promise of

[1] A memoir of her husband, written by Mary, Countess of Lovelace, pp. 24-5. (1920.)

LADY NOEL BYRON IN HER OLD AGE

From a daguerreotype

secrecy. We know the sequel to that error of judgment. Unquestionably she departed more than once from her " policy of silence " ; but nothing more can be said with any confidence.

And it is worth remarking that Arnold, though he writes of her with veneration, seems to do this against the grain. There are many stings and pricks to discount the eulogies ; for instance : " She fully endorsed the doctrine of her own personal infallibility, assumed as an axiom that she was in the right, and anyone who contradicted her must be in the wrong " ; and apropos he quotes :

> I sit as God, holding no form of creed,
> But contemplating all.

Though there is some truth in that application of Tennyson's lines, we feel that Arnold at any rate must not only have contradicted her a good deal, but have been defeated in their arguments ! He continues, as evidence of what he calls her eccentricities : " She would lie in bed late (!) She would dress untidily "—an observation which does not agree with the portrait of her given here, or with a description quoted by himself from the *Noctes Ambrosianae* :

> Her silvery-white hair lent a grace to the transparent purity of her complexion, and her small hands had a pearly whiteness. She wore a plain widow's cap of a transparent material, and was dressed in some delicate shade of Lavender, which harmonised well with her complexion.

The last impression to be gathered from that is of carelessness in dress ; but Arnold persists : " Lady Byron never fully possessed the gift of order.[1] ... A desultory state of things prevailed generally. It was no unusual thing ... for the whole of her domestics to quit their situation in a body." And he seems to feel no inconsistency when he adds : " Nothing ever disturbed the smoothness of her arrangements " !

After Robertson's death she devoted herself to her grandson Ralph King, of whom another hand than mine writes here. Her

---

[1] In that, if it was true, Ada resembled her. Lord Lovelace's letters to Lady Byron about his " Bird " are full of laments over her untidiness.

elder grandson, Lord Ockham, had for some time been a great anxiety. He had been put into the Royal Navy at the necessarily early age which too often proves to be too early, as it did with him. His desire to leave that rigidly disciplined service, though not the seafaring life, was frowned upon by his father; this resulted in the boy's flight from his ship. There is a letter from Miss Mitford (she was a friend of one of the Noel brothers) to an American correspondent, giving an account which she had had from Mr. Noel of the revolt.

> While his poor mother was dying her death of martyrdom from an inward cancer . . . her husband, engrossed by her, left this lad to his sister and the Governess. It was a dull life, and he ran away. . . . He had sent a carpet-bag containing his gentleman's clothes to his father in London. He was therefore disguised. . . . At Liverpool he was found before long . . . dressed as a sailor-boy, at a low public-house surrounded by seamen of both nations.

From Liverpool he was taken to Paris, thence to return to his ship for a twelvemonth and then decide on his future course. The consequence was that he deserted his ship, " found his way on to a small trading-vessel, and worked his way home from the Black Sea before the mast. The voyage lasted many months, during which he was completely lost sight of by his family. Finally he landed at Hull, very ill and in rags." [1] He made himself known to "some Yorkshire friends of Lady Byron's, who took him in and sheltered him until relatives and friends intervened and insisted on some provision being made for him by his father, who never forgave him."[1] Lord Ockham dropped all the social advantages of his position, and worked as a poor man among the poor—for some time in a shipbuilder's yard under the name of John Okey.

Lady Byron felt a strong sympathy with him, describing him as " simple, honest, odd "; and in a letter to George MacDonald as " a *man*, in one sense at least." To Mrs. Beecher-Stowe she said, " He is now going through an experience which may yet fit him to do great good when he comes to the peerage. . . . I think I have great influence over Ockham." He never came to the

[1] *Ralph, Earl of Lovelace.*

peerage, dying in 1862 (at twenty-six) of consumption as a result of the hardships endured at sea.

After her grandson Ralph grew up and went to Oxford, Lady Byron's life was lonely. In 1855 began the friendship with George MacDonald already touched on ; though but a pale reflection of what she had felt for Robertson, it was precious to the solitary woman—she left him a little legacy. There was Mary Carpenter, too, with her reformatory schools to be benefited, and the Red Lodge at Bristol to be bought for her.[1] But we feel that the renewal with Robertson of her emotional life was as the flash before the lamp expires ; after his death the projected memoir of herself was laid aside—only the fragmentary notes remain. When Moore's Journal was published in 1853 she wrote to Mrs. George Lamb from Esher, then her home—for the house in Brighton was given up when Robertson died :

> As to myself I have no reason to complain. It seems to be thought that a private letter of mine ought not to have been published without my leave, and especially as the letter to which it was an answer was not presented to the reader—but I am not unwilling that my reasons (my *chief* one, at least, and which no longer exists) for avoiding the public discussion of my affairs should be made known. I hear that the tone of my letter is thought cold and hard—and no doubt it was so. After my separation it was necessary for my personal security and the interest of my child that every communication I made to Lord B. should be revised or dictated by Legal Advisers—and it was no more *my own* in style, than any Deed or Will drawn up by a Lawyer with my concurrence. People are not aware that an Agreement for a Separation is invalidated by any words or proceedings which appear like a renewal of former ties.

[1] Inscription on a Tablet erected in Red Lodge Reformatory, Bristol, 1860 :

SACRED

To the memory of Anne Isabella Noel, Dowager Lady Byron, who, ever devoting the many talents entrusted to her to the service of her Master, purchased these premises, September 1854, for the purpose of rescuing young girls from sin and misery, and bringing them back to the paths of holiness.

She was born May 17th, 1792, and departed this life May 16th, 1860.

" Faithful unto death."

The letter alluded to was that refusing to read the Memoirs. Of them she added :

According to the information I received at the time the Memoirs were burnt, I had no doubt that Murray was *really* the loser, tho' Lord Lansdowne maintained the cause of Moore. The documents now produced, including a letter printed for private circulation by the present Murray, and written to Sir R. Wilmot Horton by old Murray, must I think convince anyone of that fact.

Mrs. George Lamb—the Caro George of the long-ago London Seasons, when Caro William had eclipsed the younger " little sheep "—and Miss Montgomery were the only intimates of her girlhood who survived her. Mrs. Villiers, long " immovable from infirmity," died in 1856 ; in the same year died Lord Scarsdale, one of the Curzon connection who had been in the succession to the Wentworth estates in Leicestershire. At his death Lady Byron should have been free to leave them as she pleased ; but she had allowed them to be included in the Lovelace marriage-settlement, which provided that if the wife pre-deceased her husband they should remain with him for life, passing afterwards to the children. The possibility that Ada might die before her mother, and that the estate might pass direct to Lady Byron's son-in-law, had not been thought of. . . . Her complete estrangement from him made this painful to her. " It is not a pleasant position for me," she wrote, " to be the only intermediate heir of the property."[1]

Ham Common was her abode in this year ; later she went to Hastings and moved between that and London until 1860, with an interval of acute illness in 1858. Mary Carpenter was then with her ; they had much in common, much " soul-communion " —but in this friendship as in others there is that sense of the light gone out, of the " desert spread before her " being indeed a desert. She had her old solace, work for others ; but now it was restricted by her growing infirmities. Only one Byron interest remained— Emily Leigh. A contributor to the annuity had died ; Lady Byron offered to add £10 " during pleasure " to the share she took in supporting her god-daughter.

[1] The result of the settlement was that Lord Lovelace enjoyed the estates for thirty-three years—that is, from 1860 to the last day of December, 1893.

In the last two years of her life the correspondence with George MacDonald is our principal record.   Besides her drastic criticism of his readings, there were home-truths about a drama in which one of the dialogues seemed to her " flat " ; MacDonald, as before, thanked her—but added that another friend had found the same dialogue " effervescent," so much so as rather to surprise the reader.   It was in reply to this that she recommended a course of the Newgate Calendar.   Not only in criticism was she active ; there is an amusing letter to her from " young De Morgan " (who was probably the William De Morgan of our day) about the projected purchase and furnishing for MacDonald of the De Morgans' London house.   He gives estimates of the cost of furnishing " said house imperially, regally, aristocratically, respectably, genteelly, or *decently* "—as she might decide.   The peculiar turn of humour certainly points to the writer's having been the author of *Joseph Vance* and its many delightful successors.

At this time Lady Byron was much in London.   There are frequent invitations to the MacDonalds to " share our tea-dinner at 6 o'clock," the carriage to take them home " at 8 or later."   But there seems to have been no settled home : " Leaving London at last," she writes, " only to wander about at present . . . Richmond my first stage.   *I am not at my worst.*"

Very soon after this, she *was* at her worst.   Her grand-daughter, Lady Anne King, and a friend of Mrs. Jameson's introduction, Mrs. Barwell, were with her when on the day before her sixty-eighth birthday—May 16, 1860—she died at 11 St. George's Terrace in North London.   At eight o'clock in the morning of that day Mrs. Barwell wrote to Dr. Bence-Jones : " About four o'clock she passed from sleep without a pang or struggle."   Lady Anne King wrote to Mrs. George Lamb : " My darling suffered very much, except the few hours before the end.   The end was in sleep, which passed into the sleep of death—gently and calmly."

Her grave is at Kensal Green Cemetery.[1]

---

[1] Of plain grey stone, bearing only her name: "Ann Isabella Noel Byron," and the dates of birth and death.   Beside it stands a tall marble column inscribed with the names of several members of Dr. Lushington's family.   The place was probably chosen for that reason.

If Byron had lived till then, he would have been seventy-two. No effort of the imagination can picture him old ; how little that is so with her ! Age was implicit even in her girlhood's aspect. Some symbolism there—as of the devastating storm that by its very nature is short-lived, and the torn tree that yet has permanence within its being. He swept over her like the tempest, and was gone ; broken though she was, she had withstood the visitation.

"Her life was Spring and Winter." She herself, to Byron, was spring and winter—her love the troubling breath of April, her alienation the cold stillness of November, on the brow that had so unwillingly been haloed. Could he have known, on his tormented deathbed, that one day she would write of the Deans' rejections in 1834 and 1842 of Thorwaldsen's statue for Westminster Abbey, that the empty place could have but one effect—in his own words :

> The thought of Brutus, for he was not there

... could Byron have known that nearly twenty years after Missolonghi *la fiera moglie* would so passionately uphold his memory, what an amazement it would have been to him !

May we not think of it as another message lost—the third in their strange tragedy ? His own, Augusta's, this : the message which was all the life of Thursday's Child—longest of those three lives, and ever in it the thought of him who "was not there."

> Thou art wrapt as with a shroud,
> Thou art gathered in a cloud,
> And for ever shalt thou dwell
> In the spirit of this spell.

EPILOGUE

EPILOGUE

THE NEXT GENERATION

By MARY, COUNTESS OF LOVELACE

MY recollections of what I had heard in my husband's family of his mother Ada Byron, Countess of Lovelace, are, I regret to say, very slight and fragmentary. She was a pretty dark-haired woman of graceful figure and carriage, and we may assume that she had the lovely speaking voice for which her father was celebrated and which her children inherited. To these children she was always a very dear and sacred memory, and in their hearts a halo of romance for ever hung about her name. She was reputed to have been a neglectful mother, but little Annabella and Ralph King clearly found nothing wanting. If she concerned herself little with matters of tuition and discipline, leaving these mainly to their father and grandmother, she must have known how to inspire love and—when she chose—to express it. But she led a curiously detached existence, caring little for ordinary society, or even for the more satisfying pleasures and duties of country life. She was always absorbed in study. Miss E. C. Mayne, in her Life of Byron, quotes the following from an obituary notice of 1852 : " Her genius—for genius she possessed—was not poetic, but metaphysical and mathematical " ; and herself continues : " She translated and annotated Menabrea's *Notices sur la machine analytique de Mr. Babbage* (1842)—a defence of the famous calculating machine. She was not yet twenty-eight when she achieved that feat ; but she was no pedant. ' Her manners, tastes, accomplishments . . . were feminine in the nicest sense of the word.' Unlike her father in features, she ' inherited his mental vigour and intensity of purpose '."

But her studies were not always of the profound and abstract kind. She was fond of music and at one time gave herself up to learning and practising the violin.   There is a story that rather than interrupt this practice even for necessary air and exercise, she walked for hours at a time round and round a billiard-table, playing on her fiddle.

She cared little for dress, but once at least she chose to exercise her imagination upon it.   My mother [1] used to tell how she appeared at a Queen's Ball clad in a semi-Oriental dress, evidently meant to impersonate one of Byron's heroines.   Her hair in long dark plaits, and woven and tied with pearls, hung to her waist. Descriptions of this unusual garb passed rapidly in whispers from ear to ear, and in the course of the evening the whole company managed to file past the sofa on which she sat, pretending to talk to each other, but with sharp eyes fixed on every detail of the strange and picturesque figure.   Whether she or Lord Lovelace ever became aware of the attention she excited I do not know.

Her few real friendships were with people of intellectual power.   Babbage, for instance, and Mrs. Somerville, who had a great appreciation of her.   Her mathematical teacher, Professor Augustus De Morgan,[2] said of her that if she had been a man she could have been Senior Wrangler.

It was the genius and passion for calculation which led eventually to her undoing.   To a certain extent this taste was shared by her husband, and apparently it was together that they embarked on a disastrous career of gambling on horse-racing.   The will-of-the-wisp of an infallible system led them on ; but Lord Lovelace appears to have been quickly disillusioned.   No doubt he laid his commands upon his wife to desist from betting, but unfortunately she continued to do so unknown to him ; and presently she incurred heavy losses.   In her desperate need of money she pawned the family jewels, and then implored the help of her mother in redeeming them, and in concealing the whole transaction from Lord Lovelace.   Lady Byron redeemed the jewels at the cost of a large sum, she also paid other debts, and she kept her unhappy daughter's secret.   Lady Lovelace's fear

[1] My mother's family was allied to the Kings and Fortescues (Lord Lovelace's mother was a Fortescue), so Ada's personality naturally was very interesting to them.   I had heard much family gossip about her long before I married her son.

[2] Father of William De Morgan.   See App. III.

of her husband was of that keen sort which is based on the dread
of losing love.

Theirs had been a happy marriage. We have many letters
of his, written apparently when he had left her in London for a
few days while he went down to Surrey or Somerset to supervise
the work of his estates. They breathe deep devotion. Every
detail of his life is confided to her, and they are full of tenderness
for his " Avis," his " sweet Bird," as he called her. Alas ! for
the cloud which presently fell upon all this. It did not extinguish
love, but it darkened heavily their last year of life together. In
the summer of 1852 poor Ada, already stricken with the dread
disease—internal cancer—which killed her, found herself compelled to make full confession to her husband of all her debts and
disasters. To a proud man it must have been a most bitter
revelation, especially the fact that his wife had got herself into
the toils of an unscrupulous gang of betting-men, and that to
extricate her from their clutches must prove a humiliating and
well-nigh hopeless task. In his anger at the revelation of all
that had been concealed from him, he could hardly bring himself
to feel or to express any gratitude to Lady Byron for her generosity
in rescuing his property (the jewels), or for any of the help which
she had rendered.

Meantime she also had had revelations. The son-in-law whom
she had looked to as a bulwark, whom she had believed in as an
infallible restraining and protecting force to her daughter, had in
fact led that daughter into danger. He had joined in some of
the betting transactions and later, when a supposed full statement
of financial troubles had been made to her, his own betting-debts
had been kept out of it. How could she ever trust him again ?
Also she believed that when, some months previously, Ada had for
many weeks avoided all intercourse with her, this estrangement,
which had pained her cruelly, had been caused by his influence.

And all this time Ada grew more and more ill. Her sufferings
had become daily, hourly. Death came ever nearer.

The last weeks were passed in Lord Lovelace's house at 6 Great
Cumberland Place. Though her relations with him were now
strained, Lady Byron had perforce to be his guest. Ada, in the
midst of her suffering, was most pitiable in her self-reproach, and
Lady Byron alone, with her steadfast faith in a merciful God and

in a life to come, could bring light and hope into the death-chamber. She had the supreme comfort of being able to give comfort.

Did she think enough of the misery of the man beside her ? He cannot have had much part to play in the sick-room. His daily task was the unravelling of the tangle of debts, and the desperate turnings and twistings in which the unhappy Ada had enmeshed herself. He had to try and rescue her from the scoundrels who held her in thrall, and secure that at least her deathbed should be unmolested. He could not escape from the study of every detail of her madness, nor from the bitter memory of his own share in the beginnings of it. His friend, who was also Lady Byron's, Woronzow Greig,[1] was an invaluable helper to him in the necessary investigations, and as ambassador from him to the " scoundrels." (They are never mentioned otherwise in the correspondence !) This was now all that her husband could do for Ada. There was no comfort for him anywhere. The sky was black above him.

A few hours before the end Lady Byron said in a letter :

" I write in the hearing of her groans, and of the little Bull-finch singing carelessly his wonted airs. In the next room one whose feelings are far from [being] in harmony with mine. . . ."

Ada Byron died on November 27, 1852. By her own wish, they carried her to the old Newstead country, and laid her by the father whom she had never known.

A few weeks later Lord Lovelace wrote to Lady Byron, pleading for mutual sympathy and affection in their grief. She answered that there must first be explanation of certain things in his past conduct. He answered exculpating himself. She wrote again, reiterating her view of certain events. And so these two people, often, each of them, averring their desire for peace in touching terms, drifted into the enormous error of trying to settle their differences by written explanations. For many weeks long screeds in small crabbed writing passed between them. All the events, the acts, the words of the last sad year and more, were passed in review ; and there were many points as to which only she who was dead could have given exact testimony.

---

[1] Son of Mrs. Somerville by her first marriage.

Lady Byron was the first to recognise the futility of it all. She tried more than once to end it. Woronzow Greig intervened, and endeavoured to stem the streams of argument, but he was not successful. At last Lady Byron wrote to say that she could write no more—she was ill. The battle was inconclusive, but for very weariness the combatants dropped their arms.

Lady Byron had not closed the door ; she implied that she might write again. She did not mean to be " unforgiving " ; but, as far as I know, she never did write again. I think her courage must have failed her. The contest was never renewed, but neither was the old affectionate intercourse.

She had lost a son ; and he had lost the best and most inspiring influence of his life.

Many years later Ada's son quoted from the correspondence which I have described.

Lady Byron wrote on Jan. 4, 1853 :[1] " To you, Lovelace, I have been the most faithful of friends, & at no time more actively & self-sacrificingly than in the last year & a half."

And in his answer of January 6th, 1853, were these remarkable words :

> " And yet with all your severity and coldness, which drives me into these indignant remonstrances with you, the last page of your letter is too true for me not to re-echo and confirm it. You have been too noble and generous (in some things), self-denying in all, for me not to bear ready testimony to it. In most fine qualities you have not your equal on earth, and my love for you is as ardent as ever, however you may repel it. I hold you in respect and admiration more than ever—but your want of sympathy (in spite of all your gentleness) with those who do not feel exactly as you do, has cruelly destroyed what certainty, hope, & comfort remained to me."

Lord and Lady Lovelace had three children :

Byron (Viscount Ockham) born 1836.

Anne Isabella (Lady Anne Blunt) born 1837.

Ralph Gordon Noel King (for most of his life 13th Lord Wentworth, later 2nd Earl of Lovelace), born 1839.

[1] *Astarte* (1921), p. 195.

Of the eldest son Byron, that silent and gentle rebel against the whole system of Society, and of his sister Anne (or Annabella, as she was always called until after her marriage) I have written what I could elsewhere.[1]

The third child, Ralph, was made over by his parents at about nine years of age to the care of his grandmother, and his home was with her until she died. Lady Byron having undertaken to make him her principal heir, and to provide entirely for his education and maintenance, all control over him was surrendered to her. She had a fixed belief that school-life at Harrow had had a fatally corrupting influence over Byron, and she thought that by shielding her youthful grandson from all evil contacts she could mould his character successfully under her own eyes. Accordingly " Ralph's education [2] was almost entirely bookish, sedentary, solitary. He was isolated from boys and girls of his own age, and his only contact with the male sex was in the persons of a dreary succession of tutors, only one or two of whom seem to have been at all fitted for their office. If Lady Byron showed but little judgment in the choice of these unlucky gentlemen, she could at least be very firm with them when they had proved their incapacity, and the result was continual change and the lack of any continuity and discipline, which their pupil greatly regretted in afterlife. Lady Byron, herself an only child, and mother of an only daughter, must have been gaining some knowledge of ' the human boy ' for the first time in her life. She wrote (1850-52) : ' Master Ralph is making some experiments on Tutors' nature. I could prevent them, but I do not wish to mix an element which would falsify the result.' This was sensible, and there is abundant evidence that, as time went on, a very deep affection and an amount of mutual comprehension unusual in such a relationship subsisted between the old woman and the growing lad."

He was thirteen years old when his mother died. There was no deliberate intention to part him from his brother and sister, but the circumstances of their lives had to a great extent that result. His elder brother was almost continually absent at sea. His sister he saw oftener, but though he occasionally

---

[1] *Ralph Earl of Lovelace* : A Memoir. Christophers. 1920.

[2] I quote from the above short Memoir which I wrote of him in 1920.

visited his father's house where she lived, they never shared the same home for any long period.   He used to talk sadly in later life of his longing, as a little lonely boy, to see more of the handsome stalwart brother whom he vaguely idealised and worshipped from afar ; and for the comforting presence of his beloved sister, his only intimate.

Lady Byron cannot have fully realised all this.   Nor apparently did she ever perceive that the surroundings in which she kept him were utterly dull and barren from the point of view of a boy, and furnished a poor preparation for a manly life.   These surroundings were a series of hired houses near London (for she changed her dwelling every two or three years), and apparently neither she nor her grandson ever attached themselves to any one of these temporary homes, or ever made for themselves any local occupations or neighbourly ties.   She might have made her home at Kirkby, which was now hers ; and for her grandson the active country-life and the initiation into all the responsibilities and duties which fall upon a landowner, would have been invaluable. We must, however, respect her motives for resolving not to spend her life as the chatelaine of a great house.   She desired to live modestly, so as to devote a large portion of her income to charity, and to the furtherance of education and other philanthropic objects.

The only period of his youth which stood out prominently in Ralph's recollection as one that had been in its way fruitful to him, was that of their residence at Brighton.   Young as he was, he fell under the spell of the saintly Robertson, and was intensely fascinated by his eloquence.   Lady Byron related with pride how Ralph, when he must have been about twelve years old, understood and analysed Robertson's sermons.   But she, with her fragile health, was already beginning to feel the weight of the responsibility she had undertaken.   The daily companionship of an active boy must often have sorely taxed her strength.

There is a scrap of a letter to her daughter, probably written in 1851, speaking of a possible extension of Ralph's stay with his parents ; in which she says : " As to Ralph, you are welcome to extend *my* Holidays.   They do me good.   At the same time I am only Serva Servorum—and I hope as good to be *used* as to be *abused*—more could not be desired ! "

As the years passed, the sense of being hardly equal to the charge which she had undertaken evidently grew upon her. The following letters were written by her in 1857 to her friends Arthur Mair of Edinburgh and his wife " Lizzy," who was the daughter of the friend of her childhood Mrs. Henry Siddons, and granddaughter of the great Sarah :

To Arthur Mair, Esq., Edinburgh

EAST SHEEN, *Aug.* 15, 1857.

My dear friend, I wish you to be one in *need*, for I am hardly able to bear up between illness and responsibilities—and I have thought of making you my helper under an immediate difficulty.

This grandson of mine, Ralph—lately 18—and under no control but mine, which is legally none, is I am thankful to say, free from any vicious propensity or low habit—his tastes being pure and elevated, and his desire of knowledge almost too great. But he has the oddities and wilfulness belonging partly to his age, partly to nature and circumstances. There is so much physical in the case that for some years nothing has done him so much good morally as Travelling and change of scene and associations. I have in consequence formed a plan for his going to Scotland next week, *if* you will kindly receive him on his way to the Mountains and settle his Tour with him, undertaking that office as if you were his relative or Guardian, tho' I have allowed him to travel *alone*—reserving only, as my right, to direct his course and the duration of his wanderings. He would contend for more freedom still, because he wants to be left to go, as he says, where his fancy may lead him, *unknown* to anyone. To this I cannot consent. If he is emancipated from what he felt intolerable—the restraint of a Tutor—the obligation of his conforming in other respects to what I think reasonable and right, is the greater. This is the struggle between us.

To Mrs. Mair

August 20.

I am glad to say that Ralph does not seem as averse as I feared he would be to spending 2 or 3 days with you—if they should be extended I should think it very good for him. . . .

You will " pity the sorrows of a poor old "—Granny when you think of my having, *unaided by any human being*, to manage such a big thing as he is !—and will not wonder at my wishing

to take Mr. Mair into partnership and to make you Vice
Grandmama. Really I think it would prolong my life—but
it must be done very delicately if you enter into my views.

To Mrs. Mair

LONDON, *Sept.* 10th.

Dear Lizzy,—a word in one of my spare moments *here*—I
think Shakespeare the wholesomest food in the World—and
for Ralph's mind above all, which wants to feel " the World
akin."

In regulating her grandson's religious education Lady Byron's
leading idea appears to have been to make him think for himself.
He told me that he was never subjected to any compulsion as
to Church-going or in the performance of any religious duties.
She doubtless counted on the daily influence of her own character
and the atmosphere of the society which she gathered round
her, to counteract any possibility of indifference to the subject
on his part. She knew the character with which she was
dealing, which was one of great intellectual curiosity, and of
determination to avoid all shackles in matters of opinion. In
this latter characteristic they were in complete harmony, but the
influence exercised over the boy by Robertson must have been
very welcome to her.

Without apparently feeling any hostility to the Church of
England, she was certainly inclined to dispute its supremacy ;
and she had a strong leaning towards the Free Churches, having
many friends among their members, including the Unitarians.

The following letter written by Ralph during his first year at
Oxford, shows the complete confidence which reigned between
them, and the value that he set upon her counsel :

UNIV. COL., OXFORD, *Nov.* 20th, 1859.

Dear G. M. . . . . Next Sunday there is to be a communion
which all members of the college who were not present at the
last communion are expected to attend.

As you know, I should not in any case wish to join in one,
besides which I neither have been nor wish to be confirmed,
and I believe no one who has not been confirmed can take the
communion.   (I might go back a step further, and say I never
was baptized in what would be called a valid form of baptism,

without which one cannot be confirmed.[1])   What do you think I had better do ?   Simply not to go, or to say beforehand that I cannot ?   After hearing what you think I had perhaps better also ask Mr. Donkin, as he knows the ways of the place.

I think that what has been done in Univ. reform is far from being enough.   There is not enough freedom in studies or in discipline.   There is so much restraint as to be a great drawback to the industrious, but not enough to have the least effect upon the idle and extravagant, as may be seen in the case of Sir C. ——'s son.   What a mistake it is to suppose that going to chapel so many times and hearing the same words over and over again works as an exorcism on the follies of youth like the sign of the cross to the devil !   All forcing-down of religion seems to me a mixture of blasphemy and tyranny.   Judging by its fruits, the much praised classical education of the schools has a less good effect on the mind than some freer and less exclusive system would have.   To hold that even the best of authors like Cicero, Tacitus, Plato, Homer, &c. (not to speak of Ovid, Catullus, and that kind) include the whole of knowledge and education, and that if one has not read them one is good for nothing, seems to be chaining the living to the dead.   And none of the books of the ancients are *so* needful for us to read and understand as Shakspere, Goethe, Grimm and other newer books.

We have not Lady Byron's answer, but it is pretty certain that the position taken up in this letter would have had her sympathy.   She must however have counselled some form of compromise, for there is no evidence that Ralph suffered from the displeasure of the authorities.   He remained at Oxford for many months after this.

My story must now end.   The after-life of Lady Byron's grandson is not relevant here, and I have already told it elsewhere.

To the end of his life her teaching and the lofty inspiration of her character remained with him.

MARY LOVELACE.

[1] At the time of his birth his parents had adopted the tenets of the Unitarians, and were therefore averse to Christian Baptism.

APPENDIX I

LETTERS DURING THE EARLY MONTHS OF THE ENGAGEMENT—SEPTEMBER-OCTOBER, 1814

ANNABELLA's answer to Byron's renewed proposal reached him on September 18. He at once wrote the letter we have seen at the end of Chapter VII.

Next day, and the day after, he wrote again.

I wrote to you yesterday—not very intelligibly, I fear—and to your father in a more embarrassed manner than I could have wished ; but the fact is that I am even now apprehensive of having misunderstood you and of appearing presumptuous when I am only happy in the hope that you will not repent having made me more so than I ever thought to have been again.

Perhaps in some points our dispositions are not so contrasted as at times you have supposed ; but even if they were—I am not sure that a perfect sameness of character (a kind of impossibility by-the-bye) would assure the happiness of two human beings any more than an union of temper and pursuits of very dissimilar qualities. Our *pursuits* at least I think are not unlike. You have no great passion for the *world*, as it is called ; and both have those intellectual resources which are the best—if not the only preventives—of ennui of oneself or others. *My* habits, I trust, are not very anti-domestic. I have no pleasure in what is named Conviviality, nor is Gaming nor Hunting my vice or my amusement ; and with regard to other and perhaps far more objectionable faults & levities of former conduct—I know that I cannot exculpate myself to my own satisfaction, far less to yours ; yet there have been circumstances which would prove that although " sinning " I have also been " sinned against." I have long stood alone in life ; and my disposition, though I think not unaffectionate, was yet never calculated to acquire the friendships which are often *born* to others. The few that chance or circumstances have presented I have been fortunate enough to preserve—& some whom I could little have hoped to number amongst them.

I won't go on with this Egotism. Will you write to me soon ? I shall be in London on Thursday, I think. Do not answer oftener than is least irksome, but permit me to address you occasionally till I can see you—which I wish so much—and yet I feel more tremblingly alive to that meeting than I quite like to own to myself. When your letter arrived, my Sister was sitting near me and grew frightened at the effect of its contents—which was even painful for a moment—not a long one—nor am I often so shaken. I have written—yet hardly a word that I intended to say, except that you must pardon me for repeating so soon how entirely I am

yr. attached & sincere

Byron.

P.S.—Do not forget me to your father & mother—whom I hope to call mine.

Septr. 20*th* 1814.

There is one point on which—though you have not lately pressed it—I am sure you feel anxious on my behalf ; and to this will I speak. I mean Religion. When I tell you that I am so convinced of its importance in fixing the principles that I could never have had perfect confidence in any woman who was slightly impressed with its truth—you will hardly believe that I can exact more tolerance than I am willing to grant. I will not deny that my own impressions are by no means settled ; but that they are perverted to the extent which has been imputed to them on the ground of a few passages in works of fiction, I cannot admit to those whose esteem I would secure—although from a secret aversion from explanations & vindications I have hitherto entered into none to those who would never have made the charge but from a wish to condemn rather than convert. To you, my conduct must be different as my feelings. I am rather bewildered by the variety of tenets than inclined to dispute their foundation. In a word, I will read what books you please, hear what arguments you please ; and in leaving the choice to your judgement let it be a proof that my confidence in your understanding & your virtues is equal. You shall be " my Guide, Philosopher, and Friend ; " my whole heart is yours—and if possible let me make it not unworthy of her to whom it is bound, & from whom but one event can divide it. This is my third letter in three days—I will therefore shorten it. I proceed on my way to London tomorrow. With every sentiment of respect—and—may I add the word ?—Love—

ever yours

A.I.M. *to* B.

Seaham,
Thursday, September 22, 1814.

Your letters came today, and have done me the greatest good. It is indeed a pleasure to me to write when I need no longer measure, not my words, but my feelings. When conscious that the latter *would* exceed the bounds which I had imposed upon them, I was silent. You little suspected *why*. Since I made myself yours, I have had a happiness—deep as it promises to be durable ; not a moment of doubt, nothing but gratitude for all this—so unexpected. . . . Had I *known* that you suffered, the baseless fabric would sooner have fallen. It seemed almost selfish to seek what I *felt* would be so much for my own happiness that I forgot it could be as much for yours—God grant it may ! I have been very foolish, and if you had not been wiser, we might both still have been without hope.

On *your* part everything seems explained. . . . On mine something shall be said for your satisfaction or your amusement, of that *phantom* of an attachment—a " horrible shadow " to me, since it stood between us—though I should have some obligation to it, for had I not conjured it into being, my impulse to write to you would probably not have prevailed. Till the time of my acquaintance with you I had never been in danger of an attachment. Placed by Lady Melbourne's precipitancy in a situation where I thought decision a duty, I feared to risk a disappointment to you—and though aware that you could excite affection, I doubted if your character, as I then misconceived it from false accounts, *could* support that affection in one who loves only where she can *honour*. I resolved then to resign—irrevocably I thought—all power over your affections—lest mine should become engaged to you.

Here she gave the explanation about Hugh Montgomery, already quoted from ; and went on :

Then ensued my long silence to you. At last I *did* write, still determined not to know myself ; and when you asked an explanation, I was more inclined to revive than to remove the error. A sort of quiet despair possessed me—for you had assumed an *impossibility* of renewal on your part, and you repeated it more strongly in the answer to that very letter. It haunted me till I heard from you last week, and forced me into those hopeless determinations. Mr. M. was here for a fortnight some time ago, and we were very good friends, though I could not quite forgive him for having *innocently* been your rival. It is natural that you should suppose his sister had a share in misleading me—but she never even wished for the connection. The folly was *all* mine ; you cannot condemn it more severely than I do—since it pained you as much as myself. Do not apprehend from these proofs of my potent imagination *in absence*, that it has been acting in your case. No—I remember too well what I last felt in your presence, under that coldness—my only resource and at the same time my vexation. What I may seem to feel when we meet again I cannot guess—I could shrink from it too—yet let it be as soon as possible. When you can leave London do not delay in order to prepare us for your arrival. . . . I wish you had not imagined I could repent of anything but that I have so long delayed *our* happiness. For every bitter moment which I have caused, may the rest of my life atone. My views, as you observe, are not very worldly—nor very romantic, I hope. I have formed none independently. Your observation will have taught you by what means a rational happiness can best be kept alive and cultivated, and my ideas wait to be fixed by yours. My pursuits easily adapt themselves, and to share them, of whatever kind, must be my greatest pleasure. I have told my friends and have received an answer from my Aunt—a very kind one. I do sincerely love her for her friendly conduct and feelings towards you. It appears to us that a continuance of secrecy is unnecessary.

My father is very much gratified by your answer to him. Neither he nor my mother have any wish to catechize you. To see them so happy in an event which they made it a point of conscience not to influence, is a serious addition to my satisfaction. They are the kindest of parents.

I could write to you for ever—my whole heart *is* open to you, and *will* be. But —Goodnight.

She now wrote twice running. Byron learnt from her that Lord Wentworth had been told of the engagement, and that her happiness had been made known in the village of Seaham. His comment to Lady Melbourne was : " I don't much admire this kind of publicity. . . . I quite agree with you that [marriage] were best over."

To Annabella he again wrote twice in the same day ; and (despite the issue) it was she who just then got the real man, and Lady Melbourne who got the legendary one.

B. *to* A.I.M.

Septr. 26th 1814.

Your letter has relieved me from the remaining doubts which still lingered round me—it is difficult at first to believe our dearest hopes realized. I had struggled on in the full conviction that your heart was another's, and at times in the delusion of having recovered mine ; but the sight of your handwriting, the casual mention of your name by any third person, all & every thing which recalled you to my memory—and there were few things that did not by connection or *contrast*—conspired to tell me in the sensations they produced that I still coveted " a pearl worth all my tribe." I did not require nor expect the explanation you have afforded, but it has removed a weight from my heart, and a restlessness from my brain that would have made me—I know not what. Now I am yours—and being dear to you will I hope make me better, as it has left me nothing to desire beyond deserving your affection and retaining it.

I came to town on business which I thought it as well to arrange before I proceeded to Seaham. My Agent is in the country, whence I expect him in a few days. If not, I shall join him there for a day.

I thought the delay would sit easier at present ; for if I had been with you, it had been painful to me to quit you so soon—and yet expedient—since " the heart, that little *world* of ours " is not the only world we must live in, and I have some points to discuss with him upon the subject of Newstead (which is mine again) and a property I have in Lancashire—with a view to your comfort as well as mine. All I can do shall be done, and in all my future views you must be my principal object and my tenderest care. I am glad that you have heard from Lady Melbourne. Her conduct has been uniformly kind, considerate, and even indulgent to me ; and I have only to regret the unhappy circumstances which prevent my being on the same terms of friendship with all her family. It is some satisfaction to me to have retained hers ; and had my conduct been altogether inexcusable, all things considered, I could hardly have retained it. She has much regard for you—but that is not extra-ordinary. *I* have also heard from her, and perhaps I may see her before we meet. I am anxious and shall be uneasy till I see you, yet I cannot fix a day till I have seen my lawyer—and you know " the law's delay " extends to the personal movements of its professors. I try to keep myself in patience ; but I begin to think the famous exclamation of " Ye Gods—*annihilate* both *time & space* —and make two &c."—not half so absurd as I used to do. Dearest Annabella—allow me for the first time to use that expression—do write to me, and do not grow tired of hearing me repeat, seemingly by rote but really by *heart*, how faithfully I am your most attached and unalterable

P.S.[1]—I have just been going through a curious scene. Sir W. Knighton brought Spurzheim (I believe is the name) the *craniologist* to see me—a discoverer of faculties and dispositions from heads. He passes his hand over the head & then tells you—curious things enough, for I own he has a little astonished me. He says all mine are strongly marked—but very antithetical ; for every thing developed in & on this same skull of mine has its *opposite* in great force, so that to believe him my good & evil are at perpetual war. Pray heaven the last don't come off victorious.

Septr. 26th 1814.

I wrote in the morning, but I cannot go to rest without once more conversing with you as well as I can at this distance. My letters always leave me dissatisfied—something—so much is unsaid. Since I have given way to those feelings which almost since our first acquaintance I have repressed, but never could conquer even when I thought them most hopeless, you have never left me for a moment —you never shall—you never can. *You* do not perhaps recollect the first time we ever met at Me. House, an abode with which— except in the instance of our Aunt that is to be—I cannot always

[1] This postscript is in *Letters and Journals*, iii. 137.

associate the most pleasing ideas ; but to me it is as yesterday—
although I have lived nearly a life of events since that day. You
struck me (as it is called) particularly. I did not know your name,
and the room was full of morning-visitors ; I was myself almost a
stranger & felt awkward & shy—for which I have a *natural* talent,
at that time increased by my recent return from a country where
society composed of men & women is unknown. I set you down as
the most puzzling person there—for there was a quiet contempt of
all around you & the nothings they were saying & doing in your
manner that was so much after my own heart I could hardly refrain
from telling you so—still & calm as you appeared. You went away
at last—with Miss Mercer I think ; and the moment you were gone
I enquired all the *who's* and *whats* of mine hostess. Your name was
answer sufficient, for I had heard of you long before—even while
I was abroad, through particular circumstances—little dreaming
then how much I should in future dream of you. There was a
simplicity—an innocence—a beauty in your deportment & appearance which, although you hardly spoke, told me I was in company
with no common being. Not very long after this I confided to one
whom I then thought only a friend [1] how much I admired—for I
dared not do more ; how superior you seemed to me to all I perceived in the crowds where I was wandering. At first my confidante
was all acquiescence and approbation ; but I was soon informed
that you were—but why should I retrace misapprehensions & their
consequences, for which I shall never forgive myself ? I thought
you attached and engaged—regret was useless ; but how much
would have been spared to me had I been aware that your heart was
your own—that it could even be exchanged for mine ! In very
truth—from my heart of hearts, dearest Annabella—I can now tell
you that then—at the very time when I became unworthy of being
yours—it was to you my attachment had turned—it was you from
whom it was wrenched. Those feelings cannot be quelled—only
removed ; and my sole resource was to suppose that I felt for
another the love which you would not accept.

In the autumn I was undeceived—with regard to your prepossession for another ; but confirmed by the ill-success of my kind
friend Ly. Me. in my opinion that we never should be what I still
tremulously hope—for till you are mine I shall tremble. Well—
" Rebellion lay in my way " and like Hotspur " I found it." I
became the fool of a similar delusion—loving *you* still. Since that
time I have proceeded, " seeking for rest and finding none " ; at
moments retiring within myself and gathering my thoughts and the
recollection of my passion & observations into rhimes—with which
as the world are pleased to take them well—at least in quantity—
I have only to be pleased too, and think myself a very clever
gentleman. You will think this affectation—but it is not. I have
never thought very highly of poetry nor poets—*merely as poets* ;

---

[1] This was Caroline Lamb.

and my becoming one—if indeed I am so—is the result of temporary solitude & accident. It is not " my vocation," and I once thought I was made for something better—but that is past. I yet wish to be good—with you I cannot but be happy ; but I never shall be what I would have been. Luckily I do not wish to be so now. Reflection & experience have taught me that all pursuits which are not founded on self-esteem & the good of others lead but to the same result ; and far astray as it has led me, I am thankful that the wildness of my imaginations has not altogether prevented me from recovering the path of peace.

What an unmerciful prose have I sent you, or rather am sending —but pardon me—I will compress in future my language as I have already my feelings—my plans—my hopes—my affections—into love—I could almost say—devotion to you. Forgive my weaknesses—love what you can of me and mine ; and I will be—I am whatever you please to make me. I am at least above the paltry reluctance of not submitting to an understanding which I am sure is superior to mine. I do not flatter you. I am certain that you are wiser than me—more reflective—more dispassionate—surely more good. You say that " you will look up to me." Were you my inferior I should perceive it—I should require it—but it is not so ; and yet I do not think humbly of myself when I estimate you more highly. I do not mean that *I* should rely on you for that protection which it is *my* part to give—and my pride to prove ; but that you should be not only my Love, but my first friend, my adviser, my reprover when necessary—that my head should at times be as much indebted to your counsels as my heart is to your regard. In difficulty or danger I would not call upon you to share it or extricate me—I would not throw upon you the weight of my griefs or my perils ; but I would ask you if I had done well or ill—and upon your answer would materially depend my estimation of my conduct.

I write to you as if you were already my wife. " The wife of my bosom " you assuredly are, for it does not contain a thought which I can separate from you. It is " almost at odds with morning," so —if not a Hibernicism—Good *Night*. I must try to sleep. Heaven bless and protect you. Ever your most attached
and sincere

Tuesday.

P.S.[1]—I have just heard a distressing piece of intelligence to our family. My first cousin, Sir Peter Parker, is killed in the late action with the Americans. He was a very gallant & popular officer— young & not long married—and his death will be very generally regretted. I have not seen him since we were boys, but my sister knew him very well, and I do not [know] whether—or *how* to tell

[1] In writing this news to Lady Melbourne he said of Sir Peter Parker : " . . . whom even his wife could not help loving." Byron wrote an elegy on Sir Peter.

her—or *not*. Lady Pr. was particularly attached to him. In short, it is very bitter to us all.

A.I.M. *to* B.

SEAHAM, *Septr*. 28.

I rode to meet the post, and was not disappointed. I am glad that you will be able to conclude your principal arrangements before you come, and also that Newstead is restored, if it be true, as I have heard, that you are attached to the place. It would be incredible to some people that I do not at all know the value of your property. My wishes are not of an expensive nature, and I can be " poor and content "—much more than *content*—with you ; for I dare now to contemplate a state of happiness beyond the dull resignation which was my " sovereign good," when I had no hope of being more than imperfectly your friend, and *that* I was resolved to be in defiance of the increasing danger to my own peace, as long as such a tie was possible. Thankful to be anything—rather than nothing. The situation of an only child, exposed from my birth to extreme partiality, has made me study to repress the vanity of thinking myself a treasure. I should have had less hesitation in giving myself to you if I had thought the gift of more value. But you can, *will* make me what you esteem me to *be*, however distant I may have been from the standard to which you give me courage to aspire. My powers are, I hope, in every thing superior to my actual attainments. With my purest and highest thoughts the remembrance of you has been long associated—and my incessant efforts to break the chain have proved its strength. Now let it bind me for ever.

When I write to you I seem afterwards to have omitted the greater part of what I meant to say. In truth I would say everything, and should be comfortless if I could have any reserve with you. To whom can all my thoughts be so justly committed as to my best and dearest friend on earth ? Affection without perfect confidence is a frail tenure—*with* it, the most secure. Never, I pray, withhold a question which you may wish to have me answer.

My Mother has been ill since I wrote to you—partly I believe from agitation. You will conceive that she must experience it in these circumstances, though they are " to her heart's desire." It is rarely that so fond a mother is so little selfish. Her indulgence is for my sake, not her own. Are you not afraid that such a spoiled child will prove a Xantippe ? You must console yourself with the hope that I am tired of having my own way, if that period be not to womankind like the eternally future one of Discretion. Since writing the above I have been walking this serene evening by " your own element "—though I don't think you quite Conrad, nor myself quite Medora. I am never tired of the sea—it is always an object of my *reverence*, if the word may be applied to created thing.

Perhaps because I have never seen any other grand feature of Nature save " this brave o'erhanging firmament."

A.I.M. *to* B.

SEAHAM, *Septr.* 29.

On receiving your letter I think first of the event which has so nearly touched you and yours, and feel for your Sister, whom I saw but once—at Lord Glenbervie's last year. I followed you towards the door, meaning to request an introduction to her—but you retreated and I had not courage to advance. I remember indelibly every time that we have met—that first morning too, when our impressions so well corresponded. With you, and you only, I then felt *at home*—I cannot otherwise express it. Instead of being awed or repelled as others were, I could have told you my thoughts, and perhaps your own also—those excepted which concerned me ; of them I dreamt not. My letters to my Mother at that time, for she gave them to me lately to read, show how much you had occupied my attention—my interest. Though I tried to see in you what I had heard of you, mystery & mischief, your character appeared to me very simple. Of your truth, of your deep and disinterested feelings, I never doubted. During the last part of the season you ceased to notice me at all. My interest for you had not depended on your attention—was not altered by the loss of it. At one supper party—where you sat between Lady Melbourne and me, but conversed only with her—I heard you say : " Thank God I have not a friend in the world." You knew not the pang which you inflicted on a friend so near. Those words of bitterness chilled me. When I returned home to solitude I wept over the recollection of them, and prayed that you might receive consolation from a friend below, as well as from a friend above. I did not think of myself— Love did not enter into my speculations, and was not suspected to be in yours—at least with reference to myself. . . . To those who are nearly indifferent to me I am willing enough to believe myself an object of interest ; to you, I should have deemed it the vainest presumption—not because you were " a clever gentleman," but because I already valued your *heart* too much to think of possessing it. . . . My pen is running after my thoughts till it is out of breath . . .

I will not be less your friend since I am to be—and *am*—more than your friend. . . . I *will* see your faults, though more disposed to see my own. I *have* given you proofs that I am not blindly attached—if I were, a change might be feared. In respect to the past errors for which you " cannot forgive " yourself, I would not extenuate them—I would only be your peacemaker. As I have thought of them " more in sorrow than in anger "—do you the same. . . .

Friday [September 30].

I have just had an account of a comical rencontre between your Aunt and my Uncle—Miss Byron & Lord Wentworth—at Lord Scarsdale's ; both oppressed with their incommunicable secret till they were happily relieved from the burden by a letter of mine, removing that obligation. I presume that in the joy of disclosure they " swore eternal friendship." I may as well pause here. I shall not be more willing at the end of the sheet. There is much to say of *you* and *I*—the most interesting persons in the world—at least to each other. My mother is better—still very weak.

A.I.M. *to* B.

CASTLE EDEN INN
Sunday [October 2, 1814].

I am waiting here alone—ten miles from Seaham—in expectation of my Uncle's arrival. My thoughts are with you—and you shall have them. . . .

I have something like a fear to know the day of *your* arrival. I should be unhappy if I did not expect it, yet when fixed, I shall perhaps wish that we *had* met, rather than *were* to meet. I must be thoughtless if I could be *simply glad to see you*. You will understand this too well to think it unkind.

I hear the carriage—take care of yourself and rest on the road—and think it is for the sake of her " who loves thee best."

A.I.M. *to* B.

SEAHAM, *Oct.* 3.

I know why you do not write—you think you have nothing to say that is worth saying ; and I am in the same predicament—but I do as I would be done by, and hope that *anything* from me will give you the same pleasure as I have in *anything* from you.

My Mother recovers gradually.

Lord Wentworth pleases me by his strong prepossession in your favour—he is *proud* of his future nephew. And now—no more—

B. *to* A.I.M.

Octr. 3*d.* 1814.

I am happy to hear that Lady Milbanke is better—but wish to hear that she is well—pray tell me so. . . . I am still detained here waiting for my agent's arrival. It is my intention to part with N once more. The late purchaser being unable to fulfil his engagements at the proper time was under the necessity of forfeiting £25,000—and resigning the purchase, which was hard upon him but indispensable. He may still have the option of completing his purchase if disposed and competent to renew it. When I had once determined to sell that estate, I conquered or stifled those feelings which attach one to an old patrimony—in the conviction that it was better for many reasons it should be so. My Lancashire inheritance consists merely of a very extensive and unenclosed manor with the mineral & all other rights. I wished to have sold it instead ; but was dissuaded and am still, and told that it will ultimately be very valuable, perhaps more so than the other—on account of the collieries, which have never been yet worked to the proper extent, because I could not spare the requisite sum and at the same time discharge my debts till N. was sold. A part of Rochdale, but not the most considerable by any means, has been subject to a lawsuit which I have *gained three times*, but it is not yet decided ! You *know* the *law*—this also would have been arranged by the completion of the N. purchase. My R. rights extend over better than eleven thousand acres—and these have been ours since the Conquest, I believe. They wish to enclose, but cannot without my consent. It is also further valuable on this account—as of course besides the reservation of the minerals to me, from the extent of the royalty a considerable portion of land would in that case be added. Of the actual or exact value of R. or of Newstead I cannot speak with any certainty ; it is to ascertain this, and to take the proper steps for making every settlement in my power upon you, that I wish to see my Agent and determine these points before I join you at Seaham. My debts are reduced very much within the last three years, and a few thousand pounds will cover the rest—considerably above half have been already paid. The last price of Newstead was £140,000 ; since that time land has fallen ; but I can afford to sell it for £25,000 less, at all events—and if the late purchaser renews & completes there will be no loss at all. The rents have been more than tripled—almost quadrupled ; but the income is still far short of what I should derive from the produce of the sale, besides the expense of keeping up the place in any kind of order. This is more like a *factor's* letter than anything else ; but as you said something on the subject, I thought it as well to get it over at once. Your father's agents and mine will of course canvas the business more fully. With regard to your expectations I have neither conjecture nor curiosity. My motives in addressing you were not founded upon these, and in such respects there will be no *disappointment* to me—and I will make it my endeavour that there shall be as little to you and yours as I can help.

I have said so much—at least so many words—on the above topic that I have not left myself time for others. Indeed, what I could say would be merely repetitions of that which you already know & which years (if spared to me) will only confirm. You do not yet know how dear you must ever be to

yr. most attached & sincere

A.I.M. *to* B.

SEAHAM, *Octr*. 5.

Your " factor's letter " was satisfactory (I did not mean a pun) as far as satisfaction is to be derived from pounds, shillings and pence. ... I have *some* genius for them, and when the science comes more into my practice than it has hitherto, expect to be nearly as good a proficient as if I knew nothing else, which is commonly considered the only surety for female economy. My father talks of writing to you—to suggest the possibility that a knowledge of his affairs might tend to the more convenient arrangement of yours. He is most anxious to afford every accommodation in his power, which I suspect does not extend as far as his wishes. ... I will however leave his meaning to his own exposition. My idea of pecuniary comfort is not in the more or less, but in freedom from embarrassments, which are destructive to independence.

My aversion for repetition and profession is like yours. ... There let it rest. Truth is sometimes too proud to wear the same garb which has disguised Falsehood, and I once had that pride to an extravagant degree. Disgusted by the affectation of sensibility, I suppressed every sign of genuine feeling. The habit, maintained for some years, during which I was called *a savage*, has left a difficulty or impossibility of utterance on the occasions when before I *would not* utter. I strive against it. To you it has been necessary to *say*, since, far from having the credulous vanity which leads many men to take for granted more than was ever meant to be implied, you do not readily apprehend the *existence* of what you regard as most desirable. Amongst the antitheses of your skull the Craniologist might perhaps find *humility* and *pride*—but not *vanity* surely. I begin to think that a little more of that quality would be very advantageous to us both. At least it would have brought us sooner to a thorough understanding.

My Mother is nearly well.

B. *to* A.I.M.

Octr. 5th 1814.

You will be as much surprised as I have been displeased, Dearest Annabella, to perceive in the *Mg. Chronicle* a *contradiction* of a paragraph in the D[urham] & other papers announcing our intended marriage. I have written to Perry ; but can easily *guess* the personage [1] who has thought proper to perform this piece of petty malignity—which has hurt me—but no matter—I shall probably know in a few hours whence it originated. My reasons for suspecting the personage to whom I allude are that it is not the first nor the fiftieth of these *monkey-tiger* tricks that she has played me—one

---

[1] Lady Caroline Lamb (*Correspondence*, i. 275). But he suspected also Claughton, the prospective buyer of Newstead.

in particular of forging a letter in my name so exactly that the person to whom it was addressed was completely deceived. The *cause* was a picture, and Murray (in whose care it was, and who ought to know my handwriting perfectly) was the dupe. After this (which was above a year ago) you can hardly wonder at my want of Charity on this occasion in fixing upon the same object for my present conjecture. The *fact* you may depend upon—you cannot conceive what persecution I have undergone from the same quarter, nor the pains I have taken to save that person from herself. I do not mean *very* recently ; but since my first acquaintance she has crossed my every path—she has blighted or at least darkened my every prospect. It is bitter to speak harshly of that which we once thought loved us—& yet in this instance to speak truly & kindly at the same time is difficult. I will therefore close the subject.

Mr. Hanson is still at Ld. Portsmouth's, detained by business— but I expect him daily & have written to him peremptorily. In the meantime I trust he is doing what I have desired him, & will tell me so when we meet. Nothing but this—& it is a necessary though irksome delay—detains me from you. All my connections and friends are delighted—they could not but be proud of you. My feelings are dashed with doubt. If I valued you less, I should be more confident—but you seem to me so much more than I deserve that I can scarcely persuade myself that you are to be mine. *Yours* I must be ever from my heart of hearts.

P.S.—I enclose you Perry's [1] answer, and the note (which I retain *pour des raisons*) I have seen and do not think it is the person I believed, but cannot guess the writer. Pray have I done right or wrong in this ? It could not surely be passed by silently— particularly as it first appeared in the D[urham] paper—the con- tradiction was like an insult.

As I wish to let you into the character of a man with whom I have passed much of my youth, I send you also 3 epistles of my friend Hobhouse—the son of Sir B. H. and my fellow traveller during the first part of my stay in the East. I think the dry and cynical turn of his style will amuse you ; but I can assure you he is *all heart* notwithstanding & a great admirer of you—as one of his letters will prove to you. Ever my Love—thine. Keep them till we meet.

It was now that Lady Gosford got the letter about discretion and good sense. " His great anxiety is to be free from *debts*. . . . My ready money is £16,000. I should think his annual income between 5 and 6 thousand—so we shall do very well, as I am not of an extravagant disposition."

A.I.M. *to* B.

My father was very indignant at the mis-statement, and wondered " what rascal " wanted to deprive him of a son whom I

[1] Editor of *The Morning Chronicle*.

really believe he personally prefers to any other he could have chosen, had his option been unlimited. You pleased him particularly when he visited you [1]—on his return he said that you seemed to be a most " good-natured, friendly man." You may form your own opinion of his discernment.

I wish *you* to be patient of the delays which keep us apart—yet I have not myself any patience to spare for you. I regard your absence at this time as not the least proof of attachment. I should fear for the future if you were blindly absorbed in the immediate indulgence of our wishes—there is a pleasure in saying *our*. If in this life expectation may ever rise to certainty, I am certainly yours. I would not *doubt* it for the fairest hope of other happiness, if I could conceive happiness which you were not to bestow on me. Unless your imagination has beguiled you, I feel that *I* cannot disappoint because I have never deceived. I am little changed since you last saw me, except that I have regained my health, and *now* my unstudied chearfulness. I only want to see *you* look happy.

My mother desires me to give some directions for your route. After you come to Boroughbridge, the nearest way hither is by the following stages—Thirsk—Tontine Inn—Stockton—Castle Eden—*Seaham*—I feel as if you were here when I write it. Farewell—and believe I cannot but be yours.

B. *to* A.I.M.

Octr. 7th 1814.

Mr. Hanson, my solicitor, is arrived in London, & will be glad to confer with Sir Ralph's, if he will have the goodness to favour me with his address. I believe the etiquette—in short I do not know it—but if I am wrong in addressing this to you to mention to Sir R., instead of writing to him myself, will he & you pardon it ? The fact is that I write to you less formally than I could (with all my sentiments of regard & respect) to your father ; & now I shall be quite happy to get these points of discussion out of our heads into those of our lawyers—and may *they* prosper only in proportion to their expedition !

I wrote to you yesterday, Dearest Annabella, exceedingly distempered with conjectures and choler at the contra*diction* and Contra*dictor* of the paragraph from the Durham paper announcing our intended marriage ; nor can I at this moment fix on the person. There are but—no—there can be but *one*—who could or would play such an idle & yet vexatious trick. After all, my only reason for suspecting that personage is my knowledge of her disposition—of which I must say—nothing.

It gives me much pleasure to hear that Augusta [2] has written to

---

[1] There is no other indication in the documents as to the date of Sir Ralph's visit.

[2] This passage about Augusta is in *Letters and Journals*, iii. 146.

you. She is the least selfish & gentlest creature in being, & more attached to me than any one in existence can be. She was particularly desirous that I should marry, and only regretted—what I must regret a little too—that she had not earlier the pleasure of your acquaintance. She was very anxious for the fate and favourable reception of her letter to you. Your mother " is better—but not yet well." I must naturally be very desirous to hear her amendment confirmed. This you will tell me doubtless—but soon ? Answer that question when & how you please, I shall still be dissatisfied. There is no *soon* for me till we have met—everything about me seems tedious & tiresome. When I have the honour of being presented to your Uncle Lord Wentworth I hope I shall not be unmindful of my obligation to him for his favourable opinion taken on *your word*—it is the only point on which he need doubt it. It would delight me to obtain the friendship of all who are dear to you ; but I am so unlucky in my approaches to strangers that it is one of the objects on which I am more anxious than sanguine. I have been writing on *skaits*—my paper slippery as ice and at full speed —perhaps you will think *with* them by the scrawl—but hastily or tardily believe me ever

yr. most attached
& faithful

P.S.—I cannot resist sending you the enclosed from Augusta, as it will enable you to judge of her disposition—since with me she can be under no constraint—& it will in some parts I think amuse you. " The bets " will, I hope, be soon decided. Make my best remembrances to Sir R. & let the first sentence of your answer inform me your mother is quite—*quite* recovered.

Touching to observe how literally she obeys his first command !

A.I.M. *to* B.

My Mother *quite* recovered.

Your wish in respect to a legal consultation has been anticipated. We know and care as little about formalities as you do. I am just desired by my Uncle to give you a message—that it will gratify him very much to have the honour of knowing you. In the meantime he requests you to accept his best regards.

Mrs. Leigh's letter makes me feel as if I were well acquainted with her. . . . I rely much on the *countenance* of letters, and her's *look* most kindly.

Some of the newspapers still refuse their consent to our marriage —they use me very ill, for they deprive me at the same time of my husband, and the " highly accomplished " shape in which they before presented me to their readers. These things trouble me not —yet I sympathise with the pain you must feel in suspecting an intended injury from one who has not been indifferent to you. I am truly sorry for the person who in wounding your peace, must have destroyed her own.

A feeling that it is almost useless to write a long letter—that you will hear the rest very soon—is the most welcome check to my communications. Shall I not see you in the same room where I am now writing ? Heaven bless you.

B. *to* A.I.M.

Octr. 8*th* 1814.

I have directed Mr. Hanson to communicate with Mr. Hoar in compliance with your father's kind request which I this day received. Between them I will for the present leave the discussion.

Were I to follow my own inclination—my *more* than inclination —I should now be with you and yours at Seaham ; but my presence here will forward arrangements which must be completed before we can meet free from all anxiety—& then I trust we shall meet never to part till that moment which will be bitterest to the survivor.

I have long accustomed myself to lean as little upon hope—or rather on *certainty*—as I can help. I do not foresee anything that can prevent the accomplishment of our intentions ; but if such did occur—I know not how I should bear it now ; but were I *with* you —near you—& then to relinquish you—I could not bear it at all. When I say this, do not imagine that under any circumstances *I* would now recede ; but if malice, or any of the thousand somethings or nothings which so often " give us pause " should interpose between us—it would cost *you* less (and so far be some relief to me) than if we were together only to separate.

It is for both our comforts indispensably necessary that a " freedom from embarrassments " should *precede* our marriage. This I am endeavouring—& in this the arrangements I am preparing must ultimately succeed. That delay will arise I know ; but it is expedient & must be borne, & I would much rather owe the extrication to my own endeavours and resources than to those of others—however highly I may regard them. With this view I told Ly. Me. that your situation—be it what it might—would make no difference to me further than that of parting with N. *now* instead of a few months hence ; but that I thought it better not to join you till all was settled on *my* worldly concerns.

Lady Me., with that uniform friendship she has ever shewn me, is very anxious that I should lose no time. I *will lose* none—but I would rather lose everything than precipitate you perhaps into repentance.

I do not wish you to " profess." Write to me as you feel—or if that seem more than I should request, write to me as you please— I shall find no fault. So *you* were once called a " savage." I never was called anything else, but I hope my ferocity resembles yours.

B. *to* A.I.M.

Octr. 9*th* 1814.

I have had a letter from a person [1] whose name you will guess without a large expense of conjecture. It is the first I have received from that quarter for some time, and is quiet and rational enough. The passage I have cut out refers to you, and confirms a statement which—I think—I made to you. For that reason I send it.

With regard to the writer—whom I have not seen nor heard from for months—I would fain hope that she may yet retrieve herself. I do not speak as far as regards *me*—that has of course been long over ; but on subsequent circumstances with which I have no concern except to regret that since there never were so many opportunities of amendment & remission presented to any being as to her, she should not avail herself of them. To me she has been the cause of much wretchedness not unattended with self reproach —& yet I did try to preserve her. I would have sacrificed myself at one time to have made her happier—but *that* was not called for by her connections nor even herself. Her whole disposition is a moral phenomenon (if she be not *mad*) ; it is not feminine—she has no real affection, or if any it is to the very man she has most injured, W. L. But everything seems perverted in her—she is unlike everybody, & not even like herself for a week together.

I have not discovered our paragraph-scribe. My mind misgave me it might be Mr. Claughton—on the supposition that he might conceive my marriage would interfere with any intentions of repurchase of N. on his part ; but Mr. Hanson on comparing the writing says it is unlike, and that he would not be so silly. It matters not—we shall one day laugh at it. Your " assurance," dearest A., makes mine " double sure "—but I wish our lawyers would be quicker ; my Philosophy begins to be a little fractious.

I believe you dislike bustle as much as I do. You shall please yourself & yours as to the where & when the ceremony (which I suppose you would not like to be VERY *ceremonious*) is to take place —but as it is usual to separate for a time from all but *ourselves* I wish to fix on our retreat. Newstead will hardly be in the state I could wish it to be in to receive you—but I will make it my care to provide us a suitable abode.

QUOTATION FROM LADY CAROLINE LAMB'S LETTER.

" Is it not a little strange that almost the first words you ever spoke in confidence to me were concerning Annabella ? I was astonished—overpowered—I could not believe it——."

[1] Lady Caroline Lamb.

A.I.M. *to* B.

Octr. 10.

It is as much out of the power of " somethings or nothings " to divide us, as if I were your wife. I answer for you with the same security as for myself. I am *unconditionally* yours—given by my parents as *irrevocably* as by myself. In respect to *circumstances*, believe me *they* are not so old in the ways of the world as to suffer it in any form to interfere with my dearest, my only expectation of happiness. They see me happy—and they could not bear the idea of that reverse which would follow the loss of *you* from whatever cause—whether present or absent. Do not then stay away for " somethings or nothings," from a generous, though ill-founded resolution to spare me a possibility—an impossibility and I will not name it—I am too much pained with the thought that you have even conceived it. It is true we have so often seemed irrevocably lost to each other that we have every reason to " make assurance doubly sure " when with prudence we can. If I thought that difficulties would make you love me more, I would not interpose one. Those that now exist are in the opinion of my father at least *as* likely to be obviated by your presence here as in London. He and my uncle are both *impatient* to see you. I know that *all* your conduct is regulated with a view to my good ; my only fear is that it should be a disinterestedly mistaken one—and surely it would, if you were not to permit that assistance from my father which might at least expedite the removal of obstacles, and which, *to a son*, could not and would not be regarded as a *gift*.

If you were *here* what " anxiety " would remain ? Till you are here we shall all feel *some*. . . . I speak from authority when I say that there cannot be any information relative to your *situation* which would make my parents regret for a moment that they *had* given you all that is most precious to them. They will only regret, *whatever* they can add, that they cannot add *more*. When you *know* them you will not need this assurance. . . . Tell me then if you *must* remain, or if the necessity vanishes with this letter. I can say no more—do what is *really* best, and I shall not mistake your motives.

Monday Night
[*October* 10, 1814].

I wrote all the enclosed when I first received your letter, and yet I have not exhausted the desire to write. That letter—for some reason—agitated me more than usual. I could be sad—not ungratefully so ; but it is growing too like a dream, and till your *voice* assures me, I shall dread the doubt, the very doubt, of a waking hour. God bless you—my own—my only dearest.

But it is growing too like a dream. . . . How poignantly she could express herself, when she forgot to try !

A.I.M. *to* B.
Tuesday [*October* 11, 1814].

I wrote yesterday entirely " as I felt "—and perhaps my great anxiety to relieve *yours* may have disturbed you more. You will, I know, understand the intention, if not exactly answered by the effect. I was at Elemore this morning, where I learned that my Mother had also written. Do not let us torment you with all our wishes and impati*ences*, which happily are in perfect accord. We would not render patience more difficult to you, *if it be necessary*. Mr. & Mrs. Baker, the owners of Elemore, have also an only daughter, and the *contrast* of her situation at this moment with mine, is melancholy. I was pained by a superiority *in happiness*, which she is far too generous to regard with an envious regret. I did not mean to write to you again to-day, but you will not quarrel with *this* Self-indulgence of your Annabella.

A.I.M. *to* B.
Wednesday [*October* 12, 1814].

Your letter has restored my chearfulness, which was sinking under your *doubts*.

I believe I was interested for Ly. C's escape from all the dangers with which she had encompassed herself, in the same way as you were—and I thought much more of her after a kind of request which you made to me. Do you remember saying that *you wished* I would take some interest in her fate ? I have still some compassionate kindness for her—I did not think *you* to blame in regard to her.

I am called to my Mother, about whom I still feel a little uneasiness. She is so much reduced by her late illness that everything overpowers her.

B. *to* A.I.M.
Octr. 13*th* 1814.

Mr. Hanson has just left me. He will be in Durham early next week (Wednesday I hope) to meet Mr. Hoar. He is in full possession of my intentions & the proper papers—the legal arrangement I leave to his discretion, subject to any observations your father may think proper to make. Mr. Hoar answered his letter, & they agree that a personal interview will save time & trouble. I must be at Newstead for a few days next week, after which we shall meet. My Love, I do not know how to thank you for your letter received this morning. I never doubted *you*—I know you to be Truth herself ; but I dreaded—I will not say I dread—lest a happiness which I do not deserve should be dashed from me. But I will not yield to these " thick-coming fancies "—forgive me for even hinting at them. My delays, dearest A., have arisen from various causes, &

some not very important—though equally provoking. When I addressed you from Nd. it was with so little hope that I had actually prepared everything to go abroad with my friend Hobhouse ; and now I have to do & undo fifty things connected with my then resolution. I made that as a last effort in the thought that before my return you might perhaps give me some encouragement —or by your answer crush my presumption at once ; but I had as little belief that *you* loved me—that you would be mine—as I now have that *I* can ever be another's. I will not do you nor myself such injustice as to suppose that any misconception could *now* arise, on either part. Of the state of our affections—our present feelings & our future intentions—it is for common minds to attribute little motives. I have none—nothing but wishes and fears. The former I need not repeat; the latter I hardly know how to define or to account for—except by a Superstition to which I am not generally subject. But " something too much of this." The latter end of next week I intend to be at Newstead, & as soon after as some business there will permit—at Seaham. My best regards to all around you who will receive them.

Byron's next letter, except for the postscript here printed, is in *Letters and Journals*, iii. 151. The " paragraph " referred to was one praising Miss Milbanke at Lord Byron's expense.

P.S. 2d.—I have since the morning seen the paragraph. It is just to you, & not very unjust to me—merely the old story of " the thorny paths of Satire & the gloomy recesses of Misanthropy " from which the writer hopes you will withdraw me. I'm sure so do I. He adds laughably enough, " We hope so much contradiction will not exist after the ceremony," alluding to the con- & re-contradictions.

There are also some epigrams, by no means bad & very complimentary to you in which such a " Heraclitus " as I am is made to leave off melancholy under your auspices ; and a long address in the *Mg. Pt.* to me, making me responsible for a sentiment in *The Giaour*, though it is in the mouth of a fictitious character. These " paper bullets of the brain " will not penetrate mine—and I could forgive any censure but of you.

A.I.M. *to* B.

[*October* 15, 1814].

From you—a letter. It adds somewhat to the almost invariable contentment which now is mine. They who in my calm demeanour perceived not before the want of happiness, find, from the present change, that it *was* away. The country-people, often as penetrating as physiognomists or " craniologists," say, " It does one's heart good to see *our Miss*—she looks as if she had been a wife these twenty years." They must entertain a high idea of *advanced* conjugal felicity. We shall prove it a just one if the length of trial be granted.

My curiosity has been excited by an incognito who came to this village a few days ago for the purpose of seeing me, because I am to be yours. According to the description of the woman at whose house he stopped, he was " a very gentleman," and had travelled. His interest about me was entirely for your sake, and when in reply to some enquiries his hostess assured him I was *very good*, he said, " She cannot be too good for *him* "—then spoke of you with enthusiastic praise, as if from personal knowledge. Unluckily I had made an excursion during the hours of his stay. He expressed great disappointment and went away unknown—evidently a stranger in this country. I would I had seen your nameless friend.[1]

You wish to " fix on a place for our retreat." Have you thought of any one, if Newstead would be objectionable ? I am very easily pleased as to lodgement—not prone either to make or to find inconvenience ; and the habitation which would admit you and your sister would, I should imagine, do equally well for you and me—but you will judge of its *capacity* in this respect. I forgot that as I am dignified in the *Morning Post* with the epithet of your " portly lady wife," I must require " ample room " for my reception. Total seclusion without active occupation at a period when two persons cannot have become perfectly familiarized with *each other's ways*, is perhaps, in general, not the most desirable mode of introduction. We are, I think, as little in danger as any, of feeling the disadvantages of a custom which must, for a short time, be followed.

The determination of this *where*, may not be necessary till we know more of the *when*, which rests with our lawyers—and the expediency of our situation may partly depend on the time.

My Mother has not had any return of illness, though I believe I was apprehensive when I last wrote to you. Shall I continue to direct to London when you go to Newstead ? The post between that place and this occupies four days—how long I have found them ! You would not wonder at my impatience to disconnect you and *post*, if you knew how fearful, how sickening the association has sometimes been. I have not yet unlearned to tremble as I open your " *malgré tout.*"

B. *to* A.I.M.

Octr. 16th 1814.

In arranging papers I have found the first letter you ever wrote to me—read it again. You will allow that mine appeared a very unpromising case ; but I can forgive—that is not the word—I mean I can forget even the *reality* of your sentiments *then*, if you do not deceive yourself *now*. It was this epistle to which I always recurred

[1] There is no clue to the identity of this person.

—which haunted me through all our future correspondence ; and now farewell to it. And yet your friendship was dearer to me than any love but your own.[1]

I very well recollect recommending Lady C. to your regard—or rather to your care ; but that was before I was acquainted with her real disposition, and when she—no matter what—but I thought you might do her some good, & was very sure no principle in your mind could be shaken even by the guilty—far less the *giddy*—as I then conceived her to be. It is all very well—only do not take my recommendations for the future. You would, I think, be amused or perhaps surprized if you knew how much of my late life I have passed alone.

A.I.M. *to* B.

Sunday [*October* 16 1814].

Ten or twelve days ! My thoughts are so concentered in that point—I must not feel it now, or I shall be unable to write.

I have never been covetous of praise, and except when uttered by some loved voice, I have scarcely heard it. Now I have a new pleasure in my good name—those dear words, *for your sake*. So much more of *true* kindness has been proved towards me than I knew to exist, that—I can only think it is a very kind world. You will find it so too, and *then* I may be in danger of growing too fond of it. . . . We seek no happiness which Duty shall not seal—for ever—if there be truth below, or mercy above. Rest every anxious thought on me—I could only *not* forgive you for keeping from me those cares which to soften, if not to remove, will be the work—never the task—of affection. I must to silence—there are feelings which cannot flow in words.

With yours I received a letter from Mrs. Siddons, who since I was twelve years old has loved me with maternal anxiety. She is perfectly sincere, and when her expressions exceed just bounds, it is from the spirit of poetry—in this case, also of partiality. I will enclose the letter, and though without intimate knowledge of her character, you cannot know how *natural* it is, you will at least see how *kind*. I like to hear from many voices that *you* are " happy " in my attachment, as *that* has been a point of my persevering scepticism. I must not now affront the little world of opinion, and you too, by a doubt of my own perfections ; and indeed I am very well content to believe in them, to the best of my abilities. If all articles of Faith were as seductive, who would not subscribe ? With all my *perfections* on my head, wishing very much to share the *burden,* let me be

Most affectionately yours

---

[1] This paragraph is in *Letters and Journals*, iii. 154.

Octr. 17*th* 1814.

In my last letter I mentioned Mr. Hanson's intention of meeting Mr. Hoar on Wednesday next. He has since gone into the country, & writes to me that some indispensable business will delay him some days longer—but that after those he will make all possible haste in joining Mr. Hoar at Durham and forwarding our arrangements. It is impossible for me to express how much I am disappointed by these procrastinations—but words are useless, and I must not add loss of temper to that of time. I have written to him by this post, and as he appeared and appears as sensible as myself of the importance of his commission to me, I am sure he will not willingly defer his journey.

My own departure from London will take place about the same time—and I shall shorten my stay at Newstead, or pass it by altogether. In your last you hinted that Lady Milbanke was still weakly—I had hoped that her strength was sufficiently re-established since her visit to Elemore. If there were no other inducements for me to wish to leave London, the utter solitude of my situation, with only my Maccaw to converse with, would be sufficient—though he is not the least rational of my acquaintance. I read, but very desultorily ; and as to writing except to you—and Augusta—and where I must on duty or business, it is out of the question. However, solitude is nothing new—nor even disagreeable to me—at least it was not till now ; but I much question whether I shall ever be able to bear it again. I hope *not* to be put to the test. Write to me—if only a few words.

[*October* 17, 1814].

No letter—and none can come tomorrow. Wednesday will perhaps repay me by news of your *approach*.

Mrs. Leigh has written to me again with such confiding good-nature as prevents my *pen* from being shy, and I have answered as comfortably as if we *had* been sisters. I enclose, for your amusement at any leisure moment, some passages concerning you copied verbatim from my letters to my Mother in 1812.[1] They have amused *me* much. You will find in them some fluctuations of opinion, with an unconscious consistency of feeling. I seem very anxious throughout to assure *my*self as well as my mother that I was an *indifferent* judge—you will smile at my impartiality. Now and then it appears that I was sensible at least of your goodwill towards me, and I had also been informed of it by Mrs. Lamb, who drew more conclusions than I could admit. I believe she was very well-meaning in respect to me—and not as unfavourable to you as

---

[1] These passages will be found on pp. 36, 38, 41.

you perhaps suspect, for she did not seek to prejudice me against you. She was probably convinced by my retiring manners that you could not make any impression on my heart. Her judgments are in general *superficial*. That " which passeth show " is deeper than her penetration. You are in my " heart's *core* "—invisible to common observers. There you will be—whilst Memory holds her seat.

A.I.M. *to* B.

Tuesday Night [*October* 18, 1814].

I am thinking and feeling *in the next week*—and so are you perhaps. When I recollect our last meetings ! I never was so near losing all presence of mind. Twice before we did meet to acknowledge each other, I had caught a passing glimpse of you. You did not see me, I believe, and I hurried my Mother away, who was alarmed by my agitation. I was then ill—without *strength* enough, if I had *resolution*, for the necessary exertion. Through that season I scarcely ever went out without seeing you in my mind's eye, and fearing to see you in reality—wishing it too. All this was buried— only a deeper thoughtfulness was usually observable. . . . I do not think you are dearer to me now than you were then—the difference is that now I *know* whilst *I feel how* dear. If you had gone abroad, as I long dreaded—surely a kinder power than Chance prevented it—if you had, could there have been a change in me ? I think not, & thought not. I have some recollection of telling you in my first letter that time and distance could not decrease my regard for you. *That* was true, and in the rest there was less *misstatement* than *misapplication*—by myself I mean. I am as if talking to you—I would I were—but *next week* perhaps. . . .

I have heard with comfort of Miss Montgomery's safe arrival at Granada. W. Bankes was at Granada. I am afraid he will hear of *us* with pain—yet he cannot *lose* hope, for I never allowed it to exist. Miss M. had not received the intelligence when she wrote, & was as little prepared for it as my other friends & connections, who think me very cunning in concealing what I did not know, nor foresee. They are welcome to admire my political duplicity, but I hope my other " perfections " have more reality. Good night— bless you.

B. *to* A.I.M.

Octr. 19*th* 1814.

I return you Mrs. Sn's very kind and—after all—unaffected letter. Her style, to be sure, is vastly poetical—and her epithets would be no worse for weeding than her periods for pruning ; but then with her dramatic habits all this is but natural, and you ought to be very thankful it was not in blank verse.

Our "incognito" enquirer seems a little after the heroic mode also. Who or what he is, or how he came there, I cannot conceive nor guess. All my intimates are sufficiently acquainted with your name and " most blest conditions " to render such queries useless—nor do I know one sufficiently interested about me to take the trouble on *my* account ; and yet it could scarcely be a stranger. But be he who or what he may, it is odd enough—and of a piece with some of my past adventures, which have occasionally been extravagant as those of a dull romance.

I once thought it might be Bruce [1]—but he is not in England or at least that part of it. It was like one of his high-flown experiments. I remember when I came down from Constantinople, meeting him and Lady Hester Stanhope at Athens. Some time after, when they were embarking by night at the Piræus—just as we parted he made me (for the first time of his life) a most "eternal" profession of friendship—after which he went upon the waters, and I mounted my horse and galloped back through the olives upon a steed as black as the " Giaour's " and much on such an evening. Since that time we never met.

I am only waiting for Mr. Hanson's return to forward him, and set out myself to meet you. We should find Newstead sufficiently spacious—indeed too much so ; but not quite comfortable in its present state for a permanent residence. Besides, we should certainly grow fond of it—and it would then be disagreeable to part with it. Augusta dotes on it—that is natural—but there is no reason why you should be encumbered with our family prejudices.

I will take your word for the " world " and its kindness without desiring to prove its favours further—being only too much obliged to it for containing you.

P.S.—Assure Mrs. Siddons of my respect, and the pleasure I shall feel in improving my acquaintance with her ; and give my *duty* to our Papa & Lady M., and all our relations. If you are fond of the drama, you must see Kean. He is the triumph of mind over matter, for he has nothing but countenance & expression ; his figure is very little & even mean ; but I never saw the Passions so expressed—on the stage at least—except by Mrs. Sid[s].

A.I.M. *to* B.

[*October* 19 1814].

It is odd that my last letter should have alluded to that one which you now return. I don't wish you to " forget " any sentiments which I have ever really entertained—for those which were real, exist still. You could not indeed understand the Quixotism of disinterestedness that led me, as I believed, to preclude every future possibility of hope. Convinced that I was not fitted to be your wife—that the measure and temperature of our minds were in some points too different, in others too similar—if you still were

[1] This was Michael Bruce, whom Byron had met with Lady Hester Stanhope during his first Greek tour.

inclined to love me, was it not my duty to prevent it ? I could not however but feel it the severest sacrifice to duty. . . . I had not the consolation of thinking that you knew the exertion made for your sake—it was bitter. Whenever the recollection that you thought me attached to another occurred, a strangeness (I don't know what to call it) would seize me, and has betrayed itself in company. . . . I am sure you will never know how invariably your welfare has been my *first* object, nor how much I have suffered from the determination to make it so. I must be content with whatever share of attachment you can believe that I have felt for you. though my conduct is only applicable on the supposition of the strongest.

There can be but one respect in which I may now have deceived myself—in admitting at last with too much self-indulgence, the persuasion that you will be happy *with me.* I could not *at any time* have resisted that persuasion.

I think this will be the last letter you receive from me. If you are so much alone and not always busy, why have I not had more of your thoughts ? I shall be jealous of the Maccaw.

In my last letter to Mrs. Leigh I asked if it were possible, that she would make us a visit. Could it be ? There is no one with whom I would sooner share your society. Perhaps you could make some arrangement with her, if she would come to her sister here. Is she not shy and timid ? Her letters look so.

B. *to* A.I.M.

Octr. 20th 1814.

I have been so much amused with your " extracts," though I had no idea what an evil spirit I then appeared in your eyes. You were quite right, however, as far as *appearances*—but that was not my natural character. I was just returned from a far country where everything was different, & felt bewildered & not very happy in my own, which I had left without regret & returned to without interest. I found myself—I did not very well know why—an object of curiosity which I never wished to excite, and about a poem which I had no conception was to make such a fuss ; my mind & my feelings were moreover occupied with considerations which had nothing in common with the circle where I was whirling. So that no wonder I was repulsive and cold. I never could conquer my disposition to be both in a crowd from which I was always wishing myself away.

Those who know me most intimately can tell you that I am if anything too *childish*, with a greater turn for the ridiculous than any thing serious ; and—I could hope—not very ill-natured *off the stage,* and if angry never *loud.* I can't say much for these qualifi- cations ; but I have such a regard for yours that I am sure we shall be a very happy couple. I wish you had a greater passion for governing—for I don't shine in conducting myself, and am very docile with a gentle guide.[1]

One of Augusta's friends writes to her & says she is afraid now I am to be married, "that I shall become a good sort of man"—an awful anticipation ! The P.R. has been at Brocket & talked on the subject to Ly. M., by no means ill-naturedly—as is his usual way, & might be excusable enough as far as *I* am concerned. Among other things he said, "Between her prose and his poetry what may we not expect ? "—as if we were to do nothing else but make books ! I am sure the employments the *Morning Post* found out for us would be much more useful & quite as entertaining—particularly the care of the poultry &c. &c.

I am only waiting for Mr. Hanson's return to set him off, & follow myself. If, Dearest, these men of parchment can *settle* us, or put us in the way of being settled within a reasonable time, you will perhaps not long defer taking a name to which you will do more honour than has been conferred upon it ¦since its first inscription in "Domesday Boke" with the signature of my Progenitors Erneis & *Ralph*. So you see your Papa—& the papa of all my papas were synonimous (*sic*).

P.S.—Oh, I must tell you one of my present avocations. [Douglas] Kinnaird (a friend of mine, brother to Lord Kd.) applied to me to write words for a musical composer who is going to publish the *real old undisputed Hebrew melodies*, which are beautiful & to which David & the prophets actually sang the "songs of Zion "— & I have done nine or ten on the sacred model—partly from Job &c. & partly my own imagination ; but I hope a little better than Sternhold & Hopkins. It is odd enough that this should fall to my lot, who have been abused as "an infidel." Augusta says "they will call me a *Jew* next."

A.I.M. *to* B.

Friday [Oct. 21, 1814].

If you should be in London still on Monday, do not be disappointed by this short letter, written in the conviction that you will not receive it there. Yours of the 19th has given me this hope which I shall indulge and conclude.

Byron's next letter (of October 22) is in *Letters and Journals*, iii. 159-60, except for an expression of his "increased impatience" ("I cannot remain much longer here") and the following words : "'My thoughts'? I have written to you daily, and am only fearful of tiring you with words. You do my Maccaw much honour, but are quite right to avail yourself of the only opportunity you could ever have of exerting the amiable passion of which you menace him with being the object."

[1] From opening to here is in *Letters and Journals*, iii. 157-8.

A.I.M. *to* B.

S. *Octr.* 22, 1814.

My Uncle is obliged to leave us next week, and is in despair lest you should not arrive before he *must* go. It is odd enough that my task should be to pacify the old ones, and teach *them* patience. They are growing quite ungovernable, and I must have your assistance to manage them.

To your epistle this day I have only to answer that when other delays are at an end *I* shall make none, but enter into the contract of " obedience " (for I *do* perform the other conditions) as willingly as you can desire.

A.I.M. *to* B.

Sunday [*Oct.* 23, 1814].

I do trust that this letter will return to visit you here, but I want to communicate so much that I must for a few minutes fancy it is not in vain to write.

Of our meeting—I have no doubt that we shall prove admirable philosophers on that as well as former occasions when we have been so successfully *indifferent*. We perhaps resemble each other in being the coolest when in truth we were not calmest. I never like to MAKE *scenes* even on the most favourable opportunities—when a " Heroine " would say and do most, I generally say and do least. One of the causes of my long supposed obduracy. I wonder you never heard of it, for I had lost *that* character, with some very unamiable additions, but a short time before you knew me. . . . I cannot say how kind Mrs. Leigh has been to me—it will not be forgotten.

O for tomorrow's post ! I walk to meet it every day, and sit in the blacksmith's cottage till it arrives. A woman came in also a few days ago, and not knowing me, began to enquire about the " bonny lad " who was to *tak awa* the " canny hinny."

A.I.M. *to* B.

One believes every word which Mr. Hobhouse writes, because there is not a word too much. . . . The prospect of so early an introduction to him gives me pleasure. Is he determined to wait till the ceremony ? *We* (for we are monstrously harmonic) should be gratified by a visit from him *before* the *fatal* day, if he would accept the invitation of your future wife, and be *her* guest before he is *yours also*. This I must leave to your persuasive powers.

So I wrote to you in the fit of melancholy recalled by association with less happy moments ? I might as well not have sent the " blue devils " to the post ; though, as they evaporated by that channel, *you* will not wish them to have remained with the right owner.

No more " heroic " visitors—nor " heroic epistles." You will be entertained with many of my congratulatory addresses. . . .

I am afraid my Uncle must go on Thursday—he has business in the South. That he is not *angry* with you for his disappointment you will believe when I tell you the object of his visit to Durham this morning—to exact a " solemn promise " from Mr. Hoar that he would not delay our Settlements a single moment beyond what the business positively required. He says *his whole heart* is in the " consummation devoutly to be wished."

P.S.—I have heard more of Bankes at Granada—he is living there in a beggarly, eccentric fashion. My news had not reached Miss M., for whose *glad* answer I am rather impatient, as she has uniformly, decidedly, and singly maintained that you and I were the persons in the world best suited to each other. I used to laugh at the opinion, with a very ill grace.

B. to A.I.M.

Octr. 25th 1814.

It is with great regret that I shall miss meeting Lord Wentworth at Seaham—but so it is. I could till now fix no precise day—and whatever appearance or consequences these delays may have or create, I must bear them. Hanson, whom I have been expecting & urging from day to day, now writes that he is ill, but will send his son. This will not do. It was his duty and is to be present and to meet Mr. Hoar in person—and he shall do so, or it shall be our last difference. Whether the man is mad, or only wishes to make me so, I know not. I have been acquainted with him since I was ten years old, which gives him a kind of claim upon what good-nature I possess—which he is pushing a little too far. However let that rest. I will set off on *Saturday*, and leave out Newstead & Newmarket on my way, which I had at first intended to visit. If I can get away a day before, it shall not be lost ; but I fear that I cannot remain at Seaham under the present circumstances above a few days. Nothing would have made me deliberate so long, but the hope that when we did meet the previous pause would render parting again unnecessary. But these things we can discuss in person.

If you can, convince your father that he cannot be more vexed than I. No wonder he is so—in short I can only say that I meant all this for the best, and my meaning turns out, I think, like one of those " good intentions " with which the Portuguese proverb tells us that a certain place (never to be mentioned by divines to " ears polite ") is paved.

I make all my apologies to your father rather than to *you*—for I am very sure *you* know me too well not to understand my feelings on the subject without further explanation. The very circumstances that might appear tardy on my part are in fact a proof of my impatience, for it was to render all further interruptions & delays unnecessary that I submitted to these. But enough of this. If I am alive, I will set out on Saturday.

P.S.—The oldest friend [1]—that is the earliest, though not the kindest I ever had—is now lying between life and death a few streets from me. She was seized with a fever and delirium about a fortnight ago. I only heard of this within these few days. Her husband (from whom she was separated) & her mother are now with her. Her life has been a melancholy one, though on her part blameless. I have not seen her for several years, and probably never may again—nor do I wish it ; but I always wished her happy & to live while life would make her so.

You will think my letter—at least the postscript—a collection of casualties and melancholy accidents ; but—did you know Lady Rosebery ? Very young, very pretty, & very unwise, it should seem—for the " on dit " is that she has gone off with Sir H. Mildmay (her sister was his late wife). I foresaw this in the summer ; and all I can now say is—that I hope it is *not* come to pass, and it is not unlikely to be false, having been in the Newspapers. If it turns out so, I ask her pardon—& yours at any rate—for repeating such gossip.[2]

B. to A.I.M.

Octr. 27th 1814.

My Love—Mr. Hanson is on his way from Devon at last, but if he does not arrive before Saturday I shall not wait for him. Augusta wishes me so much to pass that way that I shall make " mine inn " at her abode for a short time—and thence to our Papa's. I console myself for not being in time to be presented to Ld. W. with the thought—not very agreeable after all—that perhaps he would not have liked me ; and though I prefer the old school & courtly deportment of the past generation, I can't flatter myself with the hope of commending me to its good graces by a display of my own —if I may so quibble upon that important word in Ld. Chester-field's dictionary. You laugh at me about your serious letter—which is very mischievous ; it made me quite elegiac—not in words, though. Don't you think it a little odd that I have not once woefully balladed your eyebrow ? One can't paint a storm upon deck, though one may in port from recollection ; neither could I (almost a professed scribbler as I have been) ever rhyme or write upon any subject upon which my heart was set, till it was lost or won and some time had elapsed. And yet I have dealt less in *fiction* than most bards—I will venture to say than almost any of *the day*.

[1] Mrs. Chaworth Musters.

[2] Referring to this gossip in a letter to Lady Melbourne, he said : " [Sir Hal and the Countess Rosebery] slept at Eaton . . . in the most decisive way, so that all appears quite regular. Don't you think they are not much better than some people you may have heard of, who had half a mind to *anticipate* their example, and don't yet know whether to be glad or sorry they have not ? " (*Correspondence,* i. 286).

How sorry I am that Hobhouse is not in London ! He would be so pleased with the prospect of seeing you—and yet I don't know. He is—when & where he likes—so very pleasing that I think it may be as well not to present him till I can introduce you by our name. " Did Michael Cassio, when you wooed my Lady, know of your love ? " Oh no—not at all. What a world of tragedy would have been saved, could the Moor's ancient have received that response.

As I do not know the distance, I cannot fix day & hour ; but I shall probably arrive in an Evening—not late—at least too late. I bring no servant except my valet ; the others I shall leave here or at Newstead. A thousand thanks to you for calling me " Byron." It sounds (it never sounded so sweetly to me before) as if we had been married already. I hope Mr. Hoar will keep his promise of speed ; I have been scolding Hanson till my rage is quite exhausted, & he seems (upon paper) in great haste & contrition. The person I mentioned in my last is better—but still very ill & weakly. Her loving Lord has left London & her in this state ! And yet this very woman made his fortune, & brought him love & beauty besides. " These be your Christian husbands ! "

Upon this ominous note their correspondence before his visit closes. It should be said in defence of Byron that his letters to the always dilatory Hanson were frequent, and became ferocious, during the long delay.

APPENDIX II

MONEY-MATTERS

AFTER the separation in 1816, both sides held themselves to have been aggrieved by the marriage-settlements. There was no reason for this attitude on the Byron side, for he had " indignantly refused " to allow any part of Sir Ralph Milbanke's estate to be secured to him as a set-off to the £60,000 settlement on the Newstead estate made to his wife. He could have exacted some such arrangement, and was urged to do so by Hanson.

In 1841 Lady Byron made the acquaintance of Mme. Swanton Belloc, who had translated Moore's *Life of Byron* into French. In a letter to Ada of May 10, 1841, she alludes to this, and adds that Mme. Belloc had libelled her " most unsparingly " in a biography published some years ago : " not, however, maliciously, for she is an estimable person and full of feeling."

Lady Byron's statement as to the biography is strongly disputed by Mme. Swanton Belloc's grand-daughter, Mrs. Belloc-Lowndes, who writes in January 1929 : " I am *quite* sure that [my grand-mother] never wrote a biography of Lady Byron. If she had, my own mother,[1] who knew Lady Byron (before her marriage to my father) would certainly have told me so. . . . My theory is that the ' biography ' was an article, or perhaps a series of articles, on *Lord* Byron. . . . My grandmother wrote constantly in the French reviews of her day. . . . My own mother was brought into contact with Lady Byron (who, I think, then lived at Brighton) because of their mutual interest in the emigration of poor children (to Canada). My English grandfather, Joseph Parkes, a Taxing-Master in Chancery, knew Mrs. Leigh well."

In Lady Byron's letter to Ada she goes on : " Mme. Mojon " (whom she had known intimately for many years) " has begged me to mark the passages in Mme. Belloc's work which were positive misstatements, and I felt bound to do so in relation to the calumnies of which Mrs. Clermont is the object. ' *Cette mégère* ' is the appellation given her."

[1] Mrs. Belloc-Lowndes's mother was Miss Bessie Rayner Parkes.

That certainly seems to indicate that Lady Byron had had the book in her hands ; but neither Mrs. Belloc-Lowndes nor myself has been able to trace any such biography.

At any rate, Lady Byron also gave the following paper to " Bianca Milesi Mojon " on May 10, 1841—the date of her letter to Ada. Apparently the statement was drawn up in refutation of some-passages in Mme. Swanton Belloc's biography—or article.

My fortune (*dot*) given by my father on my marriage was £20,000, which was entirely at Lord Byron's disposal.[1] It was not certain at that time that I should inherit from Thomas *Noel*, Lord Wentworth, my uncle. My father's name was then simply Sir Ralph Milbanke.

My pin-money, by the marriage-settlement, was £300 per ann.

My jointure (*douaire*) £2000 per ann.

Lord Wentworth died in 1815—a few months after my marriage. He left a large property to my mother for her life, and afterwards to me for my life ; then to a collateral branch of the Noel family, the Curzons ; and *only if that branch becomes extinct* will the property revert to my daughter. The condition of the inheritance was— to take the name and arms of *Noel*.

My mother, who was about 55 when Lord W. died, was from that time called Lady Noel instead of Lady Milbanke, and my father Sir Ralph Noel ; but neither Lord B. nor I assumed the name of Noel till after her death.

It was discovered by Mr. Hanson, Lord Byron's solicitor, a short time after Lord Wentworth's death, that though it was Lord W.'s intention to make *me* his heir, the will was so worded (having been made before the marriage was contemplated) as to place the property *wholly in my husband's power*. By my separation a few months afterwards, I therefore left my future fortune to my husband, and it was at his option to make a provision for me out of it or not. What I asked of him was to allow me during my mother's life £200 per ann. in addition to my pin-money (£300 per ann.) as I could not have maintained myself and my child properly for less than £500 ; and my father's previous embarrassments deprived my mother of the power of assisting me out of Lord Wentworth's property. I obtained this £200.

I also required that after my mother's death Lord Byron should consent to submit the question—" What portion of my fortune he should in equity allow me " (without entering into the merits of the separation) to arbitrators appointed by him and me. After publicly refusing, he at last signed an agreement to that effect.

My Mother died in 1822, when the arbitration took place—and half of the inheritance was assigned to me. My aged father was then dependent on me, his own estates not being cleared from debts.

[1] Subject to the settlement.

Lord Byron died in 1824—when I came into possession of the whole of the Wentworth property, and also of course of my jointure £2000 per ann., which I relinquished to the present Lord Byron. The Wentworth property, being for my life only, did not enable me to make any provision out of it for my daughter by will.

Lord Byron bequeathed all his property to his sister Mrs. Leigh, and her family for ever. Ada inherited nothing from him ; but £16,000 had been settled upon a daughter by the marriage-settlement.

The amount of the property bequeathed to Mrs. Leigh in present and in reversion was more than £100,000.

(See Dallas's Life, vol. 1, p. cvii.)

APPENDIX III

THE MATHEMATICAL GENIUS OF ADA,
COUNTESS OF LOVELACE

In 1844, Professor Augustus De Morgan wrote as follows to Lady Byron of her daughter's mathematical genius:

I have never expressed to Lady Lovelace my opinion of her as a student of these matters. I always feared that it might promote an application to them which might be injurious to a person whose bodily health is not strong. I have therefore contented myself with very good, quite right, and so on. But I feel bound to tell you that the power of thinking on these matters which Lady L. has always shown from the beginning of my correspondence with her, has been something so utterly out of the common way for any beginner, man or woman, that this power must be duly considered by her friends, with reference to the question whether they should urge or check her obvious determination to try not only to reach, but to get beyond, the present bounds of knowledge. If you or Lord L. only think that it is a fancy for that particular kind of knowledge, which, though unusual in its object, may compare in intensity with the usual tastes of a young lady, you do not know the whole. And the same if you think that desire of distinction is the motive, science one of many paths which might be chosen to obtain it. There is easily to be seen the desire of distinction in Lady L.'s character; but the mathematical turn is one which opportunity must have made her take independently of that.

Had any young beginner, about to go to Cambridge, shown the same power, I should have prophesied first that his aptitude at grasping the strong points and the real difficulties of first *principles* would have very much lowered his chance of being senior wrangler; secondly, that they would have certainly made him an original mathematical investigator, perhaps of first-rate eminence.

The tract about Babbage's machine is a pretty thing enough, but I could I think produce a series of extracts, out of Lady Lovelace's first queries upon new subjects, which would make a mathematician see that it was no criterion of what might be expected from her.

All women who have published mathematics hitherto have shown knowledge, and power of getting it, but no one, except perhaps (I speak doubtfully) Maria Agnesi, has wrestled with difficulties and shown a man's strength in getting over them. The reason is obvious : the very great tension of mind which they require is beyond the strength of a woman's physical power of application. Lady L. has unquestionably as much power as would require all the strength of a man's constitution to bear the fatigue of thought to which it will unquestionably lead her. It is very well now, when the subject has not entirely engrossed her attention ; by-and-bye when, as always happens, the whole of the thoughts are continually and entirely concentrated upon them, the struggle between the mind and body will begin.

Perhaps you think that Lady L. will, like Mrs. Somerville, go on in a course of regulated study, duly mixed with the enjoyment of society, the ordinary cares of life, &c., &c. But Mrs. Somerville's mind never led her into other than the *details* of mathematical work ; Lady L. will take quite a different route. It makes me smile to think of Mrs. Somerville's quiet acquiescence in ignorance of the nature of force, saying " it is $\frac{dv}{dt}$ " (a mathl. formula for it) " and that is all we know about the matter "—and to imagine Lady L. reading this, much less writing it.

Having now I think quite explained that you must consider Lady L.'s case as a peculiar one I will leave it to your better judgment, supplied with facts, only begging that this note may be confidential.

APPENDIX IV

HISTORY OF INDUSTRIAL SCHOOLS

By Lady Noel Byron

It appears little known where, and by whom, the idea of Industrial Schools for the poor was first conceived and carried into effect ; and yet a knowledge of the origin and commencement of these Institutions . . . is necessary for a right comprehension of their purpose, especially to those who wish to establish such schools. We therefore propose here to enter into a more detailed account than has been given by the various biographers of M. de Fellenberg, of the circumstances out of which arose the first idea of Industrial Training, subsequently carried out in his great undertaking, the establishment of his Agricultural School at Hofwyl in Switzerland.

Early in the year 1798 Switzerland, whilst at peace with the French Republic, was invaded by a numerous French army on the most frivolous pretexts. The French Republic was at that time ruled by a band of robbers called the Directory, and it was customary to make all the countries to which France had given freedom, pay for that gift with heavy contributions, the greater part of which found its way into the pockets of the Directory. At that time Switzerland was the only country with which France had not yet interfered ; but as the people—but lightly taxed—enjoyed great prosperity, there was a fine opportunity for plunder. The peace with Italy had thrown a considerable French army out of employment, a little change and refreshment was deemed desirable for the soldiers, and it was quite in accordance with the morality of the French Republic of that day to make the discovery that the troops might be properly quartered in Switzerland. A pretext was easily found ; it was the old fable of the Wolf and the Lamb.

First among the Swiss Cantons which offered the most energetic resistance to the encroachments of the French Directory, stood Unterwald—and fearful was the vengeance of the enraged French soldiery. The unhappy country was ravaged with fire and sword. The inhabitants who did not fall in battle (and women as well as men took part in the combat) fled, some into the mountains, some into the churches ; but the sanctuary proved no place of safety for these latter, and they became a prey to the flames or to the bayonets.

None but children were spared by the infuriated soldiery, and after the departure of the French, troops of these houseless orphans were seen wandering about amidst the ruins of their former homes. A cry of compassion resounded throughout Switzerland.

The first philanthropist who came to the succour of these helpless little ones was Henry Pestalozzi, who had shortly before this period completed his studies for the Church, but had utterly broken down in his probationary sermon. This circumstance had blighted his future prospects in such a seat of learning as Zürich, and he did not know whither to direct his steps. The path of Theology was closed to him, but not that of practical Christianity. He converted his little property into money, tied up his bundle, and set off for Canton Unterwalden, to become the guardian of the poor deserted children there. It was an inclement season, but with the help of some kind-hearted friends he succeeded in raising a shelter for his new family amid the ruins of the village of Stanz, and here he fed, clothed, and housed the homeless little ones and formed them into a school. Daily more and more flocked around him, and he was obliged to consider how he could bring them under some kind of discipline. The only help he could obtain was from the children themselves, and he took care to select those who showed most intelligence, and exercised most influence over their companions. These he made his assistants in giving lessons, as well as in the necessary occupations of the little household, such as keeping the place in order, mending the clothes, preparing the food, collecting wood, etc. He soon added the cultivation of a piece of land. The little colony then assumed the character of an orderly community.

In the meantime patriots from various parts of Switzerland had arrived in Stanz, bringing provisions and stores of all kinds. By degrees the fugitive inhabitants returned from their places of refuge in the mountains, and all fell back into their former way of life. Pestalozzi's school was welcome to all, as long as the children were fed and provided for there. But Pestalozzi's funds were at last exhausted; the assistance of other philanthropists was required by the returning fugitives, so that the school could no longer be maintained. Thus, to the great sorrow of all, Pestalozzi saw the day arrive when he was obliged to separate from his beloved children. However, the recollection remained as a living picture in his mind; and was to him much what to Adam must have been the remembrance of the lost Paradise which he was to regain by the sweat of his brow. It gave a distinct and tangible form to his deep inward longing to serve his fellow-creatures; it became the subject of his dreams and of all his plans, and he seized upon whatever promised to bring him nearer to the desired end with the eagerness of a ship-wrecked mariner who grasps the frailest plank which the storm casts within his reach. His hopes and projects likewise formed the chief topic of his conversations with his friends, of whom he found many after the events in Unterwalden; but to most of these his words were riddles, for to understand them it was necessary to have experienced, like Pestalozzi, what a powerful means for training lies in labour for bread, when it was directed by a skilful hand. By all true philanthropists, however, the full value of his achievements in Unterwalden was recognized, and caused his unsuccessful examination sermon to be forgotten. When he made known his plan for an Educational Institution, the government of Canton Berne offered him the use of the Castle of Burgdorff for his purpose ; and although the dissimilarity was great between this castle and his barn at Stanz, he seized the offered plank and opened a school at Burgdorff.

Pestalozzi's reputation having been further heightened by the publication of some striking popular works, such as *Leonard and Gertrude*, he soon obtained many pupils, and among the number some belonging to the most influential families. He was thus enabled to carry out that part of his educational system which he called " *die Anschauungs Lehre* " (teaching by touch, sight, smell, etc.) ; but his method of industrial training he could not put into practice, for his pupils were mostly sons of families above the necessity of supporting themselves by manual labour.

The new system introduced by him soon excited public attention. Young men of the class of teachers began to collect round him, and possessed themselves of his method with more or less success, hoping thereby to make their fortunes in the novelty-loving world ; but amongst all these, there was not one capable of comprehending his great idea of making labour, and more especially agricultural labour, a principal means in the education of youth. Indeed of what avail would it have been to him in his castle, had he found a congenial spirit—there was not a foot of ground in which anything could be planted !

The opportunity soon, however, occurred of carrying out the aim of his heart, to explain which we must go back a little.

Amongst the acquaintances Pestalozzi had made in earlier times, before he went to Unterwald, was that of the family of Tcharner of Wildenstein. Tcharner, who was then Bernese Landvogt, appeared to realize his ideal of what a governor should be—such as he had drawn in his most celebrated work, *Leonard and Gertrude*, in the character of Arner. Through this family he became acquainted with that of M. de Fellenberg, who succeeded Tcharner in the governorship of Wildenstein, and a young Fellenberg became one of Pestalozzi's most attentive listeners. This young man accompanied him on several journeys, and was one of the few who afterwards entered into and adopted his idea of Industrial education. His way of carrying out Pestalozzi's idea was, however, a circuitous one. Though educated with a view to entering political life, the influence of his mother (who was in the constant habit of saying to him : " The rich have always helpers enough, help thou the poor ") had implanted in him the germ which enabled him to receive and comprehend the ideas of Pestalozzi. His childhood, moreover, fell in the time of the American War of Independence, in which his mother took the liveliest interest, her sympathies being enlisted on the side of the Americans, and thus Washington became the hero of his early youth. It is not surprising that with this early bias Fellenberg should, like so many idealists of this time, have been carried away by the principles of the French Revolution, and that he should have anticipated nothing less than the regeneration of the world. It was during the French Revolution that he studied law at the University of Tübingen in Germany. His landlord was a blacksmith [or locksmith], a good and industrious man, who, being blessed with a numerous family, found it very difficult to keep his head above water. One evening, when Fellenberg came home, this man came to him trembling with agitation and told him that all his tools and stock in trade would be sold by auction the following day to pay his debts, if he could not find someone to help him out of his troubles. The sum required for doing this was two hundred florins, and it so happened that this was the exact amount possessed by Fellenberg at the time. Nevertheless, recalling his mother's words, he helped the poor man out of his distress.

Emanuel de Fellenberg returned home from the University just as the difficulties of Switzerland with the French were commencing. He heard at the time of Pestalozzi's undertaking in Unterwalden, and was vividly reminded of his former acquaintance with the philanthropist ; and other circumstances were not wanting to confirm the bent of mind which changed his path of life from that of a politician to that of a philanthropist.

The tremendous war-taxes which the French Directory exacted from the Swiss, and the pressure of the military occupation on the country population, brought Switzerland to the brink of despair, and it was resolved that an embassy, consisting of the first men of the country, should be sent to Paris to entreat the Directory to lighten the burden. Fellenberg accompanied one of the delegates in the capacity of Secretary, and had thus an opportunity of learning to know the vaunted French freedom in its true character. One morning, while he was conversing with a member of the Directory and endeavouring to make him feel the insupportable oppression which the Republic and the Army was exercising over Switzerland, he observed that the Director occasionally interrupted the conversation by whistling, or by opening a window to make enquiries of a groom how his favourite dog and her puppies were going on ; and the astonishment of the young secretary was great to find that one of the " Fathers " of the French Republic should devote more attention to a litter of puppies than to an oppressed and suffering people.

The experience of French liberty and of the general political tendencies of the time, which Fellenberg gained during this visit to Paris, gave him the conviction that his path must be in another direction ; and he returned to Switzerland more than ever determined to serve his country in the spirit of his mother's saying. Soon afterwards he married a granddaughter of Tcharner, the friend of Pestalozzi, and was thenceforward brought into frequent contact with the latter. About this time also Fellenberg's father, who was professor of law in Berne, purchased the estate of Hofwyl, not far from that town, in order to afford his son an opportunity of commencing the activity he so much desired. The distance between Hofwyl and Burgdorff is only 9 English miles, and thus Pestalozzi and Fellenberg became neighbours. This led to lively intercourse between them, and Pestalozzi exerted his influence to induce Fellenberg to turn his estate to account for the realization of his favourite idea of industrial education.

Although by this time Pestalozzi had secured competent assistants, it so happened that each of these assistants fancied himself at least a little Pestalozzi, who owed to the father Pestalozzi just as much subordination as seemed good to himself, and no more : and thus a few years after its foundation the Institute already presented a picture of anarchy which Pestalozzi, conscious of his own diminishing powers, despaired of subduing. His hopes therefore turned to Fellenberg, to whom he proposed to cede the entire management of the Institute, provided the government of Berne would agree to give him in exchange for Burgdorff a former convent belonging to it, called München Buchsee and situated close to Hofwyl. The government consented and Fellenberg likewise entered into the plan, but upon condition that he should be empowered to dismiss any of the teachers who should refuse to conform to his regulations. The condition was assented to, and Pestalozzi removed his Institute to München Buchsee, only ten minutes' walk from Hofwyl. Here Fellenberg had an opportunity of becoming thoroughly acquainted with Pestalozzi's method, of judging of its weak as well as its strong points, and of entering into Pestalozzi's further schemes ; and there can be little doubt that the favourite idea of the latter would have been carried out at Hofwyl under his own eye, had the character of the two men been such as to allow them to work together with success. But in daily intercourse it soon became evident that this was not the case. Pestalozzi's excessive soft-heartedness led him to regard as tyranny the consistent carrying out of a plan, while Fellenberg's systematic energy bore but impatiently Pestalozzi's indecision, and demurred against it as causing loss of time. Under such circumstances it was not difficult for Pestalozzi's assistants to persuade him that he had fallen into the clutches of an intolerable tyrant, from which he ought to extricate himself at any cost ; and in consequence he accepted an offer made by the government of the Pays de Vaud to cede to him the Castle of Yverdun on the lake of Neufchatel, for the location of his Institute.

Thus ended the connection between Pestalozzi and Fellenberg, without, however, any personal quarrel having taken place between them ; and Pestalozzi was very much gratified when in the year

1806 Fellenberg sent one of his sons to him for education, accompanied by a young man whom he wished to learn Pestalozzi's system.

Meanwhile Fellenberg, left at Hofwyl, had come to the full determination to begin the work of industrial education, and it only remained for him to find an able assistant who could take the post of " Father " in relation to the pupils, and as such embody his idea. After long search among the numerous class of young men devoting themselves to education in Switzerland, he at length met with one equal to what he desired, and became acquainted with him in the following manner. Pestalozzi's method of teaching had excited great attention among all persons engaged in education throughout Switzerland, and it seemed so simple to lead the pupil, by exerting his own will and reason, to assist in the work of instruction that even mediocre teachers could only wonder that the idea had not occurred to them long before, as the number of children collected in a school had always rendered some such method highly desirable. Many therefore endeavoured to apply what they heard of this system, apparently so simple, to the subjects then taught in their schools, such as reading, writing, the catechism, etc., but soon found that the matter was much more difficult than they had imagined. Numbers were in consequence anxious to study the Pestalozzian method under Pestalozzi himself ; but this was attended with more expense than the majority could afford ; for the pecuniary affairs of the Institute were so reduced by daily mismanagement that Pestalozzi could not admit any such supernumeraries except for high payment. This led Fellenberg to think of commencing at Hofwyl a course of instruction in the Pestalozzian method, partly with a view to affording earnest teachers the means of improvement, partly in the hope that among the numbers who would probably avail themselves of the opportunity, he should be able to find some man with capabilities answering the requirements of an assistant in his own particular object. He communicated his scheme to Pestalozzi, who was delighted with it and sent him as assistant a young man from Prussia, by name Zeller, who was thoroughly acquainted with his method, and an enthusiastic admirer of it.

Fellenberg was thus able to open his course of instruction on the 1st of May, 1806. In a little wood beneath great linden trees, he had had a cottage built on twelve posts and with a shingle roof. The upper storey served as sleeping-room for the teachers who came to attend the course, the ground-floor as schoolroom. The hours from 5 to 7 and from 8 to 12 in the morning were devoted to lessons. In the afternoon the teachers worked in the fields and garden of Hofwyl. In the evening they prepared the vegetables for the next day's meal. During harvest-time they helped in the fields the whole day. In this way Fellenberg endeavoured to show them how he would like an agricultural school organized, and for the same purpose he gave them every morning a lesson in agriculture, and conversed with his hearers on the topic of agricultural labour as a valuable aid to education. Each evening he also talked over with them the labours of the following day ; and thus he led his pupil-teachers to do their work with a full knowledge of its use, to take pleasure in it, and to recognize how advantageous to themselves would be knowledge of the means of making the soil more productive, as the greater number of schoolmasters in Switzerland depend chiefly on a few acres of public ground for their subsistence.

Though proceeding in this way in accordance with Pestalozzi's ideas, Fellenberg carried out these ideas to a greater extent than Pestalozzi himself could have done ; for while Pestalozzi built his system of education on *the perception of the senses (Anschauung)*, making this perception the ground-work of memory, and former systems had concerned themselves only with the memory and with subjects which could not be made objects of sensual perception, Fellenberg went further than Pestalozzi inasmuch as he added *action* to *perception*. " For," he said, " what has been practised, and practised with thought, will be retained more firmly by the memory, and will constitute a more trustworthy experience, than that which has only been seen or heard." To sum up, earlier methods made the *ear* and *words*, Pestalozzi made the *eye* and the *image*, and Fellenberg made *action* the foundation of memory.

Zeller adopted Fellenberg's improvement with the readiness of one really desirous of knowledge, and brought his objective teaching as far as possible into relation with the daily labours of the pupil-teachers, thus making his lessons more interesting and animated.

As many as thirty men joined in the first season's lessons ; and as these, on their return home, spread the knowledge of what was going on at Hofwyl, the following spring no less than eighty teachers presented themselves to attend the course. This placed Fellenberg, as a private individual with private means, in a somewhat difficult position and caused him some pecuniary embarrassment, which on one occasion was relieved by the opportune repayment of the 200 florins, with interest, which he had several years before lent to his landlord in Tübingen.

A variety of work being necessary to enable Fellenberg to carry out his plans, he was led to enter upon various undertakings which perhaps he would not otherwise have thought of. Among these was drainage, at that period effected by means of stones or wooden channels ; and the Hofwyl land being extremely stony, this served two purposes at once. The drainage water was also turned to account in watering the low meadow-lands ; and thus Zeller obtained opportunities for extending his object-lessons, to which were joined instruction in drawing, which was regarded by Fellenberg and Zeller as a connecting-link between *perception* and *action*.

The second course at Hofwyl was attended by a schoolmaster named Wehrli from Canton Thurgovie, who, though an elderly man, on hearing of the new method of teaching had travelled on foot a distance of about 150 miles in order to avail himself of the opportunity of improving himself in his profession. This Wehrli proved himself one of the most zealous and attentive pupils, and endeavoured to make himself thorough master of all points that were new to him. When Fellenberg from time to time expressed his intention of carrying out the system of industrial training as soon as he should be able to find a competent assistant, it was always old Wehrli who had the most questions to ask in reference to the subject ; and towards the close of the course he told Fellenberg that he had a son whom he could recommend as likely to prove the efficient helper he wanted. Fellenberg invited the son to Hofwyl ; and shortly afterwards there appeared before him a youth of eighteen, with a pleasing expression of countenance and modest bearing but fearless glance, who said he was commissioned by his father to enter the service of M. de Fellenberg, who would tell him in what capacity.

Young Jacob Wehrli was not long in comprehending what Fellenberg required of him, and soon expressed his great desire to be put at the head of some boys with whom he might work. Fellenberg, on his side, was so convinced that his undertaking could not but result in success that he did not hesitate to give the first beggar-boy who presented himself to Wehrli as a pupil, and Wehrli commenced his task fully persuaded that it would be an easy matter to change even the most unmanageable beggar-boy into an industrious member of society. Indeed the first few weeks of kind treatment and (let it not be forgotten) good food, seemed to produce the effect which Fellenberg and Wehrli expected from their system ; but this result was in a great measure attributable to the fact that Wehrli shared all the occupations of his pupil, so that when the latter felt weary or idle he was spurred on to activity by the feeling that it would be a shame to let his master go on working alone. However, after a few weeks, when the food and kindly treatment were no longer new, the beggar-boy began to long for his former " free life," and instead of working he would go in quest of birds' nests (the eggs in which had formed the luxuries of his vagabond diet), or he would seek out a snug corner to sleep in. It is true that when Wehrli said to him : " Those who will not work shall not eat," he would take up his tools again ; but as his mind was not in his work his labour was worth nothing, and Wehrli came to the conclusion that he should not attain his purpose in this way. At length it became necessary to let the boy in reality experience the effect of his idleness by making him go to bed one evening without his food. This he thought too hard. " What," said he to himself, " I am deprived of liberty, and must hunger into the bargain ! " And very early the next morning he absconded.

Wehrli was now without a pupil, and Fellenberg was much disappointed at finding that the beggar-boy had not known better how to appreciate his kindness. The next experiment was made with the son of an industrious labourer. To train a *labourer's* child to industry would seem a simple matter ; but tho' the boy was willing and

senses, or as he termed it, *physical perception*, which can advance to *mental perception* only through manifold exercise ; what the eye sees must be thoroughly comprehended by means of Feeling (Touch), Hearing, Smelling and Tasting, in order that the verbal description of the object and its properties may be perfectly understood. This being accomplished, the teacher must proceed to numbers and measures, and lastly drawing must come in to complete the external image.

From this short sketch of Pestalozzi's method of Objective Teaching, it will be seen that this method was especially calculated to qualify and prepare the scholar for the study of natural science ; and it being evident that Agriculture constitutes the richest mine for the practice of Objective Teaching, Pestalozzi could not fail to look with satisfaction upon Fellenberg's agricultural school at Hofwyl, as a further development of his own system.

Fellenberg continued his labours at Hofwyl up to the year 1844 ; and offshoots of his establishment being successfully at work throughout the greater part of the Cantons of Switzerland and in many of the adjoining countries, he could look back upon his life with the consciousness of having begun a work which would steadily advance and develop through the inherent truth of the principle it represented.

It is characteristic of the effect produced by Pestalozzi's and Fellenberg's efforts that when, in 1844, the erection of a national monument to Pestalozzi was talked of, and men of all ranks met to consider the subject, it was agreed without opposition from any quarter to abandon the idea of a stone or bronze statue, and to raise a living memorial to the Father of Popular Education in Switzerland, in the form of an institution for bringing up poor children of both sexes in accordance with his ideas and after the model of Wehrli's school at Hofwyl.

Fellenberg's institutions at Hofwyl did not escape the fate of all human affairs. He died in 1844, and the political events of 1845-1848 caused a temporary dissolution of his schools ; but his system was too firmly established throughout Switzerland to be affected by the maintenance or discontinuance of the parent institutions at Hofwyl. That which Fellenberg wished to accomplish was attained. First—Switzerland had obtained a system of popular education founded in the requirements of the nation, and capable of independent development, as there was scarcely a place of any importance in the country where might not be found a pupil of Pestalozzi or Fellenberg. Secondly—The idea of training by *action*, by productive and civilizing labour, had advanced from theory into practice. The means which are pointed out to man for his material support were now made to serve as an effective instrument in his education ; and as the great mass of men are destined to maintain themselves by labour, the most effective means of educating and civilizing them was thus discovered to reside in a daily necessity of their life. The chief question that remained to be determined was how the leading classes of society, those who employ labour, could be trained to recognize the duty incumbent on them to educate the working-classes and elevate them morally in the same degree as they avail themselves of their labour to increase their own property. Towards the solution of this question also Emanuel de Fellenberg took the first step in the establishment of his educational institution for the higher classes described above.

APPENDIX V

A PORTRAIT MISNAMED " LADY BYRON "

THE present representatives of Lady Byron desire to take this opportunity of repudiating a certain portrait by James Ramsay which bears her name, published in Vol. IV of Lord Byron's *Letters and Journals*, edited by Mr. Rowland Prothero (Lord Ernle) and published by Mr. John Murray. At the time when it first appeared Lady Byron's surviving grandchild, Lady Anne Blunt, wrote : " This picture never could have had the remotest resemblance to my grandmother at any time in her life. That her name should have been tacked on to it has been a source of extreme annoyance to me."

Other survivors of Lady Byron's circle, notably Mr. William De Morgan, the well-known novelist, who was also a trained artist, expressed the same views. This portrait is that of a large, strongly-built, very plain-featured person, as unlike as possible to the small, if anything over-refined type to which Lady Byron belonged. It is totally unlike any other portrait of her, and there is no evidence to connect it either with her or with any other person bearing the name of Byron. Further information would be found about this matter in an illustrated article which I published in *The Connoisseur* of October, 1917, and which was later republished in a pamphlet entitled " A Portrait misnamed Lady Byron."

MARY LOVELACE.

INDEX